ORGASM AND THE

For Jane

ORGASM AND THE WEST

A History of Pleasure
From the Sixteenth Century to
the Present

ROBERT MUCHEMBLED

Translated by Jean Birrell

polity

First published in French as *L'Orgasme et L'Occident* © Seuil, 2005

Ouvrage publié avec le concours du Ministère français chargé de la culture – Centre national du livre.

Published with the assistance of the French Ministry of Culture – National Centre for the Book.

This English edition © Polity Press, 2008

Polity Press
65 Bridge Street
Cambridge CB2 1UR, UK

Polity Press
350 Main Street
Malden, MA 02148, USA

All rights reserved. Except for the quotation of short passages for the purpose of criticism and review, no part of this publication may be reproduced, stored in a retrieval system, or transmitted, in any form or by any means, electronic, mechanical, photocopying, recording or otherwise, without the prior permission of the publisher.

ISBN-13: 978-0-7456-3875-1
ISBN-13: 978-0-7456-3876-8(pb)

A catalogue record for this book is available from the British Library.

Typeset in 10.5 on 12 pt Sabon
by SNP Best-set Typesetter Ltd., Hong Kong
Printed and bound in Great Britain by MPG Books Ltd, Bodmin, Cornwall

The publisher has used its best endeavours to ensure that the URLs for external websites referred to in this book are correct and active at the time of going to press. However, the publisher has no responsibility for the websites and can make no guarantee that a site will remain live or that the content is or will remain appropriate.

Every effort has been made to trace all copyright holders, but if any have been inadvertently overlooked the publishers will be pleased to include any necessary credits in any subsequent reprint or edition.

For further information on Polity, visit our website: www.polity.co.uk

Ouvrage publié avec le concours du Ministére français chargé de la Culture – Centre national du livre.

Published with the assistance of the French Ministry of Culture – National Centre for the Book.

CONTENTS

A Year of Pleasure ix

Introduction 1

Part I   Orgasm and the West 7
1   Carnal Knowledge 13
   The birth of the individual 13
      The Renaissance or capitalism? 14
      The individual and transgression 15
      The envelopes of the Self 16
      Beyond the Subject 18
   Is it all down to sex? 20
      Foucault's paradigms 20
      The three stages of sexuality 21
      The family and the flesh 23
      Frustrated young men 25
      Sodomites: a 'third sex' 27
      A new sexual system 28
   The conquest of female pleasure 32
      The erotic revolution of the sixties 32
      'Cherchez la femme!' 34
      The fountain of pleasures 37

CONTENTS

Part II Imprints: Pleasure in Pain (Sixteenth and Seventeenth Centuries) — 41

2 Masculine, Feminine: Individuals and Their Bodies — 45

Representing and talking about oneself — 46
  The individual enmeshed — 46
The fragility of the Self — 50
The role of women — 53
  Weak women — 54
  Female roles — 55
  Women rebels — 59
The fluidity of bodies — 69

3 Carnal Pleasures, Mortal Sins — 75

Forbidden passions — 77
The joys of sex — 84
  Peasant eroticism in Somerset — 85
  Bawdy culture in France — 89
  L'École des filles, a libertine gem — 96
Pleasure and sin — 99
  Homosexuality in transition — 100
  Repression — 101
  The burning of a pornographer — 104
  Pleasure and the disruption of the established order — 106

Part III Cycles: Vice and Virtue (1700–1960) — 109

4 The Eroticism of the Enlightenment — 115

The pornographic flood — 116
  A literature of transgression — 117
  The market in desire — 118
  The books that dimmed the lights of the Enlightenment — 121
Sex within measure — 127
  Pleasure in moderation — 128
  Orgasm and marriage — 132
  The masculine double standard — 134
  No pleasure outside the vagina — 138
  The crusade against onanism — 141
The art of the 'I' — 146

CONTENTS

Whores, drunks and lecherous apprentices	146
Demonized biographies	149
The pleasures of the imagination	153

5 Beneath the Victorian Veil (1800–1960) — **156**

Controlling sex	158
Social roles	158
The new medical religion	160
Nudity and body hair	162
Sexuality, a shameful, even fatal, sickness	164
The age of anxiety	165
Semen wasted, death assured: the great fear of masturbation	169
Venal pleasures and fallen women	178
Through the looking glass	183
Walter the Victorian	184
The 'hell' of sex: pornography prospers	189
Making the 'transgressions' ordinary	192
Proletarian pleasures	196
The ebbs and flows of desire	202

Part IV Revolutions? The Heritage of the Sixties — **205**

6 The Era of Pleasure (From 1960 to Our Own Day) — **211**

A sexual bombshell: the Kinsey Report	212
The origins of the 'culture wars'	213
Homosexuality and masturbation	216
A hidden erotic culture	219
The survival of a sexual double standard	222
The discovery of the female orgasm	224
Female pleasure	225
The contraceptive revolutions	227
Good vibrations	228
Towards a new sexual contract?	230
Changes to the code of love	230
The right to sexual pleasure	232
Gay marriage	234
Erotic equality and simultaneous orgasm	238
The sexual revolution today	240

Conclusion: The Narcissistic Society — **245**
    The values of the hedonists — 246
    Narcissism and culture — 251

Notes — 259

Bibliography — 286

Index — 302

A YEAR OF PLEASURE

The abbey of Thélème exists. Rabelais would have loved to spend a calm and productive year there, as I did, in a select society, doing what he wanted, on the sole condition of residence. At the Institute for Advanced Study in Princeton, I found peace of mind, the warmth of friendship and the refined taste for all the pleasures of the intellect; those of the body too, sometimes, as long as I avoided the excess of powdered garlic in the sauces of the remarkable restaurant and as long as I did not too openly display a penchant for artificial paradises. No one who has not seen 39 pairs of eyes range from his own glass of wine to 39 other glasses of water can appreciate the power of personal self-control under the weight of social pressure! To conform becomes a joy, or at least a relief.

In this Eden of researchers, with its huge libraries open day and night, even on Sundays, work becomes an ethic, an art of living, even a sign of predestination for the heirs of the Protestant spirit. Confronted with this world, the European hedonist finds plenty to incite him to efficiency. I was surprised to discover how much the enjoyment of simple pleasures is enhanced when some of them are missing. Absence and lack have taught me the full value of champagne, foie gras and aromatic cheese. I have been better able to understand, as a result, the extent to which 'old Europe' today differs from this country born of its labours, still attached to a virile and competitive view of life that leaves less space than at home for the immediate delectations. These two great cultures manage pleasure very differently, as we will see from the conclusion to this book. It was a long immersion in the United States that enabled me to appreciate this more clearly. I remember the comment of a philosopher after I had addressed my peers on the subject of carnal pleasure. At table, next day, he snarkily observed: 'I've been here for more than 30 years. It's the first time I've heard the word "fuck" in public.'

I am filled with nostalgia when I think of the days I spent at the Institute. On the path leading to my office, in front of Fuld Hall, still haunted by the shadow of Albert Einstein, I bumped into colleagues and friends every day. I talked to them often and at length, watching the antics of squirrels, birds and rabbits in spring, and in May I saw cicadas fall from the trees, insects that emerge from the ground once every 17 years only to reproduce and die in July. I wondered if these creatures, too, experienced pleasure, in particular the pleasure of sex; but without talking about it too much to my American colleagues, for fear of being considered too French, too interested in subjects best kept for the privacy of the bedroom...

May all those who helped me to conceive and write this book find here the expression of my sincere gratitude:

Tzvi Abusch, Engin Akarli, Markus Asper, Vivian Barnett, Paolo Berdini, Sylvia Berryman, Glen W. Bowersock, Michael Broers, Caroline Walker Bynum, Vincent Carretta, Pascale Chapdelaine, Caludine Cohen, Giles Constable, Patricia Crone, José Cutileiro, Monica and Joseph Davis, Laurence Devillairs, Nicola Di Cosmo, Emma Dillon, William Doyle, Veit Elm, Christine Evans-Clarke, Theodore Evergates, Vincenzo Ferrone, Robin Fox, Jane Fulcher, Henry Louis Gates Jr., Oleg Grabar, Frank Griffel, Cynthia Hahn, Ellen Harris, John Hope Mason, Jonathan Israel, Victoria Kamsler, Lauren Kassell, Tia Kolbaba, Audrey Korotayev, Thomas Kühne, Ellen Landau, Irving Lavin, Trudo Lemmens, Ki Che Angela Leung, Alexander Lingas, Richard D. Lockwood, Elizabeth A. Lunbeck, Beatrice Manz, David Marsh, Judith McKenzie, E. William Monter, Lloyd Moote, Alexei Muraviev, Philip Nord, Michael Nylan, Peter Paret, Sophie and Ronnie Po-Chia Hsia, Tessa Rajak, Amneris Roselli, Suzanne Saïd, Londa Schiebinger, Joan W. Scott, Andrew Shanken, H. Alan Shapiro, John Shepherd, Heinrich von Staden, Adam Sutcliffe, Morton White, Don Wyatt and Froma Zeitlin.

Princeton/Paris, 2003–4

INTRODUCTION

The idea of pleasure covers a multiform reality. From sensual gratification to the aesthetic delights or the bliss of the spiritual life, by way of the pleasures of the table and not forgetting the perverse thrills, the spectrum of human happiness is very varied. In ancient China, under the Han dynasty, scholars defined the term precisely by relating it to an action (to take or to seek pleasure), to a state (such as euphoria) or to feelings and needs. They distinguished three possible forms of pleasure: the immediate satisfaction of the desires; the delight associated with pride of possession, of goods and of persons (palaces and gardens, fine horses, beautiful women, magnificent robes, good cooking, exquisite wines, etc.); and the pleasure derived from a philosophical reflection on the perception of joys experienced, which sometimes led to one of them being deferred in order ultimately to obtain a more extended and more intense rapture, even to its being spurned. The great sages advised the emperors to pursue a true politics of pleasure, so as to give to the expenditure of energy, time and wealth entailed in seeking it forms likely to strengthen the state, the family and the person, rather than corrupt them.[1] They believed that the virtue and the asceticism of the Confucian way crowned the edifice that led mankind towards what Westerners would call happiness.[2]

But let me not overreach myself. This book makes no claim to range so widely. I have chosen to confine it to sexuality, returning from this perspective to a subject that has been little studied in spite of the synthesizing work of Michel Foucault in 1976.[3] Contrary to Foucault, I believe that a powerful repression of the carnal appetites was established at the very heart of our civilization around the middle of the sixteenth century, and that it only really lost ground in the

1960s. Producing a fundamental tension between the libido of each individual and the collective ideals, this process constantly promoted a powerful labour of sublimation throughout this long period, under the successive cultural covers of religion, Catholic or Protestant, of the ideal of moderation of the *philosophes* of the Enlightenment and the doctors of the nineteenth century, and of the laws of the capitalist market. On the coercive base laid down in the seventeenth century were then imposed alternate cycles of liberation and constraint, whose fluctuations I believe to be fundamental to an explanation of the general dynamism of Europe, because they persistently created the need to compensate for the mental disequilibrium they caused. On the one hand, the accumulation of unsatisfied desires during periods of intense frustration gave rise to a growing demand for emancipation, which eventually unleashed a libertine surge; on the other, many people subjected, willingly or not, to the tyrannies of moral rigour developed a behavioural structure which literally drove them forward, helping to develop their personal talents to the full in many fields of activity, such as religious proselytism, war and world conquest, artistic and intellectual activities and international trade.

Many of the classic explanations for the originality of the European experience revolve around the antagonistic pairing of spirituality and economics. It seems to me, however, that to refer primarily to Christianity or to capitalism is not wholly satisfactory, because these notions, while they describe objective realities, are also cultural products, the translation into discourse of the social and material facts whose contours they define. This is why I propose a broader interpretation which involves the totality of human relations, maintaining that the sublimation of the erotic impulses has been the basis of the originality of our continent since the Renaissance. It went well beyond the norms imposed by the theologians and governments, permanently controlling the explosive and highly destabilizing potential of sexuality by constantly adapting to major changes. I believe that its apparent form, the repression of lust, is an essential element in the invention of Western modernity and provides the key to understanding the intimate relationship forged between the spiritual and the material, the body and the mind, one human being and others. Max Weber linked the birth and development of capitalism to the Calvinist ethic, a way of explaining the European genius by religious sociology.[4] Broadening his perspective, I consider that the fundamental originalities of our collective 'fabric' are the product of an intense effort to control and reorient carnal desire; however, I see this as something consistently distilled by all the life forces at work in the common matrix for nearly five centuries, not as a simple moral consequence of the Protestant spirit. Here, I agree with Norbert Elias, who described the dynamic of our culture in terms of personal sublimation put at the service of overall progress, through 'the civilizing process',[5] but I wish to complement his work, primarily focused on the generic evolution of the phenomenon and the production of the social bond, in a way that will expose the functioning of the hidden mechanism that has allowed this evolution by taming the volcanic power of the sensual appetites. Since Freud, such an approach may appear banal. However, it remains to be explained how society, source of invisible powers, is able to channel our intimate desires so as to sublimate them and make them serve the group as a whole. My theme combines a history of sexual pleasure, a consideration of the body, both in scholarly theory and in its concrete perception, and an investigation of the human Subject, from the age of contempt and almost total taboo, in the sixteenth and seventeenth centuries, to the present triumph of narcissism.

For the purposes of this book, I have decided to restrict my study to the 500 years between the Renaissance and our own day, a period I see as possessing a profound unity, and to compare two great countries, France and England. Significantly different, according to well-established stereotypes, implacable rival possessors of the greatest world empires until recent decolonizations, both upholding prestigious traditions, they prove surprisingly similar in the matter of the perception and management of the orgasm. One Catholic, the other Protestant, their long parallel evolution encourages me to play down the importance of religion in the definition and the establishment of an identical self-control of the physical passions, culminating in the production of a 'libidinal economy' which has been the basis of the extraordinary European growth since the Great Discoveries. Rival capitals, Paris and London were its favoured laboratories. At the end of this period, the United States – both rebellious heir of proud Albion and fascinated by her French rival at the time of La Fayette – will serve as a third yardstick by which to measure both the ancient similarities with the hedonistic Old Continent and the recent increasing divergences from it.

My book is in four parts. In the first I present my thesis, through the main characteristics of the Western approach to carnal pleasure over the last five centuries and the way in which it has formed a particular pact with our civilization. Christianity tried from the beginning to confine the molten lava of the vital instinct under a carapace of interdicts and prohibitions, but it was only in the middle of the sixteenth century that the moral pressure intensified, among Catholics and Protestants alike, whose action was supported by strict new laws promulgated by the civil powers. Personal self-control and the guilt increasingly attached to immodest or obscene behaviour helped to impose a system of sexuality that was purely procreative, acceptable solely within the context of marriage, its pleasures even then to be enjoyed only in moderation. All other behaviour was condemned. Although such a glaciation of behaviour was more moralist's dream than true reflection of reality, it still contributed to the growth of an inner tension in those who tried to master or curtail their desires in obedience to the commandments of the Church and of monarchical legislation. The vital energy thus channelled was frequently reoriented to the benefit of the great collective ideals. In fact, the increasing surveillance of the body and the mind denounced by Michel Foucault had unintended positive consequences, because society benefited from the accumulation of energies that ensued.[6] It also helped to imprint deep in our culture, generation after generation, the indelible mark of the suffering at the heart of pleasure, accompanied in some people by a pronounced taste for transgression. The erotic unsayable was therefore transformed into a secret motor of human actions; it produced an instinctual personal imbalance that was more creative than destructive and it generated alternating phases of repression and liberation that enriched society. Vice and virtue succeeded one another, each in its turn putting its mark on a century, on a few decades or on a short space of time, until the 1960s, when women's sexual liberation and the unstoppable advance of the aspiration to instant happiness signalled major changes, even a revolution.

The three parts that follow describe the main stages in this evolution since the Renaissance.

In the sixteenth and seventeenth centuries, pleasure could be conceived of only in pain, sorrow or rebellion. This was not only due to the ancient Christian mentality which opposed the exaltation of the body the better to save the soul. The tradition now found a new consensus among decision-makers and men of power. States became increasingly concerned to ensure the obedience of their subjects, and the towns, thriving thanks to nascent capitalism and obsessed with economic efficiency, demanded more discipline on the part of their inhabitants. The individual emerged, because men and women were driven to affirm their existence and to experience their guilt more deeply before God, the king and the representatives of governments. Indelible imprints, the prohibitions linked pleasure closely to sin.

INTRODUCTION

Strict enforcement of the laws made only too real the mortal danger threatening transgressors, as some were publicly burned for speaking too openly about the delights of physical love. Such memories would linger in the West for a long time to come, right up to the radical changes of the 1960s. Perhaps they have not entirely disappeared in our age of epicureanism?

Between 1700 and 1960, two great cycles succeeded one another, the first of moral laxity, the second of Puritanism. The Enlightenment showed eroticism in a new light and pornography flourished, but the Victorian veil came down with a vengeance, between 1800 and 1960, concealing breasts and other things that could not decently be contemplated. Nineteenth-century medicine seized control of sexual power, which it bestowed in its entirety on adult married men. By emphasizing the natural coldness, even frigidity, of their chaste spouses, it assured the triumph of the double standard of masculine behaviour, which allowed men to have no complexes about frequenting the prostitutes who alone were capable of offering them sexual satisfaction. It imposed a form of laicized sublimation, however, insisting on the absolute necessity of moderating the instincts, because it likened sexual excess to a sickness that might prove fatal, in particular for boys who indulged in masturbation. The insistent theme of pleasure in suffering thus continued on its course by draping itself in scientific certitudes.

Since the 1960s, the old rigorist model has persisted in the United States, but in Europe hedonism rules. The basic principles governing the sexual act seem to have been transformed in the Old Continent. The human sciences now openly describe notions and attitudes that caused deep embarrassment only a few decades ago, excitedly probing into the private life of one and all, uninhibitedly explaining what was for earlier centuries a mysterious and sacred paradigm. The traditional equilibrium, anchored in the dogma of shameful sensuality and the concealed body, is seriously threatened by the sudden irruption of the female orgasm onto the public and the private stage, an unprecedented innovation with major consequences in the short term and incalculable effects in the long term. The carnal pact, basis of the social contract in our world, because it produces the conjugal tie whose importance was until recently considered primordial, is now being renegotiated by the two halves of the human race; a third actor has meanwhile emerged, the homosexual Subject, who is openly demanding his or her rights.

The whole construction has been badly shaken, in an age when navel-gazing, even egoism, seems to prevail. This conclusion raises

INTRODUCTION

questions about the huge transformations which are pulling contemporary European societies towards the good life, while the United States cultivates a nostalgia for the familial and sexual archetype bequeathed by the repressive tradition, so is much more suspicious of the lure of pleasure.

The phenomenon merits particular attention at a time when major upheavals are looming on the world stage, which call for dynamic and inventive changes to the Western model. This requirement intersects with the process by which the couple is adapting to the challenges of modernity, because the concordant discourses promoted by many prescriptive authorities urge partners with increasing insistence to separate the sexual drive for pleasure from the desire for a child. I have tried in this book to formulate a broader form of the cultural history of societies, taking account of the contributions of different disciplines and of the anxieties and questions of our times. An exchange of views is necessary to an attempt to provide new answers to one of the oldest enigmas in the world: what is pleasure and what purpose does it serve?

Part I

ORGASM AND THE WEST

The human being never exists alone. Notably gregarious, from the 'primitive horde' to the hedonistic excesses of the beginning of the third millennium, humans have constantly asked others to help them to live and to die. It is the purpose of history to examine this link, in an attempt to understand how and why a society holds together as it adapts to the inexorable passage of time.

To choose the subject of pleasure to guide such a study may seem paradoxical, inasmuch as it is a vague notion and notoriously difficult to define.[1] It is through their body and their sexuality, natural elements influenced by each civilization, that Subjects become conscious of themselves, and then form their relationships with others. A medium for pleasure and a prison for the person, the bodily envelope is also a cultural entity, an element in the community that surrounds it, a part of the political whole, a small piece of a vast territory of symbols. The persons thus defined are shaped by imperative prescripts, whether they consent to them or, on the contrary, try as far as possible to exercise their own free will.

One of the great enigmas that has tormented Westerners for two millennia, and with increasing urgency since the Renaissance, is precisely that of the relationship between the individual and the group. What is its secret cement? By what special genius has *Homo sapiens* been able to move beyond the forms of association peculiar to the advanced primates with which, contemporary biologists tell us, he shares so many genes?

The long period considered here, from Christopher Columbus to the beginning of the twenty-first century, is that in which the West imposed its mark on the whole world. The 'imperial animal' became, in five centuries, an imperialist colonizer.[2] The strange compound that was the source of this power was essentially based on a skilful and effective management of time. The West did not only invent technical and economic processes; it also developed ideals and myths, necessary to give meaning to its trajectory and to strengthen, century after century, generation after generation, the communal fabric put constantly under strain by upheavals and innovations. It has slowly abandoned the old Christian concept of the duality of the body and the soul – though something of it persists to our day – in favour of formulations emphasizing the unity between the thinking being and their world of reference – the Enlightenment, the rights of man, Marxism, liberalism, etc. The change began with Descartes, gathered pace with Newton and took the name of modern science, of progress, of the march towards human happiness. It was, in reality, a way of shedding the burdens of the representation of a finite world, where nothing mattered to the faithful except preparing for their salvation by a good death, since everything was written in advance in God's great book, from the Creation to the Apocalypse.

Pleasure was not licit in the sixteenth and seventeenth centuries, especially as individuals, closely supervised by their peer group and various tutelary bodies, were given dire warnings against the temptation of navel-gazing. The explanatory systems proposed in the eighteenth and nineteenth centuries celebrated the discovery of pleasure and that of the right to sexual enjoyment. Not only did it become easy to seek out the delights of eroticism without fear of the law or of hell, it also became possible to think openly about the phenomenon. It loomed increasingly large because it spoke both of the person and of their desires, licit or forbidden, and of the role the community ascribed to sexuality, in accord with its dominant values and objectives. It was increasingly written about, proof not of an absence of repression, but of a strong and fruitful contradiction between the new demand for liberty and the indelible mark left by the prohibitions of preceding centuries. Freud was referring to this in his own way when he emphasized the duality of the Self, driven both by the instinct for life and by that for death, by Eros and by Thanatos. It may be, however, that the 1960s marked the beginning of a true revolution in sensual pleasure in Europe.

These are the main lines of my argument in this book. Implicit also is a reflection on the invention of the human sciences, faithful companions of the promotion of the West, in order to understand why and how the Subject entered onto the scene in force; not as a creature liberated from all its chains, without God or master, but as a person strongly urged by society to be much more conscious of his or her specificity, needs and desires. The flickering light of pleasure will enable us to find and follow the Ariadne's thread that will guide us in our exploration of the dark cave of our origins. The time is ripe, because Europe faces radical challenges and unsettling competition, following the emergence of formidable rivals in other parts of the globe. Deep hidden meanings emerge more clearly from between cracks and fissures than in periods of strong convictions.

1

CARNAL KNOWLEDGE

Physical pleasure connects the person to the totality of the universe. We need to try to understand what people represent in the Western tradition, therefore, before we can characterize their relationship to pleasure. Though they use seemingly very different words and concepts, both the Christian theologians and Freud emphasize an implacable opposition between two entities constitutive of the human being. The theologians speak of the body and the soul. Freud drew a more complex distinction between the life impulse and the death impulse, but basically returned to a dualist vision by asserting both that sexuality is indispensable to the survival of the species and that it conceals a destructive potential. In either case, the space left to the joys of the flesh is much reduced. It was not until the last third of the twentieth century that there emerged ideas more favourable to the benefits of the orgasm and its crucial role in our culture.

The slow and chaotic invention of the individual is the guiding thread that will enable us to trace the logic of these changes, because the mechanism of sublimation established by sexual repression was the invisible motor driving the rise of the West until the spectacular changes of the 1960s.

The birth of the individual

The notion of the Subject has been debated by Western historians for a very long time. Very few of them, however, would date its emergence to earlier than the twelfth century.[1] This innovation was then a 'collective enterprise' linked to 'a duty to God to reform one's neighbour', which made possible the 'discovery of a model' that could lead to 'the spiritual progress of both individual and community'.[2]

The Renaissance or capitalism?

For many scholars, the real turning point came in the sixteenth century, or at least in the Italian *quattrocento*. This was the view of Jacob Burckhardt, though it has been strongly contested by some specialists in the field. For Burckhardt, medieval man was conscious of himself only through a race, people, family or corporation, whereas with the Renaissance he became a spiritual individual able to recognize himself as such.[3] This development was confined to the upper ranks of society, especially intellectuals and artists.

Like Karl Marx in his thinking about the commercial origins of capitalism, Max Weber also started from material preconditions to arrive at a sociology of religions which attributed a prime role to a new type of man.[4] For Weber, the sixteenth century was a decisive turning point, marked in north-western Europe, more precisely in England, by the introduction of a trade system which broke away from the traditional agricultural system of the Middle Ages. While accepting that monetary accumulation had existed in China, India and even on Christian soil in previous centuries, he argued that the unprecedented value attached to unlimited accumulation was a unique feature specific to the early modern West. Completely unknown elsewhere, it appeared towards the end of the fifteenth century, and was later strengthened by the Calvinist spirit, especially English Puritanism. The explanation, Weber believed, had to be sought in the Calvinist doctrine of predestination. By producing an 'asceticism in the world' opposed to the enjoyment of pleasure, it conveyed a powerful work ethic and greatly encouraged the development of a 'personality' in the 'formal psychological sense of the term'. The European venture guided by the Puritans led to the decline of communal allegiances, the separation of private life from the search for profit and the promotion of the Subject. Never sure of being saved by God, in accord with the doctrine of predestination, the Subject searched fervently for signs of success in various spheres, in particular in commerce, to try to reassure himself of his mysterious eternal destiny.[5]

A privilege reserved to creative ideas, Weber's thesis has led to much ink being spilled and has inspired numerous critiques. It was very much of its time, the end of the nineteenth century, in presenting a theory based on the primacy of economics but fruitfully nuanced by a broad religious analysis, close to what we today call cultural history.

The individual and transgression

Here, too, we need to be clear in our definitions: person, ego, Self, individual, etc. – the words are heavy with hidden meanings, accumulated over the centuries like successive geological strata. In the sixteenth and seventeenth centuries, the founding period, there were no terms with which to name the phenomenon. Further, the formulation of individualism was conceived only in two contexts, which strictly limited it. In the first, one expressed what one was within a firmly proclaimed relationship to the circles to which one belonged – family, friends, neighbours, etc. Thus the spiritual autobiography flourished not as a true revelation of the Self, but as a model of piety, held up to all. The only other means of singular expression was transgression, the questioning of religious and moral obligations. Unlike the first, it has left traces only among a tiny minority of people capable of writing and of positioning themselves on the margins of the established systems. In France, only a few men and the very rare woman, often frustrated in their hopes, dared to brave the Christian taboo forbidding one to speak of oneself, because one should always be thinking of God, death and salvation. They included Montaigne, impossible to categorize; Brantôme, author of *Les Dames galantes*, disabled as a result of a fall from a horse; the maréchal de Montluc, wounded, disfigured and disgraced; Agrippa d'Aubigné, flamboyant Huguenot, who went into exile in Geneva, furious at seeing his master, Henri IV, accept a religious peace with the Catholics; and Marguerite de Valois, repudiated wife of Henri IV, nicknamed 'la reine Margot', long banished by her brother Henri III, and a disappointed woman, eager to hand down to posterity the story of her life as she would have wished it. There were certainly others, more obscure, who gave intense expression to their singularity, as one can see from the many female passions revealed by the judicial archives.[6] But everything was then opposed to the easy articulation of individual feelings. D'Aubigné himself did not use the first person when writing *Sa vie à ses enfants* (*His Life, to his Children*). Norms and codes prevented people from openly proclaiming their independence – or made them pay a high price if they did.

In the sixteenth century, contrary to Burckhardt's claims, individuals did not achieve true autonomy. They could explore their intimate life only in conscious contact with the groups to which they belonged, under the eye of authority.[7] Women encountered additional difficulties in the course of an uncertain struggle to win recognition of their specificity and their rights, especially if they were poor and weak, since they always came up against the traditional religious obligations and family relationships organized on a patriarchal basis.[8]

In other words, the individual is not individualism. The former probably exists in all human societies, but the generic quality signalled by the second is a recent phenomenon closely linked to the history of the West. The idea appears at almost the same time in English, around 1820, as it does in French, around 1833.[9] It covered a production of meaning that would preoccupy many intellectuals in the nineteenth century, because it posed a major problem for the interpretation of the trajectory of the European dynamic. To be able to conceive of it, it was necessary to break powerful taboos that had been in place since the second half of the sixteenth century. Yet these taboos had not prevented some increase in introspection. They may even have contributed to it, by causing the persecuted and the dominated to become more conscious of their otherness.

Until the eighteenth century, the dogma of the duality of the body and the soul discouraged exploration of the inner world, which was too closely associated with sin.[10] The affirmation of the Self aroused the emotions and the passions, pleasure and pain, that is, everything good believers should suppress and tame in order to assure the salvation of their soul. The perishable flesh was the prison of the soul and it brought the human being – even the saint – closer to animality. Only scientific progress and the philosophical Enlightenment could begin to change this perspective.

The envelopes of the Self

Of the many attempts to understand the human Subject, what we need to remember is the emphasis on the special relationship it has with the West and the fact that it slowly and painfully extricated itself from the collective straitjackets between the sixteenth and the eighteenth centuries.[11] One of the richest and most fruitful discussions of this subject is that of the German sociologist Norbert Elias, inventor, shortly before the beginning of the Second World War, of the influential theory of the 'civilizing process'. For Elias, the Renaissance inaugurated a long and continuous trajectory of the growth of European culture and the individualization of the person. Life at Versailles under Louis XIV then obliged the warlike nobles to rein in their previously uncontrollable aggression and put it at the exclusive service of the monarch on the battlefield. His central thesis was to link global progress to the development of the state and the towns and to show that it resulted in the increasing acceptance of self-control on the part of those concerned. The subsequent slow retreat of brutal or sexual impulses led to the growth of peaceful social exchanges in a world in which governments claimed a monopoly of violence.[12]

Elias had an admirable grasp of the federative aspects of the sublimations that Freud discovered in each of his patients. But though he proposed as analytical tool the equivalent of the Freudian superego, or even id, he was not really interested in the ego as it was described by the founder of psychoanalysis. He focused his attention on the ways in which human groups succeeded in making their members share unifying values and in inculcating automatic mechanisms, rather than on the concrete realities of existence or the obvious contradictions between the theoretical norms and the real desires or needs of individuals. He devoted only a short section to sexuality, simply to show that it was 'removed behind the scenes of social life' by a process 'similar to that shown in more detail in the expression of other impulses'.[13] He preferred to develop and broaden his theories on the reform of violent, scatological or indecent behaviour, referring primarily to the rules laid down almost simultaneously by two famous works, Castiglione's *Book of the Courtier* (1528) and the *On Good Manners for Boys* by Erasmus (1530).

Elias thus confined himself to the level of the models disseminated among the upper ranks of European society, lacking either the inclination or the means to consider practices or describe attitudes that were condemned and slow to disappear, which would have required a patient and difficult process of information gathering. Further, he did not pay sufficient attention to what was hidden by the new approach to knowledge and power that he revealed. It was not by chance that the insidious snare of the ego appeared during the Renaissance or that it really began to develop in the second half of the sixteenth century, in parallel with the Catholic and Protestant moral chill of the era of the wars of religion. This did far more than Elias suggests to stigmatize a sexuality that the guardians of the temple no longer wanted to see displayed in public, given their inability actually to control the erotic impulses. The same normative blanket fell with an increasingly stifling effect on the succeeding generations.

Beyond the Subject

Can the human being really achieve total unity? The twentieth century has slipped imperceptibly into a narcissistic culture, we are told on all sides, including that of the exact sciences.[14] This is, in a way, the fault of Freud, who broke with the traditional Western duality opposing the body and the soul, in order to restore the repressed to its place. He distinguished the 'body-ego' from the superego or ego ideal, linked to the Oedipus complex, and finally from the profound id.

> We shall now look upon an individual as a psychical id, unknown and unconscious, upon whose surface rests the ego ... we may add that the ego does not completely envelop the id ... the ego is not sharply separated from the id; its lower portion merges into it. But the repressed merges into the id as well, and is merely a part of it. The repressed is only cut off sharply from the ego by the resistances of repression; it can communicate with the ego through the id.[15]

For Freud, pleasure was intimately bound up with the ego; it was, he said, 'the true and original reservoir of libido', and 'it is only from that reservoir that libido is extended on to objects'. But he contrasts the 'ego-instincts', leading to death, and the sexual instincts, oriented towards life. Some of the latter also operate in the ego, he maintained, later observing that the pleasure principle could in reality be in the service of the death instincts.[16]

Freud, often provocative, constructed by his own admission a mythology. While refusing to oppose the soul and the body, he surreptitiously reintroduced, it seems to me, another duality, by basing his doctrine on two antagonistic types of impulse, the life impulse and the death impulse. His major innovation with regard to the unity of the Subject did not prevent him from sometimes experiencing doubts on this matter. A brilliant innovator, he could not entirely escape the context in which he lived and worked, which made it impossible for him to develop his argument wholly without reference to good and evil. His founding texts concerning the two types of contrary impulses continued, while radically modernizing, Christian teaching on the original Fall, sin, the repression of the evil desires, the neglect of the perishable flesh and the sublimation of the passions. Far from the certitudes of the optimists of the Enlightenment, who believed in a continuous progress of civilizations, his intellectual approach bears the indelible mark of the old conception of the individual as perpetually in crisis. Accompanied by a nostalgia for the internal division of the being into two irreducible entities, already present in the myth of the hermaphrodite in Plato, this tragic vision of human existence underpins the theory of the inevitably tortured genius and links the carnal appetite closely to disease and death, as in Thomas Mann's *Death in Venice* (1912) and *Doctor Faustus* (1947).[17]

Many things are contained in the notion of the repressed, to which Freud offered the symbolic key. All human beings, he said, are driven by sexual and aggressive instincts. Unconscious causes of their actions, these can be sublimated by the superego, produced by the internalizing of common values and educational models derived from the parents. The process creates great suffering, however, as a consequence of the sacrifices demanded by society and the control exercised by each individual, which entails the loss of certain pleasures experienced by our primitive ancestors, bartered in exchange for security.[18]

In our own period, we are only able to conceive of a certain unity of the person by idealizing it and by claiming that the age of the sovereign Subject has arrived. Yet social forces and the prescriptive powers, in particular the mass media, leave it with little space for genuine autonomy. Never has the Subject been so studied, oriented, controlled and looked after as now. In the United States, the intellectuals of the last decades of the twentieth century also discovered an important generic dimension to narcissism, inventing the figure of the 'tragic man' obsessed by disintegration anxiety.[19] Thus, having left, it seemed, by the Viennese door in the age of Freud, the duality of the individual has returned through the American window. This individual is seen as fractured, wracked by despair and by the impossibility of achieving self-realization, because he lacks from the start a sufficiently coherent core of ego, for which he seeks to compensate by imagining himself as 'grandiose'. The fundamental cause is to be found in the dull and sterile monotony of exchanges between parents and children, an accusation directed at a supposed abandonment of traditional family values in North America, which seems above all to conceal a malaise in the civilization.[20] The personality in question, characterized as eminently bipolar, surely simply reflects the classic Christian opposition between body and soul, in a country which remains much more deeply impregnated by the biblical heritage than 'old Europe'.

Hallmark of our identity for five centuries, the invention of the 'I', supposed to define itself in opposition to the 'we', still manages to speak only of the whole to which the person in question belongs and of the social tie as it is conceived in the West. What is meant then, in this context, by carnal knowledge?

Is it all down to sex?

Sex is nothing, it was long decreed by normative thinking in the West, from the age of the cathedrals and of the flesh tamed by God's athletes to the stultifying pressures of Victorian England or the moral order reigning in France until May 1968. It fell to Michel Foucault, that famous tracker-down of the discourse of surveillance, to try to open up perspectives on this taboo theme. He did this in the first volume of his *History of Sexuality*, entitled *The Will to Knowledge*.[21] In this brilliant if ultimately rather disappointing book, Foucault set out to disprove the 'repressive hypothesis' prevailing in this area of knowledge.

Though useful to a discussion of the subject in the eighteenth and nineteenth centuries, Foucault's paradigms scarcely apply to the earlier period or to the second half of the twentieth century. The archetype he describes was, in reality, the product of a fundamental change which began in the populous metropolises of Paris and London around 1700, and led to a general reordering of the sexual system to the benefit of adult males through the increasingly exclusive emphasis on marriage. Not only has this archetype lost its coherence since the 1960s, under the impact of the claims of women and homosexuals, but the situation had been very different in the sixteenth and seventeenth centuries; the repression, then, which is unquestionable in my opinion, resulted less from a theoretical pressure exercised by distant authorities than from the pressure produced by the gaze of others and local codes of behaviour.

Foucault's paradigms

Foucault's sometimes rather confused demonstrations were intended to shift attention away from physical realities towards discourses, by showing that what they reveal is not censorship but, on the contrary, an increasing logorrhoea which had the effect of making sex *the* secret, because it really was the 'reason for everything'.[22] He frequently uses the word '*enjeu*' ('stake' or 'issue'), in order to emphasize the importance of the new type of relationship established in such matters between the state and the individual, especially in the case of students and adolescents. He ponders the nature of the links connecting pleasure and authority and several times repeats his central argument: the eighteenth century saw the birth of a biopower which had a profound effect on the problem of the connections between the body and the population and made sexuality its chief target.[23]

Foucault twice rather cautiously advances the hypothesis of a management of sexuality, so that it would be 'economically useful and politically conservative', the biopower being indispensable to the development of capitalism.[24] He makes no attempt to clarify further the question of the correlation between the advance of this conquering West and the management of individual carnal instincts.

Foucault completely changed his plan for the series as it had been announced in the first volume. Instead of concentrating on Europe since the Middle Ages, as he had initially intended, he devoted the two subsequent volumes, which came out in 1984, the year of his death, to Greek and Roman antiquity.[25] Among the most exciting avenues he explored in his first volume of 1976 was the idea of the ultimate sexual mystery, revealed only to the confessor or, later, on the psychoanalyst's couch, paradoxically transmitted by an ever-increasing number of works on the subject. Equally fruitful was the observation that it is impossible to identify a single cycle of repression, with a beginning and an end.[26] The principal contribution of his *History of Sexuality* lies in the four paradigms he identified, which contain, whatever he says, a strong repressive charge. These are the 'hystericization' of women's bodies achieved by medicine; the 'pedagogization' of children's sexuality, intended to curb grave dangers, in particular masturbation; the 'socialization' of procreative behaviour through supervision of the fertility of couples and their 'responsibilization'; and the 'psychiatricization' of perverse pleasure to make it easier to recognize the anomalies and the pathologies to be treated.[27]

Here we have the basic features of a central period, the eighteenth and nineteenth centuries, but they characterize neither the preceding historical period nor the one that followed. The only linear development since the Renaissance seems to me to be in the discourses confining the sexual mystery to the very heart of the ego, not in actual behaviour, which is marked by a succession of major changes.

The three stages of sexuality

Biology, the neurosciences and ethology now claim that human beings, like all living organisms, have a need for permanence, of which sexuality is a principal vector; our species seems to be alone, however, in the present state of knowledge, in practising sublimation. In Freudian terms, this not only allows a diversion of the excessive excitations but is also 'one of the origins of artistic activity'.[28] In my opinion, it has been the true motor of the European dynamic since, some 500 years ago, it came to be closely associated with a powerful effort of sexual repression that extended well beyond the scope of Christian morality. This last simply expressed a wider demand for the restoration of order in a fractured and conflicted society, just as Freudianism would later offer the industrial bourgeoisie a secularized version of libidinal economy adapted to the requirements of capitalist accumulation. Under the cloak of religion or of psychoanalysis, it invariably boils down to preaching the individual self-control of the impulses, at the cost of pain and fear, but for the greater good of the community. Are we not still to some degree heirs to this Western brand of asceticism, which makes it possible to channel the potentially highly destructive life force represented by the sex drive of individuals?

The phenomenon has a long history. The monks were its champions from the beginnings of Christianity, urging the secular clergy to follow their example by extolling the virtues of celibacy and sexual continence. Yet it was not until the Council of Trent, in 1563, that such injunctions began to be applied with increasing rigour by the clergy who, before this major reform, had often given free rein to their desires; and it was only when these notions of morality were adopted by active and growing circles among the laity that they began to play a crucial role in the European experience.

At the time of the Renaissance, the traditional Christian normative discourse warned against sensual pleasure; the ideal, for men and even more for women, was to refrain altogether and enter a monastery to assure one's salvation by denying the imperatives of the flesh. But the reality was very different. The Catholic Church considered marriage to be indispensable for those who were unable to resist temptation, so as to avoid damnation, while local authorities were largely content to impose a tacit equilibrium based on the active surveillance of excesses by parishioners as a whole.[29] Although illicit physical relations, outside marriage or without the consent of the male relatives of a seduced girl, in principle demanded bloody revenge, sexuality was in practice fairly free and easy and produced a fair number of bastards, though it was never as unbridled as amongst kings and courtiers.[30]

Things changed, gradually but radically, between the middle of the sixteenth and the end of the seventeenth century. Expressed in laws and moral regulations, a vigorous and spectacular sexual repression was put in place with the support of the churches and states now seeking to impose their will by controlling bodies as closely as souls. The pressure was greatest in the urban milieus attracted by philosophies of religious renunciation or the moderation of the appetites and consumption, which in this way differentiated themselves increasingly clearly from the aristocratic ethos of spending and ostentation. This sort of collective sublimation, sustained by individual sexual repression, in my view helped to generate or at least to reinforce the aggressive dynamism of the continent on the world stage, in particular that of conquering and colonizing countries such as France and England.

A second stage, from around 1700 to the 1960s, saw an internal reorganization of sexualities, strongly influenced by Foucault's four paradigms, but also major structural changes affecting relations between the two halves of humanity, and the emergence of a third homosexual 'gender'. This long period began with a phase of epicurean freedom, in the eighteenth century, which saw off the rigours of the preceding period, but was itself followed by a sustained period of moral constraint lasting until the great changes of the 1960s.

The 1960s – decisive turning point or simply sudden liberating upsurge before a possible nervous retreat – saw the emergence of a new European and Californian hedonistic system. Characterized by a massive effort to redefine sensualities as a result of the increasing erotic autonomy of women and the recognition of gay rights, it is spectacularly different from both the old and the new Puritanisms.

The family and the flesh

How are desire and the impulses managed by a human community? In the West, this was essentially the role of marriage, under the iron rule of the civil and religious authorities and a variety of supervisory bodies. Between the Renaissance and the Enlightenment there was a steady increase in the importance of the domestic sphere, as a consequence of the inexorable rise of the conjugal family as *the* space for private life, to the detriment of a wider sociability associated with the parish, the neighbourhood, friends and kin. The trend reached its apogee with the bourgeois household of the nineteenth century, based on the sanctuary of the home, before tailing off in the last third of the twentieth century.[31] The concept of private life has narrowed, and has also changed in important ways. In the huge cities of today, it applies equally to a majority of people who live alone, surrounded by an omnipresent consumer society, as was already the case in the early 1990s for 50 per cent of Manhattan tenants and as many as 70 per cent in Oslo.[32]

The legitimate couple is thus revealed not as a timeless phenomenon, but rather as closely dependent on the general development of civilization. From the middle of the sixteenth century to the middle of the twentieth century, the classical conjugal couple formed the primary basic unit, the preferred site for the encounter of individual bodies and norms, the sole permitted space for the expression of sexuality. Marriage and domestic life strictly confined the sexual act. To have sex, you had to marry, as is shown by the very low level of illegitimate births – around 1 per cent – in the French countryside in the seventeenth century. It seems that boys and girls remained chaste for more than a decade, on average, between puberty and marriage, because, in the absence of effective contraception, frequent intercourse between unmarried partners would have sent the illegitimacy rate soaring. What, then, did they do to resist the temptations of the flesh? Some historians claim they resorted to masturbation, or even to juvenile homosexual practices, others suggest they practised asceticism, after the example of the monks and the saints.

The seventeenth century certainly saw a powerful de-sexualization, which even affected the legally constituted couple, who were now enjoined to perform their conjugal duties without seeking sensual enjoyment. For the moralists, the latter was a sign of the fleshly excesses that degraded the human being. It was subtly distinguished from pleasure, which the doctors then claimed was necessary, for women as well as for men, in order to procreate in favourable conditions. The confessors, meanwhile, advised against making love to one's spouse too passionately and tried to insinuate themselves into the bedroom by questioning their parishioners about the positions they adopted and the nature of their caresses. The only acceptable behaviour, in their eyes, was penetration with intent to impregnate, the male on top of his partner, without seeking pleasure for its own sake.[33] Such instruction encouraged people to accept a sort of sublimation, or at least to moderate the physical appetites, in order to avoid damnation. In France after 1640, however, the weapon of the fear of the torments of hell was replaced by the new and soothing notion of the redemption of sin by grace, which helped to remove some of the guilt of couples previously bombarded with stern warnings, while still strongly urging them to control their desires.[34]

Whether or not they were applied by those at whom they were aimed, probably primarily the inhabitants of the towns, the religious prescripts were always based on a notion of a personal economy of the passions. They produced types of behaviour that were very different from those of the peasantry, for whom the repression of the 'base instincts' during a long period of celibacy was assured more by the vigilance of others than by the internalizing of prohibitions, which left them with a considerable degree of freedom.

Frustrated young men

For the rural societies of pre-industrial Europe, Christian marriage played a different role from that observed in the towns or among the elites, because it was grafted onto an original relational structure, composed of three distinct elements: married men, married women with children, and the young, mainly boys.[35] This system made it possible to manage sexuality by making it the main symbolic space for a permanent negotiation between the male age groups: in this way, adults closely channelled the disruptive erotic potential of the rising generations by confining their members within a long intermediate stage. Banded together in groups known as 'kingdoms' or 'abbeys of misrule', which by tradition they were all required to join, they champed at the bit once they reached puberty as they waited for their chance to accede to a full life, defined not only by the possession of property and power but even more by the marital status that enabled them to join the circle of the locally dominant. In compensation, these groups offered their members protection and solidarity, so they could resist the demands of parents or masters, and provided them with ample opportunity for emotional release, under the tolerant eye of the rest of the parish. In particular, their members were allowed to act as guardians of legitimate sexuality by imposing parodic donkey rides on cuckolded husbands or by drawing public attention to adulterous lovers, for example by laying a path of vegetables between the two houses. This can be seen as a way of acknowledging the frustration of their situation, since girls and married women were closely supervised by the men of their own group, especially fathers, brothers and husbands, who were quick to take bloody revenge on a lover whose activities they found unacceptable.

Nevertheless, unmarried men could take advantage of situations when vigilance was relaxed to pay court to girls, at evening gatherings, for example, or beneath their windows, and to have furtive sex with them, including in the seventeenth century, when the moral and religious codes were growing stronger. Although their sexuality was constrained, it was by no means nonexistent. Any woman without a protector or who was inadequately defended risked the worst, as had been the case in the fifteenth century in the small towns of southeastern France, where bands of 'bachelors' engaged in collective rapes with total impunity.[36] Unmarried men also seized any opportunity that offered itself – unsatisfied wives, lonely widows, prostitutes. They probably also masturbated. The sources rarely refer to this before the confession manuals of the late sixteenth century, which energetically denounce this sin. Some right-minded historians have been too quick to conclude that these new norms were rapidly enforced, especially in England under Puritan influence.[37] The rather belated inclusion of strong disapproval in the theoretical texts was primarily intended to inculcate guilt in the perpetrators and their circle, who had previously regarded such activities as banal. It even seems that in Somerset, between 1601 and 1660, 'mutual heterosexual masturbation to the point of male ejaculation may have been the sexual outlet for a considerable number of the lower orders prior to marriage'.[38] As for sodomy and bestiality, theoretically punishable by death according to harsh princely edicts from the sixteenth century on, it is by no means certain that they were really the subject of a powerful taboo in the countryside. In France, prosecutions of peasants for these offences are rare.[39] Given that everybody knew who said and who did what in a notably gregarious world, and that everybody was aware of the rigours of the law, the small number of prosecutions probably indicates a tacit indulgence in this matter. Perhaps it was encouraged by the habits formed within the male associations? It may be that grown boys, deprived of regular sexual experience and accustomed to sharing their games, their joys and their fears over long years, were sometimes tempted to seek pleasure in the arms of their companions. Finally, a different kind of release was open to them in the form of violence against their peers or against older men; not only were their neighbours largely tolerant of such excesses, believing that boys will be boys, but the king of France and the Spanish sovereign, in Artois, readily pardoned unmarried murderers for the same reasons.

There is no firm evidence that the peasant system of the three age groups existed in so distinct a form in the Middle Ages. The juvenile organizations are primarily documented from the sixteenth century on, which leaves open the possibility that they spread as a means of adapting to the later age of marriage, which was then becoming the norm, and to the erotic frustrations which resulted. They persisted for a long time, in spite of an increasingly fierce struggle on the part of the authorities against their 'indecencies' and a rapid decline from the century of the Enlightenment onwards, when the sexual system was radically changed.[40]

This system depended for its existence on both a tacit pact between the generations and the principle of the permanence of social structures, because sons reaching puberty could only accept their long marginalization in the expectation that they would one day take the place of those who preceded them. The system may appear strongly patriarchal, but it nevertheless left considerable latitude to women, because they held the key to all masculine dreams and also to pleasure. Some fathers insisted on arranged marriages, so as to unite patrimonies, but the vast majority of young men and young women who possessed very little enjoyed almost total freedom in their choice of a spouse.[41] The new husband was then left to himself, without the reassuring support of his 'kingdom of misrule', to explore the sexuality of his wife – destructive according to current wisdom – and to try to avoid finding himself with a growing number of mouths to feed. There must have been some who regretted the time of their frustrated adolescence.

Sodomites: a 'third sex'

Once again, change came from north-western Europe. While elsewhere in the continent, especially the south, the peasant tradition of the three age groups persisted for a long time to come, in Paris, Amsterdam and London, a new sexual system emerged around 1700 which was to last until the 1960s.[42] It was based on a quite new representation of masculinity which led to the promotion of conjugal marriage within the context of the bourgeois home, and to major changes in power relations and exchanges between human beings.

In the Age of Enlightenment, the most dynamic European societies prohibited classic homosexual desire. It had previously been treated with a degree of tolerance, since the virility of the man who took the active role with a youth or passive male was in no way challenged. This changed radically in London with the imposition of a total taboo on any sensual contact with a minority of effeminate males, pejoratively known as *mollies*, who congregated in specific places and presented themselves as a veritable third sodomite 'gender'. A mounting anxiety on the subject had a deeply unsettling effect on the definition and the perception of the stronger sex, which helped to change relations between its members, especially as regards friendship. The ideal masculinity, also affected by the rejection of masturbation, now excluded all ambiguity and reoriented itself towards the unproblematic use of brothels and prostitutes.[43]

Apart from the precocious emergence of a very visible homosexual minority (which Foucault and many historians date only to the nineteenth century), the most spectacular consequences of these changes were the rampant spread of venereal diseases and an increase in illegitimacy rates and extra-marital sex.[44] There were similar developments in Paris at the same time, as shown by the pederasty patrols carried out by the police and by the meteoric rise of prostitution.

A new sexual system

Human sexuality is like the mechanism of a clock, in that every movement is integral to the whole. The least modification to one part has repercussions for all the others. Whereas some groups preferred to maintain their traditions or make only marginal adjustments, others were ready to accept the culture of personal guilt and submit to the new procedures for controlling the libido this entailed.

The peasantry was slow to adopt the new ideas and, for a long time, especially in certain regions far from the big cities, maintained the equilibrium based on permanence and the control of young men by the law of communal shaming.[45] At the other end of the social spectrum, the old noble habits of excess and magnificence and of uninhibited consumption continued to inspire the libertines, who rejected guilt; Sade was merely the tip of the iceberg in this universe peopled by sybarites, and which was equally well represented in Enlightenment England by men such as Richard Payne Knight, inventor of the Worship of Priapus, and the members of the Society of Dilettanti. The rest, generally city-dwellers, more or less ensnared in the toils of a respectable sexuality, were the first really to experience the power of a sublimation previously confined to the athletes of God, but now secularized, on a cultural trajectory leading to our own era and to the psychoanalyst's couch in pathological cases. In spite of delayed marriage, the old demographic balance came unstuck around 1700–20. The population began rapidly to increase. Contemporaries became aware of the gravity of the problem. In 1798, Thomas Robert Malthus issued a strong warning about the danger of seeing the food supply run out and advocated the voluntary restriction of births. Western Europe entered a new era, that of the industrial revolution. Within the immense metropolises that were its motors, the economic take-off of the eighteenth century was preceded and then accompanied by a new conception of sexuality. The Protestant ethic in England, the Catholic spiritual reconquest in France and the invention of 'civility' all over Europe had already helped to instil the virtues of restraint and continence in some circles. The phenomenon then developed within the family.

In fact, it was the values governing matrimonial relations that changed fundamentally. Women lost much of their freedom and were even deprived of their right to pleasure in the arms of a husband. In the early stages, the witch-hunts of the years 1580–1680 helped to exorcize a fear of the devouring sexuality of the daughters of Eve, attested by the humoral medicine of the sixteenth and seventeenth centuries. One of the main accusations levelled against suspects, who were often post-menopausal, was that of having copulated with demonic incubuses, thus violating every divine law by diabolically seeking pleasure for its own sake, not only outside marriage but past the age to conceive. The judicial interrogations transposed the accusation into mythical form by making these women confess that the Satanic penis, covered with spikes and ice-cold, caused intense pain during coitus. This may be seen as a way of identifying unbridled female desire with the demonic, and of extending a terrifying metaphor which linked the 'little death' of orgasm to intense suffering, prolonged by eternal torments. This message, hammered home for over a century, helped to enhance, by contrast, the image of the good Christian wife, who saved her soul and did her duty towards God and men by getting pregnant without seeking pleasure for herself. The way was thus paved for the notion that the decent woman had little interest in sex. The idea took hold in the nineteenth century, when bourgeois morality established a very sharp distinction between the legitimate helpmeet, as chaste as she was obedient, and with little appetite for erotic play, even naturally frigid, according to prevailing medical opinion, and the libidinous prostitute. This separation of roles worked exclusively to the benefit of the dominant males.[46] They won out on all fronts by practising the double standard; the model husband could also be a passionate lover without feeling guilty that he used prostitutes. The docile wives, furthermore, were closely confined to the house, thus even better protected from the lechery of competitors, which limited the risk and fear of bastardy. Carnal pleasure, lastly, was directly associated with prostitutes, a way of devaluing it and of claiming that the quest for it devalued any woman, even if she sought it in the conjugal bed.

At the same time, another crucial change affected unmarried males. Contrary to what Foucault believed, the restriction of their sexuality did not date from the late establishment of a biopower in the nineteenth century. The process began with the 'confinement' of a small number of them in the boarding schools and colleges of the sixteenth century, then intensified under the influence of various social agencies. The end of a professional army in France under Louis XIV and the efforts of the Church to moralize young men and women all over Europe, together with the strengthening of urban guilds, all combined to produce a stage of life which had not previously been clearly perceived as such. Slowly, the 'bachelors' of the 'kingdoms of misrule' became adolescents, gradually or completely separating from their peers to pass under the direct tutelage of adults. It was the sons of the privileged and of well-to-do townspeople who were chiefly affected. Although a minority of girls went to primary schools, only boys attended institutions of secondary and higher education under the *ancien régime*, where their sexual drives had to find expression within prescribed limits. Yet one sometimes observes makeshift practices designed to accommodate old habits, for example the development of collective sodomitic practices in the religious colleges or, later on, in the English universities of the nineteenth century. In other cases, the break with the past was total. This may explain the emergence after 1700 in London of a homosexual minority, driven to proclaim their autonomy and take over a space constituted as a ghetto in order to defy the prohibitions and compensate for the decline of organized youthful sociability. In addition, threats of eternal punishment or the fierce warnings of fathers, masters and confessors may have helped to develop a terror of their own body. In *The Sorrow of Belgium*, the Flemish writer Hugo Claus skilfully evokes just such a fear of sexuality, inculcated during his time as a boarder in a church school during the Second World War.[47] Internalization and suppression slowly prepared the ground for a self-awareness that could be analysed in Freudian terms. Repression and the sense of personal guilt replaced the law of shame as a way of keeping young men in check. They were still entitled to some diversions. Consorting with honest women was forbidden on principle, but there were plenty of prostitutes available. This important safety valve was not only tolerated, but encouraged, because it constituted an unarguable proof of virility at a time when the only lawful masculine sensuality was that practised with women.

From the eighteenth century on, the male 'establishment' in the big cities managed to maintain strict control over all sexual exchanges, but by very different means from those employed in the peasant world. They limited the access of young bachelors to reproduction and carnal pleasure by repressing desire, prohibiting masturbation and homosexuality and promoting an idealized definition of wives, leaving them as their only hope the resort to prostitutes – who they themselves visited without scruple before returning home to enjoy the pleasures of married life. This was a major change. It amounted to a modernization of the patriarchal system, under the influence of economic, political and religious developments. It can be argued that its persistence until the 1960s, in spite of ups and downs and increasing pathologies in the age of Freud, produced successive waves of sublimation which have contributed to the remarkable forward march of the West.

For, unlike the peasantry, which doggedly tried to resist the winds of change, industrial urban societies wanted to conquer the globe. Besides the Protestant United Provinces, the spearheads of expansion were France and England. All three founded vast colonial empires, had one huge major city and were centres for the development of commercial and then industrial capitalism and agricultural modernization. The Calvinist predestination dear to Max Weber cannot alone explain this phenomenon, given that Paris, a Catholic city, stands comparison with eighteenth-century London, as a result of the triangular trade with Africa and America and the huge profits made from Caribbean sugar. From Louis XIV to Napoleon I, the dynamism and the imperialism of France was owed primarily to its demographic vitality, which was also a factor on the other side of the Channel. Less obvious than population growth, a major factor in both cases was the transition from a peasant sexual economy, oriented towards permanence and the easy replacement of one male age group by another, to a system that was grossly unbalanced in favour of married men. Not only did adolescents now have very limited access to the pleasures of the flesh, but they might feel deep anxiety with regard to their future in an active and mobile economic world, even doubt the validity of the tacit contract of replacement imposed by their fathers at such a high price. Is this not why many of them were driven into flight – that is, a mass migration to the colonies in the case of England, military conquest in the case of revolutionary and imperial France, religious evangelization, great explorations, the colonization of the planet, etc.?

During the course of the eight or ten generations which succeeded each other between 1700 and 1960, the two implacable rivals, England and France, experienced very similar developments in the sphere of sexuality, marked by alternate phases of repression and libertarianism. It is as if the confinement and sublimation of the desires resulted, over time, in a build-up of excess vital energies, held in check until a collective letting-off of steam that led to open indulgence in pleasure. For those from the upper ranks, the process was endlessly repeated at the individual level: closely confined and strongly exhorted to develop the strict self-control of the impulses during adolescence, the Subject enjoyed all the benefits of the exercise of the sexual double standard when he married.

The conquest of female pleasure

The 1960s was a period of remarkable change in the West. The abundance of food turned its two poles, Europe and North America, into an oasis of prosperity on the globe. In spite of the poverty and marginality still visible in the streets, the majority of today's population, not only the elites, are experiencing, with the end of famine, a situation unprecedented in the history of our species. Life expectancy increased spectacularly during the twentieth century, the average currently exceeding 80 years for both sexes in the developed countries. Plague and the major diseases which caused millions of deaths have disappeared, even if AIDS and the fear of future pandemics qualify too optimistic a judgement. Further, children born since 1945 have never known war. It no longer ravages the national territories and it is exported far away from the heartlands of these two areas, which makes it easier to understand the exceptional gravity of the trauma suffered by the Americans on 11 September 2001.

Against this background of extraordinary progress, after millennia of often-extreme scarcity and deadly internecine strife up to the end of the Second World War, Western sexuality has discovered a new equilibrium. The change has happened so rapidly and so decisively that one may wonder if the 1960s saw the beginning of a true revolution. For the first time, the balance has swung in favour of women, by offering them risk-free orgasms, disconnected from procreation, if that is what they want. The entire edifice has been shaken, and the various parties now need to reconstruct their relationships with each other.

The erotic revolution of the sixties

Of the three elements of the traditional sexual system, mature men, women and pubescent boys, it is perhaps the last of the three who have been least deeply affected by the upheavals of the 1960s. As in the sixteenth century, the adolescent of today spends around a decade of his life in this insecure state, but this now represents only an eighth of the average lifespan, compared with a quarter or a third under the *ancien régime*, when married life was limited to a couple of decades. Adulthood today is long. Painful though it can be, to judge by the growth of unemployment and the incessant demands, the waiting stage for young men precedes a long period when expectations may be realized; nor should we forget the security provided by the European welfare state. Homosexuals have gained a place in the sun far preferable to that of the London 'mollies' or the Parisian pederasts of the eighteenth century. They demand and obtain respect for their difference, even the right to marry and adopt children. Only the United States firmly resists this trend, in spite of the long-time existence of large gay communities in San Francisco and New York and the measures taken in a few liberal states, Massachusetts having been the first officially to authorize marriage between same-sex partners, on 17 May 2004.[48]

The major changes concern adult men and, even more, women. In the case of the former, it is a truism that they enjoy increasing erotic latitude, now without the need for the hypocritical behaviour associated with the bourgeois double standard. The longer lifespan is accompanied by pressure from all sides urging them to enjoy and to give sexual pleasure, even into an advanced old age. This is a heavy burden to bear, creating traumas that hoards of psychoanalysts and specialists in the problems of the couple happily devote themselves to treating. The insecurity of the male Subject, constantly required to perform, makes all the media happy. Advertisements are packed with advice about avoiding, or miracle cures for, an unacceptable malfunction. A hilarious American film of 2003 describes the calvary of an ageing Jack Nicholson, still sprightly thanks to Viagra, who has to renounce the young women who pose a threat to his heart, after more than 60 years on a cholesterol-packed diet, in favour of a lover of his own age, Diane Keaton; eventually, after numerous hospital emergencies and in a glow of Hollywood romanticism, he leaves, revitalized, for Paris.[49]

We should note, however, a new phenomenon, the rapid 'democratization' of the model of the super-male, by contrast with the seventeenth century, when the sovereign had been the sole point of reference in such matters, and the nineteenth, when the pleasures of the flesh were largely the preserve of rich and powerful married men. In a context of triumphant hedonism, many Europeans demand their eminent right to instant happiness. The individual is not yet king, but wants to be. Just as the boundaries between generations and groups have been eroded as far as pleasure is concerned, and just as marriage is no longer the obligatory point of reference, especially in the big cities, so every union is now far more dependent than before on the tyranny of the orgasm. As a result, adult men now face hitherto unknown tensions which no longer relate primarily to the sharing of women, which was formerly based on the absolute power of fathers and the enforced waiting of sons. They are made vulnerable by the disappearance of the norms of the double standard of the period 1700–1960, which gave them – and only them – security. There are storms ahead for the masculine personality at the beginning of the third millennium. The rules of the game have changed beyond recognition. Women now claim the right both to pleasure and to social power, and are poised to take control of sexual relations. This means major changes to people's ideal perceptions of themselves, to relations between the sexes and to the types of behaviour previously described as 'marginal'.

'Cherchez la femme!'

Contraception encouraged the liberation of women by enabling them to join the world of individual determination of sexual identity, previously confined to men.[50] Neither madonnas nor whores, as some proclaim, they are now able to manage their reproductive function and their physical impulses themselves, instead of being collectively defined, positively or negatively, by the dominant male culture. This surely explains the fierce and sustained hostility to methods of birth control on the part of some traditional authorities. Already described as 'shameful secrets for deceiving nature' in the eighteenth century, they are supposed to be the biggest con trick ever invented for diverting humans from the path of God, or are more surreptitiously accused of offending against biological imperatives.

In the United States, opponents of abortion have never given up the fight since its authorization by the Supreme Court in 1973. A large sector of the American population, estimated at over half, is hostile to abortion and remains viscerally faithful to a puritanical view of sexuality based on unchallenged male hegemony. Bequeathed by the pre-1960s European system, it is based on a powerful sublimation of sexual needs and their diversion towards a consumer culture, leisure and sport. The frustrations engendered produce a boundless vital appetite that is expressed in a veritable religion of consumerism; housewives are both the targets of advertising and the priestesses who spread the good word, while the erotic 'marginals' constitute reprehensible heresies, devalued by massive symbolic channels, especially through a macho cult fostered by sportsmen. This structural imbalance of the personality derives from a traditional management of the sexes and 'genders', which creates a twofold fundamental tension. The first opposes mature men to adolescents, while offering the latter a real prospect of success. The second sharply differentiates the male and female roles, leaving wives with little hope of escaping the life of glorified mother, except by excluding themselves from social life or becoming a woman of easy virtue.

One can understand the extraordinary explosive power of contraception when the choice is the woman's and not at the discretion of her partner, as it was with condoms and coitus interruptus. The impact is all the greater in that so-called 'decent' women had not been permitted to dispose freely of their own body in the past, because it belonged to God under the *ancien régime*, or to her husband by 'natural' law according to the bourgeois codes of the nineteenth century. The revolution was all the more spectacular in the 1960s, when, for the first time in human history, the pill gave a genuine contraceptive choice to the second sex and when the right to abortion was forced through in its wake, in the teeth of vigorous opposition. These innovations herald the end of male control in the sexual sphere. The daughters of Eve are now free to choose the partner, forms, duration and timing of exchanges, in an equality of relationship unknown to any of their forebears, and their orgasm is no longer taboo, or even shameful, so exhaustively is it described and explained by the media and so indispensable is it proclaimed to be if a woman is to feel a 'real' woman.

The consequences are many, especially on the Old Continent. Not only are the relationships to the body and to sexuality profoundly affected, but the link between the two sexes, previously organized primarily around marriage, including in its adulterous vicissitudes, is being transformed.[51] Also changing are contacts between the generations, as a result of the number of stepfamilies, the increasingly late age at which children leave home and the significant role assumed by grandparents in the lives of grandchildren. The old notions of love have been undermined by a huge number of factors that demand adjustments, including the increasing frequency of differences of age or race, the realism of career plans and the easy separation now made between the search for sexual pleasure and the desire for a child. As if in an immense game of dominos, the whole of society is affected, shaken up and transformed, step by step, because women have abandoned the fixed roles previously reserved for them by our culture, of chaste madonna, perfect mother or prostitute. Nothing will ever be the same again, even if we do not know what choices their daughters will make from among the wide range of possibilities that will be open to them.

The changes in 30 years have been huge. In 1976, an international interdisciplinary conference on 'Le Fait féminine' was regarded as 'explosive' by its organizer, Évelyne Sullerot, appalled at the number of denunciations, moralistic sermons and threats she had to suffer.[52] Yet some of the views expressed were far from revolutionary. One of the participants could still proclaim: 'From the standpoint of selection in the human species, marriage is of capital importance: let us remember that more than 90 per cent of human beings end up by marrying and having children! It is, therefore, a good system.'[53] Problems then seen as controversial, in particular those of 'desire, eroticism, love, affectivity and creativity', had been deliberately left aside. The explanation offered was that:

> A whole 'new culture' with sometimes uncertain contours and often formidable claims has been constructed in this very field – important, certainly, but not as crucial as some would like to make it appear – of the symbolic, of the desirous, in a word, of the 'Subject'. It has rightly been emphasized that science is not concerned with the 'Subject', if we mean by Subject the individual with their little (or big) personal histories. Science deals rather with populations, with large classes of comparable experiences.[54]

Now obsolete, such remarks demonstrate that the scientific field was not yet open to a history of pleasure or of the libido because the ego was still a subject of deep suspicion among academics. Historical demography spoke constantly of sexuality, but in a disembodied manner by means of statistics and graphs. The mask of knowledge served to conceal awkward moral problems. The strong defence of the conjugal family, presented as the sole satisfactory model, was clearly a response to the attacks on it by the champions of free love after 1968. A quarter of a century later, when it is failing, and the subject of growing doubts, it is no longer so easy to believe in it precisely because desire has had its way, breaking down, one after another, the barriers erected against it over the centuries.

But is the unconstrained enjoyment of pleasure by cheating nature not dangerous for the survival of the human race? At the beginning of the twenty-first century, the question is urgent, because the only child or voluntary childlessness, combined with the desire to enjoy all the pleasures of the flesh to the full, may perhaps be indicators of an excessive surge of egoism. Some ideologies even interpret the growth of homosexuality as a factor weakening the white race. Both catastrophists and right-minded people are alarmed at seeing such signs of the decline of the Western world proliferate. What I myself find most surprising is that such fears, deep-rooted in the United States, are ultimately not more insistent in Europe, not more widely shared by the population or more vigorously debated by politicians. Is this a sign that these developments have been tacitly accepted by our relaxed civilization?

The fountain of pleasures

An increasing pleasure in attaining pleasure has for some time now been apparent. This phenomenon may not have been entirely unknown in the past, but it has recently become more widespread. It was preceded, in the first two-thirds of the twentieth century, by a marked acceleration in the swings between vice and virtue, the relaxation of morals following each time the terrible anxieties and constraints of a period of world war; a return to moral order came in the 1950s, only itself to be swept away by the liberating winds of May 1968. Since then, the pendulum seems to have got stuck at the most permissive end of the scale. Does this signal the end of the binary Western cycle which began around 1700? Does the effort of sublimation demanded during the repressive phase still have any meaning for the hedonistic Europeans of the beginning of the twenty-first century? Perhaps, as it heads for unification, our continent really has entered an entirely new phase, as a result of the convergence of three powerful processes which encourage its inhabitants to make the most of a life free of excessive constraints: the sharp decline in the influence of the churches, both Protestant and Catholic; the affirmation of a world role more focused on issues of human rights and liberties than on material or commercial progress alone; and the liberation of women, after centuries of patriarchal domination. The classic triangle composed of adult males, adolescent boys and women was based on the power of the first of the three to impose their views on the other two. Now, however, neither the second nor, even more, the third are any longer prepared to play a game they are destined always to lose. Everyone wants to get access to the delights of this world as quickly and as intensely as possible. What is the point of submission and self-torment? Why accumulate for its own sake? The strength of a civilization lies in its ability to adapt to the changes that threaten it. The capacity of Europe to respond seems to me hardly in doubt. But the historian who becomes an observer of his own times changes his trade. He can offer only a contingent opinion on a world where life is good. Changing values have become detached from the illusion of a paradise after death, to base themselves both in general humanist principles, to be shared with the whole world, and in the ability to take advantage of the extraordinary material, intellectual and ethical wealth concentrated in this temperate zone of the planet. Yet the ego still suffers from hypertrophy, which leads to a proliferation of pathologies, to say nothing of the difficulties experienced by the male sex in adapting to the enormous challenges posed by the new configuration of relationships with women. The latter are well aware that they alone hold – and risk-free since the pill – the key to the pleasure that is most sought-after, most lauded and most important in human experience: that of sex.[55]

Opening the door wide to sensuality has refined the perception of and taste for other delights. Although every imaginable rapture is directly experienced by the Subject, in his or her own body, with his or her own senses, something or someone else is still needed for this to happen. Without the collective weight of disapproval, would masturbation be any more than simply a means of obtaining release, offering a fleeting satisfaction, like scratching an itch? It is a truism to say that cultures always manipulate individuals by regulating their desires, their impulses and their needs so as to make them contribute to the strengthening of communal ties.

I am then left wondering whether the permanent flow of the fountain of sexual pleasure on European soil in the new millennium may be part of a strategy of our hybrid capitalism, strongly tinged with epicureanism, for adapting to the upheavals on the world stage. The increasing rejection of the guilt mechanism which drove the sublimation of the sexual appetites has its origins in the weakening of the great ideologies, religious and secular, which promised a radiant future on condition of an asceticism and a repression of their 'base instincts' by each individual. On both sides of the Atlantic, the consumer society actively rejects these old ideals of voluntary moderation and a libidinal economy necessary to preserve the vital flow; individuals cannot feel they exist, it maintains, without savouring to the full the pleasures offered in abundance by the capitalist manna. Yet there is a crucial difference between the two parts of the West, I believe, in the way they apprehend pleasure, especially carnal pleasure. In the United States, the vigorous resistance of the traditional symbolic envelope, rooted in religion and the patriarchal family, restricts the appetite for pleasure through the guilt mechanism that is still alive and well, and through the sublimation of the sexual impulses, at least in appearance. Europe has cast off these restraints, with the exception of minorities who retain a nostalgia for them, by choosing the path of material and spiritual consumption, which is more rewarding for those affected because it is accompanied by a widespread lifting of guilt, especially in sexual matters. Once the contradiction between the deep impulses, in the psychoanalytical meaning of the term, and the permitted forms of behaviour has been removed, individuals gain a strong sense of freedom, even if they are still influenced by powerful invisible forces, of which the laws of the market economy are one. The accumulation of things, as everybody knows, does not necessarily bring happiness. A strange melancholy can make life taste bitter for those who have more than enough of material goods, prestige and authority. Unlike the United States, where the dimension of sin is often indispensable in order to progress beyond the dreary joys experienced by satiated consumers,[56] the new European recipe combats the same risk by refusing anxiety and by increasing the impression of personal fulfilment through the lifting of many taboos. Yet, as the disappearance of repression makes sublimation less necessary, some groups may experience new forms of frustration or loss of identity as a result of the elimination of a role that had previously brought security, for example young men faced with the greater demands of girls their own age or old male chauvinists confronting the spread of feminism. Our inventive world offers them compensatory techniques, for example extreme sports or risk-taking. Both provide a frisson of danger, freely and consciously braved, to enhance the pleasure by adding the threat of an often inevitable destruction, since tobacco, alcohol and drugs slowly cause death after first giving enormous pleasure.

Pleasure, however, is well on the way to ridding itself of the heavy burden of pain and anxiety which invisible matrices have tirelessly imprinted on the mind and body of every Westerner since the seventeenth century. The orgasm is no longer hidden. It proclaims itself without shame – or almost. Only the future will tell whether this prodigious change, the work of a few decades, after centuries of alternating phases of repression and liberation, will have a lasting effect on the unified Old Continent and help it to maintain its original place in the world.

Part II

IMPRINTS: PLEASURE IN PAIN (SIXTEENTH AND SEVENTEENTH CENTURIES)

The Italian Renaissance marked the start of a new cultural process. Very conscious of the great watersheds, like every historian, I have decided to make it the starting point for my book, without claiming to discern the emergence of pleasure at this precise moment. Every human civilization surely experiences it. I wish simply to bring out the importance of a turning point after which Europe as a whole, slowly and painfully, by trial and error, and not without numerous contradictions and endless qualifications, developed a texture of pleasure different from that of the past. Ideas and practices gradually made an imprint which remained the hallmark of the West for the next five centuries and has probably not entirely disappeared today.

The experience of the pleasure of the senses came about painfully. This discreet, almost invisible watermark on the pages of the book of Europe was first applied by an incandescent mould during two troubled centuries; a concession, surely, to Christianity's deep distrust, from its origins, of the body and the volcano of passions it contains. To connect physical pleasure so closely to the feeling of death or of personal incompleteness was a stratagem of scholarship and governments which served to delay the questioning of their authority until the challenges of the Age of Enlightenment. The most significant result was to link for a long time to come Eros and Thanatos, the life impulses and the death impulses, in a strange ballet which made the athletes of God, Sade and his disciples, the heirs of Darwin, Freud, Marx, Weber, Foucault and many others dance on the same stage.

A philosophical or a theological approach might be adopted for an investigation of this Western, inextricable link between pleasure and pain. Others have done this. As a historian of culture with a particular interest in the contributions of literature, art and sociology, I will centre my argument round two convergent orders of phenomena which are set out in the next two chapters. In the first, which deals with the knowledge of the age, I will discuss the extreme difficulty of thinking about oneself, especially for women, so deep was the conviction that the body was an obstacle to Christian salvation. In the second, I turn to behaviour and describe common sexual transgressions and the strength of the repression directed against those who went too far in practising the joys of the flesh, all seen as mortal sins unless sanctified by the sacrament of marriage.

— 2 —

MASCULINE, FEMININE: INDIVIDUALS AND THEIR BODIES

The individual has not until recently had a good press, as economists, demographers and specialists in *mentalités* preferred to think in terms of large masses. They were not, after all, biographers! However, the late twentieth century has put the individual back centre-stage, especially in philosophy and politics. With the exhaustion of the great ideologies, the individual has gained ever more ground in the age of the hypertrophy of the Self. He or she must therefore be reintroduced into any temporal investigation. This was well known to Marc Bloch (1886–1944), for whom 'human flesh' was the true quarry of the historian. Scholars in the human sciences, and even more the literary specialists of the Anglo-Saxon world, are asking new and fascinating questions in this sphere.

The Subject is not a finished sculpture suddenly springing up from nowhere during the Renaissance, but the slowly modernized product of a negotiation between the community and the person. It is from this perspective that we need above all to re-evaluate the role of women, so negatively perceived by the bourgeois theoreticians of the nineteenth century.[1] One of the most important recent discoveries concerns the interaction between the two sexes, as they were conceived by the scholars of the sixteenth and seventeenth centuries, in particular the doctors, who, basing themselves on a humoral perception of the body, assigned plenitude to one sex and dependence to the other. The consequences for the mechanisms of social relations, marriage and the practice of the forbidden pleasures were huge.

Representing and talking about oneself

The perception by men and women of their singularity, even the precise awareness of themselves, certainly existed in Antiquity. Christianity introduced a growing mistrust in this sphere. St Augustine was suspicious of people's desire to fashion their own personality, which was tantamount in his eyes to building a 'ruin'. Thus introspection in the Middle Ages could almost only have as its objective discovering the extent of the sins committed, with a view to repenting them. Only pride impelled a person to venture further down this dangerous path. No doubt the reality was more complicated, and non-conformist tendencies existed, but the pessimistic model of narcissistic contemplation dominated the cultural landscape. Even the humanist optimists of the early sixteenth century did not succeed in opening up new perspectives. Erasmus, high priest of human free will and of a good God with whom one could make direct contact, free from superstition or pointless rites, was fiercely rebuked by the former monk Luther, proponent of unfree will; Erasmus, he declared, was 'not pious'.

The individual enmeshed

The Italian Renaissance had a major impact on the definition of a fledgling Self. The enthusiastic rediscovery of Antiquity was also that of the pagan gods and models, which loosened the stranglehold of the unique Christian thought-system. Humanism and art caused strong personalities to emerge, capable of negotiating with the powerful figures who commissioned them and of openly proclaiming their genius. Benvenuto Cellini, a master in every medium, wrote the story of his life with a lack of modesty and an arrogance that even the most self-important of our contemporaries would hardly dare emulate. Boastful, exuberant, mendacious, he came close to thanking God for having created such a talented individual as he. Humanist ideas swept through sixteenth-century Europe, spreading everywhere a bolder conception of the human being.[2]

Intellectuals and artists began to 'fashion' a new model man, symbolized by the cultivated giants of Rabelais or the vigorous nudes of Leonardo da Vinci and Albert Dürer. Monarchs, courtiers and men of power and wealth made a conscious effort to conform to this model. Stephen Greenblatt has traced the signs of such a 'self-fashioning' in English literature from Thomas More to William Shakespeare. Coined with both meanings of the word 'fashion' in mind, the expression indicates the formation of self-awareness, in two distinct forms. One continued the tradition of the imitation of Christ, the product of prayer, that is, of silent and purely contemplative prayer; it gained additional vigour among the Protestants, as shown by the Geneva translation of the New Testament in 1557 and by the great outpouring of male and female religious autobiography in post-Reformation England. The second emerged at the same time, but developed in painful separation from the first, at the cost of much anxiety among those who learned to 'represent' their manners or their behaviour.[3] The theoretical codes for shining in society and demonstrating the extent of one's capacities, while at the same time maintaining a courteous and polite manner, were laid out in the manuals of civility, in particular the *Book of the Courtier* of Baldassore Castiglione, published in 1528, which was hugely successful throughout Europe for a century and had a profound influence on the social elites.[4]

The emergence of the Subject in the sixteenth century was in no way, therefore, a narcissistic apotheosis. In every manifestation, it was directly linked to religious or cultural forces which promoted this sort of refashioning. Paradoxically, it was the very tightening of social control that made the sense of individuality emerge. The regulation was primarily directed at young men in the upper ranks of society. It resulted, in reaction, in mechanisms for the relaxation of tensions, for example the invention of leisure at this same period and among the same sectors of the population.[5] In short, the clearly asserted Self was a creation of the scholarship and the regulation of the age.

The great English authors of the sixteenth century constructed their personality and their oeuvre with direct reference to two opposite poles: an established authority and a detestable or hostile 'stranger' (heretic, savage, adulteress, traitor . . .). Both subject to the former and anxious to destroy the threat represented by the latter, they had the painful experience of a sort of loss of themselves, like Shakespeare exploring male sexual anxieties in *Othello* and several other plays. Even the hostility of Marlowe in the face of power has something of the force of submission. Greenblatt concludes that his research reveals not 'an epiphany of identity freely chosen', but, on the contrary, the Subject as a cultural artefact.[6] I do not share his excessive pessimism. I believe that he attaches too much importance to the theoretical cultural veil, by taking as approval the silence of those constrained or punished, when it might just as well have been prudence on their part, or even the lack of any written evidence. Further, he minimizes the contrary effect produced by the attempts to control. There were many who tried to heal their tragic wounds by proclaiming their singularity against all the conventions. Unlike the great English authors hidden behind theatre curtains, or the experts in the art of dissimulation taught by Castiglione and his imitators, they got their wings burned, but expressed themselves forcefully nevertheless, as we will see in chapter 3.

The sixteenth century saw a sort of chain reaction in the production of autobiographies, one of the signs, along with letters and portraits, of a growing interest in introspection.[7] The antique models, including that of St Augustine in the *Confessions*, certainly played a part, as did printing and also the new importance of the towns, which encouraged less collective ways of life than before. Contrary to received opinion, this style of expression was not a Protestant or Puritan monopoly. Many Catholics practised it, including St Ignatius Loyola and St Theresa. Although its writers were mostly from the well-off classes, there were some from lower down the social scale. Among the Italians, first in the field at the beginning of the sixteenth century, the boastful Cellini was joined by the apothecary Luca Landucci, the tailor Sebastiano Arditi and the carpenter Giambattista Casale, among others. Elsewhere, artisans, a few peasants and also some Spanish soldiers all lined up to tell their stories. Although most writers were men, a few women of character practised the genre; in France, they included 'la reine Margot', Marguerite de Valois, sister of kings François II, Charles IX and Henri III, who wrote the first true female memoirs with skill and a discreet frisson; also Marie de Gournay, 'adopted daughter' of Montaigne,[8] and Charlotte Arbaleste, wife of the Calvinist Philippe Duplessis-Mornay. Many others could be cited, including the emperor Maximilian (who used ghost-writers), several successive representatives of the Platter family of Basle and the English musician Thomas Whythorne. There were also personal letters, developed into a major literary genre by Petrarch and Erasmus, on the Ciceronian model. They became a genre ruled by imperative conventions towards the end of the sixteenth century, when manuals known as *Secretaires* offered a range of models for the use of those wishing to address a request to a superior, declare their love to a lady or simply participate in the great outpouring of writing.

The letters most of all, but often also the life stories and other memoirs, made major sacrifices to the norms and codes, suppressing certain aspects of the real Self that were then inexpressible. Great lover though she had been, la reine Margot said not a word about her innumerable amours or even about her married life with the future Henri IV.[9] Female sexuality could on no account be displayed, whereas men boasted proudly of their conquests. A work of fiction relating anecdotes drawn from real life, *Les Dames galantes* of Brantôme, a friend and admirer of la reine Margot, testifies to this major difference in the representation of the sensual Self.

The burden of the conventions shows even more clearly in the painted or sculpted portraits or self-portraits that were produced in spectacularly larger numbers after 1500. The faces seem increasingly individualized, as we see in the case of funerary effigies, with the growing demand for a resemblance to the deceased person. Painters also liked to portray themselves, like Hans Holbein the Elder, Lucas Cranach the Younger and Albert Dürer, who also wrote a journal. The biographer Paolo Giovio collected some 400 portraits of famous people, 17 of them women, for the museum in his villa near Como. In fact, most of these works were hung in groups at the time, whether by family or by office, for example, doges of Venice or bishops, which suggests that the identities evoked were 'collective or institutional, rather than individual'. Further, editors did not hesitate to use a single illustration to represent different persons. In an irony of a sort, one of them used the same wood engraving for both the humanist Gemma Frisius and Albert Dürer, even though the latter was obsessed with his appearance and his face was likely to be well known from his works.[10]

That the individual emerged in the sixteenth century is undeniable, but it is no less true that individuals usually remained enmeshed in a dense collective web. They became visible in their own eyes only, in the first place, to meet the expectations of the powers that confined them, not to proclaim themselves the centre of the universe. That would have been offensive to God. The devout experimented only with a collective 'I'. Driven both by a personal sense of failure and by bitterness at the compromise of the Edict of Nantes, agreed with the Catholics in 1598 by his leader Henry of Navarre, now Henri IV, and obsessed by the desire to offer himself as an example to his heirs, the old Huguenot soldier Agrippa d'Aubigné, having taken refuge on his Genevan Aventine hill, wrote his autobiography only in the third person: *His Life, to his Children*. Salvation was at the price of forgetting oneself. It was not a sin of pride, however, to put one's own experience at the service of the community. The edifying autobiography flourished on this principle.

The fragility of the Self

The door was opening, however, onto inner depths hitherto kept carefully concealed. Another type of Self emerged on the margins. It took various forms, from the simple unease that encourages questioning to the clear awareness of a rejection of the conventions. At one extreme was the Subject, literally forced into self-interrogation by the criminal procedure applied in Europe during the Renaissance, in which a meticulously codified judicial torture now played an important part.[11] The underlying notion was that the suffering body told the truth, after the example of the judgement of God in the Middle Ages, or of the corpse whose wounds bled in the presence of its murderer.[12] What the judges really wanted was a confession from out of the mouth of the culprit. The technique was similar to that of confession, which became personal, auricular and private during the second half of the sixteenth century. In both cases, the authority demanded total sincerity after a labour of introspection. Far from the depths of the unconscious, which had not yet been discovered, the judges wanted to know the reasons for the acts committed and urged the accused to 'speak the truth from their own mouth'. The referent was both divine and human, moral and social. Putting someone to the 'question' was a modernized form of the judgement of God, because it, too, involved the notion of a profound unity between the flesh and the spirit, between the sincerity of the soul and that of the body, while making the suspect in question a central preoccupation of government. England alone rejected a judicial procedure of this type, in favour of trial by jury. Yet torture was used under Elizabeth I and James I in cases of high treason. This, it has been argued, is evidence of a crisis of the Subject, provoked by the consolidation of the state. Fearing dangerous subversion, the state used torture as a desperate measure to protect itself. The obsessional fixation of the senior judges on the reciprocity of the terms 'truth' and 'treason' was then imported into other spheres of life, in particular the theatre of Shakespeare. There, it was linked to the theme of marriage, also a vehicle for the notion of potential disloyalty, at a time of deep masculine anxiety with regard to the infidelity of spouses; the misogyny of Iago in *Othello* derives from this intense anguish. In this way, Shakespeare made visible on the stage, through a banal and commonplace phenomenon, the nature of a state obsessed by the fear of treason.[13]

The end of the optimistic humanist dreams, finally buried at the Council of Trent in 1563, on which Catholics and Protestants each scattered purificatory salt, was enough to destabilize the intellectuals. Thinking on the margins became increasingly suspect and dangerous. You had to toe the line as the Christian humanism of the late sixteenth century purged culture of its errors. The Religious Wars that raged obliged the individual, great or small, to keep his or her head down to avoid having it cut off. The Self bent before the storm. The radical instability of the poet ('My name is Will') presented in Shakespeare's sonnets, published in 1609, perhaps written from 1582 on, should come as no surprise. The greatest authors of the age had a fragile ego. Those who dared to say 'I', clearly expressing their desires in contradiction to the prevailing requirement to exercise self-control, always signalled their respect for the conventions in one way or another. Thomas Howell, George Gascoigne, the musician Thomas Whythorne, author of the first autobiography in English, and even more Isabella Whitney, because she was a woman and poor, all reveal a deep sense of insecurity when they speak of themselves. Born into the gentry or at least aspiring to gentry status, they remained remote from social success, in particular at court, while making their exclusion a mark of virtue and seeing it as an opportunity to assert their difference.[14] In the seventeenth century, the use of the first person singular by English authors, often influenced by Montaigne, was more common. It proclaims a clear self-consciousness, but in a context still strongly marked by collective imprints. Two contrasting types can be distinguished: the 'conservative Anglican' and the 'radical Puritan'. The former employed an 'I' that was meditative, antihistorical, symbolic and ambiguous. The latter, a more varied group, since it included the Baptist Bunyan, the independent Milton and the Leveller Lilburne, used an 'I' that was active, as simple and visible as possible and time-related, emphasizing that the speaker lived in a hostile world.[15]

Further down the same path, the emergence of the individual in the act of writing could be the result of great suffering or of a deep feeling of humiliation. La reine Margot skilfully recounts the story of her life up to her exile by her brother Henri III, who had tired of her escapades; she probably wrote to strengthen her position in the negotiations for the divorce demanded by her husband Henri IV, who wanted to marry a wife who would give him an heir. Repudiated, kept at arm's length from the throne, she decided to present an image of herself that she found more acceptable, which the public would become aware of only after her death. Agrippa d'Aubigné was motivated by bitterness at seeing his master and king betray what he believed to be Calvinist interests. Blaise de Monluc, cruel 'man of blood' according to the great historian Michelet, disfigured at the siege of Rabastens in 1570, disgraced for political reasons by Charles IX, humiliated, began in 1571, at the age of 71, to dictate the 'discourse of his life' in order to recall, with many untruths, his prowess and the services rendered to four kings. After he had painted his own portrait in this way, he was made maréchal of France in 1574 and died three years later. His 'discourse', which became the *Commentaires*, was published only in 1592.[16] Brantôme, whose works were published in 1665–6, long after his death in 1614, wrote his *Les Dames galantes* after a fall from a horse which left him disabled and put paid to his dreams of military glory. None of these tormented individuals initially aimed at a wide public. They were thinking primarily of themselves and of the edification of those around them.

Rebellion and frustration led to a type of justificatory autobiography far removed from the model of Christological humility followed by the life stories with a religious purpose. In England, nevertheless, the Quakers imbued theirs with a conscious spirit of opposition. Suffering, isolation, illness, the taste for excess and even madness may explain a propensity to tell the story of one's life.[17] The authors were not seeking only to establish an affective dialogue with the reader, as many of these works were published after the author's death, some even remaining in manuscript. Their main motivation may well have been to explore their own Self so as to understand their failures better, or rather make them tolerable in their own eyes. The act of writing can be seen as an attempt to rebuild a personality dislocated by great trials, as in the case of Monluc or la reine Margot. The individuals who embarked on such an enterprise took sole control of their existence, honestly judging the validity of their actions. If they distorted or rewrote the truth, it might be intentionally, because they had decided to renegotiate first with themselves the categories of pure and impure, good and evil, as well as the boundaries between themselves and other people. It needed a degree of pride to do this, which explains the religious prejudice against introspection if it was not constrained by the model of Christ.

What, then, can one say about women, whose very nature was generally regarded as sinful, including among Protestants, although they allowed them a little more space? What are we to think about the rebellion of those who refused to bend the knee before their husband, governments and scholarship, to the point of loudly proclaiming their singularity?

The role of women

If it was so difficult for the male Subject to construct himself in the sixteenth and seventeenth centuries, the enterprise might seem doomed to failure in the case of 'the weaker vessel'. The expression appeared in 1526 in Tyndale's translation of the New Testament. Around 1600, it meant the female sex as a whole and was employed, notably, by Shakespeare.[18] Catholic France was no different. As everywhere in Europe, the woman was considered to be the weaker half of the couple produced by God, the man the stronger. Why seek a more complex definition of what Anglo-Saxon scholars call 'gender history'? The aim is to explore the changing relationship between the two halves of the human race. A simple history of one or the other would miss the point: the changes to the system as a whole when one of its parts moves.

The inescapable frame of reference is provided by the notion of patriarchy. The subject of impassioned discussion and debate, the word can have many meanings. In particular, it acts as a cue to feminists to ostracize enemies or tear each other apart. Making no claim to objectivity, I will use it to define the evident male domination over women and children, at every social level, from the family to larger institutions, in the age of Shakespeare and the age of Molière. However the concept is far from fixed. The forms it took slowly altered during the centuries in question.[19] Its consolidation from the beginning of the sixteenth century was followed by sporadic challenges from insubordinate or rebellious women and led to some adjustments, before the major changes of the eighteenth century, which will be discussed in a later chapter. It is unfortunate that French scholars have shown so little interest in the subject, unlike their Anglo-Saxon fellows, which means that there is an imbalance in the information available. Further, the emphasis on the idea of a mounting anxiety among men about how to control the daughters of Eve in England between 1558 and 1660 is largely based on literary and normative texts.[20] In France, it is corroborated by the same sources and by engravings on the famous theme of the 'dispute de la culotte', symbol of conjugal power. Further research is needed before we can be confident that the topos – debated since Antiquity, when Aristotle was mocked for being 'ridden by a woman' – had real social impact, beyond the theatre and the double male fantasy of loss of virility and loss of power. Surely men have always and everywhere feared such reversals of fickle fortune?

Weak women

One thing is sure: no one regarded women as strong by nature. God had created her to be subject to her companion, to bear children and to remain 'in the shade of her house, which she ought to carry like the snail or the tortoise', said Laurent Joubert, physician to the king of France, in 1579. Men were stronger, they waged war, they worked and they lived out of doors, while their 'prettier and more charming' companion waited patiently for them.[21] It was divinely decreed! The justification of the inferiority of 'the weaker vessel' was wholly masculine. To centuries-old traditions, the Renaissance added the desire to confine women and girls more closely in urban worlds that were both more unstable and full of temptation than the countryside. Boccaccio's *Decameron* (c.1348–53) depicts the Italian city as a modern Babylon. The art of adultery was easier in Paris than in the countryside. Masculine anxiety may have been greater in the towns because relations were more fluid there, leading to the resigned conclusion of Panurge, in the *Tiers Livre* of Rabelais (1546), that there was no way a husband could avoid wearing horns.[22] It is significant that the new insistence on the duties of honest women emerged in the cities, not in the corrupt courts of England and France. To reassure themselves, townsmen described for their fellow-citizens the ideal contours of the female figure they would like to find by their side: the chaste wife, immune to the approaches of other men, but fertile, a good mother, generous, self-sacrificing. By contrast, they imagined the she-devil, the woman who indulged in every failing of the female nature, especially insatiable sexual desire, unless kept firmly in check by a man. Only marriage could save her from herself and assure her salvation.[23] The division between pure and impure was not new, but it acquired a new importance at this period, as shown by the progress of Marian devotion and by the great witch-hunt, which culminated between 1580 and 1630 in Western Europe. The model of the Virgin and Child defined the maternal duties of a wife who was also expected to keep herself for her husband alone and to use her body with moderation, for procreation, not for sensual pleasure. The evocation of the satanic Sabbath, by contrast, made it possible to relegate to the Devil's side those who transgressed these same rules, those who lived on the margins, without masculine guidance, such as widows, and those who were more concerned with their mortal body than with the safety of their soul. Men in towns were less likely to encounter female witches, who were mostly rural according to the witch trials, but they sought in the arms of prostitutes more voluptuous pleasures than the embraces of their chaste wife. The masculine double standard, which was probably ancient, was strengthened, so as to make even clearer the distinction between the wife and the adored mistress – 'love was for the mistress', exclaimed Lucien Febvre – or the fallen woman with sulphurous charms.[24]

Female roles

With the exception of a tiny minority vowed to celibacy in the Catholic convents, a woman's existence was wholly oriented towards marriage. She was prepared for it, she experienced it and she then often had cause to regret losing the protection of its harsh laws when she was widowed. It has been claimed that widows gained greater independence. This may be true, on condition they had the material means to survive and the mental resources to withstand suspicion and malicious gossip. Old women, it was said, had even more unbridled sexual appetites than the rest of them, especially if there was no male hand to halt their slide into sin. The accusations of witchcraft were primarily directed at a female stereotype characterized by age, widowhood and relative marginality, through loss of social ties, within a community.[25] In France, from the mid-sixteenth century to the mid-seventeenth century, the paramount importance of marriage was also attested by deeply authoritarian and immensely detailed royal legislation.[26] In England, the crisis initiated in the 1590s by the debate on divorce resulted in a new, more internalized and less visible method of social control, the family remaining the site where power was 'exercised privately in the interests of public order'.[27]

Sexual roles were thus preordained as a function of this ultimate objective. Masculinity meant the acquisition and expression of a virile, dominating, aggressive attitude, not only on the part of the young unmarried men of the kingdoms of misrule, but among townsmen, nobles and aspirants at court. 'I'm letting my cocks out, watch out for your hens!' ran a sixteenth-century proverb. The young man who raped a woman was doing what came naturally and his offence seemed excusable in the eyes of the community because his victim should never have allowed herself to get into such a situation or should have made sure she was protected by the men of her family.[28] Although sex outside marriage was theoretically a sin, it was in real life regarded as a recreation by 'adolescent' males, because, after all, 'boys will be boys'. An age of open ribaldry used a military vocabulary, or at least one of dominance, to describe the sexual assault, even when it was consensual, carried out by the strong against a weaker prey. In the France of Henri II, knights 'broke a lance' (or even several). In sixteenth-century London, verbal and physical crudity in these matters was rife at all social levels. No fewer than 130 different terms have been noted to indicate male dominance during intercourse. They largely belong to four semantic fields: to besiege, and its variants, come from the vocabulary of war; to corrupt, dishonour or undo suggest a fairly brutal form of seduction; to break, deflower, ravish or sully evoke rape and violation; the fourth group, which excludes apparent violence, still has aggressive overtones: in the works of Shakespeare, men board, have, hit, leap, ride, stuff, thrust to the wall and tumble their partner.[29] Men were expected to behave like hunters, with women as their quarry, publicly boasting of their successes in the tavern or elsewhere. Defamation cases before the London and Chichester consistory courts in the years between 1572 and 1640 bring out this male propensity to arrogance and bragging in sexual matters. Women were less likely to complain about acts of violence than to be forced to defend their reputation against calumnies. It was difficult for them to gain the sympathy of the judges, because what they denounced was generally regarded as banal, only obvious excesses being punished, including in sexual matters.[30] The same is true of France, where the husband enjoyed great latitude in the use of force to correct his wife, short of endangering her life, and where rape was extremely difficult to prove before a court, the victim being suspected of having succumbed to her innate lustfulness.[31]

The strengthening of the patriarchal system in Europe from the sixteenth century on brought out more clearly than before the difference between masculine and feminine. For men, the old pattern was preserved, but in accentuated form; their virility was already demonstrated by sexual prowess, heavy drinking and brawling within the context of the kingdoms of misrule. The changes for women were much greater and more far-reaching as a result of an obligatory recentring on the conjugal family, under pressure from the churches and governments, as demonstrated by the increasing emphasis on marriage from the mid-sixteenth century in France and the significant changes made to it in England around 1590. Although the concrete changes probably took a long time to take effect and affected different social groups differently, the home and the conjugal unit assumed an increasingly large role in women's lives. Husbands and grown-up sons could continue to move about in the external world, now the preserve of their sex, and practise the erotic double standard, but wives and daughters were in principle condemned to confinement, as regards both sexual matters and residence. The insistence on their close bond with the home was not as commonplace or as traditional as it may seem. It was less of an obligation on peasant women because of the discomfort of their homes and of the existence of a dense network of female sociability uniting them all, irrespective of age, wealth and social position. Male domination may not have been challenged in the village but it was looser there, tempered by a sort of collective female power, with its own language, its own hierarchies, its own gossip and its own meeting places, the evening get-together, the oven or the mill.[32] The towns, especially the larger ones, were less favourable to the survival of these sorts of relationship. The constant pressure on women to focus their life on the home met with a greater response there and the judicial surveillance of female excesses was performed more effectively. Although the lower-class system persisted for centuries,[33] some townswomen found their relationships with each other and with men changing. Among the pressures promoting this was the judicial system, itself rooted in moral and religious ideas. In London, between 1572 and 1640, the main accusation against women in the consistory courts was almost always that of prostitution, whether in the form of insults for which they demanded reparation or, more often, of allegations impugning their honour, which obliged them to defend themselves.[34] Unlike in the countryside, where accusations of this type were often combated by local mechanisms controlled either by the female community or by the law of male vengeance, the increasing frequency of legal actions in the towns suggests a more individual but also more generic perception of women. They became primarily the 'property' of their husband, unless they escaped his supervision to lead a debauched life, obliging the community to intervene and punish them, but more often through the medium of the judicial system than through that of family or neighbours, bypassing the principle of private vendetta. This was one of a number of slow redefinitions of the place of women in society. The emphasis was put on a stronger moral supervision. Marriage became the ideal site for the female obedience dreamed of by the political and religious authorities. Wives had to behave virtuously, modestly and humbly, accepting the tutelage of their husband as natural and normal.[35]

In England, contradictions between the Anglican and Puritan positions on marriage had further consequences. In 1597, all remarriage after divorce was declared illegal according to the Anglican canons. The queen refused to ratify this. However, her successor James I approved the principle, reiterated by the canons of 1604, which settled the matter. This position was based on a view of the indissolubility of marriage close to that of French Catholics. It ran counter to the Puritan interpretation, according to which marriage was a simple civil pact, without implications for salvation and entirely dependent on the mutual consent of the parties. The crisis left lasting traces and may have contributed to the growth of masculine anxiety in the towns and in the contemporary theatre. The redefinition of male and female identities revived fears of subversion among the male citizens most closely concerned. The malaise took the fantastical form of a fear of a seizure of power by demonic furies. The belief in the baleful faculties of a sect of satanic females, imported from the Continent, led to the persecution of women designated as witches, with a paroxysm in the last two decades of the sixteenth century. To this was added the fear of being murdered by one's wife, which gave rise to a number of lawsuits, without much justification as the criminal records reveal no increase in the number of murders of husbands.[36] The theatre also expressed a similar male anxiety. Yet is this not, perhaps, a commonplace theme, produced by dread of sexual failure or inadequacy when confronted with a partner whose carnal appetites were deemed insatiable? The stage presentation added a specifically English dimension, because the female roles were always played by boys in disguise, until the king decreed otherwise in 1660.[37]

This third sex, in a sense, which trod the boards in Shakespeare's time, was surely both an expression of male unease and a factor likely to create confusions with strong erotic undertones.[38] Contemporaries sometimes said as much. In a pamphlet published in 1599, *Th'Overthrow of Stage-Playes*, Dr John Rainoldes, an Oxford ecclesiastic, expressed alarm at seeing this transvestism exacerbate lust and provoke sensuality. A powerful taboo then attached to wearing the clothes of the other sex, especially by women, which even led to legal proceedings.[39] Young bachelors sometimes experimented with it, but in exceptional circumstances, for example during the great popular festivals of inversion such as carnival, or during the punishment rites of cuckolded husbands, the donkey ride in France, the skimmington in England. On the Elizabethan stage, the practice, highly ambiguous and heavy with symbolism, revealed a certain social unease because the resulting eroticism was associated more with the masculine character than the feminine appearance of the actor. Authors were well aware of this. John Lyly based his play *Gallathea*, in 1584, on a complicated plot in which the boys dressed as girls and vice versa, all the characters being played by boys. The opening scene explains to the audience that transvestism is illegal and that there is fierce controversy on the subject of homosexual innuendo in the theatre.

Marlowe, himself reputedly a sodomite, and described as such at his posthumous trial for heresy in 1593, openly plays on this theme in *Doctor Faustus*. Shakespeare himself draws attention to the androgynous character of the women in his comedies. Rosalind, the heroine of *As You Like It* (c.1599), hides in the Forest of Arden dressed as a man. At the end of the play, she delivers the epilogue: 'If I were a woman', she declares, 'I would kiss as many of you' as possible. The height of sexual ambiguity is reached when a boy plays the role of a woman while suggesting that he is a young man in disguise. This wink at the public created a particular sensuality, with a strong erotic charge.[40]

We may go further. In London, where the main audience for the Elizabethan stage was found, there was a gradual change in the relationships between masculine and feminine. The appearance in the capital, around 1700, of a clearly defined group of male homosexuals, a third 'gender',[41] seems to have been preceded by a sort of long, sad goodbye to earlier practices. That high point of English culture, the theatre of the age of Shakespeare, was its first laboratory, in contact with the public. The youths disguised as women foreshadowed the migration of desire towards a troubled Subject, situated at the intersection of the two sexes but primarily exhibiting the weak characteristics of the second, because adolescents were dependent beings, incomplete men, less warm and less dry than adults, in the eyes of the doctors. They also preserved memories of sensual games and sodomy from the kingdoms of misrule, which remained very active in the sixteenth century.[42] It is probable that this conjunction of meanings, around 1600, gave the strange English custom of having women incarnated by beautiful young men a singularly voluptuous content for male spectators. We do not know the reactions of the women in the audience, but could it be that they found an echo of their own dependence in that of the young men, kept firmly in tutelage by adults in real life, made stage props for all the pleasures of the imagination for their elders or their peers?

Women rebels

You can exist only through a man: this seems to be the metaphorical lesson of the Elizabethan theatre for women. In the patriarchal world of that period, they were always defined in relation to the male sex. The records – admittedly very rarely kept by women – demonstrate that this is how they were systematically presented. Administrators, clerks of the criminal court and notaries were only interested in the principal tie that revealed a woman's estate: wife, daughter, mother or sister 'of' the man who gave her her identity. The details of this identity were of little interest to them. The Christian name itself may be missing, even if the woman was very directly involved. In 1612, for example, the Paris parlement heard a case concerning a noblewoman who had been stripped naked and beaten with a bull's pizzle, threatened with death, insulted and struck with a candlestick which had broken several of her teeth; she is referred to only by her status as wife of her abuser, the lord of Cerveau.[43] Only a few of her contemporaries were named any more precisely, because of their high rank or religious vows or, on the contrary, out of contempt, in the case of servants or even more of prostitutes, who were given names like Ginger, Fat Joan or Golden Cunt. Among the lower classes, individuality sometimes seems to have been a little more marked, going by the use of nicknames, diminutives or indications of the indomitable temperament of certain viragos, like the Parisian herringmongers. The use in combination of the paternal family name and the husband's name (as in the form Joan Smith, wife of John Brown) is a sign of a double subjection to the males of reference rather than of independence. This last was almost impossible in the countryside for the so-called weaker sex, material survival requiring mutual aid in and outside marriage. Suspicion attached to a single woman far more readily than to her male equivalent. A widow, especially if she had been married more than once, was readily accused of having driven her husbands to the grave, even of having given herself carnally to the devil of the Sabbath; the widower was simply presented with a charivari if he married a much younger woman.

The principal difficulty faced by women at this period, whatever their position in the world, was that of adapting to a complex and frustrating social role.[44] Whereas a man could one day slip into a simple form of valued and coherent behaviour, that of adult, father of a family and master of the house, his wife had to accept her subordination to him and yet impose her own authority on the children, and on the servants, too, if she belonged to the middle or upper social classes. In which case she had to comply with the dominant discourse of female inferiority while at the same time making herself respected by the male servants and avoiding – no mean task – doing anything that might encourage their view of women as a sexual quarry with unslakable lustful instincts. The greatest princesses could not escape this powerful contradiction. Elizabeth I got round it by making an asset of her virginal state, but also by claiming that she had the heart of a man in the body of a woman. La reine Margot, irritated by the misogynistic pamphlet published by one of her protégés, the Jesuit Father Loryot, adopted an ironic tone of false modesty in responding to him in the *Subtle and Learned Discourse* of 1614. Unable to attack received opinion regarding the natural inferiority of women, she made a virtue of the fact: 'God is pleased by tranquil, restful and devout spirits, like those of women, not by tumultuous and bloodthirsty spirits, like those of men.'[45] She neglected to point out that this flattering portrait referred only to the model of the good wife, whereas she herself had spent much of her life on the other side of the fence, carried away by the all-consuming lustfulness generally attributed to any daughter of Eve who rejected the salutary tutelage of her husband.

Nevertheless, a number of women deliberately placed themselves outside the normative definitions of their sex. Some, and they came from every social class, simply followed their passions and their desires to lift the veil of prejudice weighing on their peers, in order to obtain what was normally denied them by convention, especially the pleasures of life and those of the flesh.[46] Others became conscious of the pain of being a woman and found an outlet in writing, even in revolt against those who oppressed them.[47]

In England, the influence of Protestant doctrines turned the family into a 'little Church', within which a deep female piety developed. This was expressed in the writing of personal 'journals' devoted to spiritual meditation and the examination of conscience. The first known is that of Lady Margaret Hoby, begun in 1599. Twenty-three are known from the first half of the seventeenth century, and many others may have been lost. Some of the authors added a more personal note to the expression of their humility. They regarded the document as their personal property, an insidious but unmistakable way of limiting the eminent rights of the husband, even if they had nothing of significance to hide. Elizabeth Walker made her husband, who surprised her in the act of writing, promise not to read her papers in her lifetime; he discovered only edifying sentiments in them after her death. Elizabeth Bury used peculiar characters and abbreviations; her husband had extreme difficulty deciphering her text after her death, only to find, in what he managed to read, 'great sincerity, humility and modesty'. Elizabeth Dunton used a sort of shorthand of her own invention and also asked for her papers to be burnt after her death.[48] It seems that the act of talking about themselves implied an element of secrecy or modesty, but not necessarily a desire to bring their Self to the attention of the public. This was more strongly felt by women than men, because the conventions urged them to silence or at least caution in self-expression, which often led them to forbid or to postpone publication of their writings. Many female autobiographies, religious or not, were printed after the death of their author, often through the efforts of an ecclesiastic anxious to make them an example of devotion.[49]

Female introspection demanded an 'other' as point of reference. Something new was born of this unequal confrontation. It was not a triumphant Self, but a consciousness of the dignity of the woman in question. Margaret Cavendish, first Duchess of Newcastle (1623–73), concluded *A True Relation of my Birth, Breeding and Life*, published in her lifetime in 1656, with a proclamation of her individuality, in direct relation to her father and her husband. As the text begins with the statement 'My father was a gentleman', we may speak of a masculine framing of her existence, even if the duchess was famous for her extravagance and suffered for it.[50] The stories left by Anne Clifford and Mary Rich make it possible to explore the only strategies then available to those who suffered. Anne Clifford bowed her head before the storm without ever yielding on essentials; Mary Rich practised duplicity in self-expression, a form probably more common than that adopted by Anne Clifford, but which has left few documentary traces.

Lady Anne Clifford (1590–1676), Countess of Dorset, Pembroke and Montgomery, daughter of the Earl of Cumberland, is an extraordinary and fascinating figure. Her autobiographical accounts are made up of at least four parts written at different times in her life. The most detailed, her private diary, survives only in an eighteenth-century copy and was not published until 1923.[51] It begins by describing the funeral ceremonies of Elizabeth I, which is highly significant, as we will see. The Countess probably wrote primarily for her own personal satisfaction and so as to see clearly into her own mind, which was deeply troubled by severe trials. A cultivated woman and a great reader, she made no attempt to get her work published, although she was quite as wealthy as her contemporary, Margaret Cavendish. It is not impossible that the manuscripts served as a basis for discussions with family or friends, or were even shown to a restricted circle, like those of Monluc or Brantôme in France; she presents herself as modest and discreet in her journal and she bows to the received conventions regarding the position of women, although her pugnacity was quite extraordinary when something that really mattered to her was at stake.

Aged 26 in 1616, Anne had been married since 25 February 1609 to Richard Sackville, Earl of Dorset, whom she respectfully calls 'my lord', and by whom she had a daughter, 'the child', born on 2 July 1614. The death of her 'dear mother', Margaret Russell, on Friday 24 May 1616, 'between the hours of 6 and 9 at night', allowed her to locate herself very precisely in space and time. The entry made on this occasion notes that her mother had died at Brougham (a castle situated south of Penrith, in Cumbria), in the same chamber in which Anne's own father had been born, and that this was 10 years and 7 months after his death, and 13 years and 2 months after the death of Queen Elizabeth. Anne herself was then 26 years and 5 months old and 'the Child two years wanting a month'. There is no mention of her husband. On 29 May, she heard from the mouth of a messenger the details of the sad event, which she received as 'the greatest and most lamentable Cross' that could have befallen her, and read in the will that her mother had asked to be buried at Alnwick. This was added cause for distress, because she would have to be carried there and because she would not be buried at Skipton, where Anne had been born, on the southern edge of the Yorkshire Dales, 100 miles from Brougham. She saw this as a baleful sign that she might be dispossessed of the inheritance of her forefathers.

Her identity was closely linked to her paternal inheritance, the vast north-western barony of Cumberland, which extended from Skipton in Craven to Broughton in Westmorland. The title deeds, dating from the reign of Henry II, allowed her to inherit, after her mother. But the will of her father, who had died shortly before Anne reached the age of 16, stipulated that the whole of the estate should pass in the male line to his brother and then to the latter's son. The death of Margaret Russell made the matter urgent. Anne refused to allow herself to be dispossessed, arguing that she was the sole living direct heir of the third earl of Cumberland, her two brothers, Sir Robert and Lord Francis, having died young. Although she here refers to her daughter in an impersonal fashion, the diary reveals a deep attachment to the child, who was named after her grandmother, and whom Anne would refer to as 'my lady Margaret' from the evening of her fifth birthday. Queen Elizabeth appears as a deeply venerated icon. The journal opens with her death in 1603, and an observation regarding the hour at which she learned of this event, in the same room in which she long afterwards received the news of the death of her mother, makes it possible to see how Anne deliberately placed herself in the protective shadow of these two figures. At the age of 12, she had been received at the court of the Tudor queen and she seems to have retained a vivid memory of this event; her relationship to these female images combines filial feeling for her mother and deep admiration for the woman who had governed England 'with the heart of a man' in the body of a woman – a sentiment that might well, as we will see, be applied to Anne herself.

In the brief entry for 24 May 1616, Dorset, the husband, is neither mentioned nor defined by his age. Yet he cuts a fine figure, in 1613, in a painting by Sir William Segar that presents him in splendid court dress. Anne resented the fact that he gave her only lukewarm support in her claims to her northern inheritance, that he expected to administer the lands in his wife's name in the event of success and that he immediately asked her to sign a document leaving everything to him if she died without an heir. The threat seemed to be confirmed by the 'sign' she detected on 29 May. Not only did she feel isolated in the house of her husband at Knole, in Kent, but her notes reveal in veiled terms a trial of strength that had been going on for some time with 'my lord', because her mother's illness had become known some weeks earlier. Anne had been warned in letters on 9 May that her mother was in danger of death. That same night she received a message from Dorset telling her that he had decided to send their daughter to live elsewhere and that he forbade her ever to return to Knole. Anne notes simply that this was 'a very grievous and sorrowful day' for her. On 11 May she took advice on the subject of what she called 'the business' of her northern inheritance, the cause of the dissension with her husband and the affective blackmail he was practising through the child. Dorset blew hot and cold, reversing his decision to send their daughter away, but getting his friends to intervene on his behalf with Anne. She stood firm, while feeling that she was 'condemned by most folks' for her attitude, so much so that she wrote, laconically, on 12 May: 'I am like an Owl in the Desert.' Stubbornly to oppose a husband, and also the last wishes of a father, was neither easy nor common.

Anne only rarely speaks about herself. More prone to doubt than to self-satisfaction, she is often content to reveal her happiness in an occasional ironic touch, without comment. On 11 May 1616, when Dorset sent her conciliatory signals from London, together with proof of his powerful allies, because he enclosed the wedding ring of the recently married Lord Treasurer, she notes that she sent him her own wedding ring in return. Or again, on Easter Day 1617, she reports that they had had a great 'falling out' in the afternoon after taking communion together in the morning, but that she had worn her white satin gown and her white waistcoat throughout. The day before, 19 April, she had once again refused to give in to her husband's entreaties, telling him she 'was in perfect charity with all the world'. By such little touches she expresses her conviction that she was in the right, in the eyes of God and the eyes of man. Her determination was remarkable. She refused to give in for 41 years, in spite of setbacks and suffering.

The death of her mother brought things to a head. Francis Clifford, the paternal uncle, seized some of the property. To avoid a duel between his son and Anne's husband, James I himself intervened. At Dorset's request, he received the couple on Saturday 18 January 1617. Dorset agreed to submit to the king's judgement, whereas Anne refused to renounce her Westmorland inheritance as long as she lived. No argument could dent her resolve. On Monday 20 January, the king received them a second time, around 8 in the evening, in the presence of the relevant relatives of Anne and several men of law. She stubbornly replied once again that she would never agree to lose Westmorland. She stuck to her guns in spite of the intense irritation shown by the king and in spite of the attempts of some of her family to persuade her. She later learned that the royal decision was to come to a compromise without her, since she would not consent. She confined herself to concluding in her journal, with relief and apparent humility, that neither she nor anyone else thought she would have got through the day as well as she had. She seems to have received the secret support of the queen, who, she says, had whispered to her not to trust blindly in the king.

In March 1617, James I ordered Anne to leave her lands to her uncle, Francis Clifford, in exchange for which Dorset would receive £20,000 in compensation. The stubborn Anne continued to resist, come hell or high water. On 23 April 1617, at Easter, she notes that her husband did not sleep with her as he should have done; he was attempting sexual blackmail. This too failed. At least, he joined her the next night. Anne thus continued valiantly to behave respectfully towards him, as she had done in the king's presence, without ever relenting in her opposition to her father's last wishes. There is no need of a psychoanalyst to tell us that, fundamentally, she was refusing to submit to male, royal, paternal or marital law. Nevertheless, she lost the battle and her inheritance, though not the war, which would end to her advantage more than 30 years later.

Between 1617 and 1624, she gave birth four more times and saw three of her children die, leaving only Isabella, who survived into adulthood, like Margaret. Her husband died in 1624. In June 1630, after a widowhood of six years, she was married a second time, to Philip Herbert, Earl of Pembroke and Montgomery, born in 1584, a former favourite of James I, by whom she had two children. The marriage was not particularly happy. This was in part because, at the Revolution, Anne was strongly royalist whereas Herbert supported Parliament. Her uncle, Francis Clifford, died in 1641, followed by his son Henry in 1643. Anne then inherited everything she had claimed for so long, but had to wait for the Civil War to end before she could take possession of her lands. In 1649, the energetic Anne arrived at Skipton Castle, which had been besieged and slighted, leaving her second husband behind; he died the following year.

Free at last, at the age of 60, she restored her northern castles, Pendragon, Appleby, Brough and Brougham, and then, in 1655, Skipton itself. Cromwell did not want the castle to be rebuilt, but in the end he let her have her way, out of respect for the only woman who had ever dared to oppose his wishes. Once again, Anne had shown the most powerful man of the age that she would never give in. Alone of her sex, in spite of every male misgiving, she reigned over a vast English barony, building and restoring churches and establishing almshouses for the poor. She died on 21 March 1676, at the age of 86, in the room in which her father had been born and died, in Brougham Castle. In a last twist of fate, she left the inheritance to her daughter, now Lady Thanet, whose son, Nicholas Lord Thanet, seized the properties by force on his mother's death, upsetting the order of priorities Anne had laid down.[52]

Another sign of her indomitable temperament was her commissioning of a painting in 1646, the 'Great Picture', to commemorate her victory.[53] It is in the form of a family triptych and it is heavy with symbolism. In the centre are Anne's parents and their two sons, who died young; the father, George Clifford, third Earl of Cumberland, who was often absent and preferred to leave his inheritance to the male line of his family, is a little off centre, to the right; Margaret Russell, the mother, points to her elder son, Lord Francis, beside whom stands Sir Robert, the youngest of her children. On the wall behind them, four portraits, grouped in pairs, are all of women, aunts of Anne: two Cliffords (Baroness Wharton and the Countess of Derby) and two Russells (the Countess of Warwick – also named Anne – and the Countess of Bath). The gently ironic message is that they are secretly watching over the rights of their niece, dispossessed by the will of her father and the law of men, but who had finally triumphed over all obstacles. Lady Anne herself is shown on the left-hand panel, aged 15, when she should have inherited her paternal properties; above her are shelves full of books and two portraits of her tutors, including Samuel Daniel. The right-hand panel celebrates her victory at the age of 56, her right hand placed on some books lying on a table, many others piled on two bookshelves above; just above her right arm, two little portraits placed between the books she so loved, those of the poets in particular, show her two husbands. Anne allows herself the pleasure of a malicious wink by thus demonstrating her conjugal loyalty, but hanging 'my lord' and his still living successor like trophies from her painful past, at the very moment when she knew she was at last free of all shackles and in a position soon to attain the happiness she had so long desired by reigning in person over her Westmorland estates. It is difficult not to conclude that she had achieved something extremely rare in the seventeenth century, a victory over all the men who had tried to bend her to their will, the king, her father, her two husbands and Oliver Cromwell. Yet she had done so without ever abandoning an attitude of obedience towards them, as towards God. It is by no means certain that this had always been feigned. This is sometimes suggested by her resort to irony, but her tone is equally sincere on many other occasions when she expresses doubts about her actions and worries about the conventions. It did not stop her from giving everything a female imprint, her own, that of her daughter whom she made her heir, and that of the aunts on the central panel of the family painting of 1646. A hybrid figure, a rebel often taken aback at her own audacity, it is very probable that she was sustained by the image of the great Elizabeth I, the only woman not of her family in relation to whom she locates herself on learning of her mother's death. Would she have had the strength to go as far as she did without this most prestigious of female models, who had herself been forced to insist on her rights to the royal inheritance?

While obstinacy could prove effective, on condition of possessing money, patience and talent, it was easier for a woman who was rebellious but conscious of the dangers she ran to opt for a strategy of seeming submission. Before a court, female defendants knew that to conform to the model of natural weakness expected by the judges would win them some sympathy, unlike an attitude of defiance. Records making it possible to identify a consciously constructed duplicity are, however, rare. The case of Mary Rich, Countess of Warwick, is made all the more interesting, because it reveals both the lived reality and its idealized reconstruction. Mary Rich was the author of thousands of pages of manuscript comprising her private diary, which she wrote almost daily for some ten years, beginning on 25 July 1666. In addition, she condensed her entire personal history, from birth to an advanced age, into a short autobiography of 40 pages written seven years before her death, around 1671. From this date, therefore, she was writing the two documents simultaneously, and she records the same chronological information, on her youth in Ireland and London, her controversial marriage to Charles Rich, the death of two children and her widowhood. The chief difference is in the way she describes her married life. In the autobiography she presents her husband as a gallant romantic hero, whereas the private journal portrays him as violent and tyrannical. In the autobiography she presents herself as a lively, confident and fulfilled woman, living out a great passion, whereas the journal entries reveal a chronically depressed, disappointed and bitter wife. The choice of these two opposed styles is difficult to understand. Mary Rich seems to have found it hard to accept that her marriage, a love-match disapproved of by her family, had ended in affective failure, after endless disputes. The private journal clearly acted as an outlet for her frustrations and her sufferings.[54] This is quite often the case with this form of writing, not intended for public consumption. In this way, the women who practised it were, like Anne Clifford, healing hurts in their love life, linked to work or deeper still. The mystery thickens in the case of the autobiography of Mary Rich, composed in parallel, which makes the deliberate choice to idealize reality. Is this true duplicity? Or a pathological fracture of the Self following a particularly painful failure which may have made her bitterly regret a choice condemned by her family? Or a reimagining through writing of what might have been, in order to leave a beautiful memory of herself and her life? Unlike the journal, the autobiography assumes an audience to appreciate it. She may also have been motivated by a desire to relive a lost dream, to preserve the nostalgia for it on paper and, in so doing, to recover a self-esteem damaged by the many negative details recorded, over the last five years, in the hundreds of pages of the private diary.

Whatever the answer, the example of Mary Rich shows the extent to which suffering could help the Subject to reach a clearer perception of herself. Even more than the men of the sixteenth and seventeenth centuries, women had extreme difficulty in establishing their identity, between normative ideals and concrete realities. The 'weaker vessel' had to endure the violence of the 'lord and master', regarded as a normal part of married life, not to speak of the disappointments associated with the male practice of the sexual double standard. Yet she was expected to submit and to suffer without complaint. This was the price of saving her soul, because her body tugged her naturally in the direction of hell.

The fluidity of bodies

'Every man is as a spunge, and but a spunge filled with teares', preached John Donne in a Lenten sermon in 1623.[55] A great reader, Anne Clifford – who had met the great man on 27 July 1617, after a Sunday sermon – was familiar with such ideas, developed by all branches of learning at the period, with medicine in the vanguard. The lessons of Galen and Hippocrates dominated description of the body, which was seen as full of fluids but open to the air that traversed it, its frontiers being porous. All the liquids circulating inside it, sperm, milk, sweat and tears, could turn into each other and become blood, so the various physical processes, alimentation, excretion, menstruation and lactation, were believed to be homologous.[56] This humoral body was closely dependent on the balance of its internal temperature: feeding was seen as a coction (cooking), sickness as an excess or lack in this sphere. Ancient medicine added to the picture the four constituent elements: heat, dryness, cold and moisture. The first two defined the virile adult, the last two his partner. The polarization sustained a thinking of difference, which ethnologists observe in many human societies in a variety of forms: man is situated on the side of strength, purity, heaven and God, whereas the concept of woman evokes weakness, impurity, water, land and the devil.

It has been claimed that Galenic physiology contains only a single sexual model, the differences between the two halves of the human race being only of degree and not of kind.[57] It is true that the medical and scholarly discourse evoked a continuum,[58] from the very hot and very dry, hairy and dark-skinned super-male to the most feminine of women, blonde and light complexioned. Between these extremes came hybrids with less evenly balanced humours: brunette women, with a lot of hair and hard breasts, who developed these features from an excess of heat; old men, weakened by age and colder than the norm; little boys, not yet warm enough (and kept in skirts until they were 7); young men, in the process of slowly gravitating from maternal moistness towards the calorific apotheosis (the definition of homosexuality was then essentially a question of age); and effeminate men, whose internal fluids resembled those of women. In the eyes of the doctors, the sexual organs of women appeared to be exactly the same as those of men, simply hidden inside. This is why Montaigne could ironically advise young girls not to jump up and down too energetically if they wanted to avoid the fate suffered by one such, whose 'shameful parts' had descended when she did just that. And in his *De Humani Corporis Fabrica* (*On the Fabric of the Human Body*), published in 1543, the famous anatomist Andreas Vesalius showed an excised vagina which had exactly the same shape as a penis.[59]

Discourse should not, however, be confused with reality. The theory of the unique sexual model was much criticized because it did not allow for the concrete experience of the body. Without questioning the importance of the theory of the corporeal flux, what matters is that the humoral language constructed personal practices that were always turbulent, even dramatic, including for those who saw themselves as normal according to received ideas.[60] Thus the banal, ordinary definition of virility in Augsburg in the sixteenth and seventeenth centuries emphasized its hot and violently disruptive character.[61]

The question needs to be relocated within the framework of the Western definition of the Subject. Since Plato, man had been seen as the site of a constant struggle between the body and the soul. The battle only intensified in the century of the religious Reformations. Calvinist theology made a major contribution by urging Christians to master their physical needs and desires so as to avoid the ravages of sin. In his *Religio Medici* of 1642, Sir Thomas Browne exclaimed that he sometimes felt a hell within himself: 'Lucifer keeps his court in my breast!'[62] The statement may be interpreted literally. At the same period, the French Catholics were finding the mark of Satan on the skin of witches, and exorcists were making the nuns of Loudun or Louviers, allegedly possessed by the Devil, vomit up demons, toads and snakes. On both sides of the Channel, the immortal soul was increasingly mistrustful of the snares of the flesh. But science had advanced since the Renaissance. It began to explore the interior of the human body after the publication, in 1543, of the treatise of Vesalius, *De Humani Corporis Fabrica*. The period up to about 1640 was one of the emergence of a new curiosity about this subject. Civilization being a whole, other spheres of knowledge were also affected. Some painters flaunted a 'culture of dissection', like Caravaggio, in 1603, in *The Incredulity of St Thomas*, or Rembrandt in *The Anatomy of Dr Tulp* of 1632. The fact that Caravaggio had failed to get from the Jesuits the commission he had hoped for, so he could paint a resurrection of Christ for them, shows that his approach deviated from the principles of the Counter-Reformation. His St Thomas is painted with a very realistic attention to 'surgical detail', the finger of incredulity pushed into Christ's wound. To mix the sacred and the profane in this way was bound to disturb many of his contemporaries. Further, the artist had drawn on a knowledge of autopsy considered sacrilegious by the Church. Had he not, one day, the story ran, forced his assistants to stand around a decomposing corpse? A new phase in the development of the scholarly gaze at the physical envelope began with the discoveries of Harvey and the thinking of Descartes, which led to the body being perceived as a machine. William Harvey published his ideas on the circulation of the blood, *De Motu Cordis*, in 1628. The famous *cogito*, 'I think, therefore I am', of Descartes dates from 1637. Yet the earlier vulgate was only slowly overturned, especially as some of its defenders explained that a machine had to have a creator.[63]

Contrary to a received idea, the sixteenth and seventeenth centuries did not represent an age of medical knowledge set in stone. This same was true of relations between the body and the soul, hence also with perceptions of masculine and feminine. The whole of Western civilization adapted to these slow, muted changes. The conception of the world gradually shifted from the image of a divine circumference, the universal macrocosm of which each human microcosm was the exact reflection, to a consciousness of the existence of frontiers, of breaking points. The stage plan attached to the manuscript of *The Castle of Perseverance*, an English play from the first quarter of the fifteenth century, shows a circle – that of the earth, surrounded by water. At the centre of the circle is the castle, beneath which is the bed of Mankind. The first printed map of the world, of 1472, is configured in the same way. Other examples of medieval manuscripts show a similar arrangement, with Jerusalem at the centre of a disk on which the three continents then known, Europe, Asia and Africa, are represented. Geography and the theatre offered observers a mirror of themselves. Also significant in this context is the invention by Inigo Jones in 1605, at the English court, of the stage in the Italian fashion. Destined to prevail in the second half of the century, having proved deeply disorienting to its first audiences, it drew a precise line of demarcation between the actors and the hall, creating a new, unified and stable perception of the human being. The effect was heightened by the new recourse to the soliloquy, as in Marlowe's *Doctor Faustus* (*c.*1588), which strengthened the effect of interiority and was increasingly to the taste of the public.[64] The old cultural traditions did not, however, disappear overnight. In a very different sphere, that of the anatomy lesson, the iconographical representations of the early seventeenth century retain a concentric arrangement inherited from Vesalius: the corpse is at the centre of *The Anatomy Theatre of Leiden* of 1610, surrounded by banks of circular tiers, in the middle of a square room, where the curious wander about outside wooden barriers.⁶⁵ The commitment to the traditional circle and the position of the dissected body surround with divine signs an act which many considered sacrilegious, because one was daring to look inside a creature fashioned in his image by the Creator. In *Portrait of the Image of God in Man*, of 1627, John Weemes (or Wemyss), an English theologian, turned the argument on its head to reconcile anatomy with religion by claiming that it made it possible to know more about the work of the Almighty.⁶⁶ The taboo has not entirely disappeared in our own day, because the inside of the body, which a twentieth-century surgeon described as a 'Medusa's head', reminds the observer of his human condition.⁶⁷

Fears and prohibitions were even more strongly associated with women's bodies than with those of men. The Dutch physician Levinus Lemnius (1505–68), author of a book famous throughout Europe, *The Secret Miracles of Nature*,⁶⁸ claimed that the latter smelled naturally good, unlike the former: 'Woman abounds in excrements, and because of her periods she gives off a bad smell; also she makes all things worse and destroys their natural strength and faculties.' Like Pliny the Elder, he believed that contact with menstrual blood destroyed flowers and fruit, dulled ivory, blunted knives and drove dogs mad. Following Henricus Cornelius Agrippa, he added to this list of disasters the death or flight of bees, the fact that warmed linen turned black, the aborting of mares, the sterility of she-asses and, more generally, the impossibility of conceiving, even claiming that the ashes of sheets stained by menstrual blood took the colour out of purple and flowers. Further, he extended the idea of noxiousness to the female smell strictly speaking, itself a product of the coldness and moistness peculiar to the sex, whereas the 'natural warmth of man is vaporous, soft and sweet and almost as if saturated with some aromatic odour'. Unlike the male, therefore, the female had a nasty smell, to the point where her approach dried up, spoiled and blackened nutmeg. Coral went pale when she touched it, whereas it turned redder on a representative of the stronger sex or if a grain of mustard was inserted into it.⁶⁹

In other words, the female body made men uneasy. This led to its being dissected with particular enthusiasm, especially in the United Provinces and England, where the Protestant culture emphasized original sin. The anatomists tried to discover the mystery of the origin of death, result of the sin of Eve, while also searching for the proofs and causes of women's rebellious nature.⁷⁰ On the English stage, women were represented – by boys, as we have seen – as 'leaky vessels', which added the dimension of incontinence to their structural frailty ('weaker vessels'). Full of fluids, linked to the movements of the moon which regulated their inner seas, they appeared almost like the constantly emptying barrels of the Danaides. In a treatise published in 1625, *The Anatomie of Urines*, James Hart followed common medical opinion in seeing their micturition as lighter in colour but greater in quantity than that of men, due to their colder temperament. This feature was the butt of many jokes. One proverb ran: 'Let her weep, she'll piss less.' The other female fluids were equally superabundant. Shakespeare explains in *The Merchant of Venice* (c.1596–8) that a male body that bleeds resembles that of a woman. Gail Kern Paster thinks that such allusions to incontinence and the humoral profusion are part of general trend designed to produce a feeling of embarrassment – from which she takes the title of her book – in the Elizabethan theatre audience.[71] It is an attractive hypothesis. It complements that of Norbert Elias on the civilizing of manners, which began with control of the natural functions, as Erasmus had emphasized in 1530 in his *On Good Manners in Boys*. It also builds on and nuances the observations of Mikhail Bakhtin regarding the 'grotesque body' of the people, open and spilling out all its excretions.[72] Between the future triumph of personal self-control, imposed by the gradual instilling of a culture of guilt, and the law of collective shame characteristic of rural worlds, the intermediate notion of embarrassment makes it possible to define a period of transition. It primarily concerned the Londoners who watched the plays of Shakespeare and probably also many inhabitants of European towns who were beginning to adapt and modernize their behaviour.

This feeling of embarrassment in the face of excessive bodily functions that would be better concealed was also something that the Flemish and Dutch painters who followed the Elder Bruegel tried to provoke, especially in the seventeenth century. The pissing man frequently shown in the peasant scenes of genre paintings was meant to help the owners of the paintings, often middling or well-off townspeople, to differentiate themselves from such rustics by laughing at their attitudes. In the nineteenth century, those who inherited paintings often simply erased crude details which were now no longer acceptable in their society.

The definition of pleasure, especially sexual pleasure, is closely linked to the way the Subject perceives him- or herself and their body. Stephen Greenblatt has spoken of a 'caloric model of sexuality' in the Renaissance.[73] Lemnius, the Dutch physician quoted above, says in *The Secret Miracles of Nature* that the origin of desire lay in the brain and the liver, but that man achieved an erection thanks to an effect of superior warmth coming from the arteries of the heart. For both the doctors and the authors of conduct manuals, the sole aim of sex was reproduction. So the act of love had to be effective. For this, it was necessary for the partners to achieve a simultaneous orgasm, which allowed the best possible coction of the two 'seeds' – women being believed to produce seed, too. Thus the preliminaries should not be neglected, although no text of the period refers to the clitoris. Overall, the effort expended was exhausting, especially for the man, the quality of whose sperm diminished if he indulged immoderately in the pleasures of the flesh. Scholars debated the intensity of pleasure within the couple with equal gravity. The most generally held opinion was that the female experienced greater pleasure because she ejaculated her own seed while also receiving that of her partner.[74]

The medicine of the day was essentially one of evacuation, to purge the sick of superfluous fluids by means of bleeding or clysters. Though roundly mocked by Molière, it may have had unforeseen erotic consequences. Some documents, such as almanacs, associated purging with coitus. The almost daily use of laxative techniques involved an ambivalent bodily experience, mingling satisfaction and shame, producing voluptuous sensations on therapeutic orders, so to speak.[75] There is no reason not to believe such a claim. Some observations made during the course of this chapter on the subject of the female roles played by boys in the theatre and on male homosexuality in the kingdoms of misrule suggest that anal satisfactions, real or imaginary, were by no means rare. Also, the harshness of the legislation against sodomy in both France and England resulted in very few cases in the criminal records. Girls also received the clyster; did they, too, get pleasure from it?

3

CARNAL PLEASURES, MORTAL SINS

FANCHON: But when all is said and done, these girls who are so timid and so frightened of getting pregnant, what can they do to manage without a man when they get the urge and it overwhelms them to such an extent that their cunt is on fire and there's no getting any relief whatever way you rub it?
SUZANNE: I tell you, cousin, there are some who have never been touched by a man and who still manage to give themselves a good time and pleasure themselves, without fear of all that.
FANCHON: But how can they do that?
...
SUZANNE: The girls who can't get hold of statues [the preceding anecdote describes the use by the daughter of a king of a male figure in bronze equipped with a huge penis carved from a less hard material] make do with dildos, or simple contraptions of velvet or glass made in the shape of a natural male member, which they fill with warm milk and use to arouse themselves as if it were a real penis. The others use saveloys, or big four-for-a-pound candles or, if they haven't any of those, they put a finger in their cunt, as far up as they can, and make themselves come that way. And lots of poor girls who live alone against their will, and all the nuns who only see the world through a hole, are forced to do this and can't banish temptations any other way, because, since fucking is as natural as eating and drinking, once they're past 15 they're no longer innocent, and they have to cool their vital natural heat.[1]

L'École des filles (*The School for Girls*), the short anonymous text from which the extract above is taken, appeared in 1655. A great tracker-down of forgotten libertine writing, which shocked him while arousing his curiosity, Frédéric Lachèvre (1855–1943) proclaimed it the first practical manual of eroticism in French. But it is more than that. This little work is extraordinary in every sense of the term, in the very strict censorship it suffered, in the tone and quality of the presentation and in the intentions of the author (or authors). At a time when manuals of etiquette designed to instruct the 'gentleman' citizen in pleasing and well-controlled behaviour were hugely popular,[2] the author offered, with heavy irony, a lesson in a sentimental education that was both very carnal and wholly devoted to the sexuality of women. For the first time, a male writer (it would appear) invented the body of a woman and her right to erotic sensations. The book explores this unknown continent in great detail and with a disarming simplicity of expression, uninhibitedly calling a spade a spade. It is a pity there was no equivalent for boys, no *École des garçons*. Molière, soon after, in 1661, offered a school for husbands (*L'École des maris*), followed by one for wives the year after that. He, too, proclaims the legitimacy of the quest for love of Agnès, the heroine of his *L'École des femmes*, but in doing so he stays close to the precepts of good manners; in Molière, the virginal Agnès dreams only of lawful delights and desires within marriage.[3]

This is very far from the case with Fanchon, instructed by her cousin Suzanne. Eating, drinking and fucking, she says, are natural. The lesson, as we will see, recalls that of the libertines of the age, in particular the baron de Blot, who died in 1655. Although the religious and moral norms, the conventions learned and the law of the land all defined excesses in such matters as mortal sins, there were other voices that demanded access to sensual pleasure for the human being, in particular for women. Molière says this too, cautiously, through the question posed by the innocent Agnès on the subject of love: 'A sin, you say? But why, if you please?'[4]

L'École des filles will serve as Ariadne's thread to this chapter.[5] Historians, who are generally more austere and certainly less curious than Frédéric Lachèvre, often take at their face value the rodomontades of the moralists. But life is not necessarily as straightforward as the latter like to claim. The harshest criminal laws are only applied strictly and for a long time if they are genuinely accepted by the populations concerned. By forgetting this, some authors of brilliant syntheses on the family and sexuality have seen their work sink gently into oblivion.[6] Nevertheless, like them, we have to start with the theoretical and judicial facts in order to assess the power of the prohibitions: the pleasures of the flesh were grave sins in the monastic

Christian tradition, which was extended to a sector of urban society and a minority of the peasantry under the impetus of the religious Reformations. The realities then intrude, because there were many, sometimes even systematic, transgressions. The data culled from the French and English judicial records can be compared with the lessons of L'École des filles. Seen from this perspective, the erotic work focused on the female orgasm becomes also a sort of ironic, slightly nostalgic digest of a carnal experience that was much more widespread than has been claimed, including among the peasantry, in contrast to the moral freeze that was in the process of imposing new rules. The end result of such tensions was to connect for a long time to come the notion of sexual pleasure and that of sin and punishment: sex in pain became the prerogative of those men and women who resisted, body and soul, the growth of prohibitions and taboos. Long before the marquis de Sade, the seventeenth century discovered the resort to pain and blood in order to heighten the sensations, in the *Dialogues of Luisa Sigea*, also known under the title of *Satyra sotadica*, published in 1660 by Nicolas Chorier.[7]

Forbidden passions

Christianity has, 'from the beginning, opposed the spirit to the flesh and waged war on the flesh in the name of the spirit', says Jean-Louis Flandrin. Doctrine and practice were established in the age of the monks, between the sixth and the eleventh centuries. Under their influence, the celibacy that they had voluntarily chosen became the purest ideal, whereas marriage was to be regarded as a lesser evil, and even as a trap when it resulted in pleasure. 'We do not claim that marriage is culpable,' explained Gregory the Great, but 'it cannot take place without carnal pleasure', which can 'in no way be without sin'. The faithful were urged to consider the words of the Apostle Paul: 'But if they cannot contain, let them marry.' The sacrament was holy, admittedly, but the conjugal prerogatives should still be used with moderation so as to avoid sin and damnation. This is why the Church put such strict controls on marriage, increasing the number of prohibitions on consanguinity and affinity and extending the periods of obligatory continence, during festivals and fasts, in particular the long periods of Lent, before Easter, and Advent, in the lead-up to Christmas. The monks had transposed their own voluntary sacrifice into a rule of periodic continence 'almost as hard as their own', imposed on all married couples.[8]

Once the matrimonial doctrine had been laid down, it was not deferred to quickly or completely. In the seventeenth century, the Western peasantry in particular still largely resisted the pressure. It was stepped up, however, following the Reformations. Protestants and Catholics vied with each other in zeal by claiming to assure Christian salvation more effectively than their enemies. Marriage increasingly attracted their attention. On the papal side, the battle for control of the continent intensified from the mid-sixteenth century on. The intellectuals of this generation often rejected the irenicism of the Erasmians, that is, the optimistic conception of relations between the Creator and humankind. This way of thinking had dominated the humanism of the 1520s, in the wake of Erasmus himself, of Thomas More in England, of Rabelais in France and of the painters who now dared uninhibitedly to portray nudity, such beauty testifying in their eyes to God's goodness and power. The giants of Rabelais were a metaphor to affirm that human beings had ceased to grow smaller, as had been – and would again be – believed, because they were lit up by the sun of the spirit, under the benevolent eye of He who had created them in his image. Their heirs of the 1560s saw things very differently, as they observed the religious chaos then turning into terrible and cruel wars of religion, in France, England and the Low Countries. One of them, Pierre Boaistuau, bemoaned 'this piteous tragedy of the life of man'. He was quite clear where the blame lay: 'But see, first, from what seed he is engendered, if not of a corruption and infection? What is the place of his birth, if not a dirty and unclean prison? How is he there in his mother's womb without resembling anything but a vile mass of unfeeling flesh?' This unhappy state of affairs was the result of his being 'sustained by the menstrual blood of his mother, which is so detestable and foul that I cannot repeat without horror what is written about it by the philosophers and doctors who have dealt with the secrets of nature. But let those who are curious about such things read Pliny.' The child came into the world after a long time spent feeding on 'this venom', during a pregnancy that is likened to a sickness where 'corrupt and depraved humours abound' in the maternal body. The 'tragedy of human life' was overwhelming: 'To the point where, if we consider with care all the mystery of our birth, we will recognize the truth of the old proverb that says we are conceived in foulness and corruption, born in sadness and pain, and nourished and raised in anguish and toil.'[9]

At the Council of Trent (1545–63), the canons of 11 November 1563 emphasized the indissoluble and monogamous sacrament of marriage. In parallel, French monarchical legislation regulated marriage with increasing rigour from the reign of Henri II on. An edict of February 1557 (new style) prohibited clandestine unions, 'which daily, by a carnal, indiscreet and disorderly will, are contracted in our kingdom by children, without and against the wishes and consent of their fathers and mothers'. The guilty minors, that is, sons under 30 or daughters under 25, were to be disinherited. Even those who were of age were still 'required to seek the advice and counsel of their said fathers and mothers'. The subsequent blizzard of texts indicates they were not as effective as had been hoped. In 1579, the ordinance of Blois made the agreement of tutors, guardians and close relatives obligatory for orphans, including for widows under 25, also the presence of four witnesses at the ceremony, after publication of three prior bans. It formally prohibited marriages *de praesenti* (that is, using words in the present tense) conducted before a notary, a sort of trial marriage then common which allowed the future spouses to cohabit and have sex before receiving the sacrament. An edict of 1606 repeated all these requirements, under pain of annulment. In 1629, the Code Michau emphasized once again the need to 'maintain the authority of fathers over their children'. Other ordinances from 1639 on returned to the intractable problems of clandestine marriages and lack of parental consent. The persistence of the royal legislators indicates that marriage was a major preoccupation of the monarchy under the last Valois and the early Bourbons. The ordinance of 1579 described simply as rape any matrimonial commitment made between minors without the permission of the family, which made it possible to seek its annulment before the parlements.[10]

These measures reveal wider religious and cultural changes, equally visible in a new literary and artistic insistence on the theme of voracious female sexuality: for those who could not take the veil, marriage was the sole bastion of their eternal salvation. The monastic morality of periodic continence applied to couples took the form of a growing fear of the hell of the lower regions of the body. Everyone should beware of the devil who slumbered there, women more than men, because they were unable to curb their lustfulness alone. In the deeply troubled times of the confessional confrontations and wars of religion, the old message of the sermons against sin took on a more alarming aspect and circulated much more widely, in particular in the towns threatened or besieged by enemies of the faith. The terrifying images of the punishment of sinners emerged from the churches, where they had been painted with great realism at the end of the Middle Ages, to insinuate themselves into people's consciousness.[11]

The bonfires of witches which became increasingly common in Europe after the decades 1560–80 spread everywhere the stereotype of the old debauched peasant woman who gave herself to Satan in order to thwart the divine plan and help to destroy humanity. This was another way of claiming that her sex was dedicated to death even when giving life, because witches were accused of killing unbaptized babies and handing them to their master to be turned into diabolic unguents. All these fantasies came together in what was primarily an urban justificatory masculine discourse, spread by books and images. It gained considerable credibility because it was now upheld not only by ecclesiastics but also by doctors, legislators, judges and authors of literary fictions, like Rabelais in the *Tiers Livre*. Parisian engravings spread it widely and made it accessible to those who were unable to read. An analysis of 6,000 images produced between 1490 and 1620 brings out two very contradictory definitions of femininity. The main one, visible in two-thirds of the works, turns women into she-devils addicted to the seven capital sins. By far the most common was lustfulness, followed in descending order of frequency by envy, pride, idleness, avarice, anger and greed – a fascinating catalogue of the forbidden pleasures leading to eternal damnation! What the prevailing culture particularly stigmatized was the 'natural' propensity of the daughters of Eve to indulge unrestrainedly in the pleasures of the flesh. This was to its own advantage, obviously, because this imaginary model of the 'prostitute' reputed to lie dormant in every woman authorized men to practise the sexual double standard and to consider as easy pickings any woman not protected or supervised by a husband. The remaining engravings studied, a little over a third, glorify the virtuous matron, chaste but fecund; not the wise virgin, who makes few appearances, but rather the ideal spouse, faithful to her husband and, above all, maternal. Unlike other female vessels, constantly pierced and always on the lookout for sexual gratification, her body was closed to temptations, gave birth in obedience to the divine will and then nourished.[12] A good wife and a good mother, courageous even to the point of sacrifice, she had the characteristics of those whose soul would be saved because they meekly accepted the masculine tutelage that was indispensable to lead them along this difficult path, contrary to their rebellious and eminently sinful nature.

European art developed these features, emphasizing fecundity and lactation, systematically opposing the mother to the whore.[13] From the mid-sixteenth century on, willowy young women with small high breasts, like Botticelli's Venus, the perverse Eve frequently painted by

Cranach the Elder or the models of Jean Gougon in France, gave way to the fuller, rounder forms of the Second Fontainebleau School or of Rubens in the cycle dedicated to Marie de Medici for her palais du Luxembourg. This triumphant flesh announces that the receptacle of femininity, too open by nature, can be closed by force of virtue. The fluids thus retained will no longer change into impure menstrual blood or the voluptuousness of the senses, but will concentrate, filling out the figure, to the benefit of the nurse alone. As we have seen, all the organic liquids were identical in the eyes of the doctors, and all capable of turning into blood. The milk of the mother was analogous to the sperm she was believed to ejaculate during coitus: the one sublimated the other after procreation. Here we see the coherence of the discourse on marriage. The aim was to enhance its status and call it holy, in spite of the sin associated with the pleasure taken during sexual relations. Representatives of the churches and judges were given the task of applying the accepted canons so as to prohibit and punish the search for pleasure alone, inside and outside the sacred conjugal tie.

Sexual repression is clearly attested to by the criminal records of the sixteenth and seventeenth centuries. In France, the law and courtroom practice gradually established a very negative vision of the excesses of the flesh, reinforced by the activities of confessors, who took a close interest in the sexual practices of couples.[14] The system came to maturity in the reign of Louis XIII. In 1609 the jurist Claude Le Brun de la Rochette published, in Lyons, *Le Procès civil et criminel*, which distinguished four main types of crime. *Paillardise* covered a range of sexual transgression and was less often prosecuted than assaults on the person and theft, but more frequently than divine or human lese-majesty.[15] A ranking order of cases was established, primarily according to the threat posed to the sacred principles of marriage. Masturbation was an offence in the eyes of the judges, the first rung on the repressive scale, but too difficult to detect to be effectively prosecuted. Next in order of importance came debauchery, that is, sexual relations outside marriage, followed by concubinage, adultery and bigamy, variously punished according to region and court, but always stopping short of the death penalty. This was applied in cases of rape, male or female homosexuality (sodomy within marriage was less serious and so left to the confessor), incest (between parents and children or brothers and sisters) and bestiality (the animal in question also usually being killed). Further, a royal edict of 1557 ordered the execution of mothers who had given birth outside marriage, having concealed their pregnancy from the authorities, if the child died, irrespective of the reason. In the vast area of its jurisdiction, which extended to almost half the kingdom, the parlement of Paris ratified about 1,500 death sentences for this offence between 1557 and 1789. Lastly, the male and female witches condemned to be burnt for divine lese-majesty were assumed to have had carnal relations with a demonic incubus or succubus, according to need, during the Sabbath. The confessions of the women witches before the court often refer to a very painful pleasure, the diabolic penis being described as icy cold and bristling with spikes.[16]

With the exception of concealment of pregnancy and infanticide, sexual crimes have left relatively few traces in the judicial archives. The most shocking in the eyes of the magistrates, sodomy, bestiality and incest, are very rarely mentioned. The possible destruction of the archives to avoid preserving the memory of such scandals is only a partial explanation. Prosecutions really were exceptional, which implies a tacit tolerance, especially in the countryside. Rape is rather better documented: 18 out of a total of 641 criminal appeals in 1567, 13 out of 673 in 1568, before the parlement of Paris, according to my own sampling. Cases were again notably fewer in the countryside. The act may have aroused a little more indignation in urban circles, but capital punishment was still rare. It is recorded three times in two years, that is, in 10 per cent of arrests, always where there were aggravating circumstances. The same is true of the seven men condemned to the galleys, the rest being banished, whipped or simply released.

The presence of adultery in the same sources reveals the new interest in the purity of the marriage sacrament after the royal edict of 1557. In 1567 and 1568, 33 persons were accused, 18 of them women. Yet the harshest punishments inflicted consisted only of sending two men to the galleys and banishment for two years in the case of an unmarried woman who had sinned with a married man. The others sentenced suffered banishment, fines, public whipping or public shaming. The authorities were primarily interested in the double breaking of the conjugal tie in an urban context: 11 of the women prosecuted were from towns as against 7 from villages; 11 were married, 4 were widows and 3 were spinsters. Peasants comprised more than 80 per cent of the population, yet were clearly less often prosecuted, which reveals that religious and moral supervision was less rigorous in the rural world than in towns, rather than a lesser propensity to sensual sins in the former. A century later, around 1670, adultery rarely figures in the appeals heard before the parlement of Paris. A practice linked to the mastery of the husband over his partner seems to have become established: a deceived husband could confine a guilty wife in a religious institution for two years, then have an absolute right to decide either to leave her there for the rest of her life or take her back into the marital home. It goes without saying that the opposite situation is never found.[17]

In the end, it is far from easy to arrive at a clear interpretation of all these phenomena. Those who argue for austerity can see them as evidence of a spectacular rise in moral standards among the population in general. I myself suspect, rather, that the paucity of cases in relation to the millions of men and women living within the jurisdiction of the parlement of Paris signifies the exact opposite, that is, that sexual behaviour had changed very little in essence. Nevertheless, the normative pressures were probably a source of unease for those who now knew that they were acting in a way that was condemned by the law and by the Church. By seeking to make people admit their sins, auricular confession, which was now presented as a Christian requirement and duty, probably added to this unease. It must surely have helped to develop a new sense of guilt. The confession manuals taught priests insistently to question people, especially women, about the sexual positions they adopted, any possible attempts by the man to avoid leaving his semen inside the woman and other uses of the body regarded as degrading. Sadly, satisfactory evidence about actual attitudes in Catholic France is lacking. Only the Protestants, increasingly in a minority after 1598, have left written traces on this subject in the records of their consistories.[18]

The evidence for England goes some way to compensate for these drawbacks. The sacrament of marriage was the subject of fierce debate between Puritans and Anglicans at the end of the sixteenth century, as we have seen. The Anglican position prevailed in 1597 and was ratified by James I. In 1604, the canons of the Anglican Church imposed a view of the indissolubility of marriage that was close to that of the French Catholics: publication of intent three times in succession during divine service in the parish church; respect for the prohibited degrees of kinship; the necessity of parental consent if the future spouses were under the age of 21. Further, canon 109 instructed the churchwardens, of whom there were usually two per parish, to report to their superiors any scandalous conduct on the part of the faithful, such as adultery, prostitution, incest or 'any other uncleanness and wickedness of life'. The bishops established systems of surveillance. In 1630, for example, the bishop of Bath and Wells asked for a detailed account of every type of immorality, including simple fornication, attempts on the chastity of women, lewd behaviour by men or women, pregnant girls, suspected fathers, young men who married these debauched girls to hide the sin of the father and inefficient or unlicensed midwives, together with the names of those who had given material support to any such offenders. The purpose was not to find proof but to oblige those who were denounced by public rumour or gossip to defend themselves before the religious authorities, because 'common fame' was in itself a fact that they should be able to explain.

Although marriage ceased to be a sacrament at the time of the English Revolution, following the Presbyterian ordinance of 1645, little changed in reality. Nor did the act of 1650, intended to suppress the abominable sins of incest, adultery and fornication, make much difference in practice, because the sanctions it laid down were so harsh. It stipulated the death penalty in the case of the first two, except if a male adulterer was unaware that his partner was married or if the husband of an adulteress had been absent for three years. In practice it was often only the punishment for fornication that was enforced, as in Somerset: three months' prison and a year's probation for the simple fornicator; whipping, the pillory and branding with the letter B and three years' prison for a brothel-keeper, who risked death if he re-offended. Though in theory concerned only with the crimes of rape and buggery with a man or an animal, in practice the civil magistrates exercised considerable influence in all sexual matters in their capacity as guardians of the peace. Further, Tudor legislation had given them full responsibility for the problem of bastards, not only to punish guilty fathers but also to assure the subsistence of the children and prevent them from becoming a charge on the parish. In Somerset, the two types of court concerned, the lay quarter sessions and the ecclesiastical consistory courts, have provided Geoffrey Quaife with an abundant and suggestive harvest of documents for his study of the sexual life of the population between 1601 and 1660.[19]

The joys of sex

There is a well-established view that the population, especially in the countryside, was subjected to and largely accepted the moral reformation of the years 1550–1650, so that they appeared less crude and less impulsive to subsequent generations. The notion of the civilizing process developed by Norbert Elias, though largely based on the changes at the French court under Louis XIV, seemed to lend support to this view, as did Mikhaïl Bakhtin's nostalgic evocation of a scatological and sensual popular culture, of which Rabelais was one of the last survivors.[20] In England, Puritan morality was established, we are told, including among the lower social orders.[21] The example of Somerset between 1601 and 1660 proves the opposite and casts serious doubt on such historical reconstructions.

Peasant eroticism in Somerset

The county of Somerset, with a population of some 200,000, was subject to close moral surveillance, like the rest of England. The exhortations of the Anglican bishops were here particularly detailed. One gets the impression that nothing could escape the eyes of the Church, made easier by the mechanisms of gossip, rumour, the bragging of men in their cups and deathbed confessions. But the repression was hardly commensurate with the effort expended. Admittedly, the potential punishments – admonition or penance – were not much of a deterrent. The latter was the usual penalty for incest, fornication and adultery. It consisted of two public ceremonies within the parish, a third in the cathedral and sometimes, in the most serious cases, a fourth in the marketplace. If the Anglican authorities demonstrated a liberal attitude towards marriage and sex from the mid-sixteenth century on,[22] it was because they knew that they were unable fundamentally to alter the behaviour of the faithful. Life was hard in peasant society, before and during the English Revolution. Violence was latent, always ready to explode. The abuse of strong drink, especially beer, was a scourge, vigorously combated by the authorities, but with limited success because it was a refuge, even a sort of narcotic, easing the strains of contemporary life.[23] Similar features are found at the same period in the county of Artois, under Spanish then French rule after 1640.[24] They were probably typical of rural areas in the West at the time.[25]

Sexual life in Somerset emerges as distinctly liberated. Quaife even concludes that the peasants were predominantly amoral, with the exception of the daughters and wives of the yeomen farmers, who were more influenced than the others by the moral tendency. The gentry also felt the effects of the greater strictness, but constituted, with the yeomen, only a tiny minority. Yet at first sight the demographic characteristics give the impression that sexual desires were tightly controlled. Bastards were rare – around 3 per cent on average for the period as a whole, with a downward trend reaching two-thirds between the first and last decade of the period in question. Pre-nuptial pregnancies, where brides had married when already pregnant, accounted for at most 16–25 per cent of baptisms, depending on the parish, which is in line with the observations of Peter Laslett for England as a whole. With figures of between 18 and 20 per cent, Laslett saw the seventeenth century as part of a long period of decline in this phenomenon, compared with the 32 per cent of the years 1550–99 and the later steady rise, peaking at 39 per cent in the period 1800–49.[26] The situation seems to have been very much the same in France at the time of Louis XIII and Louis XIV, where the rate reached a maximum of 3 per cent in Lower Normandy and often fell elsewhere to 1 per cent of births. Anticipations of marriage by young people in France never exceeded 5–10 per cent, that is, they were notably fewer than in England.[27] When we move from the demographic sources to the records produced by the English system of ecclesiastical surveillance, however, the picture is very different.

At every social level, men behaved with great sexual freedom both before and during marriage. They saw women, whatever their rank, as legitimate objects of desire, whom they could try to seduce if they could get them alone, even if they were married. Many men could not understand why they were in the dock over something so trivial; everybody did it, said some, so there couldn't be any harm in it; others even claimed they had their wife's permission. Thus, to explain their behaviour, they drew on a view of women which emphasized their natural lecherousness and their constant search for a partner capable of satisfying their lust. They themselves were quite normal, simply too 'hot' at a given moment, so they had needed to cool their ardour by a quick fuck; one promised a girl he lusted after that it would only take a minute, if she would be kind enough to step into the next room. The pleasure of the man was defined as a right, without any real regard for the partner. Many were vain enough to describe their exploits in detail, in the tavern or elsewhere. A certain peasant of West Hatch, for example, bragged that he had for 20 years been the 'seeker of the chastity' of various women, unmarried or not. The double standard, which would become the norm in the nineteenth century, was unnecessary in a world of such tacit tolerance. As for the women, while their desires may have gone unrecognized in the male discourse, they were often quite capable of imposing them themselves. Women from the lower orders enjoyed active sex lives. Many of them, too, freely boasted about their sexual prowess. Others openly complained about a husband who was too old or who failed to perform his conjugal duties or who practised coitus interruptus or even one who had a 'small privy member'. They only confirmed masculine convictions regarding the insatiable erotic appetite of their sex. It is true that the new norms tried to impose the model of the respectable wife who reserved her favours for her husband alone, and with the sole aim of procreation, at least in yeoman or gentry families. A man's honour, by contrast, was never damaged by his carnal needs. A man who impregnated a girl was expected to marry her if neither was married; if he was already married, he was simply expected to be concerned for the child's future and contribute financially to its upkeep, so that peace and order would continue to reign in the community. Only fear of venereal disease acted as a real curb on the sexual freedom of men.[28]

Other details emerge from these records. Male homosexuality, in theory a capital offence, made only two appearances at the Somerset quarter sessions. Similarly, incest was less strongly disapproved of than in subsequent centuries and is very rarely mentioned in the ecclesiastical records.[29] Sodomy was not, it seems, an erotic outlet for unmarried men, as has been suggested for France.[30] Or was such behaviour simply too common and too banal for it to be included in the denunciations demanded by the authorities? Masturbation was very common, not only as a release for the frustrated but more generally as a prelude to full sex. The manual stimulation of the penis, the clitoris or the vagina is attested to in a wide variety of circumstances. Prostitutes practised it and accepted it readily. The absence of underwear made things easier for the enterprising male in every conceivable situation, for example on horseback. Sometimes, they tried to provoke a girl or a woman to go further by exposing their member, sometimes manipulating it in front of her, more often guiding her fingers towards their penis, placing it in her hand, or even on the shoulder of a married and seated parishioner in one case recorded. Although women only rarely exposed their private parts, they readily allowed them to be palpated or explored. The happy beneficiaries boasted about this freely, with copious comments. One remarked in public that 'Mary Pittard's thing is as soft as a feather pillow', after exclaiming to Mary herself that she had a 'soft cunt'. Some men groped every woman they could get close to. One man was denounced for having held onto the sex of a girl so long that she eventually pissed in his hand. Quaife thinks that these generally accepted liberties, practised by boys for the decade or so between puberty and marriage in the form of mutual masturbation or the manipulation of female genitals, may have affected their later erotic life. It was not uncommon, he argues as proof, for brutal sexual assaults to focus on such acts: after a long drinking session in a tavern, for example, six men held a servant girl down on a table so that they could each in turn explore her 'privities', then pour their glass of beer over them, except for the sixth, who simply touched her, claiming to be the most honest of them all, before drinking his beer.[31]

Reciprocal caresses between women are very rarely mentioned in the documents. There are almost no references to bestiality (one single case) and none to oral practices. For the young bachelors of Somerset, heterosexual masturbation to ejaculation seems to have been the main way of satisfying their desires. Chasing after married women came a close second. Young men and adults had plenty of opportunities to test the faithfulness of the latter and many women yielded to their advances, sometimes in their own home, more often nimbly profiting from favourable circumstances. The inventiveness shown in this matter would have tempted the pen of Boccaccio, or Brantôme for *Les Dames galantes* or Marguerite de Navarre for the *Heptameron*: the guilty pleasures were snatched more or less anywhere, at home in the absence of the husband (sometimes deliberately sent elsewhere), up against the wall of a castle, under a hedge, inside a stable, in a tavern (often), even in the toilet of an inn. The sexual positions recorded were not confined to the missionary position, because, when time was short, the partners made love standing up, leaning against a tree trunk or a manger or a stile (in this last case, the lover had to make his lady-love 'hold up her leg' before he could do it) or even on a staircase.[32] *L'École des Filles* describes such practices, even sometimes emphasizing the special quality of the pleasure to be gained from furtive lovemaking, when fear of being surprised had a galvanizing effect on Suzanne's boyfriend.

Popular sexuality in the county of Somerset emerges as extremely colourful and very varied. Prostitutes played a significant role, including in rural parishes, and their activities were far from being as despised as the Puritans claimed. There were four different types: the poor itinerant women who went from place to place, offering their services at fairs or markets or in taverns; the public whore operating from an inn or a brothel; the private prostitute who devoted herself to one man, sometimes two men, for a few weeks or a few months, before moving on to try her luck elsewhere; the village easy woman, fairly discrete, often a widow, who offered her body in exchange for services such as milking her cows or harvesting her corn, and whose door was always open, the salvation of many a married man or inexperienced youth. Mary Combe belonged to this last category, but in a particularly flamboyant way. She frequently appeared before the justices without suffering any very heavy penalties, which suggests a degree of tolerance for her activities. The wife of an innkeeper, she frequently put her hand inside customers' breeches; she was in the habit of wandering around the parish naked and often lay down in the road with her legs spread apart, calling out to passers-by, 'Come play with my cunt and make my husband a cuckold.' In 1653 she organized a drinking session to which she invited only cuckolds and cuckold-makers. She was also alleged to lift up her clothes and sit astride any man she found lying on his back. She was ready to demonstrate her contempt for her enemies by spattering their houses with her excrement or by lifting her clothes and pissing in front of them. Many Somerset women, especially in Wells and Glastonbury, displayed a sexual and bodily freedom as aggressive as that of Mary Combe. One was said to be 'so hot in her seat' that she would lie with any man in the open highway. The weakness of the legal action against them suggests that they were publicly flaunting a feminine subculture that was to some degree tolerated, though very different from that of the Puritan wife of a rich yeoman.[33]

It is abundantly clear that the inhabitants of Somerset did not conform to the strict morality defined by the law and the religious regulations. The complaints of frustrated wives reveal that contraception was practised, in the form of abstinence or, as is frequently stated, by the man's withdrawal or coitus interruptus. The authorities seem not to have been unduly concerned. In France, the manuals for confessors insist on the need to condemn this grave sin, which resulted in the loss of semen and hence of a life. Little is known, however, about the realities, before the remonstrations of the eighteenth century against the propagation of 'baleful secrets' in the countryside. Outside marriage, sometimes even within it, attempted abortions are frequently mentioned in the Somerset records. Many women knew various formulas, which seem often to have been effective, even if many women rejected them, from fear of physical damage more than eternal damnation.[34]

Bawdy culture in France

For France, records as rich as these are lacking, but an abundant erotic literature enables us to discover a culture of pleasure with very similar general features. Some famous authors wrote in this genre, including Mathurin Régnier and François Béroalde de Verville in the first decade of the seventeenth century. More often, the prudent cloak of anonymity made it possible to offer the public the *Copie d'un bail et ferme, fait par une jeune Dame de son con pour six ans* (*Copy of a lease and farm, made by a young Lady of her cunt for six years*), published in 1609, or *L'Origine des cons sauvages et la Manière de les apprivoiser* (*The Origin of wild cunts and how to tame them*), published simultaneously in Lyon and Rouen in 1610. Under Louis XIII, we may note René de Menou, Claude d'Esternod, Jean Auvray, Charles Sorel, Charles Sigogne and, above all, Théophile de Viau, author in 1622 of *Le Parnasse des poëtes satyriques* (*The Parnassus of the satirical poets*). Anonymous opuscules also flourished, such as *Le Réveil du chat qui dort* (*The Awakening of the sleeping cat*) (1616), *La Permission aux servantes de coucher avec leur maîtres* (*The Permission to maidservants to sleep with their masters*) (1620) and *Le Parnasse des Muses* (*The Parnassus of the Muses*) (1627), while a canny bookseller collected the best pieces of Sigogne, Régnier, Motin, Berthelot, Maynard and other bawdy poets to produce, in 1618, *Le Cabinet satirique* (*The Satirical cabinet*). A genre existed and it was popular, to judge by the numerous editions and reprints, now preserved in the forbidden books collection of the Bibliothèque nationale in Paris. In the middle of the century, *L'École des filles* and the writings of the baron de Blot became famous, the former being translated into English in 1656, the year after it first appeared. Under Louis XIV, there were many new editions, especially of the works of Théophile de Viau, and many new successes, including the tales of La Fontaine in 1685 and *Vénus dans le cloître ou la Religieuse en chemise* (*Venus in the Cloister, or the Nun in her Smock*), attributed to François Chavigny de La Bretonnière, around 1682.[35]

At first sight, authors and readers were very different from the English peasantry of Somerset. Many nobles wrote erotic verse and prose. This is hardly surprising, since many writers came from their ranks and, furthermore, the aristocracy had a very strong oppositional culture until the Fronde.[36] This type of bawdy literature was fiercely prosecuted by the authorities. The two supposed authors of *L'École des filles*, Michel Millot, controller-paymaster of the Swiss Guard, and Jean L'Ange, gentleman servant of the king, belonged to this milieu. Other writers were citizens, sometimes with aristocratic connections. Their public is more difficult to define. It came primarily from the well-off and literate townspeople, who formed a very small minority. It also included some famous persons, such as the poet Scarron and the finance minister Fouquet: the former was in possession of eight bound copies of *L'École des filles* and the latter received one of them, which he gave to a mistress, in whose home it was found by the police in 1661, after the minister's disgrace. It has even been suggested that Françoise d'Aubigné, granddaughter of the Huguenot

Agrippa and Scarron's wife, might be the author of or model (Fanchon) for the book. The hypothesis has now been abandoned, Michel Millot probably being the sole true author. It was not without its amusing side given that Françoise would later marry Louis XIV, turn into the deeply pious Madame de Maintenon and open a school at Saint-Cyr for the daughters of impoverished noblemen.[37] At least she had had the opportunity to read the book when with her first husband, and perhaps she was able to give the Sun King the benefit of her knowledge.

Taken as a whole, the literature offers a masculine representation of pleasure, while allowing that of women its due, in particular in the jewel of the collection, *L'École des filles*. The picture it paints is so close to that revealed by the sources for Somerset that one may suspect the existence of a veritable erotic culture, widespread in many social milieus, among peasants, townspeople and aristocrats, and inconsistent with the repressive principles promoted by English Puritanism or the French confession manuals.

Without any false prudery, the poets sang of the beauties of the female sex and urged their readers to savour the joys of physical love. In his *Parnasse*, Théophile de Viau wrote of his sweet contentment of seeing a bold cunt burning for action and begging for the caress of a penis, and poetically evoked the orgasm ('my victory') and the pleasures of remembering it afterwards.*

What men wanted was penetration, in the classic position, the man lying on top of the woman. In *L'Académie des dames* (*The Academy for Ladies*) (*c*.1680),[38] Tullie and Octavie sing its praises:

> What is there, I ask you, said the latter, sweeter than to be naked beneath your lover? To be almost smothered by the weight of his body? ... Ah! how sweet it is, Tullie, to watch each other die, and come back to life a moment later. He who takes his pleasure behind, he has only a single pleasure; but he who loves the front, he tastes all the pleasures together.

The rejection of anal sex is clear. Tullie describes an episode in Italy when her partner had sodomized her by force: 'Never had I accommodated such a terrible guest, he made me burn.' At her cries,

---

* Quel doux contentement voir une grosse fesse, / Une motte vermeille, un con audacieux, / Qui brûle de combattre, et d'un ris gracieux, / Appelle un vit nerveux pour lui faire caresse! ... Quand verserai-je au bout de ma victoire, / Dedans la fleur le cristal blanchissant, / Donnant couleur à son teint pâlissant, / Et du plaisir une longue mémoire?

the lover changed his strategy, returned to 'the scene of his usual refuge, and there he filled me with a celestial manna, a thousand times sweeter than the nectar of the Gods'. Yet the 'Florentine game', as it was then called, the Italians being 'very prone to enter by the back door', was not totally rejected. The same Tullie describes another more agreeable experience, 'because the game he played with his member around my buttocks, together with the frequent entries and exits he made to and from my behind, gave me a feeling I much enjoyed'. Might the frequent use of the medical clyster explain this sensibility? However, there were strong moral grounds urging its rejection. Tullie herself describes it as a 'shameful pleasure which kills a man because he might have made one' and as a 'dirty pleasure' that stifles, as it were, an as yet unborn child. The erotic discourse fully accepted sexual pleasure, but as a means of procreation, in line with the medical opinion of the day. The 'arse-pokers' were in bad odour because, explains Tullie, they act in that way 'to satisfy their lascivious appetite', because the back entrance is very tight – unlike the genitals of Italian and Spanish women, which are larger than ours, she mockingly adds.[39]

Masculine sexual morality is clearly asserted by Claude de Chouvigny, baron de Blot-l'Église and familiar of Gaston d'Orléans, born in 1605, dead in 1655. A libertine in every sense of the word, a debauchee and an atheist according to his many enemies, he mocked everyone and everything and denied the immortality of the soul and the existence of paradise. One of his songs, of 1643, defames the queen, Anne of Austria, who he accuses of fornicating with her principal minister:

> The balls of Mazarin,
> That fine man,
> Do not labour in vain;
> Because, with every shove,
> He makes the crown move.
>
> This buggering villain,
> This worthless Sicilian
> Is like a dog on heat;
> Upon my word, what a farce!
> He is up our Spanish lady's arse!*

---

*Les couilles de Mazarin, / Homme fin, / Ne travaillent pas en vain; / Car, à chaque coup qu'il donne, / Il fait branler la couronne. / Ce foutou Sicilien / Ne vaut rien, / Il est bougre comme un chien; / Elle en a, sur ma parole, / Dans le cul, notre Espagnole!

In search of a pardon, in 1652, the baron could think of nothing better than to address a song to the outraged queen in which he professed his high regard for her posterior and her cunt:

> I said nothing wrong, so don't take offence;
> My esteem for you is always immense,
> Your backside I much admire
> Also your cunt, which is on fire.
> The Mazarins, they have lied,
> So cease to chide!
> The Mazarins, they have lied,
> I have too high a regard for those two neighbours, placed side by side.*

His master himself, whose homosexual tastes are well known, did not escape his sarcasms. Gaston protected him, nevertheless, which explains how the baron de Blot could die peacefully in his bed, in his master's house, having frequently and loudly proclaimed his credo:

> As for me, I drink, I laugh, I sing.
> And I don't care a fuck what happens. (1648)

> But I know very well that you live happily,
> If you drink, eat and fuck. (1650)

> All I ask of the Lord.
> For my happiness,
> Is to be a drinker, a fucker,
> An unbeliever and a sodomite,
> Then to die
> Then to die
> Then to die a sudden death!†

In a last piece of scoffing, he described Paradise as a place where 'everyone would fuck an Angel whose cunt smelled of orange blossom'.[40] Eating, drinking and fucking were the supreme pleasures

---

* Je n'ai rien dit, ne vous déplaise; / Je vous honore infiniment, / J'estime votre fondement / Et votre con chaud comme braise. / Ils ont menti les Mazarains, / Ne faites donc plus la mauvaise! / Ils ont menti les Mazarains, / J'estime trop ces deux voisins.
† Pour moi, je bois, je ris, je chante, / Et je fous ce qui se présente. (1648) Mais je sais bien qu'on vit content, / En buvant, mangeant et foutant. (1650) Je ne demande au Seigneur, / Pour bonheur, / Que d'être buveur, fouteur, / Incrédule et sodomite, / Puis mourir (*bis*), / Puis mourir de mort subite!

of life for the baron de Blot, not counting that of living on a knife edge, because his declarations could easily have earned him the death penalty, so insistently did he hound Mazarin and call the queen a whore. It was all down to whether you were powerful or poor; others were burned for less.

Although so very male and so full of admiration for the virile 'sword of love', the erotic literature recognized the eminent rights of the weaker sex to pleasure. The texts use almost as many different words to describe the natural parts of women (200) as those of men (about 250). Some 300 verbs or expressions were used for the act of love. Armed with his natural knife, his skin flute or his hammer, and with his cymbals of lust, his balls of Venus, his bollocks or his globes, the man went for a ride, fought, rubbed the fat, took, amused himself, shook, possessed the ring, the shop, the brazier, the fire, the cat, the slit, the crystal flower, the tasty morsel, nature, the magnificent palace, the little hole or the dark paradise of his lover... The most frequently used terms were *vit* (rod), *con* (cunt) and *foutre*, 'which meant putting the penis in the vagina and ejaculating without delay'. Masculine pleasure was often seen as rapid; that of his partner was slower and accepted diversity. Wives were advised to choose a discreet lover the better to achieve this, since with the husband it was a matter of conjugal duty, and less agreeable, which suggests that the male writers extolled the virtues of the double standard because it was even more to their advantage than to that of the weaker sex. Yet they were able to recognize women's needs. The fat Marion presented in an anonymous poem recalls the historical figure of Mary Combe, in Somerset: having found the phallus for which she had fervently searched, she loudly proclaimed her joy at seeing this 'prick red as a ruby'; having tried it, however, she was disenchanted: 'It isn't big enough; I like the candle better, or the velvet job I rub myself with.'[41]

The description of solitary female pleasures or the occasional advice to 'rub yourself in front' rather than risk a pregnancy was an absolute taboo for right-minded people. It is likely that the facetious contract published in 1609, establishing the rights over the cunt of a lady for 'six consecutive years and six harvests, the one after the other', would have appalled them. It takes the form of a lease signed before the appropriately named notary, Goodtimes, and employs all the proper legal terminology:

> That is to say, a small plot called the cunt, which abuts at one end another called the arse, adjacent to two others called the buttocks,

situated close to the Longraisse, on condition that the said plot called the cunt will have its watercourse to secrete day and night through the conduits and that it will be shorn of mature forest, which is called hair, twice a year: that is, in the month of May and in the month of February, and that it will be guarded by good and sufficient guards, by reason of the wild beasts which enter and damage it, as do lice, fleas, crabs, nits and other vermin. The said aforementioned plot is situated at the base of the stomach, six inches below the navel, and in it there is a fine meadow with a spring in the middle and a fine house to accommodate the farmer, with an upper chamber, lower room, room at the side and all-purpose room, and a larder behind which is not for everybody, with the aforementioned adjoining properties and on condition that if the said lessor is not well and duly paid by the said lessee, [she] may resume possession without any costs, damages and interests or return of proof, restitution of money or any security.[42]

The references to the non-use of the back larder and the possibility of breaking the lease if the lessor is not well and duly paid are a reminder that the physical delights so gleefully evoked here exclude anal sex and require constant practise, also demanded by many Somerset women. The word 'pleasure', repeatedly used in the libertine corpus, is presented as a requirement for women, a sort of compensation for braving the pains of childbirth, prime purpose of sexual relations according to the majority of the authors. Thus female adultery is excusable in their eyes, given that the only legitimate role for a girl was to marry, and that the supreme carnal satisfactions were rarely associated with the married state. 'Sin makes love live, the marriage bed makes tenderness die', wrote Bussy-Rabutin. In *L'Occasion perdue et recouvrée* (*The Lost Opportunity Recovered*) (1651), a play which caused a scandal, the great Corneille himself attached great importance to simultaneous pleasure, essential to conception according to the doctors, which he sublimated to make it an experience of closeness to God. His lovers 'swooned with pleasure' from an excess of happiness; five or six times, they 'died and came back to life'; they lay 'mouth to mouth and body to body, sometimes alive and sometimes dead'.[43]

Sin and 'the little death'! The orgasm was not only a delight of the pleasure-seeker or a cry of despair like that of the baron de Blot. In the Baroque age, it constantly preyed on people's minds, either to be rejected with horror as the work of the devil or to express a mystic experience in which souls and bodies merge, as said by Corneille.

L'École des filles, *a libertine gem*

In 1655, the most famous and most influential of the erotic books of the period, *L'École des filles*, condensed all these lessons to perfection. Short, incisive and highly descriptive, it offers a complete sexual and amorous education to a young and innocent virgin, Fanchon. It is in two parts: in Part 1, she learns from her cousin Suzanne everything she needs to know in order to engage in her first encounter with Robinet, a young man who desires her. In Part 2, deflowered and already an expert, she discusses all matters sexual with Suzanne. At a time when the short story was in its infancy and conduct manuals for the noble or citizen 'gentleman' were proliferating, this book falls midway between the two genres. Like all the works of the period devoted to the subject, and like John Cleland's *Fanny Hill* a century later in England, it contains a wholly masculine body of knowledge, observed and concrete, on the subject of feminine pleasure. It is paradoxical that none of these authors really focuses on men, although they are of course present, implicitly, in the libertine tales.

As naive as the Agnès of Molière in *L'École des femmes*, Fanchon listens as her cousin tells her about sex. Suzanne explains that there is a special pleasure, which is at its most intense with young men. With a husband, it's good, she admits, but wives discover even more agreeable sensations with 'gentlemen, who do it to them secretly, because the husband doesn't want to'. This was the opinion of the peasant women of Somerset, too, and of the young lady who leased out her cunt for six years in 1609. The lesson becomes more explicit: 'This thing, then, which boys piss with, is called a penis, and it's sometimes known as the member, the hose, the main nerve or the love gun; and when a boy has nothing on, you see it hanging at the bottom of his stomach like a long cows' teat, in the place where we have only a hole for pissing.' Fanchon then learns that the lover 'lies down like that on the belly of the girl and sticks into her, into the hole she pisses through, this long thing, with the greatest pleasure and delight in the world'. She explains exactly how it is possible to push in such a limp organ. Then Suzanne describes the woman's sex organs: 'I call it a cunt . . . and it's called putting the penis in the cunt . . . but be careful not to talk about it in front of people, because they say that these are bad words which make girls blush when someone says them aloud.' The orgasm she describes is a moment when 'the tickling seizes them in such a way that they swoon with pleasure and make little jerks as they discharge through the holes what tickled them so much, which is a white liquid, as thick as soup, which they both emit with inexpressible delight'.[44]

Penetration in the missionary position, followed by the simultaneous ejaculation of the two semens, which procured a twofold enjoyment necessary to conception, was what both the medical literature and the descriptions of the peasants of Somerset defined as normal sexuality. Like the Somerset peasants, Suzanne's lover varied their positions, doing it standing up or, if he was in a hurry, throwing her onto a chair, a mattress or even the first place he found. He had told her a hundred times, she claimed, 'that he had more pleasure doing me furtively like that than otherwise'. The mutual manipulation of the genitals seems very important to Suzanne, who frequently goes into detail: while putting her tongue into the mouth of the boy, the girl, 'running her hand over his thing, that she takes hold of through the flies', makes it go hard by stroking it just two or three times. Her lover, she adds, liked to put his 'hand on her pussy, which he pinches and curls for a while with his fingers', then he kisses her, touches her buttocks, sucks her breasts and looks at her naked from every angle by the light of a candle. 'Afterwards, he makes me take hold of his thing, which is stiff.' He puts it between her thighs or her buttocks, kisses her, whispers sweet nothings and finally fucks her.[45] Juvenile sexual culture seems to have been based on such risqué fondling and games, often furtive to avoid the wrath of a father or a husband, which gave a special flavour later on to furtive pleasures and those accompanied by a sense of unease or danger. The strongest feelings seem to be associated with the transgression of prohibitions, both social and religious. The amorality flaunted in *L'École des filles* perfectly matches that of the peasants of Somerset at the same period.

In the second dialogue, Fanchon, no longer a virgin, begins boldly to give lessons. She explains that the word *besogner* meant 'to put the penis in the cunt, move it about and ejaculate, and that on its own it says more than all the others; that *foutre* meant simply to put the penis in the cunt and ejaculate, without moving it about; that *chevaucher* meant to put the penis in the cunt and move it about, without ejaculating; and that *enfiler*, *enconner* and *engainer* all meant the same thing, simply to put the penis in the cunt, without the other two. Suzanne goes one better by explaining that you also used the words *baiser*, *jouir*, *embrasser* and *posséder*, because they were more respectable in public or between lovers than *foutre* and *chevaucher*. Robinet had done a good job! He had taught Fanchon how to enjoy herself so that she 'swooned with delight', and also how to slow down or speed up. Having put some wadding under her left buttock, some wool under her right buttock and some cotton under her rump, he said aloud in succession the names of the three materials, changing the order at will, so as to make her move skilfully. She also says he knew how to take her or caress her through a slit in her clothes, even when they were both in company. Suzanne, for her part, doesn't like men who cry out during the act, even less those who get someone to spank them so as to get it up. The two naughty cousins then discuss the length and the size of penises and the dirty words men say out loud when they are making love. Suzanne says it is 'to make their victory more famous' and also because, in that state, all they can manage is words of one syllable, but that, at the end of the day, there are no dirty words between lovers.

They discuss numerous other aspects: dildos of velvet or glass or even the finger to achieve pleasure for a woman; men ejaculating between the thighs of their partner or the little piece of linen put over the tip of the penis to avoid a pregnancy; the position where the mistress straddles her lover because they are so much in love that they want to swap sexes and 'turn each into the other'. A little philosophy never comes amiss, and Suzanne defines love as 'the desire of one half to serve its other half'. Here, the Neoplatonist theme of fusion to recreate the androgyne after the death of its two separated parts resurfaces in the form of lust transmuted into 'spiritual idea or vapour', before becoming the white rain that leads to sexual pleasure. And Suzanne adds that, if for some men, 'all their joy is in the arse or between cunt and balls', you can also believe 'that the soul is dragged down by the strength of the pleasure and is as if torn from its seat by the close attention it pays to this so longed-for union of the two bodies, which happens in this place; so it comes about that it no longer thinks of itself and leaves the faculty of reason empty and devoid of its presence'.[46]

Here, Corneille's embrace of the souls comes close to the thinking of Suzanne, true philosopher of the boudoir, or rather to that of the author of this amazing *L'École des filles*. It offers women abundant and detailed advice on how to love and be loved as well as possible. Its highest praise is reserved for penetration, face to face, for the purposes of procreation and the enjoyment of lovemaking. Variants and sensual preliminaries with mutual erotic caresses are described in detail, not forgetting solitary female pleasures. The position where the mistress gets on top of her partner is discussed at length, in order to explain that it is perfectly all right, even though it is strongly condemned by religious morality as an abortifacient through the loss of semen. The references to contraceptive possibilities do not stop impregnation from being described as the ultimate purpose of coitus, the gratification of the senses adding an extra dimension of feeling, a joy lavishly praised, a compensation for those who will suffer in childbirth. Contrary practices such as heterosexual sodomy are criticized, even though they can provide some agreeable sensations. The great crimes in the eyes of the law, homosexuality and bestiality, are passed over in silence, as is oral sex, because they all prevent the birth of a child. In spite of the aura of scandal that surrounds it, the book does not present a particularly daring sexuality or one that is remote from the practices of the day. It was simply too bluntly expressed, with too much emphasis on the carnal passions, at a time when censure was directed both at the words and the things and when, at least in appearance, a thick moralizing curtain was being lowered, destined to conceal a pleasure that the Tartuffes of this world could not see.

Pleasure and sin

Medical opinion and social practice were agreed, in the sixteenth and seventeenth centuries, that the orgasm, both male and female, was a necessity. Scholars and theologians alike believed that the ultimate purpose of sexuality was reproduction. This could take place in optimum conditions only if the partners experienced together the same delicious excitement, as they each ejaculated a semen that resembled a thickish milk. I rather doubt, however, that the men and women of this period really regarded their bodies as identical, that is, as variations on a single theme.[47] The illusion derives from the fact that it was only men who spoke about such matters, including in the erotic literature. The woman's view is entirely absent. It can only be approached through the explanations of the stronger sex, who sometimes emerge as notably attentive to the wishes and pleasure of women, as in *L'École des filles*. Taken together with the raw data gleaned for Somerset, such formulations suggest the existence of a specifically feminine erotic culture. Sometimes exuberant, as in the case of Mary Combe, referred to above, it was based on a healthy sexual appetite, which reinforced the male stereotype of the insatiable daughters of Eve. We get glimpses of masturbatory practices, secret abortifacients and sensual techniques on their initiative that are not confined to the male model of domination and vaginal penetration with a view to a quick shared climax, with little thought for the possible consequences of pregnancy or venereal disease. We lack a systematic study of the subject. At all events, there is nothing to prove that women became sexually passive during the course of the seventeenth century or that they ceased to engage in heavy petting or mutual heterosexual masturbation, as many historians argue in the case of England.[48] It may well be that what we see is more the dominant moral discourse in the process of becoming accepted than real changes in behaviour.

Homosexuality in transition

The steady increase in repressive pressure throughout this period is unquestionable, but its effects were not everywhere the same. In Florence, there was a high degree of tolerance for homosexuality in the fifteenth century. Those who practised it actively did not appear in any way abnormal; rather, they demonstrated their membership of the stronger sex, for whom penetration was a dominant value. The passive young boys were hardly guiltier in the eyes of the community, because they were only just emerging from the wet and cold world of femininity. Only sodomized adults incurred deeper disapproval, by betraying the masculine model. In 1542, a harsh law, the first of its type, punished by death the activities of those over the age of 20 if they committed the crime for a second time, whereas others risked death only on a third conviction. Further, the judges were instructed to vary their severity according to the quality of the persons, the duration of their vice, the number of their partners and the practices in which they had indulged. Convictions were numerous for a decade, then declined sharply from the 1550s on, remaining at a fairly low level throughout the seventeenth century.[49] The long-term trend suggests a degree of collective tolerance towards those who committed what was a very common offence. Nevertheless, the feverish activity of the 1540s lingered in the memory as a result of the severity of the punishments inflicted on a small number of men. Things were not quite as before. It may be that historians are letting themselves be misled by the sources if they put too much emphasis on the formal severity of the punishments, which were comparable with those elsewhere in Europe. In France, for example, such offences, theoretically inexpiable, are rare in the judicial records. The discrepancy points to a fundamental contradiction between the desire of the authorities to stamp out such activities and a widespread tacit indulgence; the few spectacular trials, which often involved aggravating factors of a different type, marked the boundaries not to be crossed rather than aspiring to eradicate the phenomenon.

If we try to imagine what the Florentines felt after 1542, it is possible to speak of a modified continuity; modified not so much by coercion, taking account of its limitations, but by new and guiltier perceptions of homosexuality. For those involved, the real danger was not all that much greater than it had been before, but their mental security was seriously disturbed by the fear of sanctions. One historian of the eighteenth century claims that people of quality took fright and fled the town in large numbers, which explains, he believes, the leniency of the judges after a few years of active prosecution, so as not to damage trade and industry.[50] It is likely that the atmosphere changed after the middle of the sixteenth century. Although the sin in question was probably committed as frequently as in the past, it was now accompanied by a new sense of unease heightening the consciousness of a difference, an abnormality, paving the way for the birth of a marginal pederast world in the large towns of Europe at the beginning of the eighteenth century.[51]

The same ingredients are found in England and in France, where the less advanced state of research makes it impossible to paint as detailed a picture of the struggle against sodomy. In both countries, the denunciation of the pleasures of the flesh became active and constant from the second half of the sixteenth century, but the level of repression fluctuated, as in Florence. The greatest effect was on the representation of the self, by linking desire and sexual enjoyment ever more closely to sin and suffering; to the point where some individuals were driven far from the beaten path in the attempt to fulfil themselves in spite of the constraints, at the risk of losing themselves.

Repression

René Pintard has remarked on the incoherent manner in which the legislation against impiety and evil morals was applied in France.[52] The erudite libertines of the first half of the seventeenth century, La Mothe Le Vayer, Gassendi, Naudé and many others, who held a heteroclite collection of opinions distinct from that of the religious majority, had, in his eyes, one thing in common: that is, that they suffered, hesitated and fought.[53] Accused of impiety, they risked harsh penalties. Following in a long line that had begun with St Louis, the ordinance against blasphemy of 19 May 1636 laid down graduated fines up to the fifth conviction, when the culprit was also exposed in an iron neck collar; on a sixth conviction, he had his tongue slit with a hot iron and was put in a pillory; at the seventh, his lower lip was cut off; at the eighth, his tongue was torn out. 'Enormous blasphemies' were more serious and could be equated with atheism or heresy, or even defined as 'crimes of divine lese-majesty', which were punishable at the will of the judges. Seven persons were put to death between 1599 and 1617, sixteen between 1618 and 1636 and eighteen between 1637 and 1649. The Fronde brought a pause, free of convictions, followed by seven death sentences for blasphemy between 1653 and 1661. The erudite or spiritual libertines were not the only ones to feel the wrath of the magistrates; their rather too ribald fellows were also targeted.

Théophile de Viau, born in 1590 to the lesser Protestant nobility of the Agen region, a court poet and pensioned by the king in 1618, was exiled from the kingdom a year later for having produced 'poems unworthy of a Christian'. His enemies accused him of debauchery. In 1622, *Le Parnasse des poëtes satyriques*, a collection published in Paris by two associates, caused a scandal. It contained works by Théophile. The volume begins with a very free sonnet which is attributed to him: 'Phyllis, everything is fucked up, I am dying of the pox...'. While the duc de Montmorency kept him concealed at Chantilly, Théophile was tried and sentenced to death by burning; his books were to suffer the same fate. In his absence, an execution in effigy took place in the place de Grève on 19 August 1623. Later, Théophile was arrested, imprisoned for almost two years in the Conciergerie and finally sentenced to banishment by the parlement of Paris on 1 September 1625. He died on 25 September 1626. The only one to be prosecuted of those accused in connection with the *Parnasse* (which was reissued in 1623, at the least proving the interest of the public), he was a convenient scapegoat at a time when the monarchy and the Church wanted make a spectacular example. Only his protectors in high places saved him from an ignominious death at the stake.[54]

Repression was a fact. But it was neither constant nor methodical and it frequently spared those protected by powerful patrons, noble writers in particular. The baron de Blot, a familiar of the king's brother, could dare, therefore, without undue anxiety, to insult Mazarin, refer in 1653 to 'our whore of a queen', sing 'I don't believe in the other world' and mockingly observe, still in 1653, that 'Jules [Mazarin] has returned to Paris / And got back on his beast [Anne of Austria]', among many other jokes, impieties and blasphemies.[55] A lecher, the word 'fuck' was never off his lips, and he made it his philosophy. It was also, for him, a way of burning the candle at both ends, fast, with the prickly pride of an aristocrat who (sometimes) used the familiar *tu* to Gaston d'Orléans and who provides the key to his despair:

> This world is only misery,
> And the other is only a chimera.
> Happy is he who fucks and drinks![56]

Others, who are often ignored by our classic handbooks of literature, felt the same way, such as Jacques Vallée, Sieur Des Barreaux (1599–1673), and Denis Sanguin de Saint-Pavin (1595–1670), authors of libertine poems, who nevertheless enjoyed a reasonably peaceful existence until a respectable old age.[57]

In 1655, as order was restored after the Fronde, many others slipped through the moral net. This swooped down very selectively, totally ignoring the baron de Blot and many of his disciples, but seeking to capture the supposed authors of *L'École des filles*. The case has been reconstructed on the basis of the trial documents.[58] On 12 June 1655, after a denunciation by the bookseller Louis Piot the Younger, the civil and criminal lieutenant general of the *bailliage* of the Palais, in Paris, arrested Jean L'Ange, squire and gentleman servant of the king, for having tried to sell copies of this work contrary to good morals. Under interrogation, L'Ange stated that the true author was Michel Millot, controller-paymaster of the Swiss Guard, who had borne three-quarters of the cost of publication, he himself having provided the rest and copied the manuscript with his own hand for the printer. A third culprit, Claude Le Petit, a young man barely emerged from the Collège de Clermont, was also named. To escape the censor, and lacking the necessary license to publish, the indication of the printer did not mention Paris or give Piot's address, but ran simply 'At Leiden'. A total of 250 copies had been printed on ordinary paper and 50 on strong paper, destined for notables. On 7 August, sentence was passed in the absence of Millot, who was in hiding. Pronounced impious, injurious to the Christian religion and contrary to good morals, the book was to be burned on the Pont-Neuf. For having written it and for having had it printed and sold, the two supposed authors were to be harshly punished. Millot was to be 'hanged and strangled if he can be found, if not hanged in effigy from a scaffold to be erected in the same place'; his property was to be confiscated to the benefit of the king and he was fined a total of 400 *livres parisis*. L'Ange was to make honourable amends, kneeling and bareheaded, in the hall of the *bailliage* of the Palais, then be banished for three years from the *prévôté* of Paris and fined 200 *livres*. The printer Piot escaped punishment because the law guaranteed the denouncer against any damage to his person or property. The sale of the opuscule was also prohibited to any bookseller, on pain of death. The prosecutor had asked for this punishment to be extended to anyone who kept a copy at home, but in vain – which was to the benefit, as we have seen, of the poet Scarron, who had eight bound copies, and the powerful Nicolas Fouquet, *surintendant des Finances* since 1653, who had received one of them and given it to a mistress.

L'École des filles was hardly unpopular with the public, as is shown by the reissues of 1667, 1668, 1671 and 1686. The strict censorship of the age of Louis XIV was hardly over-zealous in its case, since the seizures carried out in Paris between 1678 and 1701 resulted in the confiscation of only two copies, from a single owner.[59] From the beginning, the case seems to have been handled cautiously by the authorities, perhaps because of the protection in high places extended to the accused, in particular to Fouquet. Nor did the prosecutions greatly disturb the cultivated world. They are not mentioned in *La Muse historique* of Loret, or in *Les Épîtres* of the bookseller Lesselin, or in various verse gazettes of the year 1655. It was a case of apparent severity but tacit indulgence. The work found a place of honour in a sort of virtual 'forbidden books collection' older than that of the Bibliothèque nationale. It circulated illicitly, appreciated by connoisseurs in intellectual or worldly circles. And it enjoyed a dazzling subsequent career, still prosecuted but repeatedly reprinted. A Belgian edition of 1865 was condemned for outrage to public morals and good manners by the Seine magistrates' court, and an adaptation, also Belgian, modernized in 1863, was similarly condemned five years later by the court of Lille.[60]

The burning of a pornographer

Claude Le Petit (1638–62) was not as lucky as Millot. Named in the case, he dedicated a madrigal to Millot, which appears at the beginning of *L'École des filles*, but which was probably not included in the original edition of 1655.[61] The first verse sets the tone: 'Doomed author of a doomed book...'. A young libertine fresh from the Collège de Clermont, Claude tried to live by his pen, writing *L'Heure du berger*, a comic mini-novel – his own description – in which he spoke of carnal pleasure and lust. On 29 September 1661, a certain

Jacques Chausson, known as des Étangs, was burned in Paris for the crime of sodomy and the attempted rape of a young boy. He had also supplied *mignons* to the baron de Belleforte and the marquis du Bellay. Claude dedicated a remarkably vulgar sonnet to him, lauding his courage and his refusal to heed the objurgations of the confessor.*

In 1662, driven by financial necessity, Claude, then a lawyer of barely 23, joined up with two equally young printers, Eustache and Pierre Rebuffé, in order to bring out a text with the title *Le Bordel des Muses ou les Neuf Pucelles putains*, which begins with a 'Sonnet foutatif', every line of which but one begins with the word *Foutre*.† Claude and the two printers were arrested and quickly sentenced, on 26 August 1662, before the criminal court of the Châtelet of Paris. As 'the public had need of examples', at the time when the young King Louis XIV was seeking to assert his personal power, after the disgrace of Fouquet, Claude was sentenced to make honourable amends in public before the main door of the church of Notre Dame, then to have his right hand cut off and be burned alive in the place de Grève 'for having written the book entitled *Le Bordel des Muses* and other writings against the honour of God and his saints'. He was accused, therefore, of a very serious crime of divine lesemajesty. Eustache Rebuffé was to be whipped and then banished for nine years from the town of Paris, while his brother Pierre escaped with a simple admonition to be administered in the chamber of the council and a prohibition on repeating the offence under pain of punishment.

The three young men appealed before the parlement. The ruling was given with unaccustomed rapidity, on 31 August. The original sentence was confirmed in full. However, benefiting from the *retentum*, which was then considered an alleviation of the torture, Claude 'would be secretly strangled at the stake' before feeling the heat of the flames. The execution took place on 1 September. A few hours beforehand, Claude Le Petit had managed to secure an interview with the baron de Schildebeck, whom he had known in Germany, getting him to promise to publish his *Bordel des Muses* and telling him where he had hidden a copy.

---

* L'infâme vers le ciel tourna sa croupe immonde; / Et, pour mourir enfin comme il avait vécu, / Il montra, le vilain, son cul à tout le monde.
† 'Foutre du cul, foutre du con, / Foutre du ciel et de la terre', and so on for a dozen more lines.

Pleasure and the disruption of the established order

This terrible example was necessary, said a correspondent of the chancellor Pierre Séguier, to curb 'the unbridled license of the impieties and the audacity of the printers'. You could die for pleasure, or at least for speaking about it too freely, under the young Sun King! The case was exceptional, because Parisian society and the court were far from prudish in general. It was the impiousness of the condemned man and the danger of subverting the moral order that the erotic discourse concealed, rather than its bawdiness, that was the target, and the reason for creating a lasting memory of the terror in those who watched the execution. The political and religious authorities were particularly sensitive on this issue, which recalled and perpetuated the disorders of the Fronde. In both France and England, a 'pornographic turn' can be detected between 1650 and 1660.[62] Nicolas Chorier, in *Satyra sotadica* (1660), made a clear change of gear, though locating his work in a family setting, like *L'École des filles* five years earlier. The attitude he advocated was not only amoral, it now included all the perversions that might gratify the senses: lesbian love, sodomy, multiple copulations, flagellation and more subtle forms of sadism. Added to which, he suggested that social relations were merely façades to facilitate the achievement of sexual gratification, including in the case of the local priest. The horrified Church found itself directly implicated, in an increasingly explicit manner, in other works, such as *Vénus dans le Cloître* in 1683.

As the execution of Claude Le Petit reveals, the gnawing anxiety of the authorities was that they might be destabilized as a consequence of challenges to the principles of obedience on which they depended.[63] More than a simple pornographic flood, we should speak of a new desire on the part of the civil and religious hierarchies to institute a tighter system for supervising the social tie, especially in the very large towns such as Paris and London. In France, the erudite libertines were increasingly viewed as enemies of the established order. However, this world was also that of bawdy writers such as Claude Le Petit. Not only did he poke fun at the authorities, mock their highest principles and seek sympathy for a sodomite executed in 1661, but worse, he represented a perversion of the intellect and of culture. Well educated, a lawyer and a poet, Le Petit pitted his appetite for liberty and his youth against the advance of the religious and political moralization that was gaining ground after Louis XIV seized personal power in 1661. The space for liberty was shrinking. An eye of the king was imposed on Paris: the *lieutenant de police*, instituted in 1667. All non-conformists, from simple marginals to organized movements like Jansenism, were urged to fall back into line.

This society, in its attempts at greater constraint and stricter control, inevitably aroused stronger oppositional feelings in some of its members. The civilization of manners was emerging, based on the imperatives of court etiquette and the courtesy manuals intended for high society, such as that of Courtin. Published in 1675, reprinted seven times in the next ten years, the *Nouveau Traité de la civilité qui se pratique en France parmi les honnêtes gens* was aimed at the wider urban audience that wanted to imitate the royal model.[64] This was a world in which sex should be practised discreetly and according to the rules laid down by male Christian morality. Yet among some nobles frustrated in their 'duty of revolt' after the Fronde, among the libertines, in the Cartesian science that threatened theological certitudes and among those forced to adopt a lower profile than before, rebellious attitudes emerged. For some, 'pornography' was a vehicle. It had been linked from the beginning to attitudes hostile to the increasing concentration of power. Sexual practices and the way they are conceived reveal the nature of the social relations of which they are part.[65] Civility was certainly destroying the taste for Rabelaisian scatology and teaching people how to speak about sex modestly, in words that were acceptable in public, as Suzanne had advised Fanchon when suggesting she choose words less shocking than 'fuck' or 'screw'. Nevertheless, those who liked to proclaim and make love lustily, but were prevented from doing so by moral censure and the law, were not always ready to submit. Some of them decided to risk their all, if need be, in a bid to reconquer the free space they were refused.

It is unlikely that the dark continent of evil thoughts disappeared in the second half of the seventeenth century. It became less visible to escape the repression, while waiting for better times. This hidden face of modernity was symbolized both by anti-establishment thinking and by the physical taste for pleasure. Though caricatured by their enemies, the libertines were actually the link between the mind and the body, until the *philosophes* of the next century. Some of their erotic writings conveyed a philosophy of life, a bitterness of man without God that the baron de Blot concealed beneath the outpourings of sensual delight. In 1660, Chorier linked all the perversions to a fierce critique of the hypocrisies of polite society. The pain of having to obey unacceptable orders and constraints culminated in libidinous demands, a sort of release for the tensions. More generally, on both sides of the barrier between those who upheld the norms and those who transgressed them, sex and sin were more closely associated than before; more painfully, too. The prohibitions, more loudly and more forcefully proclaimed, were resolutely ignored by some, who set out to discover secret joyful pleasures; like that of reading – sometimes with one hand – the forbidden books that the law never managed to burn in their entirety.

In this regard, France and England changed in parallel. The French erotic successes were very quickly sold or translated on the other side of the Channel. Samuel Pepys bought a copy of *L'École des filles* on 8 February 1668, which he read and then burned so 'that it might not be among my books to my shame'.[66] A hidden erotic culture circulated freely and constantly between the two countries. Just as the French Bibliothèque nationale organized a 'Collection de l'enfer' in the nineteenth century to house this outcast literature, so the British Library created the 'Private Case', which contained no fewer than 1,920 documents in French and English, alongside a mere 127 in German and 38 in Italian.[67] After Italy in the Renaissance, France in the seventeenth century served in its turn as paragon in this sphere; England then produced its masterpieces, including John Cleland's *Memoirs of a Woman of Pleasure*, better known as *Fanny Hill*, published in 1748–9.[68]

Though prohibited and suppressed, pleasure continued to haunt the West, with which it had formed a close and troubled relationship in the sixteenth and seventeenth centuries.

Part III

CYCLES: VICE AND VIRTUE
(1700–1960)

Appearances are often deceptive. The libertine, frivolous and pornographic eighteenth century, which contrasts in France with the era of great moral austerity that preceded it, established a very controlled view of pleasure. The same was true of England after the Restoration of 1660. In both countries, or, to be more precise, at the heart of both their capitals – urban monsters without equivalent elsewhere in Europe – a system of sexual economy was slowly put in place that would dominate Western conceptions and practices until the 1960s.

The dozen or so generations that succeeded each other during this quarter of a millennium inevitably display very diverse characteristics, even huge differences. Yet they were all marked by one and the same cultural trend which conveyed a conception of virtue determined to triumph over vice. This expressed in new terms, adapted to a rapidly changing urban world, the religious and moral prohibition that had weighed heavy on sexual enjoyment outside Christian marriage in the preceding centuries. It offered a philosophy of the happy medium, liberated from judicial and penitential punitive harshness, preferring the personal moderation that resulted from self-control and an inner sense of guilt. Promoted by dynamic social sectors whose core groups were recruited from the *philosophes* of the Enlightenment and the middling ranks of the large towns, it linked sexuality firmly to the quest for happiness here on earth, rather than in the next world. To speak of the bourgeoisies in this context would be reductive, so fluid and so shifting is the notion throughout the long period under consideration. Nevertheless, the groups in question displayed original features in the management of the sexual passions, in opposition both to the aristocracy and to the majority of the peasantry.

VICE AND VIRTUE (1700–1960)

Around 1700, Europe entered a new era of accelerated change in every sphere. Among the most important for the subject of this book is the expansion of the very big cities, linked to commercial capitalism and the strengthening of states. Motors of growth, they attracted streams of rural immigrants and offered lifestyles of a quite new type. A consumer society began slowly to emerge, at least in England. The people who lived crammed together within city walls led different lives from those in the country. They practised sex with fewer moral constraints but with more unease and a deeper sense of the ephemeral, particularly among the very poor. The contrasts increased in number, as did the occasions for mixing with people of very different social conditions. Eating, drinking and making love, to paraphrase the baron de Blot, had a different feel to them in the towns than in the villages or castles. As a consequence of such feverish urban activity, the repressive pressure was relaxed in practice, though remaining strong in theory. Licentious authors were no longer burned in France; at the most, they were – sometimes – put in the Bastille. The straitjacket burst open at every seam, despite the best efforts of the lieutenant of police specially charged with keeping watch on Parisians. Like London, Paris became a world so complex that it was impossible to control it completely. It exploded into riots and major disorders whenever there was an execution or a crowd panicked. Under cover of the philosophical Enlightenment, the evil-minded, the rebels of every sort, the eccentric and all those who lived – by choice or not – on the margins of the law could prosper. A decision from on high triggered a brief wave of repression which could never solve the problem once and for all, because the population reverted to its old ways once the storm had passed.

The immense living entity of more than half a million Parisians or Londoners constantly fluctuated between a fairly routine vice and a virtue as precious as it was rare, because the realities prevailed over the law and moral conventions. These more or less regular swings provide the structure for the third part of my book. Those who wished to avoid excess in order to achieve happiness, even simply a happy life, cultivated the virtuous ideal and patiently urged it on others. Continuing the old ascetic effort of the monks, though in a very different form, in accord with an economic principle derived from commerce, they wanted to stamp sexuality with the seal of moderation. The age of controlled pleasure was about to begin! However, their actions resulted more from a considered decision than from a fear of punishment or hell. This explains both the virulence of the battle against masturbation and the promotion of the masculine double standard. The latter made it possible to step up control over wives and mothers while offering husbands the legitimate outlet of the use of prostitutes. Now less bound up with religion, the dogma of the inferiority of women took two forms, each the subject of an abundant justificatory social discourse. On the one hand, married women must be protected against temptation and against themselves by being confined to the home; on the other, the whore, an increasing presence in city streets, concentrated in her person the negative features, notably perversity and an insatiable sexual appetite, that had earlier been imputed to all the daughters of Eve.

This model was in sharp contrast both to the relatively lax and amoral popular peasant practices observed in seventeenth-century Somerset and to the incitements to unconstrained enjoyment offered by nobles such as the baron de Blot and Michel Millot, probable author of *L'École des filles* (1655). Neither of these traditions entirely disappeared. In both Paris and London they continued to produce lively erotic subcultures. The first, numerically important, was characteristic of the poorer townspeople, often recent immigrants, for whom lovemaking was of necessity often rapid and furtive. The second, involving a much smaller group, provided the figure of the debauched aristocrat, or the London 'rake', who scorned both the laws of man and the laws of God, and was strongly disapproved of by the moralists but generally tolerated, including in the most amazing excesses. Both groups were characterized by the absence of constraints, even by sexual 'prodigality', in the case of the poor so as to introduce a little enjoyment into a hard life, in the case of the nobles so as to pursue an ethic of largesse contrary to the principles of economy extolled by the bourgeoisie. In this complex situation, strategies took shape which did not prevent the representatives of each group from sometimes being affected by features derived from elsewhere. The great French cuisine, for example, a refined pleasure which had been primarily the preserve of the world of aristocratic magnificence since the reign of Louis XIV, aroused passions among the prosperous peasantry as well.

4

THE EROTICISM OF THE ENLIGHTENMENT

To appreciate the importance of the erotic transformation of the eighteenth century, we need first to consider the pornographic flood. Appearing around 1650, then gathering pace, it put its mark on the age of the *philosophes*, even intensifying in revolutionary France. Whereas it had initially expressed resistance to Church and state, it was increasingly oriented towards the more specific rejection of a too controlled or too sublimated sexuality. This was a period of profound change in the relationship between body and soul, in which the Self gained greater importance and shifted from the margins towards the centre of society. A revolution in desire began to take shape on both sides of the Channel. Fundamental but concealed, it accompanied the relaxation of religious and political constraints, to replace them with a more personal moral economy. It was structured round new 'gender' relations between the two halves of humanity, and even with a third male homosexual world that was in the process of becoming ghettoized. New internalized prohibitions aimed to turn men away from sodomy, even active, and in particular from masturbation, which was the subject of an extraordinarily repressive offensive. The growing practice of the masculine double standard also kept women in increased subjection; it replaced divine law with a 'natural' principle of weakness that justified the necessity of marriage and motherhood, while isolating the detestable aspect of femininity and adding it to the image of the prostitute or loose woman. Such an adaptation of the old paternalist model to the mental and social changes under way was not universally accepted. Sexuality increasingly assumed forms dictated by social class, explained Bernard de Mandeville in the *Fable of the Bees* (1714). Building on the system of courtesy, the new way was, like it, predominantly if not exclusively for the use of the expanding urban population. It remained surrounded by clusters of different sensualities. The mass of the population was reluctant to follow advice that suited neither their traditions nor their needs, so much so that they were subjected to a string of offensives to make them fall into line. The refined, the aristocrats and the courtiers continued to behave with such visible triumphant exuberance that it seems, in both France and England, to characterize the century of the *philosophes*, making it an age of pornography and eroticism. However, the most powerful impulse to change came from those who sought a harmonious balance of the passions, a middle way, in order to achieve happiness. Their efforts did not prevent the headlong rush for enjoyment in which many of their contemporaries were caught up, but they put in place a principle of the self-control of pleasure which developed in parallel with the 'civilizing process',[1] though in the form of a sinuous rather than an ascending line, virtue never succeeding for long in completely vanquishing vice.

The pornographic flood

Works of pornography of a very different type from the bawdy tales of earlier centuries made a sudden appearance in the mid-seventeenth century, as we have seen. One of their principal features was a challenge to the established authorities and rules: Eros rebelled against the oppressive conformisms.[2] The attack became fiercer in 1683 with *Vénus dans le cloître ou la Religieuse en chemise. Entretiens curieux . . . par l'abbé du Prat*. Here the Church was rebuked directly, two years before the rigours of the revocation of the Edict of Nantes, when the Sun King was at the pinnacle of his glory. Attributed to Jean Barrin, or sometimes to François Chavigny de La Bretonnière, the book presents two nuns aged 19 and 16 engaged in three conversations in a convent. Exchanging kisses, they talk about the necessity of keeping up appearances but also that of 'allowing something to the body's sensual side, and having pity on our low spirits'. Some visitors – an abbé, a Feuillant monk and a Capuchin friar – arrive to do just this with the younger of the two, Sister Agnès, at the instigation of the older, Sister Angélique. There are no obscene details, even though the two heroines discuss erotic subjects. They find *L'École des filles* 'not nice' and are even more critical of Chorier's *Satyra sotadica*, because 'the pleasures we take should be constrained by the law, by nature and by prudence'.[3]

A literature of transgression

Pornography is a literature of transgression, but it first developed according to the rules of a system of good manners that prohibited any reference to the perversions, which explains the criticism of Chorier's book, the only one so far to have dared to do so. Authors used this form to express ideas that were unconventional, sometimes heretical or close to the free thought of the spiritual libertines, and also their faith in science or in natural philosophy, against the established authorities. In the years 1650–90, the pornographic message spread at the same time and in the same places as the new scholarly discourse, that is, in the large towns where social networks were changing, where life was more atomized and more individualized and where the need to conceptualize the body and space in order to perceive one's own being was emerging.[4] The weakening of the concept of sin – similarly linked to urban and scientific developments – also played a role. In England, it was not simply a reaction against the Puritanism of the time of Cromwell, because the pornographic wave came from France even before the Restoration, in the 1650s, and continued for a century. Chorier's book was translated with the title *Venus in the Cloister; or, the Nun in her Smock* in 1683, the same year it appeared in French in Cologne; it was reprinted in 1724 and 1725, leading the government to legislate against obscene works. All over Europe, but especially in Amsterdam, Paris and London, there emerged the new idea that nature and the senses should be preferred to the laws defended by the established authorities, a way of distancing oneself from a society based solely on hypocrisy or appearances.[5] Paradoxically, it was the tightening of the political, religious and moral censorship of the written word and the intensification of sexual repression that gave rise to this pornographic literature.[6] It was the tension between authority and transgression that gave it life and conferred on it an important cultural status, as testimony to the discrepancy between principles and reality.

The repression acted more as a spur than as a truly dissuasive force. In spite of police surveillance and the seizures of prohibited works, the trade in pornographic books and images was very active, a sure sign of the growth of a market large enough to justify the risks incurred. In Paris, its principal centre in the eighteenth century, its production and sale involved organized groups consisting of up to a dozen persons, which was unknown for other types of prohibited writing. The sex trade in all its forms loomed large in the street culture of the French capital. *Guides roses* enabled the connoisseur or the curious to find the addresses of brothels or prostitutes. After 1789, in imitation of London, there appeared lists of famous whores, with their prices and attributes. Forty of these have been identified from between 1789 and 1792, including *Étrennes des grisettes*, *Almanach des demoiselles de Paris* and *Tarif des filles du Palais-Royal*, with the addresses, prices, characteristics (blonde, brunette, young, etc.) and specialities ('a very active *citoyenne*', 'a fiery cunt', 'a madame by day, a monsieur by night', etc.).[7]

The pornography of the eighteenth century has been defined as 'the written or visual presentation in a realistic form of any genital or sexual behaviour with a deliberate violation of existing and widely accepted moral and social taboos'.[8] Between 1660 and 1800, its popularity steadily grew in England. Many translations of ancient or contemporary authors, especially French, were published. The phenomenon can be explained both by sexual repression and by a more insidious censorship of literature in general, which was purged of anything to do with sex, just as good manners required that the routine functions of the human body and the extremes of pleasure be ignored.[9] As well as expressing resistance to moral and religious dictatorships, pornography catered for a lively curiosity that was no longer easily satisfied by the street spectacle or by printed works. The genre flourished, as a result, furtively, it goes without saying. Become a voyeur, the reader could tremble with anxiety without having to face the harsh punishments awaiting those who did actually indulge in such turpitudes. Readers could also enjoy the solitary bookish pleasures that sometimes led on to those of masturbation or even frenzied sexual activity, like Monsieur Nicolas in the fevered imagination of Rétif de La Bretonne.[10]

The market in desire

Generally regarded as saturated with repetitive clichés, pornography never stopped changing and adapting to fresh times in the century of the *philosophes*. It may be that this was simply a generational effect, with new developments emerging as each cohort came of age. In the absence of detailed research, it is impossible to say. At least two turning points stand out, one towards the middle of the century, the other in 1789. The first corresponds to the simultaneous publication, in 1748, of the profession of materialist faith of La Mettrie, *L'Homme machine* (*Man a Machine*), the same author's *L'Art de jouir* (*The Art of Sexual Pleasure*) and, in England, the *Memoirs of a Woman of*

Pleasure by John Cleland, famous under the title *Fanny Hill*. Pornography seems by then to have become an end in itself. The work of Cleland adopted the new literary techniques of realistic narration, but it does not really tell the story of a prostitute of the period, nor, above all, does it mark a serious break with the erotic traditions established a century before. Neither the world of the streetwalkers nor that of the courtesans frequented by upper-class rakes is accurately described: Fanny never gets pregnant, she avoids venereal disease and drunkenness and she ultimately makes a love match with her first customer; added to which, she shares the pleasure of her clients. Cleland here stays close to the sexual system evoked in *L'École des filles*, which avoided all perversions and emphasized the woman's right to orgasm. He offers an idealized male version of the latter, assuming it to be more intense the larger the penis, and he does not describe the clitoris in as much detail as the male member or accord it much importance, claiming that the woman climaxes only as often as her lover.[11] If the break with the Christian tradition is obvious, *Fanny Hill* is hardly innovatory on the subject of relations between the sexes, a full feminine existence being linked in the traditional manner to marriage, admittedly for love. Having run through the gamut of depravities, Fanny is redeemed through married love. Her originality is simply to have been successively devil and angel, mistress and wife, which posed no threat to the masculine double standard that was then on the way to becoming established.

It is difficult to know how many erotic works were published. One scholar has proposed the figure of 25 French titles between 1714 and 1749 and another 22 between 1741 and 1797; there is some duplication in these two lists, which are not exhaustive.[12] They include some great names and some famous works of literature: the *Histoire du chevalier des Grieux* (*The Story of the chevalier des Grieux*) by the abbé Prévost; Marivaux, for *La Vie de Marianne* (*The Life of Marianne*) and *Le Paysan parvenu* (*The Upstart Peasant*); Crébillon fils, author of *L'Écumoire* (*The Skimmer*), *Les Égarements du coeur* (*The Wayward Head and Heart*) and *Le Sopha* (*The Sofa*); the marquis d'Argens with *Les Nonnes galantes* (*The Bawdy Nuns*) and *Thérèse philosophe* (*Thérèse the philosopher*); Diderot, with *Les Bijoux indiscrets* (*The Indiscreet Jewels*). Of the pornographic literature strictly speaking, the true jewels, frequently reprinted, are *L'Histoire de Dom B..., portier des chartreux* (*The Story of Dom B..., porter at the Charterhouse*), published in 1741 by Jean-Charles Gervaise de La Touche; the *Mémoires turcs* (*Turkish Memoirs*) of Godard d'Aucour in 1743; La Mettrie's *L'Art de jouir* of 1748; and Fougeret de Monbron's *Margot la ravadeuse* (*The amorous adventures of Margot*). The 25 works listed for the earlier part of the century were translated into English after 1728, most of them between 1735 and 1749, evidence of a lively interest in the subject at the period. In 1748 and 1749, seven titles published in France were almost immediately made available in English. Perhaps there was a 'Fanny Hill effect'. Among those works not honoured by a translation was *L'Art de foutre ou Paris foutant* (*The Art of Fucking or Paris Fucks*) by Baculard d'Arnaud (1741); perhaps it was too coarse for English readers?

The pornographic flood seems to have abated a little in France by the end of the reign of Louis XV, then resumed with renewed vigour at the beginning of the next reign. Apart from Sade, two prolific writers stand out: Andrea de Nerciat published in 1775 *Félicia ou mes fredaines* and several volumes of a similar type, up to *Mon noviciat ou les Joies de Lolotte*, in 1792; Mirabeau followed close behind with *Érotika Biblion* in 1782 and *Le Rideau levé ou l'Éducation de Laure* in 1785. To which may be added, in 1775, *La Foutromanie* of Gabriel Sénac de Meilhan, *L'Anti-Justine* of Rétif de La Bretonne (1797) and two anonymous tales, the *Confessions de Mademoiselle Sappho* (1789) and *Caroline et Belleval, ou les Leçons de la volupté* (third edition in 1797).

Far from stemming the flow, the French Revolution intensified the taste for sexuality. Not only did the number of publications rapidly increase, but there was a new emphasis on vice, first in the social and political critique of the *ancien régime*, then from the more overtly sexual perspective of challenging every taboo.[13] This trend spread throughout Western Europe and gradually created the modern meaning of the word 'pornography'. Used for the first time in France in 1769, by Rétif de La Bretonne to describe a work dealing with prostitution, it meant something quite different in 1806: texts or images disturbing the social order and contravening morality. In England, the word was not used until the end of the nineteenth century. A verdict of 1728 against the editor Edmund Curll, who had published a lampoon judged obscene, defined the field in question and served as a precedent until the Obscene Publications Act of 1959. Whereas the courts had previously refused to punish acts of this type, the paucity of English translations of French pornographic books between 1728 and 1735 attests to a fear of prosecution; their proliferation in the 1740s suggests the restoration of a high level of tolerance. It was only at the end of the century that the situation changed, with the foundation in 1787 of the Proclamation Society, created to punish vice and immorality, which, for the first time, attacked publications capable of poisoning the minds of readers, especially the young. However it was not until the appearance in 1801 of the Society for the Suppression of Vice and the Encouragement of Religion and Virtue that tangible results were achieved. The growing antagonism between France and England probably played a part by making even more suspect a literature consumed on a large scale on the other side of the Channel.

The trend was increasingly for the market to become purely pornographic. Andrea de Nerciat, for example, is remarkable for a lack of interest in the public life of his day, unlike the revolutionaries who had used the genre to reach a popular readership and make it aware of social and political problems. After 1795, works were published that explored new sexual pleasures that had previously been passed over in silence by the best examples of the genre: bestiality and transvestism in two anonymous works published that year, *L'Enfant du bordel* (*The Child of the Brothel*) and *Éléonore ou l'Heureuse personne* (*Eleanor or the Happy Person*), transsexualism also in the latter. The heroine, Éléonore, is admittedly both a child of the brothel and the illegitimate daughter of a nobleman, and one recognizes a parody of the edifying stories of orphans then enjoying huge popularity. Only sadism, torture and death went unexplored, except by Sade,[14] which tells us a good deal about the capacity of this type of literature to adapt to prevailing cultural trends and to a society that was rejecting the old prohibitions but not accepting the decadent eroticism of the divine marquis. Damaged by divorce and awaiting the Napoleonic reforms, marriage was no longer, for a while, a major preoccupation. The libertine Thérèse the philosopher was replaced by the depraved woman with Lesbian tendencies, prostituting herself out of self-interest in order to ruin men and destroy their virility. Although she still had a long way to go before becoming the vamp, that is, the female vampire who loved to suck the blood of her masculine prey, no pornographic heroine since the mid-seventeenth century, not Fanchon in 1655, not Fanny Hill in 1748, had issued such a challenge to the system established for the greater glory of men; but the latter were well able to defend themselves, in the next century, as we will see.

The books that dimmed the lights of the Enlightenment

What excites the people of one period may leave those of another cold. What was it that made the contemporaries of the Regent,

Philippe d'Orléans, Voltaire and Andrea de Nerciat, swoon with delight? Given the impossibility of analysing the sensibilities of each generation, I will confine myself to an overall view in an attempt to grasp the distance that separates these people from ourselves. Where did the scandalous begin? An eighteenth-century engraving attributed to Ghendt, after a gouache of P. A. Baudoin, *Le Midi*, shows a young, richly dressed girl lying stretched out on a garden lawn, in ecstasy, her right hand pointing to a book lying open on the ground, one leg raised, her left hand buried in her skirts: she is having an orgasm, having aroused herself after reading a sulphurous tale.[15] What is important is not so much the signal the artist gives to the viewer, the voyeuristic dimension (similarly suggested in Fragonard's *Le Verrou* of 1775–7), as the gulf created by this image in the mind of a twenty-first-century reader: she's having an orgasm, so what? What was once a jewel of intellectual refinement, a joke at the expense of the taboo on autoerotic pleasure, an evocation of the delights of transgression, the eyes of the ecstatic woman gazing at an external observer, is now no more than a rather banal image, with scarcely any erotic charge. In an age of widespread nudity, in summer as in advertising, and of hardcore films, the picture can only be perceived as tame; except, perhaps, in puritanical America, shocked by the bare breast of Janet Jackson fleetingly revealed during the televised Super Bowl half-time show on 1 February 2004, a sight that provoked howls of indignation.

We have to apprehend licentious literature in the same way. It has lost much of its corrosive power in two centuries because the society whose vices it describes and whose taboos it breaks now exists only in history books. It has left us legacies, however, including a certain frisson at the mention of unusual attitudes. The pornography of the eighteenth century took five main forms and employed a variety of media to spread its messages, in particular poetry, facetiae, prose and images.[16] The latter, which often went with the text, were frequently derived from the famous sexual positions of Aretino. They might also nestle surreptitiously in the corner of a painting or an engraving, be disguised to thwart the vigilance of the censors and give added pleasure to connoisseurs by making them share the secret, and the sensations of the hidden observer, thus intensifying the sexual frisson. This is what is customarily called the spirit of the eighteenth century, frivolous and libertine, concealing the barbed remark under the semblance of politeness, devotion or obedience. Not everyone could easily decipher such signs. To understand them, you had to be part of the privileged world of wealth, birth and intelligence. The works, including the most seemingly salacious and crude – books of fucking that would have pleased the baron de Blot – were not intended for the use of the common people, for the vast, illiterate rural majority populating France. Levels of literacy were higher in England, where 62 per cent of men and 38 per cent of women could read in 1750,[17] but here too it was a minority interest. London and Paris were almost alone in providing a discreet and refined public able to appreciate such treasures.

The first of the five types consisted of medical or paramedical works: sex guides or sexological treatises, dealing mostly with masturbation, flagellation or strangulation. The battle against onanism was such a major preoccupation of this period that this sin condemned by medical science deserves a separate discussion. Flagellation was so popular in England that it became a national stereotype in the eyes of her – obviously facetious and unjust – neighbours, and it sold well. In 1718, Edmund Curll, famous editor of risqué books, published *A Treatise of the Use of Flogging in Venereal Affairs*, for which he was prosecuted. The opuscule was reissued in 1761 with a promotional note before the title page claiming that this technique increased the pleasures of love, and an engraving showing a kneeling gentleman, his bare backside being whipped by a girl who is looking at a woman sitting on a bed, waiting until he is sufficiently aroused to join her. Specialized brothels, the bagnios and seraglios of London, offered connoisseurs refinements such as these. A treatise falsely attributed to the abbé Boileau, a doctor of the Sorbonne, but actually written to ridicule Catholic religious practices, was translated into English in 1783 with the title *The History of the Flagellants*.[18] Pain as an aid to orgasm is also the subject of a short text of 46 pages published anonymously in 1791 under the title *Modern Propensities; or, An Essay on the Art of Strangling*. . . . The second part deals with flagellation, the third and final part with suffocation, which, it says, produced an interesting reaction by titillating the reproductive organs, which helped criminals face the final agony. The gentleman who did not wish to lose his life through this practice was advised to have recourse to the nostrum of Dr Martin Vanbutchell, sold under the name of 'Vanbutchell's Balsam of Life'. In 1793, *The Bon Ton Magazine* published two articles, one on the 'Origin of Amorous Strangulation', the other on the 'Effects of Temporary Strangulation on the Human Body'. As for the women who wanted to arouse themselves, they could buy dolls with a cloth-covered cylinder instead of legs, which were on sale in St James's Park according to a French traveller of the years 1713–14.[19] The dildo in question was no doubt as effective as the books read with only one hand...

More traditionally, the second and third pornographic strands were anti-religious and anti-aristocratic. They followed in the footsteps of the libertine literature of the previous century. The rake openly frequented impious clubs, which were forced to be more discreet after 1720, and went in for atheism, blasphemy and anticlerical satire. He was caricatured by William Hogarth in 1732 in a series of eight engravings with the title *A Rake's Progress*. Drinking, gaming, wenching and blasphemy were his principal occupations. From aristocratic or wealthy families, well travelled and multilingual, such men reproduced the behaviour of the debauched French aristocracy, in spite of the antagonism between the two nations.[20]

Less specifically English and Protestant than tends to be believed, pornographic works attacking the sexual excesses ascribed to Catholic monks played a major role in this world. In France, the tradition is widely attested for the sixteenth century in the writings of Rabelais or the *Heptameron* of Marguerite de Navarre, sister of François I, which was often reprinted in the eighteenth century. It is also found in the *Histoire de Dom B..., portier des chartreux*, published in 1741 by La Touche. Saturnin, the hero, equipped with an abbreviated name whose meaning is not hard to guess ('bugger' means sodomite), is the son of a nun. During the course of his adventures, he discovers his mother in a secret cell where the monks keep their mistresses. He takes part in orgies, for example with six nuns at a time, gradually exhausting his vital forces by such excesses. After raping a nun, he flees to Paris, where he discovers his sister-in-law Suzon in a brothel. Although she warns him that she is suffering from a venereal disease, he sleeps with her. They are both thrown into prison, where Suzon dies. Saturnin falls ill, has to agree to be castrated to survive, then returns to the monastery where he spends the last year of his life serving as porter (hence the subtitle) and writing his memoirs. The work is ambiguous; it lauds erotic freedom and makes pleasure a veritable new religion, but it ends with a return to the order transgressed with the cessation of all sexual activity. Indeed, it concludes with a sort of eulogy of moderation, made obligatory by castration: extreme human passions cannot bring happiness. Though fiercely parodying faith, it develops the morality of the *philosophes* and the middling urban classes, who were then coming into their own. Beneath the pornographic veil, it demonstrates the absolute necessity of self-control in order to avoid all the miseries suffered by Saturnin, who thought he could pleasure himself for ever but began increasingly to suffer.

Turning to England, it is not difficult to imagine the contents of *Father Paul and the Blue-Eyed Nun of Saint Catherine* (1770) from the engraving in which the libidinous Father Paul, seated in an armchair, eyes burning with desire, clutches, beneath her half-naked breasts, the body of a superb and ecstatic nun whose hands are joined, all in a convent setting that only aggravates the carnal sin.[21]

English anti-aristocratic pornography was also deeply rooted in a French tradition, that of the *chroniques scandaleuses*. These salacious little stories about the court at Versailles delighted English readers. It was in this way that the Frenchman Morande, having fled to England in 1769, attacked the moral corruption prevailing in his country. He had a great success in 1771 with the publication in London of two pamphlets, *Le Philosophe cynique* (*The Cynical Philosopher*) and *Le Gazetier cuirassé, ou Anecdotes scandaleuses de la cour de France* (*The Journalist in a Cuirasse, or Scandalous Anecdotes of the French Court*). Madame du Barry provided him with an inexhaustible supply of jokes. He maintained that she was the illegitimate daughter of a servant girl and a monk, and described her career as a whore and a courtesan, her lesbian relations with girls and the methods she used to retain the king's affections (perfuming the interior of her genitals and douching them daily with amber). When Louis XV tried to proceed against him, Morande announced the imminent publication of the *Mémoires secrets d'une femme publique* (*Secret Memoirs of a Whore*), meanwhile offering his manuscript to the highest bidder. In 1773, the affair assumed an air of farce when some agents of police were sent to arrest him; Morande informed the London papers that the French were trying to kidnap émigrés who had fled the tyranny of their prince, which won him huge popular support and forced the policemen to beat a hasty retreat, leaving Morande holding onto the money he had borrowed from them. Despatched to reason with him, the best Beaumarchais could do was purchase all the copies of the pamphlet from him, at a high price, and agree to grant him the pension he had requested. Morande later changed sides and became a secret agent for Louis XVI.[22] Which only goes to show that pornography opens all doors and can work wonders for its authors!

A popular ancestor of the stories of the marquis de Sade, the fourth group of scabrous writings combined sex with blood and death. It comprised a wide assortment of works and lampoons which recounted the exploits and misfortunes of the criminals executed in London for rape, incest or adultery ending in murder. There was a comparable phenomenon in France, which led to a flourishing trade in short one-off pieces and engravings, often at the foot of the scaffold or bonfire. England also had vast official collections, like the four volumes of *The Tyburn Chronicle* of around 1768, or the five volumes of *The Newgate Calendar, or Malefactor's Bloody Register*, of around 1773.[23] This is a complex category, which also included famous authors like Daniel Defoe, and I will discuss it more fully at a later stage, because the reading of the accounts combined with the spectacle of the execution had a major impact on the definition of the Self, by linking the bodily depravities of the culprits to sin and by serving as a negative model for the right-minded.[24]

A fifth type of pornography was based on marriage and the battle of the sexes. This category also includes the literature devoted to 'criminal conversations', the term used for infidelities, and the writing and images dealing with prostitution, cuckoldry and the battle for power within the household, what the French called the *lutte pour la culotte*. In England, it primarily developed in the last decade of the eighteenth century and achieved wide circulation in the caricatures of Newton and Woodward. In Richard Newton's *Wearing the Breeches*, of 1794, a powerfully built woman, her weight firmly on her right leg, which is placed well forward, hands on hips like a theatrical braggart, observes with ironic amusement the futile fit of rage of her puny little, sullen-faced husband, standing before her like a boxer knocked off balance. The roles seem to be reversed, if we are to believe these engravings. In Woodward's *The Padlock* (*c*.1800), a man-wife who has put a giant chastity-lock on her husband tells him with a satisfied air that he won't be able to run after the housemaids any more.[25] Prostitutes were given special literary treatment, because their biographies were usually relocated in a moral – or sham moral – framework. This allowed Daniel Defoe to judge it respectable to write *Moll Flanders* and *Roxana*, and John Cleland to conclude *Fanny Hill* with a eulogy to reciprocal married love. Nevertheless, the life of the high-class courtesans had the perverse charm of the *chroniques scandaleuses*, as in the *Genuine Memoirs of the Celebrated Miss Maria Brown*, of 1766, which was attributed to John Cleland as a way of increasing sales.[26]

The flood of pornography in the eighteenth century brought few innovations before the great watershed of the French Revolution. Clichés and stereotypes abound and the double standard reigns in these risqué books, which do not question the male and female sexual roles set in stone for generations. The outpouring of eroticism primarily reveals that sex outside marriage was increasingly seen as in bad taste, a sign of depraved tendencies. The repression became more insidious and more persuasive than in the two previous centuries. The age of executions, censorship and the fear of hell was succeeded by the age of personal restraint. The forms of control changed because the growing success of pornography helped to discredit the authorities, who were unable effectively to impose their prohibitions. Things essentially continued as before, but adapting to the spirit of the times. As marriage remained the touchstone of society, the most arousing eroticism was that which made it possible to dream of additional paradises, in the arms of a prostitute or loose woman, but without seeking the extreme depravities of the perversions surrounded by taboos: homosexuality, anal and oral sex, bestiality, torture and murder. The English went in for flagellation rather more than the French. It was for a long time a common punishment in English schools, like the 'reasonable chastisement' permitted to parents by an act of 1860 and which the House of Lords refused to prohibit on 5 July 2004 by 250 votes to 75.

Pornographic literature and art were also outlets for those whose sexuality proved too routine, which explains its growing audience. They did not, however, truly take their consumers out of themselves, far from their culture, but simply a short distance onto the margins, where the pleasure of minor transgression was added to that of the discovery of little-known sensualities. Only with the Revolution did authors go significantly further, as far as the real perversions. Early in the nineteenth century, the Napoleonic iron fist in France and the rise of the societies against vice in England cut short these hesitant beginnings. The ambiguous dialogue then resumed between those who believed in reproductive conjugal sex and the amateurs of more intense, more refined or cruder pleasures taken in the arms of fallen women, before returning quietly back home. Most works of pornography shared this collective duplicity, now based on natural law, medicine and philosophy, and no longer on religious or political authority. Worn out by pleasure, cut off from himself by a medical punishment to save his life at the cost of his 'indiscreet jewels', Dom Bougre was the unhappy hero of a skirmish with the prohibitions, because he had been unable on his own to acquire enough self-control to resist temptation and achieve happiness by observing a middle way.

Sex within measure

Societies never evolve as one. Libertines and Puritans coexisted in eighteenth-century England, just as the French debauchees had critics of equal importance. It was the same in the nineteenth century: the Victorians were capable of having a ball or leading a secret life, while pornography never went away, despite being increasingly under attack. In the age of Voltaire and Hogarth, the demand for liberty seemed self-evident, without necessarily making profound changes to the cultural fabric. In the sphere of pleasure, which effectively meant relations between the sexes and the marriage question, the religious and moral censures lost much of their power. The controls reappeared, however, in other forms, aimed as much at stifling the desire for sexual pleasure, so it did not prove too destructive for society, as at reinforcing the subjection of women in the name of 'scientific', medical, philosophical and natural principles.

Pleasure in moderation

At first sight, the inhabitants of big cities in the age of Enlightenment had ample opportunity to find enjoyment, in a society that was wealthier, comfortable or luxurious for the rich, better fed and enjoying population growth. In both London and Paris the upper classes had access to vast possibilities for merrymaking and sensual pleasure, especially after the disappearance of the strict moral codes, in 1660 in England with the Restoration and in 1715 in France, when a festive mood succeeded the gloom of the last decades of the reign of Louis XIV. In London, large crowds, sometimes as big as 100,000, flocked to watch public hangings at Tyburn or bouts of bull- or bear-baiting. As in Paris, cafés, taverns and gardens were well frequented. Nighttime offered the louche pleasures of the many brothels and places of ill repute, such as the Haymarket, Bankside or Covent Garden. Sex was everywhere in gallant society. Under the Regency, it erupted in the crude, often obscene, works of Gillray, Rowlandson and the Cruikshank brothers. Hedonism rules in the gallery of debauched and dissolute characters drawn by Hogarth. A hell of gambling, a masculine culture of drinking and casual sex, all amply described in the *Memoirs* of Samuel Pepys in the seventeenth century and William Hickey in the eighteenth, present a picture of a frenetically licentious society. Love affairs were generally tolerated and led to little or no guilt. Nevertheless, the conventions required that the language employed should not be filthy, but rather filtered through the models of ardent love and romantic passion, as in Cleland's *Fanny Hill* or the *Life and Opinions of Tristram Shandy, Gentleman* of Laurence Sterne (1760–7). Good manners and sensibility permitted the expression of individual passions as long as they did not question the social order too fiercely. At this price, carnal pleasure became a 'must', for women as well as for men, especially in refined circles. The number of brothels steadily grew (at least 3,000 establishments were listed by the police in 1859) and more than 10,000 prostitutes walked the streets (around 80,000 in 1859). A long period of 'incredible hedonism' preceded the strict morality of the Victorian age. The incisive art of Hogarth captured the mood, as in *Bleak Morning in Covent Garden, after the Dissipation of the Night Before*, in which desire still smoulders around a wood fire, as lingering revellers still fondle and kiss girls at the door of a coffee house; nothing can stop their lustful ardour, not even the lugubrious first light of day just visible on the horizon.[27]

Paris was very similar, in size and in the concentration of pleasures to be found there, the huge numbers of prostitutes, the taste for sensuality in every milieu, the gambling, the drinking and the spectacle of public executions, which gave a frisson to the debauchees. Eros and Thanatos formed an indissoluble couple in the West, where life was short, on average twice as short as today, and where venereal and other diseases were a constant threat and the tragedies of existence were many. Blood, filth and pain were the other side of the coin, which only added to the importance of instant pleasure, liberated by the loosening of repressive constraints, against a backdrop of the unease of those who clung to the fading religious message.

People of quality, who had time on their hands, invested huge psychic energies in the pursuit of personal passions and pleasures. The erotic became a central aspect of their identity, in the context of a culture that sharply distinguished the roles of the two sexes and even accentuated this difference, towards the end of the century, by creating radically separate spheres.[28] But erotic freedom always risks coming into conflict with the collective aims of a society. The regulation of this potentially explosive phenomenon, capable of transforming a community into an anarchic aggregate of uncoordinated pleasure-seekers, was effected by means of subtle mechanisms which replaced the old censures. The theoretical element was provided by a philosophical debate on the pursuit of happiness. The subject permeated thinking, because it loomed large in the daily realities. Even though it did not appear in the Declaration of the Rights of Man of 1789, the right to physical pleasure was openly claimed. The British literature of the Enlightenment that was devoted to good manners saw it both as a civilizing force and as a legitimate source of enjoyment. For James Boswell, there was 'no higher felicity on Earth'. Dr Erasmus Darwin, paternal grandfather of the author of *The Origin of Species*, described it as 'the purest source of human felicity, the cordial drop in the otherwise vapid cup of life'. In London, between 1811 and 1820, under the Prince Regent, known as the 'Prince of Pleasure', drinking, eating and making love were joyfully indulged in, without attracting fierce criticism.[29]

The ideas of Bernard de Mandeville (1670–1733), which were highly controversial in his day, had already introduced this question into a wider intellectual debate. Born in the Netherlands, this doctor lived in London and wrote works of satire. He cynically advocated the quest for personal power, honour and fame. For him, there was always a powerful hedonism behind disinterested morals. Fascinated by the control of the carnal passions, he developed a sort of treatise on sexual economy, *The Grumbling Hive* (1705), which he then repeatedly revised. In 1714, the work took the title *The Fable of the Bees: or Private Vices, Publick Benefits*. It was further expanded in later editions, and translated and published in France in 1750.[30] For Mandeville, men and women were always on heat and constantly seeking to satisfy their sexual hunger. In consequence, all social institutions were based on hypocrisy. Far from condemning this situation, he proposed accepting it, because it was necessary for humans to seek pleasure, vanity and ambition, on condition it was under social control. Private vices would then bring public benefits by putting the egoism of each individual at the service of the common good. Individualism was integrated into an image of the hive, a world paradoxically united, because if some attended only to their appetites and others to collective goals, this composite whole, even if conflicted, received overall an additional input of energy. Fiercely attacked by the defenders of Christianity, Mandeville's message met with increasing favour. In 1776 Adam Smith offered a not dissimilar vision in *The Wealth of Nations*. In parallel, another critical strand inaugurated by Joseph Addison, founder of the short-lived magazine, *The Spectator* (1711–14), which had enormous influence and was imitated all over Europe, ridiculed both Puritan excess and aristocratic libertinism. He advocated a middle way, because he believed that the pursuit in moderation of sober and rational joys produced a more sustained pleasure. Urbanity, good manners, reason and restraint were the best guarantees of what was beginning to be called happiness. It seemed possible to attain it in the here and now, rather than delay it in the improbable hope of a Christian paradise.[31]

In France, the *philosophes* explored the same question at great length. They revisited ancient Epicureanism, 'which consists of preferring, to an always unstable pleasure, that absence of emotion which leaves the conscience like a calm sea and brings the end of anxiety in the fading of desire'.[32] It was in this context that pleasure assumed a role of supreme importance. Madam de Puisieux decreed it indispensable to loving happiness, in *Le Plaisir et la Volupté*. Voltaire devoted his Fifth Discourse to it and claimed, in a letter of June 1738 to the Crown Prince of Prussia, that he saw it as proof of God's existence, 'because, physically speaking, pleasure is divine, and I hold that every man who drinks Tokai wine and kisses a pretty woman, who, in a word, has agreeable sensations, must recognize a supreme and beneficent Being'.[33] On the Christian side, Pierre Bayle proposed, in *Les Dialogues entre MM. Patru et d'Ablancourt sur les plaisirs* (1701), an amiable and flexible morality based on three rules: moderation, relative rarity and facility. Without ranking them, he listed 12 different types of happiness: love, the table, music, conversation, reading, spectacles, gaming, the countryside, virtue, friendship, study and daydreaming. Others, like Dupuy in 1717 (*Dialogues sur les plaisirs*), distinguished the raptures of the senses, the mind and the heart. Gourcy wanted to spiritualize the first by associating them with the other two, 'so as to give them delicacy and solidity, and make them worthy of man'. The majority of authors believed that one should take pleasure without abusing it or succumbing to passion.[34] Reserve was equally admired in England, since Locke, who had developed the Pythagorean idea that temperance could heal the body, physical or political, of its ills. Writers as diverse as Mandeville, Woodward, Cheyne, Defoe and Swift professed similar principles.[35] Enjoyment was not, therefore, accessible to all. Only the 'perfect man is voluptuous', proclaimed Rémond le Grec, in 1719 in *Agathon, dialogue sur la volupté*. In 1746, the chevalier de la Morlière offered a 'manual of enjoyment' in his novel *Angola*: everything is false in a world entirely devoted to pleasure, where the end of the ball reveals the disaster hidden beneath the mask, 'like the sickening spectacle of a ruined cocotte'. Rousseau and his disciples, meanwhile, preferred to celebrate virtue as the supreme joy, the poet Edward Young asking, 'What is pleasure?' and replying that it was virtue under a gayer name. But the edifice was shaken at the end of the century, most notably by Sade, whose ideas justified the unconstrained expansion of the individual, the pure hedonism and the contempt for the social rules that were revealed by the criminal scenes he described.[36] However, the divine marquis left only a small sulphurous stain on the cultural fabric. The defence of balance and the happy medium was as strong as ever in the next century.

Orgasm and marriage

The devil is in the detail. Western sexual norms seem not to have changed radically during the eighteenth century, in terms of relations between the sexes, except for the greater subjection of women, in spite of the outlets offered by a certain moral laxity in both London and Paris. Nevertheless, a slow and silent revolution changed the very motor of relations between men and women, young people and adults and the different social categories.

The various discourses helped to obscure these changes. The weakening of religious moralities was offset by an insidious mechanism which promoted marriage and the fixed conjugal roles, through the prevailing sentimentalism of the age, in the form of romantic love. This did not affect only the social elites, consumers of novels and romances. Ordinary people, too, were caught up in this trend and prompted into affective growth, like the muslin-maker Louis Simon in Maine.[37] This was in a context of the concentration of scientific, medical and literary works on things of the heart – not the blood pump discovered by Harvey, but a much less localized organ, which replaced the soul, discredited by its long association with the rigours of religion, as a way of describing the turmoil of love. An analysis of the titles of French books published since the sixteenth century reveals, for the period 1723–89, the frequent appearance of love (cited 367 times) and marriage (143 times), the irresistible rise of the heart (208 occurrences) and sentiment (179), the notion of pleasure, in the singular or the plural, occurring a mere 69 times. The reality was more mundane, as prenuptial pregnancies and illegitimacies rapidly increased in number in the last century of the *ancien régime*, especially in the countryside, but also in London, where the incidence of bastardy had previously been very low.[38] Perhaps the steady advance of romantic love was a discreet cultural veil thrown over facts dimly perceived by the new moralists, protagonists of moderation and temperance. At all events, the two phenomena went hand in hand. They came together literally in the figures of the debauchees who progressed towards a sort of laicized redemption, returning to the role laid down for them in nature. Dom Bougre, the porter at the Charterhouse, was forced to go down this route by castration and awaited death on re-entering his monastery. Fanny Hill, the repentant prostitute, chose her own destiny by making a happy marriage which offered her both the joys of tenderness and skilled but legitimate carnal pleasures.

The main innovation with regard to marriage in the eighteenth century was the emergence of the right of the woman to pleasure. Perhaps as a concession to those now increasingly confined within the institution, orgasm began to be seen as lawful in itself and not simply as indispensable to procreation. Until now, confessors had warned couples against seeking orgasm, some even seeing it as a mortal sin. In 1584, the Franciscan theologian Benedicti fiercely condemned all excess: 'A man should not use his wife as a whore, nor should the wife behave towards her husband as if to a lover.' He adjured couples not to 'make your bed your God'. Every erotic extra was criticized. The only acceptable position was that in which the male straddled his partner, so as not to loose the semen but also to avoid a breach of the natural order, leading literally to the world being turned upside down. The Jesuit theologian Sanchez, an authority in the matter, even claimed that the biblical Flood had been caused by women, 'transported with madness, [who] had abused men, the latter lying beneath and the women on top'.[39]

The *Tableau de l'amour conjugal* of Dr Nicolas Venette (1633–98), published in 1686, broke with this tradition. It was enormously influential throughout Europe, as more than 30 reissues, translations into Dutch (1687), German (1698) and English (as *The Mysteries of Conjugal Love Reveal'd*, in 1703) and numerous adaptations show. There was a Spanish edition in 1826 and it subsequently became the 'Bible of the French peasantry'. Dr Venette discusses, in turn, the mechanics of sexual intercourse, the results of copulation and their social implications, paternity, inheritance, divorce, etc. His outlook remains very male, for example when he claims that the mere sight of a penis drove women wild with desire, but he accepts that men and women were equally lascivious. In his eyes, young men were satyrs and women were constantly seeking love, because their sexual organs rendered them insatiable. The crucial difference lay in the ways this need was expressed: men, who were stronger, were more quickly satisfied and exhausted; women were capricious, jealous and vain, less capable of self-control. Venette earnestly put the case for sexual intercourse, in the case of men to preserve their health and avoid a sudden death, in the case of women to protect against melancholy, hysteria and the 'green sickness', or chlorosis. Yet he advised avoidance of excess and the poison of sensuality, through observance of the golden rule of moderation, because the most lascivious of the animal species, such as the hare and the sparrow, lived the shortest lives.[40]

Although he freed pleasure from guilt, Venette reinforced matrimonial morality by claiming both that true virility lay not in erotic capacity but in that to father children, especially boys, and that wives were incapable of controlling their natural lustfulness themselves. The wife, he said, 'is like a weathercock that turns in the slightest wind, and that would certainly be swept away by the storm if the rod supporting it did not hold it fast'.[41] The lasting success of his book was probably due to its combination of paternalistic traditions and innovations as agreeable for couples to read about as put into practice. Although he preferred the classic position, with the man on top, as the most normal and the most voluptuous, he also advocated sex lying on the side or from behind. In the latter case, he was daring to go against the vigorous condemnation of theologians, insisting on its advantages, because 'the womb is much better situated for conception', the semen naturally running deep into the vagina, even if the pleasure was less, or so he believed. On the other hand, he was in full agreement with the confessors and erotic classics such as *L'École des filles* in rejecting all extra-vaginal ejaculation, describing sodomy as an 'enormous crime', because 'one never conceived that way', and raging against the 'impure commerce' of fellatio, which, he said, produced warts on the penis. His great skill was to replace condemnation of the sins of the flesh when not wholly devoted to procreation with a more soothing vision, in which 'conjugal caresses are the key to married love' and are 'truly of the essence'.[42] Making concessions in this direction, yet insisting on the need for moderation, like the confessors before him, he preserved the dogmas of the inequality of the spouses and the condemnation of all sexuality that was not reproductive. The technical medical discourse he promoted replaced that of the theologians to serve as the basis for an allegedly 'natural' order of things, which in practice reinforced male domination in marriage as in society.

The masculine double standard

The end of the eighteenth century saw a laicization of discourses on the body, linked to the major upheavals of the political, social and scientific revolutions. They adapted with great flexibility to the new realities, confirming male domination through marriage and sexuality, even reinforcing it with new arguments. What changed was not so much the substance of relations between men and women as their mechanisms. Male power was no longer based on Holy Writ but on the internalizing of 'gender' values that emphasized the natural inferiority of women. While the frontiers between the two worlds were strengthened, the system of ideological subordination created constant anxiety in those who exercised control, driving them to be for ever seeking proof of the obedience of those under their rule.[43] In spite of their growing antagonism, France and England developed in a remarkably similar manner, with differences only of detail, which explains why Dr Venette had so many readers on this side of the Channel. The years that saw the rejection of the French Revolution in England were also those of the emergence of a provincial middle class destined to dominate the Victorian scene, which differentiated itself from the aristocracy and the gentry by a set of domestic values in which the male and female spheres were clearly separated. The culture of this politically and socially highly ambitious group was distinguished by three features: trade, rationality and moderation. The last of these is very reminiscent of 'moderate' French philosophical thinking on the subject of pleasure and the need to control its use closely. The ideas preceded the social formations. The change had begun long before, at the time of the crisis of European consciousness, between the end of the seventeenth century and the 1720s. It took concrete form in five slowly implemented innovations: the masculine double standard, the confinement of women within marriage, the ferocious battle against masturbation, the emergence of a group of socially ostracized male homosexuals and the intensification of masculine anxiety in the face of the colonized, but still dangerous, feminine world.

The double standard is, in a sense, a laicization of the traditional division of women into two contrasting types, one good and submissive, the other rebellious and diabolical. All women were carriers of original sin thanks to the sin of Eve, but those who married God in a convent or who patiently submitted to the salutary tutelage of a husband were saved, whereas the rest, driven by their lewd instincts, were irremediably damned. Admittedly, such ideas did not prevent either the Suzanne and Fanchon of *L'École des filles* or the libidinous and loudmouthed peasant women of Somerset from giving themselves a good time. This was still the case after the spread of the secularized theory that distinguished pure women, the sort you married and then kept under close control, from impure women, prostitutes or simply women who were free with their bodies, the sort you had orgasmic sex with before returning to the virtuous conjugal hearth, at peace with oneself.[44]

It goes without saying that women did not, in principle, have the right to this sort of dual personality. They were obliged to opt for one or other of the two roles laid down for them. It was easy for them to fall short and pass to the other side of the looking-glass, much harder to contrive to redeem themselves from a life of sin, like Fanny Hill – whereas males could and must play both roles in succession to be perceived as real men. We should not, however, forget social status. The double standard involved a morality of appearances and discretion in the quest for pleasure and it was primarily important to the middle classes and the aristocracy. It had long been practised by debauched courtiers, in both France and England, and by their wives. At Versailles under Louis XIV, said the marquise de Sévigné, they laughed at anyone who loved their spouse and showed it in public. Things were very different among the people, because the duplicity the system demanded was not to their taste. Marriage did not prevent men from openly seeing every woman as potential prey or girls from liking to vary their pleasures, in seventeenth-century Somerset or in London at a later date. In the English capital, a particular form of popular divorce existed, the public wife sale, usually after a prior agreement. The practice is clearly attested between 1750 and 1850, with some earlier examples. A certain Thomas Carter, for example, obliged to marry Rebeccah Riddle in 1777 after presenting her with a bastard child, left her, then bought Mary Collingham from her husband for a bottle of beer in 1783. The newspapers began to report these practices in the 1730s. A sailor returning from China found his wife married to another man, persuaded his rival to give her back, changed his mind and eventually sold her for two pounds of beef sausages and a crown's worth of gin punch. The public ritual became more elaborate after 1790, with the agreement of the purchaser. Thomas Parsons publicly auctioned his wife of five years by whom he had two children, marching her with a halter round her neck to a public house in Whitechapel, where, in return for a gallon of beer, he handed her over to a customer with whom he had already made an agreement. Another man exposed his wife with a rope round her waist in Smithfield market for a quarter of an hour, then sold her for a guinea to a man who wanted her, because a lawyer had told them that the sale would only be valid if it was conducted in a public place. In some cases, the sale was to the highest bidder; one wife, perhaps unusually beautiful or good with her hands, was sold to a tailor who outbid eight competitors.[45]

The 'bourgeois' double standard was very specific in nature. It was not based on the frantic search for pleasure peculiar to the debauchees of high society, even less on the piling up of sexual conquests to proclaim one's virility, as was the way among the English gentry or the French and English peasantries. It was linked to a morality of constraint and self-control that was widely disseminated both by the books of etiquette and good manners and by the philosophies of happiness in moderation. It primarily concerned men engaged in commercial capitalism, who knew what being economical meant, who had a taste for financial risk and who, in England, also sought for signs of predestination in material success. For them, the wife so carefully chosen was not for sale, but she had to be constantly supervised, kept like an idol in the sanctuary of the home, where she produced children while also ensuring the well-being of the master of the house. Her sphere was the private and enclosed world, whereas the husband conquered the external world, before returning to savour the tranquillity of a family life that was increasingly appreciated.[46] She could give him conjugal pleasure, if they followed the advice of Dr Venette, through respect for the norms of decency and politeness. However, the competitive masculine lifestyle caused men much anxiety, which they had to cope with while always keeping up a good front, sign of success, and avoiding all excess in accord with the morality of moderation learned from the conduct guides and literature. In this stressful existence, the most effective outlet was the resort to prostitutes. This did not give rise to feelings of personal guilt or social disapproval; everybody did it, especially the dissolute aristocracy. Whorehouses and refined brothels on the French model proliferated in London. Paris was no different. For the members of the middling classes, those some French historians call the 'frustrated' bourgeoisie, often remote from power but economically extremely dynamic, the haunts of ill fame became indispensable complements to the home. Husbands went there to relax on a regular basis, young men went there to learn the rudiments and techniques of love before marrying the sweet little virgin who was lined up for them. What they all found was a cure for anxiety. This had actually been heightened by the strengthening of tutelage over all women, some confined in the domestic sphere, others in that of prostitution, because their growing subjection gave rise to a disturbing fantasy, making men fear a possible rebellion of the oppressed. This system, which steadily developed throughout the nineteenth century, had the effect of making men two-faced, the good father of the family transmuting at night into a resourceful frequenter of brothels. It explains the boom in pornographic literature, the sudden emergence of which around 1650 and growing success in the eighteenth century corresponded, paradoxically, to the establishment of the exacting philosophy of the moderation of the passions. This type of eroticism reassured men by celebrating their lust and often depicting the female body as an object.[47] It had female readers too. However, it is far from certain that this is proved by the prints and engravings that show a woman masturbating as she reads pornographic literature, which might equally well be pandering to a male voyeuristic fantasy. This produced, in due course, the clientele of Freud, since neither the strict subordination of women nor the split personality of men was easy to bear without neurosis. In addition to which, the ferocious battle against masturbation and the inculcation of deep guilt at the slightest inclination towards their own sex, was aimed to forbid men any sexual impulse that did not lead them to a woman, legitimate or not.

No pleasure outside the vagina

The outlawing of masturbation and homosexuality, a corollary of the establishment of the double standard and the demand for 'moderation' in the sexual appetites in order to attain happiness, primarily affected men. The condemnation applied to both sexes, but it was of much greater social and cultural importance for men than for women, because it was intended to educate them to enjoy vaginal sex alone. Described as onanism, the absolute taboo encompassed both the sin of self-abuse and that of sodomy. It derived from the religious prohibition on spilling semen outside the receptacle intended to receive it, and in the name of which homosexuals had been burned in the two previous centuries. Although such punishments were no longer enforced, the battle against the phenomenon was actually intensified by being aimed at all men, to make them feel guilt, and no longer at a few exceptions punished as an example. It can be seen as an expression of the anxiety of the upholders of the new morality, concentrating their hostility and their fears on what was to them an abnormal group, those who took their pleasure outside the vagina, chosen as scapegoats because they transgressed the most important taboo.

In London, the construction of the alterity of these outcasts was a consequence of a 'gender revolution' which developed in three stages, corresponding to three successive generations.[48] The first was that of the emergence of a sodomite minority. By 1720, the 'molly houses' were the scene of a flourishing homosexual subculture, associated with the taste for flagellation, a service offered in many brothels.[49] In parallel, heterosexuality became an essential principle among the majority of men in all social classes. In the second phase, some from among the middling and landed classes experimented with romantic monogamous marriage. The concept had long existed, for example in the plays of the 1690s, but it had encountered strong moral resistance, and it was only in the middle of the eighteenth century that it came into its own. Theoretically exclusive, it seemed to forbid the use of prostitutes, in contrast to the practices of the mass of the male population, constrained only by fear of sexual diseases; they would discover it in their turn half a century later. The third and last generation was dominated by the growth of Sapphic relations, among the nobility and the middle classes. As a result, other parameters of sexual life also changed. The illegitimacy rate, which had been surprisingly low in London until the 1750s, now rapidly rose. Sexual diseases, a direct consequence of the explosion of prostitution, were spreading fast by the 1690s. They first affected the debauchees, hence their generic name of the 'Gentleman's Disease', then spread to the population as a whole, even the very poorest by about 1790. One popular belief in this connection horrified the affluent, that is, the idea that intercourse with a virgin cured venereal disease; it led, after 1720, to an increase in the number of abductions of pre-adolescent girls aged 13 or less, which is attested by the judicial records.

The rise of romantic love, which was equally visible in France, including in the countryside after 1750, had two indirect consequences. First, this new view of conjugal relations made the partners more demanding of each other in matters of sentiment. Divorces for incompatibility increased in number in England from the mid-eighteenth century. Infidelity itself changed its meaning. Prosecutions for adultery practically ceased in London in the 1730s, because the legal authorities no longer wished to meddle in what they now viewed as a private matter; which is not to say, of course, that behaviour was becoming more restrained, especially since the women of the capital had more freedom than most and plenty of opportunities to sin. However, the double standard had the effect of restricting their movements outside the house, to ensure their unimpeachable morality. The chaste, desexualized and maternal wife, capable of resisting masculine advances, was imagined on the mythical model of the eponymous heroine of Samuel Richardson's *Pamela: or, Virtue Rewarded* (1740), who staunchly resists the assaults of her lecherous employer. For those who believed in the moderation of the passions, cuckoldry was no longer a matter of honour involving the perceptions of others, but increasingly an inner shame, caused by the feeling of having failed in a relationship based on reciprocal affection. At the same time, the bourgeoisie and the landowning classes differentiated themselves by this means from the upper-class debauchees, whom they found both effeminate and obsessively adulterous.[50] They loudly proclaimed a domestic ideology which kept the feminine icon apart from the depravities of the street and offered her a privileged relationship with a chosen and loved partner, on condition she accepted the duty of not deceiving him and of tenderly attending to his needs and healing the little hurts of his daily life. This can be seen as a subtle way of subjecting the wife, both herself enclosed and closed to the desires of other men, to an even stricter subordination than in the past, all the more so as it was consented to and based on the idealization of the husband. In other words, the definition of the role of each member of the couple was no longer dependent on the fear of punishment or of hell, but on an internalization of the rules deemed to distinguish the stronger from the weaker sex.[51] The courtesy manuals, literature in all its forms – from *Pamela* to *Fanny Hill* – and the medical treatises – of Dr Venette among others – established the codes which made it possible to inculcate from the cradle these two contrasting roles. This aspect of the 'civilizing process' was neglected by Norbert Elias, who wrote before the discoveries of gender historians.[52] It made a huge difference to women, who were bombarded with an abundant literature intent on instructing them in their duty. Conduct manuals for women flooded the market in ever-increasing numbers from 1670 to 1800, along with medical works which learnedly explained the sexual differences,[53] not forgetting the periodicals, the romances, the novels and the paintings and engravings.[54] The daughters of Eve were no longer demonized as they had been in the seventeenth century, but they paid a heavy price in increased subjection.

The second unforeseen consequence of romantic love was to allow the emergence of a new type of masculine friendship, devoid of sexual ambiguity. For those who shared an exclusive love with their sweet little wife, it was perfectly acceptable to form a deep affective relationship with men of their own age, or adolescents, and invite them regularly into their home, without fear of being accused of homosexual tendencies. This, it has been argued, would explain the growth of fierce disapproval of the sodomitic and masturbatory practices, individual or collective, which had been common among young unmarried men before the first decade of the seventeenth century.[55] Every virtue having its down side, the valorization of male camaraderie had the perverse effect of allowing the male best friend to be one of the few, if not the only, representatives of his sex who was able to have close contact with the wife in a degree of privacy. All that was needed was for married love not to come up to expectations for an even closer relationship to develop between the wife and the alter ego of the master of the house. This sort of love triangle could amount to a sort of homosexual rape of the latter, through the body of his wife, by the man who thus enjoyed his relations with the couple twice over.[56] Without necessarily going so far, the idea at least expresses a masculine fantasy of the period, even of our own. The ideal wife, enclosed and closed, who could not confront the gaze of outsiders alone, was surely at risk of fixing her desires on a familiar, sometimes a servant, more often a friend of her husband. At least, in the latter case, he was of her own rank and she might hope to form a second romantic liaison of the same order as the one which had disappointed her.

Although Paris is less well documented, it seems to have been little different from London. The masculine double standard and the subjection of women allowed the middling ranks to assert their originality vis-à-vis both the courtiers, as debauched as the British rakes, and the common people, with their lax morals. Prostitution flourished, the high-class brothels even serving as models to be copied in London. The actresses at the Opéra and the demimondaines were reputed to do honour to the libertine reputation of the French capital. The police directed by the lieutenant-general instituted under Louis XIV used them to spy on strangers or act as *mouches*, that is, informers. Male homosexuals formed groups with their own recognition signs, preferred places and language, in other words, their special culture. This is demonstrated by the 'pederasty patrols', when the agents of police passed themselves off as 'buggers' to entrap sodomites and compiled astonishingly detailed reports of their activities. However, the subject has been less fully researched than in England.[57]

The crusade against onanism

If there is one area in which sexual repression was particularly apparent in the Enlightenment, it is that of the sin of Onan, in other words, masturbation. We need to remember, nevertheless, that the peasants of Somerset had had no inhibitions about masturbating in the seventeenth century and also often felt up women's bodies or sexual organs.[58] The Catholic confessors tried to forbid it, but without much success. For the civil authorities it was a minor crime, and they admitted defeat before the difficulty of punishing an act so easily concealed. As a lawyer from Artois resignedly observed in the 1630s, it was extremely difficult to discover the 'self-abuse' or 'filthiness' of a man who 'arouses and strokes himself to an emission, to the point of ejaculating his semen'.[59] Those who masturbated probably felt quite safe. This is suggested by the curious erotic misappropriation of a famous English medical treatise published in 1684, *Aristotle's Master-Piece*, which was largely devoted to explaining reproduction and the pleasures to be enjoyed with a woman; the annotations left by John Cannon, a Taunton apprentice, at the beginning of the eighteenth century, reveal that the book was used as a reciprocal aid to masturbation by a group of young lads.[60] Which only goes to show how the definition of pornography changes over time!

Once seen as banal, even as an acceptable sexual outlet for young peasants as they awaited marriage, itself increasingly delayed, masturbation became a serious taboo in England at the beginning of the eighteenth century. It continued to be disapproved of by right-minded people for a very long time to come. Freud himself believed there was a danger of it corrupting the character.[61] Around 1710, an anonymous pamphlet appeared in London with the title *Onania; or, The Heinous Sin of Self Pollution, and all its Frightful Consequences in Both Sexes Considered, with Spiritual and Physical Advice....* The supposed author, Bekker or John Marten, was a quack. A total of 2,000 copies were printed, which were intended to help sell cures; it was a great success, with a score of editions,[62] and some German translations. The offensive against masturbation was exactly contemporary with the definition of a group of gays in London, the 'mollies'. In fact the etymology of the word is discussed in the pamphlet. In no discernible order, in 40 pages, a fifth of them tables, it provides a number of anatomical expositions, followed by long sections on widowhood and prostitution, before tackling wet dreams and masturbation itself. This manual 'pollution' primarily affected adolescents, but also adults and old men. The edition of 1723, advertised as the eighth, included what purported to be letters written by male readers who confessed they had begun to masturbate between the ages of 11 and 17, usually around 14 or 15. Some had started of their own accord, but most claimed they had been initiated within a circle of friends. A similar collection of fake letters at the end of the century came up with very much the same age range, between 8 and 15, as the most common starting-point for this vice, while confirming that it was usually learned from someone else. No one seemed to be unaware that many boys masturbated in their youth. The *Nymphomania* of Bienville, published much later (1771), described the same phenomenon among girls.[63] Female masturbation was less strongly disapproved of, however, just as lesbianism was more readily tolerated than male homosexuality. As we have seen, pornography either avoids describing such things or condemns them, as in the case of an act of sodomy between young men in *Fanny Hill*, the norm of reference always remaining vaginal penetration.[64]

Other medical texts of the first half of the century indicate that onanism, now the accepted term, had become a major problem. The vehemence of the authors was now directed against its consequences. They claimed that the practice ruined the health, especially in the young, whose growth it slowed, and that it caused illnesses, especially epilepsy and convulsions, even death. A similar concern began to be felt in France following the translation in 1746–8 of the medical dictionary of Robert James. The campaign against masturbation took a different turn in France, however, because the 'patient' was presented by Rousseau and Tissot as a victim of the depraved social order that turned man away from his true nature. Paradoxically, this discourse has been seen as eminently liberating, on the grounds that it opposed 'the real pleasures of moderation' to debauchery as much as to continence and that it replaced coercion by a discipline that was freely accepted. I myself see it as primarily an expression of the measured morality of the middle classes, accompanying their battle to substitute vaginal pleasure alone for all other temptations. In 1762, Tissot informed Rousseau that his book on onanism, published two years earlier in Lausanne, had been prohibited in Paris, like *Émile* not long before.[65] If the campaign against masturbation did not have the wholehearted support of the authorities, it is because it came to have what they saw as an unacceptable erotic dimension. Works denouncing the solitary vice proliferated, nevertheless, in Europe and in the United States. From a few titles per decade before 1760, the number rose to 12 in the decade 1760–70, to 25 in the last decade of the century, remained at between 10 and 20 per decade between 1800 and 1860, before climbing to 20 and then 25 between 1870 and 1890.[66]

The high point of the genre is *L'Onanisme* of Dr Samuel-Auguste Tissot, published in Latin in 1758, then in French, in Lausanne, in 1760. Banned in France, its third edition was published clandestinely in Paris in 1764. An English translation appeared in London in 1761.[67] Several studies have shown that Tissot was simply reformulating in medical and philosophical terms knowledge and prohibitions that had previously been described in theological terms. Like the confessors before him, he criticized masturbation because it led to a squandering of the semen. Only the morality changed, being now a matter of the person, no longer of collective Christian salvation. Tissot enjoyed a huge public success, perhaps because his dramatic picture of the sufferings of the masturbator took over from the old descriptions of the torments of hell. It was hardly innovatory to describe the body as a machine or combine this notion with the hydrostatic theory, itself heir to that of the humours. Tissot claimed that, for this mechanism to function efficiently, there had to be a balance of its fluids. But 'our bodies lose continually, and if we cannot make up for our losses [by the process of nutrition], we will soon fall into a mortal weakness'. Thus one should avoid 'copious evacuations', in particular of semen, which was the most 'worked' of the humours. For centuries, he said, it had been thought that 'the loss of one ounce of this humour enfeebled more than that of forty ounces of blood'. In contrast, 'milk is of all the humours the least worked'. It is easy to recognize the old notion of the inferiority of women, now demonstrated by science. Tissot was forced into contortions on this point, however, because, like his predecessors, he accepted that the daughters of Eve also ejaculated semen during intercourse. This led him to conclude that milk should not be expelled too copiously, for fear of exhaustion. It, too, should remain in the reservoir. The ideal state for a woman was thus maternity, followed by lactation, the latter a subject of renewed interest following the diatribes of Rousseau against the wet-nursing that was current among Parisians of all social categories. Tissot specified that if you were forced to have recourse to commercial milk, 'the female who provides it should be healthy and of good conduct'.[68] There could hardly be a clearer formulation of the natural nurturing role of the mother and the superiority of the male, while also lauding a 'reasonable' ideal of the conservation of the humoral 'capital' and rejection of waste. It was ideally suited to the ideas and practices of the middle classes and the upper bourgeoisie engaged in commercial capitalism, who were anxious to strengthen their position by the accumulation of wealth and knowledge.

Masturbation appeared so dangerous to Tissot because it did not produce the 'invisible torrents', a sort of exchange of energy through perspiration during coitus. In addition to which, it made women indifferent towards 'legitimate pleasures'. Some women even practised 'another dirtiness, that might be called clitoral', because their organ, normally small, was of 'unnatural size' and they used it like a penis with other women. This idea had existed in previous centuries, when sapphism or tribadism were in principle punished by death. Male masturbation engendered a fatal disorder, with convulsions, slavering and 'epileptic paroxysms'. Such men could be recognized by their pallor and their effeminate air, given that they 'lose, and get nothing back'.[69]

It is difficult to see Tissot as a liberator of Western sexuality. Rather, he was the champion of a controlled middle way to the pleasure to which the new urban elites in London and Paris aspired in the years before the French Revolution. With the aim of combating all erotic excess by instilling a salutary fear in his readers, Tissot quotes the case of a man scarcely recovered from illness who died the night he paid 'conjugal tribute to his wife'. Another succumbed after 'an excess of women and wine'. A third, who had similarly indulged and suffered from gout, was afflicted 'with a general trembling immediately after coitus'. The pleasures of the marriage bed should also be enjoyed in moderation, because whoever was too energetic in his lovemaking died a painful death; this had been the fate of one young husband after a continuous fever accompanied by red blotches and swelling of the face, and of another after 'a violent pain in the backside'.[70] He who lived by the sword...

On both sides of the Channel, the doctors of the Enlightenment played a crucial role because they alone seemed to be responding concretely to the growing sexual anxiety of the better-off sectors of the population. Impotence, infertility and venereal disease are recurring themes of the age.[71] To which were added more diffuse anxieties, linked to the perception of the changes taking place and a possible revolt of the oppressed, that is, wives confined to the home, mollies and sodomites, boys deprived of solitary pleasures, though it was well known that many practised them. The advocates of a cleaned-up morality and the supporters of a balance of the passions combined to bring about a major upheaval, without really wishing it. Their demands weighed heavily on women and on young unmarried men. The traditional constraints – arbitrary justice, fear of hell, subjection to the father, obedience to the husband – were losing their power. Social control was being reconstructed on different foundations: reason, knowledge, medical in particular, love marriages, personal attachment and sentiment as the basis for love, paternity and friendship. A new and more refined mixture was emerging from the cauldron of the past. Relationships between the sexes and between age groups were changing, almost exclusively to the advantage of adult men. In 1796, Anne-Louise-Germaine de Staël (1766–1817) wrote a treatise on the influence of the passions.[72] She sublimated happiness by the imagination, which she believed was more important in women and almost exclusively oriented towards love, whereas for men it was primarily a weapon for public recognition. In elegant and novel terms, she explains the influence, through the romantic vision, of the 'natural' gender differences, the man turned towards the world, his partner, mother and wife, towards an inner universe devoted to great literature and the transmission of culture to the next generations. She did not describe the extent to which this distinction based on philosophical arguments produced tensions and anxiety among men. The perception of the self changed profoundly in the social groups most subject to the tyrannies of moderation.

The art of the 'I'

The sentimentalism of the eighteenth century paved the way for autobiography. Completed in 1771 and posthumously published between 1781 and 1788, the *Confessions* of Jean-Jacques Rousseau are classically credited with being the first real autobiographical account.[73] The phenomenon is actually much earlier, especially in England, but for a long time it encountered stubborn resistance, many Christians seeing it as an unacceptable narcissism which distracted from the path to salvation. Courtesy literature tended in the same direction, by advising that one conceal one's emotions or passions beneath a polite urbanity and by decreeing excessively personal manifestations of the body or the spirit unacceptable. The reluctance to allow people to look into themselves led to dreams being classified as vulgar and something not to be mentioned in polite conversation.[74] This is why the Self emerged only with difficulty, initially in the reprehensible form of the sulphurous stories of prostitutes, licentious apprentices and even demonized criminals. Nevertheless, by devouring the adventures of others so different from themselves, readers learned to see themselves more clearly.

Whores, drunks and lecherous apprentices

The criminal biography was an immensely popular literary genre, especially in England. Among the characters most frequently portrayed were fallen women and idle, lazy and lecherous apprentices. Hogarth reveals what was involved in a series of engravings entitled *Idleness and Industry* (1747): the industrious apprentice marries his master's daughter and ends up as Lord Mayor of London; the idle apprentice, who wastes his time and behaves in a seriously anti-social manner, ends up on the gallows at Tyburn. Even if he starts off honest, bad company, especially an encounter with a prostitute, puts the idler on the road to ruin through alcohol and crime. The femme fatale is presented as strong, independent and without masculine tutelage, the exact opposite of the chaste, submissive, docile, loving wife and mother of the romantic literature. The biography of *Mary Young* provides the archetype; her evil influence drove even serious criminals from bad to worse. In *The History of the Remarkable Life of John Sheppard*, a celebrated robber who twice escaped from Newgate in 1724, the unhappy hero abandons his worthy employer after meeting Elizabeth Lyon, and then sinks to the level of an animal, guided by brute passions and returning to his old haunts 'like a Dog to his Vomit', as a result of which he is easily captured after his second escape.[75]

There were more than 20,000 apprentices in London in 1700, as well as an increasing number of prostitutes, probably more than 10,000 by the end the century. The two groups were indispensable, the former to economic activity, the latter to the erotic needs of men of all social classes. The danger represented by both groups was acutely felt at this period. Fear of venereal infection, transmitted to the most chaste of wives by husbands who frequented brothels, was general. The anger, the bad language and the brutality of the street-walkers, who had little to lose, was also feared. As for the young workers, who were bound by strong traditions of solidarity, they were readily suspected of rejecting all supervision by refusing *The Great Law of Subordination* – the title of a work by Daniel Defoe of 1724, in which their habitual dissoluteness was emphasized. In 1734, Samuel Richardson produced a manual of good conduct for their benefit, *The Apprentice's Vade Mecum*. They should not, he says, frequent fallen women or even marry. A flurry of similar works insisted on the necessity of protecting young men within the disciplined environment of a properly regulated apprenticeship. They expressed real social concerns regarding the special situation of London. Unmarried men and migrant workers were much more numerous here than elsewhere; two-thirds of the delinquents sentenced to be hanged had been born outside its walls. Contemporaries had a particular fear, consequently, of the lower classes, whom they viewed as typically anarchic, drunken and dishonest. The demographer Thomas Short, mistakenly claiming that the population of London was in decline, wrote in 1750 that the economic expansion of the capital was morally corrupting because it led to the poor drinking themselves to death on gin and the rich leading idle and parasitical lives.[76]

The real problem, masked by the moral topos of rural virtue contrasted with urban vice, was the place of young people in the big city, because of the steady stream of rootless persons who swelled its population. The laws of the market often doomed the new arrivals to poverty, a preliminary to theft and crime in the case of the boys and to selling their charms in the case of the girls. This double reservoir of labour and pleasure experimented with new symbolic practices. The prevailing morality invented adolescence as a time of constraints which had to be accepted by whoever wanted to succeed. It enjoined boys to avoid all sex, legitimate or not, not even seeking an outlet in sodomy or masturbation. The girls faced an even more dreadful choice. As servants, they could hope to become chaste and loving wives if they could escape the ambiguous attentions of masters and menservants. If not, they sank inexorably down into the street, swelling the ranks of prostitutes. Unlike in the village, they were not protected in case of pregnancy by a collective pressure strong enough to oblige their seducer to marry them or accept responsibility for the upkeep of their child. As a result, many outcasts of both sexes were ejected from the normal economic circuits. For the well-off and the right-minded, this growing cohort of malcontents, marginals, lecherous apprentices and fallen women could only intensify the latent dread of seeing them turn on their masters. Nor was the fear of venereal disease deliberately transmitted to a gentleman by a hate-filled whore pure fantasy.

It is hardly surprising that many metaphors to describe the great European cities conjure up images of an infernal abyss filled with every vice, or of a gigantic womb that swallowed up human beings. The old fear of an all-consuming female sexuality was transposed onto the urban monster as a whole. The theme of the body, human and collective, became literally an obsession. In England it haunted the writings of Defoe, Swift, Smollett, Sterne, Fielding, Richardson and many others, as well as the engravings and paintings of Hogarth. Defoe even called for a plague to help purge London of all these organisms that filled it. Urban morbidity provoked reactions of horror and rejection. In 1721, Thomas Lewis, in his *Seasonable Considerations on the Indecent and Dangerous Custom of Burying in Churches and Church Yard*, recommended ending the practice of burying people inside or close to churches, to avoid a fatal corruption. It was the same in Paris; however the decision taken in 1776 to remove the cemeteries outside the cities led to riots, because the lower classes did not see things in the same way and wanted to keep their dead close by.[77]

Demonized biographies

The fascination for the public spectacles of execution and bodily mutilation did not disappear in the eighteenth century. Though criticized by the *philosophes*, most notably Voltaire, and by the squeamish, they continued to attract huge crowds: 40,000 spectators, including 2,000 children, turned out to see a Protestant pastor hanged in Toulouse in 1746. In London, the executions at Tyburn were equally popular.[78] The notions of balance, moderation and temperance formulated by the thinkers of the age had little impact on the practices of the masses, for whom the sight of blood and death still held great evocative power. A new literary genre, the criminal biography, used this very taste for blood to urge its readers to exercise greater control over their passions. Taking over from the long tradition of the 'spiritual biography' in England, it involved the reader in a way that could lead to a sort of recognition of his or her own Self. Defoe's *Moll Flanders* employs this technique: the heroine, in a familiar progression, journeys from innocence to experience and finally to repentance.[79]

The increasing severity of the judicial legislation led to an increase in the number of death sentences between 1680 and the 1720s in London, particularly against thieves, 'stinking, dangerous beasts'. The condemned men and women were always invited to make a public speech of expiation before surrendering their soul to God. There were similar developments in Paris, with an increase in the number of executions for theft and the desire to make the culprit participate in an edifying spectacle. The 'testaments of death' preserved in the archives of the parlement are not a record of the last wishes of the criminals but rather notes jotted down on the spot by the clerk who accompanied them to urge them to repent publicly and make honourable amends before the crowd. However, the only works dealing with this phenomenon for the French capital remain unpublished.[80]

In England, apart from the literary transpositions, there were three different types of accounts of events, compiled respectively by the administration, the chaplain and journalists. The official *Proceedings* were sold to the public, in particular to the lawyers attending. They always included the composition of the court, a summary of the case and the verdict. They became increasingly detailed and vivid, the two pages of the late seventeenth century becoming an average of 48 pages by 1730. The accounts of the Newgate chaplain, which usually appeared the morning after the execution, concentrated on the condemned man or woman, in the tradition of the spiritual biography. They were designed to demonstrate the criminal's fall and their degree of repentance, because only those who repented from love of God, rather than from fear alone, could achieve salvation. Neither series is complete, and they do not cover the provinces. As for the newspapers, they make the condemned person into the hero of a story, seeking something sensational and blood-curdling for the front page, adding stereotyped engravings in which the actors converse in balloons, as in the modern strip cartoon. The writers felt free to side with the victim, express their horror at the culprit and pass moral judgements. It was not unknown for them to reveal some admiration for the most celebrated brigands, such as Jack Sheppard and Mary Carleton.[81]

These three sources gave rise to some hugely popular works. They included simple anonymous collections of trials, like *A Compleat Collection of Remarkable Tryals*, in 1718, *A Compleat Collection of State Tryals*, which appeared the following year, and later in the century, *The Tyburn Chronicle* (1768) and *The Newgate Calendar* (1773). They all have the same structure, presenting in succession the origins and youth of the personage, episodes from their deplorable life, their arrest, their trial and their execution. Others works were more elaborate and signed. Their authors trawled the records for information to serve as a basis for stories that were in part imaginary, taking as their models much-loved popular heroes such as Robin Hood or Moll Cutpurse, who had not always been criminals but who had fought against the authorities. In 1719, Captain Alexander Smith told *The Lives and Histories of the Most Noted Highwaymen...*, while in 1734 Captain Charles Johnson collected nearly 200 brigands for his *A General History of the Lives and Adventures of the Most Famous Highwaymen, Murderers, Street Robbers, etc.* In a preface, Alexander Smith emphasized his edifying objectives, which did not prevent him from including often highly scabrous details, in order, he claimed, 'to instruct and convert the corrupt and profane individuals of this licentious age'. His stories gave the public what it wanted: a little violence, a little pornography, some humour and a lot of action. Entire passages from the *Proceedings* or from the confessions before the chaplain were sometimes incorporated. To these were added ridiculous, even grotesque, episodes, which are sometimes repeated verbatim in different lives of criminals, in order to make people laugh at them and establish a healthy distance between them and the reader. Readers were hardly tempted to take these sulphurous heroes as examples, given that none of them ever escaped the gallows;

the wicked were always punished. Also, as the century progressed, they tended to fall into standard stereotypes, dominated by the figures of the apprentice who goes to the dogs, and the fallen woman, a prostitute and a thief.[82] Thus, the genre reveals the same fears as the conduct guides, the moralizing works and great literature regarding the grave threat of subversion represented by wayward apprentices and women living outside the sacred ties of marriage. Turning them into figures of fun may have helped to allay these fears.

Revealed by the criminals' pathetic end, when they spectacularly accepted their responsibility, the underlying moral of these texts is that of the necessity of self-control as opposed to destructive individualism.[83] The torn social fabric is mended by the culprit. One may speculate about the precise effect produced in the mind of the reader by the pejorative use in the documents of the notions of 'private person', depraved 'human nature', 'private passions' and 'appetites and inclinations', opposing an intemperate 'private' use of oneself to the necessities of public order and morality. It is not impossible that there were readers who identified with some of these tragic creatures, out of admiration for their strong, sometimes even charismatic, characters. The success of the genre at least indicates a widespread fascination, probably oscillating between dreams of risk-free transgression and the satisfaction of seeing crime punished, the licentious apprentice and the lost woman paying the price for their deviance. A masculine fantasy, the rebellious woman was put back where she belonged and finally agreed to accept the way of the world. It is by no means certain that women readers saw things from the same perspective. Did the wives confined within the cage of marriage perhaps experience a few frissons at the tales of forbidden adventures and inaccessible erotic passions? At the very least, it was easier and less shameful for them to buy and devour these books openly than it was to procure works of pornography.

Great writers took up the theme. Among playwrights, Gay presented *The Beggars Opera* in 1728 and Lillo *The London Merchant* in 1731. In the literary sphere, Fielding published *Jonathan Wild* in 1743, while Daniel Defoe (1660–1731) was clearly fascinated by the subject, which he dealt with many times in a highly original manner.[84] Contrary to the accepted conventions, the heroes presented in these long stories went unpunished. Further, Defoe, a highly individualistic and devout Protestant, made his readers consider the story as a fiction and exercise their freedom of judgement by surprising and even shocking them. In the preface to *The Fortunes and Misfortunes of the Famous Moll Flanders* (1722), he explains that his ambition was to cause us 'to be more present to ourselves'.[85] *Colonel Jack* (1722) provided him with an opportunity to engage in a complex play on the concept of the person. When Jack, overcome with remorse, returns the money stolen from a poor widow a year earlier, he addresses his conscience mentally using 'I', but addressing the widow uses 'he' and 'him' to indicate the thief, who is actually himself. It is not simply a subterfuge in order to attribute the crime to a person unknown. More subtly, Defoe employs the 'I' in the register of moral failure and the 'he' to express repentance and the hope that God may pardon such an act.[86] He may have got the idea from the very real confessions of certain criminals, who revealed a similar confusion, a loss of sense of identity at the moment of a murder or soon after. The eponymous heroine of another of his books, *Roxana* (1724), explains, furthermore, that 'Sin and Shame follow one-another ... like Cause and Consequence'.[87]

Colonel Jack is a distant ancestor of Dr Jekyll. He may not suffer from a true split personality, but his moral being is deeply disturbed by remorse, because he has succumbed to the sirens of his narcissistic and infernal Self. Such an excess is directly connected to the crime and, through it, to the Christian tradition of the sin of vanity. That is, contemporaries, as they read about his adventures, could receive the singular expression of the self, the too strongly asserted 'I', only as an eminent mark of transgression, on the path to crime and disaster. The old religious opposition to the arrogant affirmation of the Ego was alive and well. Transposed into the cultural language of the middle and upper classes, it still constituted a taboo, now based on decency, good taste and the internalizing of the passions advocated by the civilizing process.[88] Yet Defoe's readers were, paradoxically, cultivating their specificity, because they were learning to explore their inner world while being warned of the dangers this entailed. The contradiction was to prove fruitful.

The golden age of highwaymen tales, illustrated in France by the famous figures of Cartouche, broken alive on the wheel in 1721, and Mandrin, executed in 1755, was drawing to a close in England by 1740. The public was probably saturated, so many stories of this type had the newspapers published. One of the last spectacular examples was Sixteen-String Jack Rann, hanged in 1774, famous for his showy elegance and the eight strings with silver tips that adorned the knee of each of his boots, and gave him his nickname. It is possible that the decline of the genre was linked to the disappearance of its symbolic usefulness. On both sides of the Channel, the new type of crook in the latter part of the century was the great forger, from a respectable background, practising a more refined type of crime which directly concerned the preoccupations of the middle classes and highlighted the danger of economic individualism.[89] Further, the myth of the repentant criminal, of the sinner turned saint at the moment of death, was probably beginning to bore the general public, all the more so as it was easy to suspect that it was all a pious fraud. It was increasingly difficult to believe in the man who was supposed to have declared that his execution was 'the happiest Minute of my Life'.[90] In London, the curious could flock to Tyburn and watch much less edifying scenes, difficult to conceal in spite of all the precautions and all the entreaties of the officials and the chaplain. In the last third of the eighteenth century, lastly, introspection became more common, even if it often still met with social disapproval. Jean-Jacques Rousseau shocked people by speaking of the uneasy pleasure he felt when being spanked and found himself isolated for having dared to read his *Confessions* aloud in public. Others invented more discreet ways of talking about themselves and about sexuality, by taking the path of sublimation.

The pleasures of the imagination

The pleasures of the imagination became increasingly important in the eighteenth century. They were directly linked in contemporary thinking to the pleasures of the body and of sexuality. Thus, moral decadence was generally associated with the theatre, the opera and dancing. When d'Alembert, in an article on towns in the *Encyclopédie*, regretted that Geneva had banned the theatre, he attracted vitriolic condemnation. In England, reading novels and romances was often associated with immorality. Some French engravings linked it to female masturbation. The fear that the nation might be weakened by luxury and comfort, imported from foreign parts, resurfaced with every major crisis: the Jacobite Rebellion of 1745, the loss of the American colonies, the French Revolution. As elsewhere in Europe, the culture of the upper classes was effectively cosmopolitan and heavily influenced by France. Works by Voltaire were found in 80 per cent of 200 English libraries, according to one study; Rousseau was one of the most popular authors in Britain in the last quarter of the eighteenth century. The elites spoke and read French or bought the translations that were quickly available. Anna Larpent, who kept a private journal from 1773 on, got through more than 440 volumes in 10 years, among them almost as many works of French fiction as English, including Rousseau, Marivaux, Marmontel, Voltaire and 36 plays of Corneille. She read aloud to her daughter or her husband, who did the same for her, and also to the whole household, servants included. History, travel literature and belles-lettres were all then highly popular. Books on these subjects were by far the most borrowed from the Bristol subscription library between 1773 and 1784, with 521 titles taken out a total of 9,439 times, as against 82 works of theology taken out 606 times. On both sides of the Channel, polite society established a common behavioural system defined by the 'arts of conversation'. The fine arts and imaginative literature were central to it, and the aim was to produce refined, pleasing and virtuous persons. This could not fail to give rise to some unease: did the public role not risk destroying personal identity? Lord Shaftesbury feared that this might happen to him as a consequence of his desire to please others: 'Resolve, therefore', he wrote, 'Never to forget Thy Self!'[91]

This context, favourable to the printed word and to the image, encouraged the rapid growth of an artistic appetite that extended beyond the restricted circles of the patrons of the arts, the aristocracy and the court. In France, the royal collection – which there were plans to open to the public under Louis XVI – represented a model for a growing number of rich aesthetes. In London, it would be more accurate to say that their fellows revealed a double passion, for art and for the 'fair sex'. The Society of Dilettanti, originally a convivial group of diners, rapidly became a very wealthy club which patronized modern painters and collected ancient Greek works of art. If all 'connoisseurs' were not libertines, a very large number of them were enthusiasts for eroticism. This was true of the Earl of Sandwich, Frederick, Prince of Wales and the Prince Regent in the days of Napoleon I. The European 'grand tour' was both an intellectual training and a romantic initiation for young aristocrats, especially in southern climes. Mothers feared seeing their sons become the *cicisbeo*, or languishing lover, of some fateful Italian beauty, fallen completely under her spell, like Horace Walpole with Elisabeth Capponi in Florence, between 1739 and 1741. The study of *virtu* was assuredly tainted with sensuality. This was how the future amateurs of female nudes, phallic objects and voluptuous depictions on Greek and Roman vases formed their tastes. Sir Francis Dashwood, Baron le Despencer, one of the founders of the Dilettanti, was painted by Hogarth, in the 1750s, as a priest venerating, not Christ, but a little nude female figure, wholly exposed to his gaze, which suggests a confusion of carnal desire and the desire of the collector. Another member of the Dilettanti, Richard Payne Knight, published and distributed in 1786 *An Account of the Worship of Priapus*, which had a notably provocative frontispiece. Right-minded people choked with indignation as they read ironic asides about the pleasures of the priesthood or saw it suggested that the crucifix was a symbol of the organs of generation. The cult of Priapus, shared by the Catholic Charles Towneley, actually revealed an old dimension of male aristocratic culture that was given a certain respectability at the end of the century by its association with research into the origins of mythologies and religions.[92]

The scandals surrounding the worship of Priapus or the hedonists who made their sensuality into a new religion signal the return of a culture of desire. It was no longer necessary to conceal women's breasts. On the contrary, the feminine bust and the naked body came back into fashion. For a privileged minority, all over Europe, it seems, the distance between the representation and the living flesh shrank, to the point where contemplation of the treasures of the past became the antechamber to erotic excitement. Those who were called debauchees or libertines confused the object and the subject. They appreciated the academic image or the literary account in a 'pornographic' manner, refusing to let their enjoyment be constrained by norms or rules, in contrast to the citizens who practised the moderation of the passions. As for philosophers, writers, artists and the wealthy bourgeois of the big cities, they turned towards sublimated satisfactions, sometimes gently eroticized, but unthreateningly so. The ground was being prepared for the new aesthetic delectation, the contemplation of the work of art becoming the joy of looking, the evocation of the beautiful, a disinterested pleasure.

5

BENEATH THE VICTORIAN VEIL (1800–1960)

If one were forced to choose a single term to characterize the civilization of France and England in the age of the triumphant bourgeoisie, it would have to be 'Victorian'. The notion is not restricted to the reign of Queen Victoria (1837–1901), strictly speaking, if it is defined as a state of mind whose rules and norms weighed down on the English and French populations as a whole. I have decided, therefore, to analyse the phenomenon between 1800 and 1960. The two countries each had their distinguishing features and sometimes significantly different timescales of development. In England, the commercial and industrial middle classes were quicker to make their influence felt than in France. In the latter, the revolutions of 1830 and 1848 and the Commune made for a much more uneven development. Nevertheless, the cultural roots of the principal colonial rivals on the world stage continued to be closely intertwined. With many and often significant variations which are not central to my thesis, both countries discovered and explored the Victorian view of life.

This vision, which had originated in the ideas of the eighteenth-century *philosophes*, conveyed a message of moderation, economy and the management of the instincts. In this way, the bourgeoisie and the middle classes developed an original mind-set. They broke with a religion of fear while clearly distancing themselves from the idle nobility and from the mass of the population, whom they saw as rough, disturbing and dangerous. As well as the philosophical literature and the intellectual sociability of London and Paris, the concept of good manners made a major contribution to the development of this new sensibility. Slowly and surreptitiously, the definition of the Self moved towards an approach to the personality that was based on the control of the impulses, the tyranny of appearances and the division of the world into two spheres, private and public. In both Paris and London, two cities experiencing spectacular growth, such a distinction was as opposed to the promiscuity of the 'dangerous classes' as it was to the largely unconstrained and much more worldly aristocratic model. Among equals, the art of conversation was also that of the dissimulation of the emotions. The bourgeois 'tribes' protected themselves against the dangers of the urban jungle by a double barrier created by the cult of the conjugal home and individual self-control.

The result was a perception of the body and of pleasure that was based on restraint and sobriety, in contrast to the systematic prodigality of the nobility and the lower classes. Between 1800 and 1960, five or six generations in succession confronted a repression of the pleasures of the flesh which generated a discourse of extraordinary virulence; it aimed to make sexuality a shameful disease and caused traumas so severe that it needed Freud and his cohorts of disciples to treat them. A real fear of the loss of vital substance led the right-minded urban minority to elevate medicine into the new religion of modernity. Coitus was declared to be dangerous, even lethal, and prescribed only in small doses. All excess was to be avoided, especially masturbation, which, quite simply, led 'patients' to their death. The worm was in the bud, however, because erotic duplicity, in accord with the masculine double standard, was practised by the good and worthy father of the family who went out at night in search of the delights of venal love.

Perhaps the Victorian age would be better characterized by the image of the veil, modest but begging to be raised, rather than by a firm and fixed morality. A journey through the looking glass shows just how intense the taste for pleasure remained. Brought up according to the strict morality of his class, 'Walter', pseudonym of the extraordinary narrator of My Secret Life, who claimed to have known more than 1,200 women, was both direct heir of the debauchees or libertines and also cultural intermediary, because he learned popular lore in the arms of maidservants, farm girls and London prostitutes. The amateurs of eroticism turned to pornography to assuage their passions, the pleasure only enhanced by its being forbidden. The peasants and the workers, caricatured as beasts thirsting for sex, alcohol and violence, at least displayed their own significant characteristics in this sphere. The history of pleasure, lastly, is not linear. Cycles of repression alternated with outbursts of sexual laxity during the century and a half under consideration here. The principal turning points came at the end of the nineteenth century, when the medical discourse radically changed, and in the first half of the twentieth century, when the middle classes, then economically and socially triumphant, saw cracks gradually appear in the rigid morality they professed and when they lost control of medical knowledge in the face of the general advance of hedonism, including in their own ranks. Nothing can ever completely control the sexual urges, the body always demanding its dues. Societies impose, or try to impose; human beings dispose, adapt, make do and mend and invent.

Controlling sex

The concept of bourgeoisie is multiform and difficult to apprehend. In the ambitious synthesis of Peter Gay, often more descriptive than explanatory, the word is at once a term of reproach and a source of self-respect. In France, England and Germany in the nineteenth century, those who recognized themselves to be bourgeois felt a sense of moral superiority with regard to the decadent aristocracy and the respectable working class, but were deeply hurt by the sharp 'bourgeoisophobe' criticisms of the intellectual avant-garde represented by Gustave Flaubert or Friedrich Nietzsche.[1] Gay also rightly points out that their addiction to collecting works of art was 'an emblem of individualism triumphant', and that the 'hypertrophy of inwardness' developed within them an increasing control of their aggressiveness, which was at its most conspicuous in sport. He is much less convincing when he tries to rehabilitate the idea of sexual pleasure within the legitimate couple. The possibility cannot be denied, but nothing proves that it was a dominant tendency. The example of the American Mabel Loomis Todd, which is presented as proof, is puzzling, because, although she certainly sought sexual pleasure in the arms of her husband, she indulged in it with even greater ardour in adultery, turning the masculine double standard on its head to her own advantage. The ideal aspired to at this social level was one of 'moderation, probity and monogamy', which distinguished it from the aristocracy and the lower classes, at least until the changes of the 1880s.[2] In short, the Western bourgeoisies seem to conform to the civilizing process, even if the reality was often more complex and more varied.[3]

Social roles

Paradoxically, the emphasis placed on the personality only brought out the full importance of the group. It was not enough to be born a bourgeois. It was just as important to be recognized as a member of the 'tribe' of reference.[4] For this, one had to acquire, within the family and in selected schools, an art of detail, combined with a specific technique of self-control, so as to demonstrate in life the mastery of a public and a private role. Thus individuality was strongly affirmed, in the context of a very powerful culture, as if an actor with a strong personality were to take on a preordained role that left him little room for manoeuvre. The obligatory code was that of secrecy, applicable both in the business world and within the family. It was the need to keep a constant watch on oneself, so as always to behave in the way that was expected by others, that led to the development of self-consciousness.[5] The 'tyrannies of intimacy' thus led the nineteenth-century middle classes to valorize a 'culture of personality' – the first step towards the 'intimist idolatry' that prevails at the beginning of the twenty-first century. It was not at all a withdrawal from the public sphere but simply a strategy for adapting to a philosophy of restraint placing particular value on the economy of the impulses. The norms of good manners erected into an absolute and self-evident rule the superiority of civility over the savage and bestial nature of the primitive human being or the coarseness of the peasantry and the working class. The admirable man portrayed in the *Usages du Monde*, a famous manual of good manners attributed to the baronne Staffe in 1899, should have the ability to make you forget that he had a body.[6]

The effect on respectable women was even greater, at a time when the fear of involuntarily or chaotically expressing one's bodily needs or personal feelings, even within the family circle, was general. A German physician, Dr Carl Ludwig of the University of Marburg, related 'green sickness', the result of feminine constipation, to the fear of accidentally farting after eating, leading to a constant tensing of the buttocks. 'White sickness' allegedly afflicted women who did not get enough sun because they were afraid to go out, for fear of being spied on by strangers. It is surely more likely that they were primarily suffering from the masculine pressure on wives to stay within the home. Feminine hysteria, a subject of consuming interest to nineteenth-century scholars, makes sense in the context of a familial intimacy marked by constraints so heavy that they easily brought on depressions.[7]

The hypertrophy of the bourgeois Self, we should be clear, was not a highly personal self-expression, which was the preserve of artists and writers who disclaimed their origins, such as Flaubert. Subjects were urged to reveal their full potential within the confines of a well-defined social role, not to let themselves be led by their needs, instincts, desires or passions.

The new medical religion

The desire to keep sexuality under close control was a product of such ideas. In the nineteenth century, medicine took a decisive step in this direction by assuming the power to prescribe and to guide in the name of a body of knowledge elevated into a new religion, with its chapels, its heretics and its unbelievers. It acquired and strengthened a monopoly of the bodily phenomena, while the established churches increasingly lost their influence in this sphere.[8] The weakening of spiritual constraints, especially in France after the Revolution, and even more the new ideas about a happiness accessible on earth, had freed up a vast space for belief by the second half of the eighteenth century. Alone in speaking rationally about the mysteries of the body, death and the orgasm, medicine carved out an empire for itself by responding to the anxieties of a cultivated and wealthy public, with all the more ease in that it was not, strictly speaking, necessary to abandon one's faith in order to adhere to its precepts.

Medical authority was not based on scientific fact alone. Its practitioners were also fathers, husbands, brothers and sons, usually from the middle classes. They bent reality to the cultural needs of their universe of reference. Recycling the old sense of Christian guilt regarding sexuality, they reformulated it in the form of a health regime. They warned against excessive vital expenditure, confidently taking over from the confessors and resolutely directing the private lives of their contemporaries. In particular, they advised moderation in conjugal relations. This was the case with the prolific O. Q. S. Fowler and with the hydropathist T. L. Nichols, as we see from the English editions of the latter's *Esoteric Anthropology* after 1873. Women, he wrote, were 'full of ardour' for several days a month, but relations should cease during lactation and, of course, during menstruation. He also advised avoiding excitement, dancing, immodest dress, kissing and caresses. Many wives, he claimed, were incapable of achieving sexual enjoyment in the corrupt modern world and the efforts of husbands to make them take a more active role in lovemaking risked injuring their nervous system. Further, he warned men over the age of 50 that the joys of the flesh were extremely exhausting and liable to produce paralysis or apoplexy.[9] His opinions, which were ordinary, indeed rather on the moderate side in his day, were based on a secularization of the fear of sin, translated into advice on physical hygiene. The fear of disease and death replaced that of eternal damnation. It caused deep anxiety, which medical science claimed to allay by counsels of moderation, a sort of 'libidinal economy' before the expression was invented. The doctors were only transposing into the physical domain the dominant bourgeois thesis to the effect that saving made it possible to draw maximum dividends from the prudent accumulation of capital. Thus they defined sexuality as a disruptive force, potentially dangerous to the health, which must at all costs be watched over and contained.[10] This idea went back a very long way, to the medieval monastic tradition. It expressed a fear of uncontrollable sensuality, directly linked to the representation of the Self and of society. The orgasm could evoke for the individual a loss of self-control and become the emblem of the disorder of the world if pejorative moral or scientific formulations aggravated this feeling. The inner turmoil produced fantasies about the genital organs, and about the Other of the opposite sex or a different race. Art and medicine took up these ideas and turned them into the dominant discourse on sexuality.

In the nineteenth century, the necessity of female sexual pleasure to successful conception was gradually questioned.[11] Some, like Dr William Acton (1813–75), author in 1841 of *A Practical Treatise on Diseases of the Urinary and Generative Organs in Both Sexes*, even claimed that normal wives lacked sexual desires and simply submitted to their husband, for his pleasure alone. 'Love of home, children, and domestic duties', declared Acton, 'are the only passions they feel.'[12] The best way of reducing sexual desire within the couple was for the wife to conceive every second year, because during the following nine months she would feel little sexual excitement. Acton seems here to be fulfilling an old masculine dream of almost total control over a wife who was regularly pregnant or nursing. Not all his fellows shared his views. A more common belief was that woman were not innately frigid, but that their appetites were dormant and in need of awakening to make them 'become vibrantly alive', which it was easy be do. Men, for their part, were ardent but clumsy and impetuous, like orang-utans trying to play a violin, in the famous image of Balzac.[13]

Neither the abandonment of the theory of the humours nor the decline of the sense of sin prevented doctors from adopting the thesis that sexuality was extremely dangerous and quite different for men and for women, though with very different arguments, it is true. Men were by their nature 'hot rabbits'; women, who were colder, performed their duties as wife and mother without undue difficulty, attaining satisfaction of the senses if their partner knew how to bring this about with tenderness and delicacy. The picture would be idyllic but for one unfortunate feature: conjugal harmony and sexual moderation were accessible to men only at the price of the regular use of prostitutes. Was it not necessary for them to be initiated in youth, then regularly to purge a 'hydraulic' machinery under permanent pressure, the chaste wife being unsuitable for the purpose? This double standard testifies to masculine domination, because wives had no moral right to seek pleasure other than in the arms of their lord and master.

Nudity and body hair

The sexual repression of the Victorian age was firmly implanted in reality. There is abundant evidence of the control of the body. Modesty was one of the great productions of the age. People had bathed in the nude up to the reign of Louis XIV (1643–1715), but half-glimpsed flesh became shocking in the nineteenth century. French judicial records provide many examples. A weaver from Meuse, for example, claimed he could not endure a young neighbour walking about in a room without curtains or shutters, her breasts visible under her chemise: 'I was so shocked that I thought, for a moment, of closing the shutters.' He may not have been entirely sincere, but he was at least articulating the norm that should be observed, rather than extolling the charms of the young woman. Total nudity was redolent of the brothel. Virtuous women were ashamed to undress in front of their husbands. In the 1930s, one such confided her feelings to an abbé, asking him if a husband had the right to demand this, or force her to dance with him naked. In Great Britain, total nudity during sexual relations was regarded as the ultimate in naughtiness throughout the nineteenth century. For pornographic writers, the erotic climax came, after the most extravagant sexual games, when the man lifted the last veil of feminine modesty, the lady's chemise, at the end of the century.[14] On both sides of the Channel, fantasies on the subject were many and powerful. In France, prosecutions of works that showed or suggested nudity, deemed to be obscene, increased in number. A report of 1884 criticized an engraving, *La Méprise*, which showed a woman in a shift, on a bed, her left hand between her thighs, the tail of a cat close by.[15] England was no different. Here, nudity took refuge in mythological paintings, a sort of substitute for the forbidden. Lord Leighton, president of the Royal Academy, who died a bachelor in 1896, pursued feminine beauty in the sublimated form of Venus, Ariadne or Andromeda, not without provoking the ire of some churchmen. The pronounced English taste for depicting very young girls was due to the fact that they had no pubic hair, the height of indecency, because it recalled the animal nature of the human being. It is claimed that Ruskin, an art critic accustomed to juvenile female bodies, was unable to consummate his marriage to Effie Gray due to the shock of seeing her adult pubis. It may not be true, but it is not impossible. Visiting the gallery of the Royal Academy in 1868, the very year that Leighton painted his *Ariadne Abandoned by Theseus*, Lewis Carroll, the discerning author of *Alice in Wonderland* (1865), notes that he had been particularly charmed by the canvases portraying little girls, whom he also liked to photograph. In any case, the sexual exploitation of young girls was one of the principal fantasies of Victorian England, a veritable and well-documented cult.[16] One anonymous Londoner admitted that it gave him a special thrill. He indulged in it one day with delight and cruelty in equal measure, after rejecting the advances of a woman who was selling him the services of a child and who had tried to get him to change his mind. 'What the devil did you bring me here for? – it was for her, not you', he shouted. When she replied simply, 'I have hair', he peremptorily retorted: 'I like a cunt without hair', before forcing himself on the little girl without regard for her sufferings.[17]

The prohibitions led, in reaction, to transgressive writings and behaviour. British fetishists took a particular interest in women's naked feet and legs. Prudery went so far as to have table and piano legs covered, which gave a peculiar erotic charge to any glimpses of flesh. Speaking of the subject in a magazine, even at the cost of contortions to stay within the law, was enough to arouse the erotic imagination of the reader. In 1879–80 *The Pearl* pointed out that there was no country in the world where ladies were more curious about their legs than England – because there was nowhere on earth where they had greater reason to lift their petticoats to avoid dirtying them, thanks to the famous English weather. One can only imagine the shock felt by appalled readers of the highly respectable *Daily Telegraph*, victim of a misprint, when they were told that 'women's tights must not be pushed too far, nor stretched too wide'. The owner, Joseph Moses Levy, promptly decided to create the post of chief reviser to prevent such an obscenity from occurring again.

Any verbal reference to the lower half of the body or its functions was then considered a sign of a bad education. In England, discreet allusion was the rule: a prostitute was never a whore, but called an 'academician', or a 'cat' if she was drunk; 'glue' meant venereal disease, a vulva was called 'leather' and 'to be in his altitude' was used of someone who was drunk. Female breasts were referred to as 'globes' or 'hemispheres', or as a 'milk-shop', a 'feeding bottle' or a 'baby's public house', which at least describes their nursing function. When John Thomas met Fanny, Mary Jane or Lady Jane, the penis had entered the vagina. To 'urinate' was to 'plant a sweet pea', 'shake hands with an old friend' or, more often, to 'spend a penny'.[18]

Other evidence reveals the imperatives of morality. In France under the Third Republic, novelists and doctors constantly urged women over 40 to renounce the pleasures of the flesh. In 1926, a mayor of Yonne was surprised to find a widow, 'a woman of 50, lavishing sweet nothings on a man of 45'. As for kissing on the mouth, it scandalized most French men and women throughout the nineteenth century. In Yonne, a judge referred without comment to the exposure of a penis before a young peasant girl, but made a big issue of an obscenity he found unacceptable: 'He put his tongue in her mouth!'[19]

Sexuality, a shameful, even fatal, sickness

Many Victorians would have liked copulation to be a criminal offence, it has been claimed.[20] Numerous doctors regarded it as, at the very least, a serious illness, and the cause of a deep if vague anxiety, even among those who did not indulge in the depravities denounced by the censorious. Sex was taboo, shameful, disturbing and difficult to deal with. The collective disapproval was primarily focused on masturbatory practices, which were denounced in quite terrifying terms by the medical profession. The young, especially boys, were inundated with distressing images. Pornography and the use of prostitutes – the former confined to a small number of consumers, the latter common and taking many forms – were two of the chief ways of relieving anxiety. Even more discreet, but on the increase, perversions like flagellation, sadism and masochism testify to a growth of neuroses at the end of the nineteenth century. Freud came at the right moment to offer his services to the European middle classes, who no longer knew which way to turn and who begged, at the dawn of the twentieth century, if not for sexual liberation, at least for a little consolation.

The age of anxiety

Sexuality has a frightening dimension. Cultures can seek to play it down or, on the contrary, make it a central plank in their discourse on the social tie. Western Europe in the nineteenth century opted for the latter. The age of industrialization, of optimism, progress and science, of the emergence of socialist utopias and the growing rejection of superstitions was also the age of torment in the sphere of physical pleasure. Many Anglo-Saxon historians emphasize this dimension, which has received little attention in France.[21] Yet the ideas and practices of the period were very similar and equally traumatizing on both sides of the Channel, especially in the case of masturbation. It is possible, however, that a lighter touch in all things erotic persisted in French civilization, in spite of the spread of Victorian norms. Further research is needed.

Imperial England had a particular fear of sex because people dreaded its uncontrollable and destructive power. The Victorian age was an 'age of anxiety', when anything associated with carnal desire was perpetually surrounded by prohibitions and confusion, even by a sense of danger, ruin and disaster, produced by the feeling of living in a world of pain and difficulty.[22] The cultural and social consequences were particularly serious for women.[23] The unease derived essentially from a sort of perversion of the ideology of accumulation peculiar to the middle classes. It expressed a more general fear of loss, dispossession and poverty. Thus the most common English colloquialism for the orgasm until the end of the nineteenth century was 'to spend'. The notion lingered, even when the expression was displaced by the modern term 'to come'. The medicine of the age saw the body as a machine, so much so that male ejaculation was seen as a mechanical movement resulting in a loss of substance and power. This helps explain the insistence on the need for sexual economy. The world of pornography offered an exactly inverted image by creating a utopia, a 'pornotopia', of erotic plenty, where nature assumed a gigantic female form and enthusiasts worshipped an immense erect god penis. Such a fantasy could only be conceived by people suffering from extreme privation, by men literally famished for sex.[24] The authors and consumers of the genre were only a minority, admittedly, but the symptom is nevertheless revealing as to the passions concealed beneath the modest Victorian veils. It is a commonplace to insist on the hypocrisy of the middle classes. Their members must, however, have been conscious of the existence of a double reality to practise this duplicity with such consistency. They were not performing their roles for themselves alone; they also wanted to appear good, noble and pure, in their vocabulary, their heart and their deeds, in the eyes of posterity.[25] In other words, they were posing for history!

Through the looking glass, the frustrations were immense. Society remained deeply constrained. Moral rigour was upheld by the law. In France, divorce had not survived the revolutionary period. In England it was very rare in the nineteenth century: 7,321 cases are recorded between 1858 and 1887, that is, 50 times fewer than in the United States between 1867 and 1886. The Matrimonial Causes Act of 1857 officially established a double standard of morality, because an adulterous man could be divorced only if he was guilty of another offence, whereas infidelity by a wife was in itself legal grounds for divorce.[26] The paucity of cases underplays the practical results of the Act, but it calmly transcribed the fundamental unwritten rule to the effect that the respectable wife must sacrifice any desires she might have for the good of her husband and children. Only the man had the right to a double life, his lapses, though ethically blameworthy, enjoying both tacit and legal indulgence, in particular in the case of the use of prostitutes. It was the same in France. A 'new demand for prostitution' developed from the 1860s, which was the result of *'the numerical growth and above all the increased wealth of social groups within the bourgeoisie'*.[27] Dr William Acton, who had studied in France, found the situation comparable in both countries. While disapproving of the use of prostitutes on moral grounds, he took an active part in the discussions that led to the Contagious Diseases Acts of 1864, 1866 and 1869. As a result, in areas with concentrations of soldiers and sailors, prostitutes were subject to medical supervision and obliged to accept treatment at government expense if they suffered from venereal disease.[28]

The official attitude adopted by the English and French authorities was a sort of 'civilized morality' based on twin pillars: the conspiracy of silence and the double standard of behaviour.[29] The 1850s and 1860s were its apogee. In spite of the growing protests and the numerous projects for its eradication, prostitution was openly on display in both London and Paris. In France it burst onto the scene in great literature around 1876–9. Brothels make frequent appearances in the work of Joris-Karl Huysmans, Edmond de Goncourt, Émile Zola and Guy de Maupassant. *Marthe*, *La Fille Élisa*, *Nana*, *La Fin de Lucie Pellegrin* and *Boule de Suif* were published at almost the same time, while the comte d'Haussonville signed articles devoted to debauchery and vice in the *Revue des Deux Mondes*. Though this has been seen as a political victory over censorship at a time when the Republic was being consolidated,[30] it primarily marked the triumphant affirmation of the masculine double standard, more openly proclaimed than under the Second Empire. The whole of Europe was implicated. In 1886, the German psychiatrist Richard von Krafft-Ebing (1840–1902) published *Psychopathia Sexualis*. This book, which became famous as the first medical classification of sexual disorders, openly defends the theory that 'the man who is ruled by his sexuality can find satisfaction everywhere' (a clear allusion to prostitution), while the woman is 'tied to one man', especially in the upper classes; Krafft-Ebing also observed that 'love is for a man almost always only an episode next to which he has many and important interests, while for a woman it is the main object of her life'.[31]

Far from being typically British,[32] such a sexual differentiation of genders is a Western invention of the nineteenth-century middle classes. Replacing the notion of sin with an equally strict lay morality, upheld by medical authority and by the law, they firmly asserted the special rights of the male by separating procreation and pleasure, to his greater advantage. The main innovation was the distinction between two diametrically opposed types of woman, good and bad, whereas the Christian moralists of the past conceived only of one unique female, sinful and lustful by nature, both angel and devil. Was this simply an adaptation of patriarchal power to new social, economic and religious conditions? It is more useful to ask why and how such conceptions were able gradually to spread to other social categories.

It was probably towards the middle of the nineteenth century that they became more widespread, at the time of the economic and political triumphs of the European bourgeoisie. The morality specific to one group then became a system of power based on medical knowledge that spread to the rest of the population. Its success was probably due to the fundamental ambivalence of the message. Though sacred, and acceptable within the context of legitimate marriage, sexuality was seen as dirty, disgusting and dangerous when carried to excess, in masturbation, adultery – pejoratively called 'criminal conversation' in England – or prostitution. Everybody could recognize a little of themselves in this, from the libertines thirsting after eroticism to the most moralistic believers, by way of the working classes who knew all about the realities of venal love and venereal disease. As Freud had not yet plumbed the depths of the unconscious, the classification of women into two groups, the pure and the depraved, mothers and whores in a sense, also served to reassure men by giving them the feeling that it was easy to understand the mysteries of the other half of humanity. The explanation was all the more acceptable because it continued the Christian view that opposed the immaculate Virgin Mary to Eve the temptress.

Touchstone of the whole structure, the domination exercised over the weaker sex was visible at every level. The ideal modest wife, maternal and almost saintly, assured the repose of the weary capitalist warrior by confining herself to the home, refusing any guilty passion and using her body with him wholly lawfully but in moderation. The thinkers of the age – doctors leading the way – increasingly described the worthy woman as a creature without urgent sexual needs or desires.[33] Available, loving, faithful: no male had ever dared dream of such bliss in previous centuries! The exact opposite of the virtuous wife was the libidinous whore. She collected and concentrated in herself all the negative features previously attributed to women as a whole. A putrid creature whose odour indicated moral corruption, she literally had a bad smell. Further, she had something of ordure about her, because she helped the social body to expel the superfluous seminal fluid which risked causing it to rot: Dr Fiaux spoke in this connection of a 'seminal drain'. Some nineteenth-century scholars, like Alexandre Parent-Duchâtelet, even on occasion likened her flesh to that of a corpse.[34] Pestilence, putrefaction and decomposition: these are precisely the features attributed to the devil in the sixteenth and seventeenth centuries.[35] The stink of the harlot conjured up a whole series of ancient, vague and active existential anxieties connected with death. She could not but be viewed negatively, as a result, even though many contemporaries contemptuously accepted that she rendered a great service to the community. That essential feature of Western culture, the morbid dimension of sexuality, is hinted at here. A convenient scapegoat, the prostitute now carried alone the burden of original sin, liberating her chaste bourgeois sister from the burden of desire. With the whore, the pleasure was uneasy, certainly, but intense, and she knew how to take her own. She remained, nevertheless, fundamentally one of the dominated, the most despised sector of femininity; but also the most lusted-after, she who sold herself at the market price.

All these various constructions of meaning engendered many frustrations and some serious traumas. Victorian anxiety developed as strongly as Victorian sexual repression. Women were the worst affected, but virile sexuality was far from easy to handle. The law of silence, the need to assume different personalities in the home and in the brothel and the unease created by the moral conscience or by religion could not but be disturbing to those affected. To cut a fine figure in all circumstances, as the code of manners required, was not easy. The rapid growth of transgressions and perversions, especially sadism and masochism, at the end of the nineteenth century testifies to this. Many people developed more ordinary neuroses. It is not surprising that the age of psychoanalysis began at precisely this point, after two generations of rigorous moral constraint and self-control, inculcated from infancy in order to entrench the masculine and feminine ideals. Freud and Krafft-Ebing began to treat people who did not dare to use their genital organs or who felt traumatized when they did, believing they might die of a surfeit of pleasure.

Semen wasted, death assured: the great fear of masturbation

As it did to the Christians of earlier centuries, the body seemed dangerous to the Victorians. This was not because it turned people away from eternal salvation but because it constituted a capital, a mechanism to be managed to maximum advantage, or, as Balzac lamented in his novel of that name (*Peau de Chagrin*), published in 1831, a 'magic skin' that shrank with the passage of time. The education of the senses was, therefore, an education in saving. Medical thinking fostered a fantasy of loss leading inexorably to death. Such was the fate of a man who took an aphrodisiac containing Spanish fly. 'Driven mad, he approached his wife 87 times during the night; he also spilled a lot of sperm in his bed: Cabrol, summoned next morning to treat him, saw this new Hercules, far more famous than he whose exploits had amazed Antiquity, achieve three further successive ejaculations by rubbing himself on the foot of his bed. Death soon intervened to terminate this erotic crisis.'[36] This tale was taken seriously by many contemporaries. They were firmly persuaded that erotic excess was a sort of mortal sickness. The mercantile and industrial age was simply embroidering on the theme of the infinite danger of pleasure and reforging the old link established in the West between carnal pleasure, pain and death.

The sense of touch, directly linked to sensuality, was regarded with deep suspicion. The art of the Renaissance had already invested it with an alarming quality by representing it, in the figure of Eros or Cupid, as the port of entry not only to ineffable joys but also to terrible suffering. A painting of Agnolo Bronzino, *Venus, Cupid, Folly and Time*, shows Cupid kissing his mother, Venus, on the mouth, his right hand on her left breast.[37] This lascivious pose is emphasized by the signs of lust and decay, evoked by the masks of age and disease at the feet of the goddess, the scorpion's fang on her left and the presence of Vulcan, her cuckolded husband. The episode has been interpreted as an allusion to the transmission of syphilis by sexual contact. Believed to darken the skin, the fatal illness, or *morbus gallicus*, is incarnated by a black man with his head in his hands, in an attitude of despair, behind Cupid's back.[38] In the following centuries, the pox continued to be closely associated with sexual excess, for example in the work of Hogarth. The anonymous English treatise *Onania*, of about 1710,[39] followed by the work of Tissot on the same subject in 1758, focused the dread on masturbation, which became a cause of physical disaster. So as to accentuate the dramatic contrast between a healthy skin and that of the 'invalid', the successive editions of Tissot in the nineteenth century used pictures.[40] In 1836, *L'Onanisme; ou dissertation physique sur les maladies produites par la masturbation. Nouvelle édition annotée d'après les nouvelles observations par les docteurs Gottlier, Vogler, etc.* (*Onanism; or a physical dissertation on the illnesses produced by masturbation. New edition annotated on the basis of the new observations of the doctors Gottlier, Vogler, etc.*) offered two graphic images: in the first, a vigorous and dashing young man of fashion struts his stuff: 'He was young, handsome and a picture of health.' In the second, he lies on his bed of pain, naked, his flesh bearing the terrible marks of his vices: 'He battles with death.'[41]

Masturbation obsessed the doctors of the nineteenth century. This resulted in the artificial construction of an obsessional pathology comparable to the collective witchcraft fantasy which had been responsible for so many deaths in the sixteenth and seventeenth centuries. In both cases, a profoundly detestable Other was produced, morbid because of their sexual deviance, doomed to destruction by the dominant scholarship of the age. The witch was accused of giving herself carnally to the Devil by abandoning the Christian faith, masturbators of abandoning the virtue of moderation to the point of exhausting their vital forces and dying an early death. In different cultural packaging, each in tune with the dominant ideas of its day, the same moral lesson underlay the argument: sexuality is dangerous and infinitely destructive if not strictly controlled. Yet it is difficult to know at all accurately what concrete effects such ideas had. All we have are the anguished confidences of transgressors who feared the consequences of their acts. The young Gladstone, a student at Oxford, noted in his journal for 1 April 1831 that the solitary vice, to which he referred only in very veiled terms, constantly returned.

He wanted to obtain God's help, because he feared for his salvation. Henri-Frédéric Amiel, who feared he was dying as a result of such practices, expressed his anguish on 12 June 1841: 'Nothing is more horrible than to feel one's life fatally seeping away, a few nights deprive me of several years of life . . . I see myself dying.' Next day, he tries to reason with himself: 'Above all, I must live, that is, put a stop to these losses; a single emission, according to Tissot, is equivalent to four ounces of blood. My vein is thus open; not to make an effort, to let go, that would be suicide, because the result is certain.'[42] In both cases, education played on the terror in the attempt to dissuade the young men from wasting their substance by indulging in self-abuse. Religious or secular, the pedagogic discourse was based on a medical imagery that was truly repressive.

In the nineteenth century, childhood evoked an image both of purity and of latent corruption. In England, the former found expression in the cult of the little girl without pubic hair, or in the story of *Little Lord Fauntleroy*, by Frances Hodgson Burnett, which appeared in 1886. At the opposite pole were the children who polluted and degraded themselves, fell ill and bore on their skin the 'stigmata' of their condition. Invented by Charcot for this very condition, the term implicitly referred to the *stigmata diaboli*, the marks left by the devil on the body of witches, in counterpoint to the sacred wounds of Christ. The internal disorder thus appeared on the flesh. On 20 January 1904, the famous medical journal *The Lancet* published an article accompanied by a picture that showed the damaged skin of an hysterical child.[43] The obsession with 'repeated touching' led to the gravity of the consequences being distinguished according to sex. In the case of little girls, the doctors contented themselves with evoking a pre-defloration, described as a withering in moral terms. 'The habits of self-abuse have for a long time wizened her organs', we read in a medical report for the court of Meuse, in 1876, referring to the daughter of a gas-worker of Ligny. In boys, the consequences were more serious, such tendencies indicating, it was believed, a real mental imbalance. A paedophile imprisoned in Paris in 1876 had probably been reduced to this state, explained the expert consulted, because 'the genital perversions seem to have appeared in him at the age of 14 or 15. He had very actively indulged in onanism up to the age of 16.' The magistrates adopted exactly the same language and identical arguments. Though unanimously and unquestioningly condemned among the bourgeoisie, masturbation seems to have been condemned much less systematically and more selectively among the working classes. The practice was observed without undue concern in the very young and seems to have been tolerated as a temporary phase among the unmarried. It should, however, remain discreet. Children who touched themselves in public, even just to scratch, were usually reprimanded and punished by their parents. Exhibitionists were not seen as mentally deranged, but they shocked people by rejecting the norms of modesty and were universally condemned. As for the husband who pleasured himself in full view of his wife, he often deeply wounded her by making her feel she was of no account.[44]

The offensive against masturbation was probably so aggressive because it was so ineffective. Boys and girls of all social classes masturbated spontaneously before adolescence without feeling any guilt, unhesitatingly admitting it in court if they were questioned. To the Argenteuil judge who asked her, in 1873, to describe her 'habits', a little girl of 10, the daughter of well-off farmers, replied that she knew that many of her friends did it and that her uncle had taught her how. In 1891, an Avignon magistrate who questioned a peasant girl scarcely any older about the fact that she was no longer a virgin received this reply: 'It's me who did it to myself when I was little. I rubbed myself sometimes with a finger and one day I tried to put a carrot in my genitals, but I couldn't get it in, because it hurt.' Flaubert describes the collective games in the lavatories of his college, where boys smoked and 'jerked off'. Some scholars even claim that the literature denouncing such perversions was, in reality, a dubious genre, its hidden aim being 'the sexual stimulation of the reader';[45] in fact, the sort of book you read with one hand! The hypothesis seems excessive if applied to the intentions of the authors. It is less so when one considers how they were read, because, under the *ancien régime*, medical treatises were often used as manuals of instruction in forbidden practices. With the intention of enabling couples to procreate in the most favourable circumstances, they described in detail the positions and types of behaviour likely to discourage conception. *Aristotle's Master-Piece*, for example, advised men not to withdraw too quickly after coitus and women to avoid moving or sneezing. It was hardly difficult to discover contraceptive practices by reversing the advice.[46] Paradoxically, they were almost the only permissible books from which one could learn about carnal pleasure.

The anti-masturbation campaign was the result of a terrible fantasy of loss. It expressed both a fascination for and a fear of the body, a morbid curiosity about what lay beneath the surface of the skin. Many were appalled when what they found was the spectacle of corruption and death. Sex went hand in hand with moral decadence and physical decline. The vignette on the title page of the French version of Fracastoro's *Syphilis: poème en deux chants* (1840), by Auguste Barthélemy, shows a young man at the knee of a beautiful woman of fashion; she holds one hand out to him, raising with the other a flawless feminine mask which conceals her true, pug-nosed face. In 1888, Jack the Ripper murdered street prostitutes in London. The police dared reveal to the public pictures only of the mutilated faces of the victims, although they had been eviscerated and sometimes had their breasts cut off, with such skill that the perpetrator was suspected of being a doctor.[47] Never, perhaps, had the intimate link between sex and death been treated with so much indulgence as in passing from the register of sin to that of morbid bourgeois eroticism. Around 1900, lust, pleasure and death were inextricably interwoven in romantic love, in life, in art and in pornographic literature. The first cinema vamp, Musidora, in Louis Feuillade's *Les Vampires* (*The Vampires*: 1915–16), was heiress to the perverse heroines who had exhausted men in a trice by literally sucking their blood. In *La Maîtresse et l'esclave* (*The Master and the Slave-Girl*: 1903), Anne, the little street girl, drives Georges to the tomb by masturbating him with 'various procedures which stupefy'. *Enfilade des perles* (*String of Pearls*), signed Georges Lesbos, portrays a countess who got the better of a 'doughty fucker' by 'draining him of energy, bleeding his virility dry'.[48]

The terrifying medical morality was directed primarily at adolescence, an age recently 'invented' in the big cities. It expressed the anxiety of adults in the face of the rising tide of young men. Even though middle-class boys were entrusted to the care of institutions of confinement – schools, colleges, universities and boarding schools – the moral danger was still not dispelled, because such concentrations of male juveniles risked encouraging the growth of homosexuality and masturbation. The latter unleashed a 'great fear' which lasted from 1760 until the 1880s, not entirely disappearing even then.[49]

Published in Paris in 1830, *Le Livre sans titre* (*The Book Without a Title*) illustrated a quotation from Tissot: 'This baleful habit causes the death of more young people than all the diseases together.' Sixteen coloured engravings retrace the ineluctable progress of the evil on the body of an adolescent. In the first he is pink and spruce, with a fine head of curly hair: 'He was young and handsome; he was his mother's pride and joy.' By the second, 'he had debased himself . . . soon he bore the penalty for his vice, old before his time . . . his back bent'. By the fifth, he could no longer walk and his teeth were rotting; they fell out in the sixth. In later engravings, he spat blood and lost his hair, was covered with pustules and consumed by a slow fever, burned with pain and became delirious. Finally, 'at 17 years of age, he died, in terrible agony'.[50] At the beginning of the century, Dr Bernard devoted a room in his Parisian chambers entirely to onanism, evoked by wax figures: 'a young man close to death and in the final stages of emaciation through masturbation'; another 'become hideous' for the same reason; a pretty, healthy young woman, then the same woman 'six months later, now very ugly, thin and worn out as a result of indulging in the solitary vices, from which she had the good fortune to be cured by marriage'. This terror with pedagogical intent was manipulated by doctors of all kinds. It took over the manuals of hygiene intended for a wide readership. In England, that of Samuel La'mert declared masturbation to be 'the surest, if not the most direct, route towards death'; it was translated into French by 1847. Auguste Debay warned readers of his *Hygiène et physiologie du mariage* (*Hygiene and Physiology of Marriage*) against the ravages caused by the 'baleful habit' of self-abuse, because 'the victims are hideous to the eye; they inspire disgust and pity'. A huge bookshop success, with 172 editions between 1848 and 1888, more than 200,000 copies were printed.[51] English readers were similarly warned by the pedagogues of the terrible dangers they risked. In 1858, Frederic William Farrar, a master at Harrow School, devoted a novel to the story of a handsome and robust young man who gradually succumbed to the vice, *Eric, or Little by Little*. The hero progressed from trivial to more serious faults, then crowned them all by 'it', masturbation, though never named as such, finally perishing from its effects, in spite of repenting. By the time of its author's death, in 1903, the book was in its 36th edition, having fed the fears and perhaps also the fantasies of several generations of young men and adults. In the last decades of the nineteenth century, 'masturbatory insanity' was talked about in England. The alienist Havelock Ellis (1859–1939) even claimed that fatuity usually derived from the 'debility of the brain and nervous system' caused by the pernicious habit of masturbation.[52]

But how to eradicate a hidden vice? The doctors vied with each other in the imaginativeness of their solutions. The simplest and most common means, recommended by Dr Simon in 1827 in his *Traité d'hygiène appliquée à l'éducation de la jeunesse* (*Treatise of Hygiene Applied to the Education of the Young*), was to tie the patient's hands to the bed bars overnight. In 1851, Dr William Acton spoke of the 'usual procedure', which consisted of wrapping up the hands or employing a sort of straitjacket. A wide variety of more elaborate devices were also in use, although the therapeutic consensus was less complete in their case. Their aim, according to a medical dictionary of 1881, was to imprison the female or male genitals so as 'to prevent them being touched by a hand, while allowing the discharge of the menses and urine'. All sorts of pants, bandages and belts were invented. In 1860, a Parisian 'surgical bazaar' offered a wide range of methods designed to present 'an impenetrable barrier against the solitary habits condemned by religion and society'. In England, in his *On Spermatorrhoea* (1872), J. Laws Milton described preventive methods that consisted of waking the sleeper by an alarm that sounded if the penis was touched, or exerting painful pressure on it. One of his brainwaves resembles nothing so much as an instrument of torture: a ring for the penis with four spikes on the inside that caused a sharp pain in case of an erection. In a catalogue of 1904, the Parisian house of Mathieu offered various devices against onanism, including metal belts reminiscent of chastity belts, for both boys and girls, which 'are also made in the form of hermetically sealed pants'. Shackles could be added for the arms or legs and, ultimate refinement, 'metal mittens... for the hands'.[53] There were even doctors who advocated surgery, for both sexes. During a debate at the Surgical Society in Paris, on 13 January 1864, Broca announced that he had performed an infibulation to cure of her nymphomania a little girl of 5, 'highly intelligent before her harmful habit'. The use of dissuasive techniques had failed to solve the problem, because the little girl, who was very slim and supple, 'managed to insinuate her toe between the plate of the belt and the soft parts, and in this way practise masturbation'. A colleague, he confided, had recommended amputating the clitoris, but he himself was of the opinion that this would have caused 'the irreparable ruin of the organ of pleasure, which would have been excessive in the case of a little girl who might be cured'. Many who disagreed with him doubted whether this would work. One of them, Dr Deguise, asked Broca why he had not used cauterization, a method which had been successful, in his own experience, in the case of a persistent offender: 'For a whole year, in spite of the pleas of the young patient, I maintained in the canal of the urethra, by repeated cauterizations, an irritation sufficiently painful to make any touching impossible. Today, that young boy is a young man who is grateful to me for my persistance.'[54] The calm certainty they all felt – Broca asserting in his turn that 'infibulation is a palliative operation which preserves the future' – attests to clear medical consciences during the cruel treatment of what was seen as a very serious illness. In England, infibulation was also practised on boys. In 1876 Dr Yellowlees boasted of the 'spirit of remorse' manifested by his patients during the painful operation. He explained in 1892 that this consisted of passing a sort of metal safety pin through the foreskin. Clitoridectomy, he added, still had its advocates but was not thought to be effective, unlike the painful cauterization of the urethra.[55]

It is an appalling picture. The historian cannot help but see it as a veritable collective neurosis of the medical establishment, rooted in a deep anxiety about sexuality in general. Masturbation provided an opportunity to talk openly about a taboo subject. In England, those who broke the law of silence in this way, like George Drysdale, Samuel La'mert and the leader-writers of *The Lancet*, deplored the deep reticence of the profession in the face of sexual disorders. They were themselves suspected of being not altogether normal for taking an interest in such subjects. Havelock Ellis encountered deep hostility and had great difficulty in finding a publisher for his *Sexual Inversion*, the first volume of his enormous *Studies in the Psychology of Sex*. Published in 1897, it was prosecuted for obscenity the following year. The idea that only cranks could write about problems so shocking was deeply entrenched in the Anglo-Saxon psyche in the Victorian period.[56] It is by no means certain that it has since disappeared.

As for the ingenious devices supposed to eliminate self-abuse, they were rarely used, if only because of their prohibitive cost. The electric alarm that went off in the case of an erection, perfected by Dr Milton, cost a small fortune – £5 – in 1887. Such contraptions belonged in large part to the realm of fantasy. One is even inclined to wonder whether their learned inventors did not perhaps derive some enjoyment from battling against an evil from by which they may themselves have been afflicted. Was it a way of exorcizing temptation? Or of suppressing feelings of guilt or shame by projecting them onto the Other, the adolescent male? This is by no means impossible at the period when Krafft-Ebing was describing the growth of sadism and masochism. Like those who indulged in such perversions, the public interested in anti-masturbatory devices was certainly small and extremely discreet. It is difficult to take this any further, even more difficult to determine the role of the horror of the self, or of the fear of damnation or of physical decline, in such behaviour.

The repressive tide began to turn in the 1880s. Sir James Paget, surgeon to Queen Victoria, found masturbation disgusting, impure and vile, but no more dangerous than ordinary sexual relations conducted without excess. At most, it risked exhausting the very young if they indulged too frequently. Charles Mauriac and Jules Christian were of the same opinion. There was no major scientific discovery to prompt this shift in attitudes. Some of the proponents of the old ideas also experienced a change of heart. In a new edition of his book *The Pathology of Mind*, in 1895, Maudsley abandoned the theory that masturbation led to madness, as he had claimed a quarter of a century earlier, now saying that it might simply be a symptom of the evil. In 1899, in the second volume of his great work, prudently published in the United States, Havelock Ellis showed that 'autoeroticism' was very widespread.

The dangers of masturbation were still denounced in the twentieth century. The medical fears took new and more insidious forms. The psychoanalysts, Freud at their head, identified a castration complex linked to a parental disapproval expressed by a threat of mutilation: 'I'm going to chop it off!' Julien Green tells how he was deeply traumatized by seeing his mother brandishing a large knife. Many children were told that it would make them fools, idiots, cripples or deaf, or prevent them from growing. Yet surveys in Europe and America established that, around 1970, an average of 90 per cent of boys and 25 per cent of girls masturbated. The level of the resultant individual feeling of fear or guilt depended on local cultural pressures and social class. It seems more common and more intense in the United States than in France, where the notion of normality has prevailed since 1968 in medical works and dictionaries.[57]

Perhaps the spectacular about-turn in medical thinking about masturbation after 1880 corresponded to the abandonment by the middle classes of cultural characteristics which had become less useful to them in affirming their cultural specificity. On the one hand, the workers' movements rapidly expanding in the last decades of the nineteenth century also sometimes explored, in their turn, the path of moralizing and asceticism as a way of preparing for the revolution. On the other, the birth of psychoanalysis cast such phenomena in a new light by making it possible to identify the hidden impulses, especially when Freud linked Eros so closely to Thanatos, which fundamentally altered his readers' ideas with regard to sex. The transference of collective anxiety onto masturbators probably proved less necessary and less effective than the exploration of personal abysses as a way of understanding oneself and of trying to heal one's neuroses. Stevenson's *Doctor Jekyll and Mister Hyde*, published in 1886 and contemporary with Jack the Ripper, reveals the unstoppable irruption of the unconscious onto the European scene. The shadows of the past have not yet, however, been definitively dispelled. Masturbation remains 'an intrinsically and gravely disordered action', according to the 1992 *Catechism of the Catholic Church*.[58]

Venal pleasures and fallen women

Prostitution evoked the second great fear of the Victorian era, that of syphilis. Yet its status was highly ambiguous, because, in spite of numerous and strong moral protests, it was often admitted to be socially useful. This was in part because the model of the pure woman – loving mother and virtuous spouse – was now linked to the notion of frigidity, or at least of a weak sexual appetite. Honoré de Balzac provides an example of such a woman in the *Mémoires de deux jeunes mariées* (*Memoirs of Two Young Married Women*, 1841–2), alongside a second, more passionate, type, who survived in the more aristocratic version of love-passion. In the *Physiologie du mariage* (*Physiology of Marriage*, 1829), he evokes the classic excuse of a headache, wheeled out at bedtime by women devoid of erotic desire who dreaded being approached by their husband. Many such women suffered from hysteria. Before Charcot and Freud, books on this subject were counted in their hundreds.[59] They crystallized a contradiction, because many flesh-and-blood bourgeois women found it very difficult to conform to the medically sanitized ideal wished on them. Their 'abnormality' was then explained by neurosis, which further reinforced the distinction established between good women and bad women. The lascivious and lustful nature previously attributed to the weaker sex as a whole was now polarized round two exceptions, the hysterics and the whores.

Paris and London were flooded with prostitutes in the nineteenth century. As the English capital grew from 90,000 inhabitants in 1801 to 4,500,000 in 1901, contemporary estimates ranged between 80,000 and 120,000 prostitutes. The police divided them into three categories: the well-dressed whores who worked in brothels, those who walked the streets and those who worked in poor neighbourhoods, who were known as 'motts'. The etymology of this word has been much debated, some believing it was a slang word for the vulva, others that it came from 'moth', to indicate both the brightly coloured appearance and the brief lives of the women concerned. One expert of the period, Dr Tait, claimed that all such women showed signs of physical decay within a year, that they were no longer recognizable after three years and that their death rate was very high. The principal dangers they faced were pregnancy and disease. The Thames carried away the corpses of thousands of their abandoned infants, while an equal number were put out to nurse in the country by women who resigned themselves to their fate. Only the most beautiful and the most intelligent, possessing additional talents, best of all a good singing voice, had any chance of bettering themselves by becoming the kept mistress of some rich man. This was less common than might be imagined, as this vast troop of outcasts was exploited without much scruple. At least they were not unduly harried by the forces of law and order. The 'Bobbies', newly established in London in 1829, practised a sort of tacit tolerance. They arrested only 3,103 such women in 1837 and 9,409 in 1841, half of whom were 'motts'. Despite constant pressure to make them take more drastic action against 'the great social evil', they maintained the same attitude throughout the reign of Victoria. The public at large had no desire for greater severity, seeing paid sex as a personal affair. Only the leagues of virtue and Gladstone were preoccupied with the lot of these fallen women of the gutter, in the hope of rehabilitating them. The results were unimpressive. Gladstone's efforts were successful in only a dozen cases in three years.[60] The real reason for these failures was the impossibility of eradicating prostitution, given that it performed an essential social function. The general indulgence manifested by the population and the authorities is explained by the need to maintain prostitution as an outlet for a sexuality that was fiercely repressed. Since the eighteenth century, as in Paris, it was easy to get hold of guides to this murky world. *The Man of Pleasure's Pocket Book* was stylistically a work of pornography but also a true sales catalogue. For a guinea, the connoisseur could procure the services of Miss Merton, whose 'sister hills' were 'prominent, firm, and elastic'. The physical descriptions put particular emphasis on the figure, vigour and energy of the women concerned, with the promise of incomparable bliss and observations on their bust, hair and even legs, a word capable of throwing a Victorian male into a tizzy. The writers sometimes got so carried away that they adopted the language of reportage to describe 'the French flesh market' or a 'convent' packed with nuns who could sing, play the piano, dance and play cards.[61]

For France, the pioneering work of Alain Corbin on the 'women of the night' enables us to appreciate the scale of the problem. Alexandre-Jean-Baptiste Parent-Duchâtelet (1790–1836) set the tone at the beginning of the century by devoting a very detailed study to the subject. He distinguished several different categories of prostitute, girls *en numéro, en carte, à soldats* and *de barrière*, for example, who could be compared to the London 'motts'. All of them had an 'ignoble origin' and had followed the same degrading trajectory, which led from disorder to debauchery.[62] Only certain women were likely to fall so low, with the clear implication that good bourgeois wives belonged to a totally different species. Prostitution was necessary, but dangerous. It was important to hide it from the eyes of respectable people and keep it closely controlled. To discipline the fallen women, Parent-Duchâtelet imagined that they would spend their entire career within four enclosed establishments, the brothel, the hospital, the prison and possibly the refuge or institution of repentance, conveyed from one to the other in a closed carriage.[63] Thus they would be disciplined and punished according to the panoptic ideology of the age.[64] This system was based on the concentration of vice in brothels, under the iron rule of the authorities. The regulationist discourse went on to become even more alarmist. Around 1871, Maxime Du Camp spoke of a sort of gangrene rising from the lower depths to invade the whole of the social body during the Second Empire. He estimated that Paris had 120,000 prostitutes, which is of very much the same order as the number suggested for London at the equivalent time. The most pessimistic experts feared a veritable invasion, a surge of whores from the red light districts and brothels, thanks to the 'unregistereds' and the fact that 'you can buy any virtue'. Under the Third Republic, ever fiercer critics used this as a pretext for trying to control every form of extra-marital sex. In 1872, Dr Homo demanded the registration of all kept women, accusing them of being disguised professionals. Dr Bertillon set about demonstrating that the use of the genital organs before the age of 21 resulted in terrible dangers to the health. Official estimates revealed a massive increase in the number of 'unregistereds' who became preponderant in the world of commercial sex around 1890–1900. The failure of the regulatory system was then patent.[65]

The prostitutes came from every social class and adapted to every sort of customer. The demimondaines – the *lionnes* and *cocottes* of the Second Empire and the *grandes horizontales* of the Third Republic – lived luxuriously in a private house or an apartment in one of the good quarters of Paris. The *soupeuses* of the all-night restaurants and the *femmes de café* were more common and more representative of the changing times. Kept women were numerous in the capital and the industrial towns. Some were fully set up by an old bachelor, occasionally even with their husband; others had the rent of a room or an apartment paid, or even just their clothes or their entertainment bought. The provincial bourgeoisie, for example in Lyons, Lille or Valenciennes, often chose their mistress from among young factory workers. Real little households were sometimes formed, consisting of an upper-class young man and a pretty, young, uncultivated working girl, which often led to misunderstandings and frustrations on both sides.⁶⁶ The class war took unexpected turns but left deep traces: the man tended to consider his partner simply as an instrument of pleasure while she, for whom he may have been the first, suffered from his offhandedness and from the fact of having been bought.

The anonymous erotic autobiography of an Englishman of good family tells a revealing story on this subject.⁶⁷ The narrator meets Molly in the countryside and makes her his mistress: 'Soon Molly went again to London, and I did the same day, but not in the third-class carriage.' Bourgeoisie oblige! He asks her to come and live with him, she agrees, and they settle down in a house. But 'she only staid with me five days. I took her to theatres and other places, but not out in the day; fed her up, and fucked her and myself out... I had the delight of teaching her baudiness (which is the main pleasure a virgin gives you over a gay woman), but she did not care about me. She was often crying, but a little friction on her clitoris usually cured that.' On the last day, 'I asked her if she was in the family way? She admitted it.' When she added that she thought the child was his, he retorted that it was more likely that it was that of another man, called Giles. He probably knew he was lying, given that he had boasted earlier of being Molly's happy initiator. She found a job, kept it for a fortnight, then disappeared. Grieved, or so he said, he started to look for her and wrote to her. He found her, in a miserable furnished room, 'overdressed'. The explanation was simple: 'Molly had turned whore.' He availed himself of her amorous skills, discovered that she had never been so voluptuous, but failed to persuade her to tell him any details of her life; 'a woman who takes to whoring takes to lying', he cynically observes. At first a little uneasy, he soon recovers his good conscience: 'I went back to my aunt's, sorry, for I seemed to have been largely the cause of Molly going astray, and did not know then that a gay life is as happy as that of the wife of a farm-laborer.' Not a word about the child she was carrying and got rid of. 'Uneasy', no more, he soon after decides to return to London, where she 'would neither let me fuck nor feel her'. She bursts into tears and admits she has had the clap. Thus, within a few weeks, the unfortunate Molly, made lustful by her relations with the man who had deflowered her, had drifted into prostitution and then faced the two worst possible dangers, pregnancy and venereal disease. Was her fate really any better than the one that had awaited her in the countryside? The young gentleman who tells her pathetic story, without remorse and in the space of a few pages, admits to a vague and fleeting feeling of guilt, but reveals few scruples in exploiting her erotic talents, before coldly moving on to other adventures.

In France, prostitution took a different form in the last third of the nineteenth century. A new type of demand emerged, linked to social changes. It no longer came primarily from the sexual needs of the proletariat that had flooded into the towns, but from the wealthy and rapidly expanding 'bourgeois class'. The supply adapted to the demand. Neither high-class courtesans nor 'clandestines', and not based in brothels, the new prostitutes tried to give the impression they had been seduced. What their clients now increasingly wanted was a simulacrum of feeling and some continuity in a relationship, far removed from the brothel. The richest clients demanded luxury or comfort as well as a sort of imitation of conjugal life, with added eroticism. This explains the growing fashion for kept women, or at least women visited on a regular basis, and also the popularity at the end of the century of *maisons de rendez-vous*, discreet houses for secret meetings that gave the illusion of an adulterous relationship or of the conquest of a woman of equal or even higher rank.[68]

The very close link between prostitution and syphilis was a major contemporary concern. The spectre of venereal disease haunted men and women on both sides of the Channel. In England the statistics are fairly well known for the beginning of the reign of Victoria; a veil of silence then gradually descends on 'the great social evil'. Fantasies persisted until the discovery of the spirochaete of syphilis in 1905, the Wassermann test in 1906 and the development of effective remedies after 1909. An anonymous doctor writing in *The Medico-Chirurgical Review* calculated that a few hundred infected London prostitutes could infect 10 times as many men, their clients, in a single night, who would in their turn transmit the disease to hundreds more women, prostitutes and wives, which would result, he worked out, in an annual total of 1,652,500 carriers of the disease. Such figures should probably not be taken too seriously, but they reveal a real anxiety, all the more acute because the masculine double standard set off a chain reaction of infection, which even affected some children through heredity.[69]

A similar hygienic terror gripped France. It permeated art and literature. Identified with the gaping vagina, the deadly 'pox' obsessed Joris-Karl Huysmans. *En Ménage*, one of his novels, describes the evolution of feminine desire in three successive, increasingly serious, stages, on the model of syphilis.[70] *Les Avariés*, a play by Eugène Brieux written in 1901 and performed in the Théatre Antoine in Paris in 1905, and the paintings of Félicien Rops similarly reflect the fascination and anxiety the subject provoked. Around 1900, the terror reached a new peak of intensity when it was discovered that the disease was extremely serious, more contagious and more long lasting than had been thought. Doctors claimed, without scientific proof, that between 7 and 8 per cent, even 42 per cent, of children died infected by their mother. Edmond Fournier 'proved' the existence of an inherited syphilitic degeneration sometimes more tragic for the grandchildren than the direct descendants. The recommended remedy was, quite simply, abstinence: 'What we must achieve is that young people marry as virgins', proclaimed Dr Queyrat in 1902, before the Société de Prophylaxie. This has been seen as 'a dissuasive strategy directed principally at the young', the excessive fear of the pox taking over from that of sin so as drastically to curtail access to carnal pleasures.[71] The intense syphilo-phobia of the turn of the century succeeded a pure repressive fantasy that had been in decline since the 1880s, the great fear of masturbation. This had channelled the energies of the proponents of moderation in the erotic appetites since the eighteenth century, just as the witch-hunt had once focused attention on the extreme danger of coitus with the devil himself, in other words, the unbridled quest for sexual pleasure to the detriment of the salvation of the soul. Could it be that the recent dread of AIDS, justified by terrible realities, unlike the two great fears that preceded it, is our own postmodern way of fearing that death is the ineluctable consequence of sexual excess?

The repressive discourses surrounding prostitution did not readily disappear in the twentieth century. The great collective fears simply shifted to other subjects, adapting to new social conditions. Thus in France the loi Marthe Richard of 1946 ordered the closure of brothels, which had been experiencing a slow death since their apogee in the middle of the nineteenth century.[72] The legislative turning point came in 1960, when the sanitary register, which recorded the names of 30,000 prostitutes, was abolished. Though tacitly tolerated, the sex trade is still described as a social evil. The law of silence and the survival of the double standard of masculine behaviour suggest that Victorian habits have not entirely disappeared from the world of commercial sex.

Through the looking glass

The other side of the Victorian picture is surprisingly varied. Real attitudes bore little relation to the imperative moral norms, as was shown, around 1890, by an extraordinary anonymous erotic autobiography, *My Secret Life*. At the oneiric level, the rising tide of pornography offered the exact opposite to the prohibitions. Further, the scholarly and medical consensus began to break down towards the end of the nineteenth century, timidly introducing desire and pleasure into the official discourse and seeking to know more about the instinctual foundations of the personality. In any case, large sectors of society had never really subscribed to the repressive discourse. For the rural and urban masses, for example, masturbation and prostitution remained fairly banal practices. They might sometimes have adapted to their own specific needs forms of censure originating with the right-minded, but their sexual behaviour was often simpler and more direct. Less constrained than ladies at this period, lower-class women enjoyed the physical pleasures, in spite of the serious dangers they incurred, and reached orgasm with ease, if we are to believe a narrator who had studied hundreds of them.

Walter the Victorian

An anonymous Victorian gentleman began to write as a way of finding out about himself. He regretted having no standard of comparison by which he could know if every man committed the same acts and had the same attitudes as he when with a woman, and he hoped his experience, committed to paper, would serve as a reference for others. Published in Amsterdam around 1890, *My Secret Life* runs to 11 volumes; the American edition of 1966 had more than 2,000 pages.[73] The book is based on a private journal begun at an early age, which the author decided to turn into memoirs of his 'inner and secret life' when he was about 25 years old.[74] 'Walter', as he called himself, without further details, was born into a wealthy upper-middle-class family at a date unknown. He lived in the reign of Queen Victoria and was still alive around 1890, when his book appeared. We learn vaguely that he had worked at the War Ministry, but he omits almost everything that would make it possible to recognize or identify the persons he mentions. He describes his sexual experiences with 1,200 women from every country – except Lapland, he regrets – with many details about his own feelings and those of his partners, not to speak of innumerable observations on every conceivable subject. His huge practical experience of the body, his own and those of the women he slept with, did not prevent him from accepting the cultural myths of his own or previous ages. Thus he admits he had masturbated regularly since adolescence, and is afraid that this will lead to madness or worse – that is, an inability to have sex. Similarly, while he describes a pleasant feeling of tiredness after bouts of sexual activity, he bemoans his feelings of depression, guilt and fatigue after a wet dream or self-abuse. The medical and social taboo seems to have been both fully internalized and constantly transgressed. Like the authors of *L'École des filles* in 1655, and like the doctors of his own day, he believes that women ejaculate at their climax. He keeps referring to the sensation of female 'seminal discharge' that he claims to have experienced himself or that his mistresses have sometimes described. Experience, it is clear, cannot rid itself of the cultural dimension. Walter reveals a theoretical ignorance that was typically Victorian, due to the law of silence applying in anything to do with physical love and to the conventions that forbade the slightest allusion to the body in polite conversation.[75] Many other observations have a ring of truth, in particular because he is capable of reporting events that reflect badly on his own virility. He had a complex about the size of his penis, which he had believed since schooldays was smaller than those of other boys, and he is constantly seeking reassurance from the prostitutes he sleeps with, without being wholly convinced by their answers, which he usually reckons to be diplomatic. He frequently wonders whether he will be able to maintain an erection, describes fiascos that had greatly distressed him and fears venereal disease. In short, he takes the opposite view to the official discourse of masculinity by revealing his weaknesses.[76]

Though primarily concerned with his own reactions, he is also keenly interested in those of his women, while still regarding them as objects of pleasure and having no scruples in paying for the services of a large number of professionals. In this, he was well and truly a man of his times. His regrets, occasionally expressed, never become remorse, even when he corrupts a healthy young country girl, a virgin, in record time.[77] After his marriage, he practises the double standard and claims to detest his wife, which it is hard not to see as a convenient way of salving his conscience. Nevertheless, his version of female sexuality is at the opposite pole from the official version, which was based on frigidity or a weak sexual appetite. Not one of his conquests conforms to this pattern. The majority of them, coming from all social classes and from different countries, achieve orgasm easily, quickly and repeatedly. He also records some rarer cases when they could not reach orgasm with him.[78] This description of a sort of equality with men in desire and pleasure, including among prostitutes, suggests we need to look again at Victorian realities. Contrary to the rules of politeness, the women Walter sleeps with are quite ready to talk dirty, at his request, when they climax.[79] Beneath the veil of prejudices, the taste for pleasure and the quest for sexual excitement on the part of both sexes shows through. We need to rethink our conception of a Victorian glaciation, which was perhaps no more than a veneer concealing a sexual appetite that could very easily be satisfied in London. Though he had many encounters with women from good society, Walter slept mainly with women from the urban and rural working classes, servants and prostitutes in particular. The crucial role of money in social relations between the rich and the proletariat is fully brought out by his account.

Walter was also a sensualist, an heir to the libertines who had experimented with every type of erotic delectation. He enjoyed extending the range of his fantasies by reading pornography. He never tired of contemplating the vulvas of his mistresses, comparing and recording the differences between their bodies and questioning them about their erotic tastes, feelings and habits. An occasional voyeur, he masturbated while watching them urinate or defecate. Sometimes a sadist, he became very aroused and brutal when he deflowered little girls brought to him by procuresses. One day, finally achieving an erection and managing to ejaculate, after several abortive attempts, he cried out in his moment of triumph, 'I've fucked you, – I'm a man you see!' He was very conscious of his male privilege, which allowed him to fuck on his own terms. This had not prevented him from feeling up some male friends in his youth. A little later, he had an uneasy experience the first time he slept with a prostitute, in the company of his brazen cousin Fred. The latter had arrived with two women. In a state of anxiety, Walter could only achieve an erection by watching his cousin's penis springing into action, which galvanized him. The two boys climaxed at the same moment, watching and touching each other during the sex act. A long time after, Walter made a conscious decision to have a homosexual experience. He saw this moment as crowning his libidinous career: 'the most daring fact of my secret life. An abnormal lust of which I have been ashamed and sorry ... tho according to my philosophy, there was and is no harm in my acts, for in lust all things are natural and proper to those who like them.' He reassured himself by claiming that it was no more disgraceful for a man to feel another man's penis or a woman to feel another woman's cunt than it was with the other sex, but he admitted that the memory of this experience made him feel an aversion for himself, produced in his opinion by 'the prejudice of education alone'. During a sexual encounter with a pretty girl, he fellated a craftsman called Jack (who respectfully addressed him as 'Sir'), 'exactly as it had been done to me' by a French whore, he says, before moving on to anal penetration.[80]

One of his chief obsessions was knowing exactly what the woman felt during and after the sex act. A glimpse of a pretty passer-by made him want to possess her, so that, he said, he could become part of her body.[81] This intense curiosity about the other sex drove him to keep on adding to his experiences. His virility was sometimes triumphant, but more often uneasy. It was sometimes tinged with fantasies of female identification, even with homosexual impulses. This is all out of kilter with the moral Victorian discourse, but very close to the erotic dream developed in pornography, where the emphasis is on elaborate sexual games and the transgression of taboos. Walter is a very lucid deviant, who frequently feels uneasy as he lives out his desires by breaking the rules of morality. Socially, he was perfectly normal, firmly fixed in his class role, which enabled him to embark on sensual experiences from a position of dominance. Money gave him the power to enjoy himself without constraints and to exploit the sexual proletariat, female or male, like Jack, a house-painter. He was surprised, therefore, when Jack began to behave familiarly after allowing himself to be masturbated. 'He had lost his modesty and with it much of his respect for me. Instead of only answering and saying "sir" he began to ask me questions.' Walter compared this attitude to that of a woman whose 'manner alters towards the man' directly he has made love to her.[82]

Unlike the pornographic heroes in books, Walter exposes himself without seeking to conceal the many contradictions that trouble him. Narcissistic and compulsive, he wearies the reader with his constant repetition of the same scenario. He was well aware of this, even wondering in middle age, in the conclusion to the seventh volume, whether he ought to abbreviate his memoirs. He says he has already omitted many pages of the manuscript, but is reluctant to remove more. He had written them for his 'secret pleasure', which had always remained as intense, even if he described the same things 20 times. Further, 'the woman, the partner in my felicity was frequently fresh and new to me, and I to her.' It was the quest for these subtle nuances that drove him on; because, even if it always ended the same way, in copulation, 'there are delicate shades of difference even in fucking which make the variety so charming, and describing them was ever new and amusing to me, when the charmer was new to me'. After experiencing contradictory feelings, a mixture of remorse, the conviction that he had done nothing wrong and the fear that being shamed, he decided to keep in the few passages dealing with pornographic images and books: 'It must remain – written by *myself* and for *myself*, none probably will ever see it but *myself* – therefore why cheat *myself*? – let it remain.'[83]

Walter the Victorian emerges as a precursor of postmodern narcissism. He is the link between the sexual libertines of the seventeenth century and the enthusiasts for sexual liberation. Yet there is one major difference, a perpetual split between his personal Self and the conventions of the age he had internalized. A prey to acute anxiety, which he shrugs off at the cost of much suffering and doubt, he is perpetually at the interface between the social role he ought to play and the desire to enjoy all the pleasures by which he was obsessed. His testimony is all the more valuable as a result. He reveals both the other side of the coin and the strength of contemporary cultural prohibitions. He has a split personality but avoids neurosis by experimenting with everything that attracts him and by spilling a lot of ink. As he himself says, he prolonged his enjoyment not only by writing about his exploits but also by reading and re-reading about them. Another major contradiction, he did not quite dare to go public but nevertheless wanted to go into print. A 'rich old Englishman' paid a small fortune to an Amsterdam publisher contacted in 1888, if we are to believe the first sale catalogue featuring the book, in 1902. This eccentric gentleman wanted to have all 11 volumes 'privately printed for his own enjoyment', on condition that no more than six copies would be struck off.[84] Though we should perhaps not take these statements too literally, because the hope was to sell a rarity at what was an astronomical price for the period, it is likely that very few copies were printed. The presence of a lengthy and detailed table of contents suggests that the author, in old age, wanted to be able to locate his memories with ease in the some 4,200 pages of the original, undated (*c*.1890) edition. We should not necessarily take at face value his frequent claims that he had toiled for his own enjoyment alone. He was obviously motivated by the desire to know himself better, because the law of silence prevented the Victorians from knowing if their sexuality resembled that of others, or not. He often explains things to himself by adding observations to passages written down years earlier.[85] Also, although he denies it, it is very likely that he had an unconscious desire to bring his erotic life to the attention of his contemporaries. Perhaps he simply felt a thrill of satisfaction at the idea of a stranger casting his eye over his pages? There is no reason to doubt that his everyday life was that of a worthy and respectable gentleman, cultivated, a traveller, a married man briefly employed at the War Office, who took great pains to muddy the waters sufficiently to avoid miring himself, his cousin Fred or the people of quality mentioned in his memoirs in scandal. His book is a fascinating journey through the looking glass, if in a rather more scabrous style than that of Alice, and it would surely repay systematic study. By writing his memoirs, Walter probably avoided the destructive neuroses observed in his contemporaries, Jack the Ripper and the Dr Jekyll of R. L. Stevenson. He would have made an excellent subject for Freud. As the clients of the budding psychoanalysis then constituted only a tiny minority in Western Europe, it seems reasonable to wonder whether many other 'Walters' may have compensated in the same way for the frustrations imposed by the restrictive Victorian codes.

The 'hell' of sex: pornography prospers

In the century of industrialization, pornography was 'embourgeoisified'. Its old connection with oppositional ideas and free thought, distant heir to the libertines of the seventeenth century, was gradually severed in the first half of the nineteenth century, while it adapted with increasing success to the commercial market. The genre flourished.[86] In England it increasingly appeared as the inverted mirror of Victorian anxieties, a sort of voluptuous utopia or 'pornotopia' transmitting the erotic 'fables' most enjoyed by adults, in particular transgression of the principal sexual taboos of the age. Its frontiers were fluid, as it included banal feuilletons with enticing titles such as *A Peep Behind the Scenes*, guides to night life such as *London by Night* or *Gay Life in London* and even works denouncing the ill effects of vice, especially masturbation, that were read for the wrong reasons and used on the sly to learn about the practices they condemned.[87] Nevertheless, the readers of erotic works, strictly speaking, remained few, and editions were limited to a hundred or a few hundred luxuriously bound and illustrated copies, sold at a high price. Henry Spencer Ashbee, under the prudent pseudonym of Pisanus Fraxi, compiled the first bibliography in the English language devoted to the subject, the *Index librorum prohibitorum*, published in 1877 by an unidentified London printer, in 250 copies. It was followed by two companion volumes in 1879 and 1885. The pornographic magazines – *The Boudoir* from 1860, *The Pearl* (1879–80), *The Cremorne* (dated 1851, in fact 1882) – were similarly expensive and restricted to a narrow elite, given the general condemnation and the conspiracy of silence in sexual matters.[88]

The world of pornography is a totally erotic imaginary world which offers men an uninterrupted succession of pleasures. From the middle of the nineteenth century, it experienced unprecedented growth, to the point of becoming a minor European industry. The sexual subculture it transmitted offered an exact reverse image of official moral positions. Thus it took the opposite view on the fight against masturbation, it described endless orgies just when medicine was warning against the dangerous effects of carnal excesses and it insisted on the female orgasm when ladies of quality were supposed to be frigid or at least uninterested in sex, and so on.[89] Right-minded people were appalled, obviously, at the harm this might do. They tried to apply the law of silence, either by prohibiting pornography or by relegating it to a sulphurous 'hell'. The word was originally used for works that had been banned and were in the Vatican library waiting to be burned. In Paris, a small collection of ribald books and drawings preserved in the Bibliothèque nationale was generally referred to by this name (*enfer*). According to Guillaume Apollinaire, this followed a decision of the First Consul, Bonaparte. Some experts date it only to the last years of the Second Empire, others to the July Monarchy. In any case, it was the positivist nineteenth century that invented the 'literary' hell. The British Library officially uses the name Private Case but unofficially that of 'hell' for a similar collection, organized at about the same time. The appearance in France in 1861 of the *Bibliographie des ouvrages relatifs à l'amour* of Jules Gay, and, in England, in 1877, of the *Index librorum prohibitorum* of Pisanus Fraxi (which ironically took its title from the Roman Catholic organ of censorship), responded to the needs of enthusiasts to be able to consult works now consigned to oblivion and silence, which it was often very difficult to obtain commercially. Apart from the books published legally, the Parisian collection included others seized by the courts or by customs at the frontiers, if they had been printed abroad.[90]

The authors were almost always men, but they expounded at length on the pleasure of women, as had been the case at the time of the 'pornographic turn' of the mid-seventeenth century.[91] The continuity in transgression is evident, in particular in the stories of convents turned into brothels.[92] Their popularity at the end of the nineteenth century was probably in part due to the rise of anti-clericalism, but erotic nuns had long haunted the European imagination and had deliciously titillated anti-Catholic sentiment in England under the *ancien régime*. In the same way, *Le Roman de Violette*, one of the great successes of the nineteenth century, attributed to Théophile Gautier, teaches a similar lesson to that of *L'École des filles*, published in 1655. The heroine, a young lady of 15, is almost the same age as Fanchon and, like her, is initiated into 'all the voluptuous perversions her ingenious lover can think of to teach her'. The novelty lay in the social morality expounded, which was perfectly suited to the age. Although her lover encourages her to reject the rules laid down by men, which 'impose chastity on young girls and fidelity on women', he still treats her as a sexual object, very like Walter the Victorian. And death awaits Violette at the end of her voluptuous journey.[93] Contemporary norms surreptitiously infiltrated sulphurous works, here providing the reader with an edifying end that took away some of the guilt of indulging in voyeurism, which had not been the case in previous centuries. Even the theme of feminine purity emerges, around 1900, in *Association de demivierges*, a work of the prolific Le Nismois (who used several pseudonyms, including Fuckwell, Tap-Tap and Léna de Beauregard).[94] Appointed almoner of the convent of Les Bleuets, the abbé Tisse forms a society that enables the inmates to enjoy themselves without fear of pregnancy. The little 'perverts' have the right to try anything, except 'the most brutal' act of all, as their lovers have to confine themselves to caresses. The prevailing morality was thus safe on one essential point, while being joyously contested on every other, all in the name of a female right to pleasure which had been an obsession since the seventeenth century in this male-authored literature. Le Nismois was surely unaware that he was rehabilitating the mutual fondling that had been the main erotic outlet of young people awaiting marriage under the *ancien régime*.

Behaviour that was 'abnormal' emerged primarily at the end of the nineteenth century. At the time when the Victorian barriers were beginning to break down and masturbation was ceasing to be a medical obsession, homosexuality and the 'perversions' began to be openly discussed. We should not be misled by the desperate efforts to stem the tide. The legislative severity was in proportion to the perceived gravity of the danger. It may briefly have checked the emergent liberalizing trend but it could not reverse it. The French censors of the years 1880–1914 were essentially nostalgic Victorians engaged in fighting a rearguard action. Among the laws of 1881, 1882 and 1898 regulating violations of the press laws, the last established a link between what was 'obscene' and Malthusianism, revealing a fear of moral decadence. This took root in the divorce law of 1804, which asserted the importance of individual liberty and the right to happiness. Pornography dealt with these burning questions in its own way by offering many portraits of adulterous debauched women, throbbing with desire, and by highlighting the worst vices, as it presented *Le Troisième Sexe* (*The Third Sex*), *Les Invertis* (*The Inverts*) or *Les*

Déséquilibrés de l'amour (*Those Unhinged by Love*).[95] The ferocity of the prosecutions reveal just how great the censors felt the danger to be. Saucy magazines such as *Le Boudoir, Le Boccace* and *Gil Blas* were their chief targets in the early 1880s. They were replaced by books, especially after 1910, with 175 prosecutions before the outbreak of war, 12 times more than during the preceding 30 years. While the laws of Jules Ferry established compulsory secular public education, and republican educational principles lauded liberty and tolerance, an effective system for censoring the written word was put in place. Its professed aims were to protect the more vulnerable sectors of society, especially the poor, young people and women, from the amoral and pornographic flood.[96] At a deeper level, it sought to stifle a challenge to the dominant value system from those who no longer believed, or had never believed, in the virtues either of the law of silence or of the sexual system based on the indissolubility of marriage, the masculine double standard and the premise of the weak sexual appetite of the virtuous wife.

Making the 'transgressions' ordinary

Incest and paedophilia are today universally and fiercely condemned. It was not quite the same in the nineteenth century. Although it sickened the moralists, child prostitution was common, and sometimes joked about in a way that would be thought unacceptable today. Oscar Wilde observed one day of a publisher of erotica: 'He loves first editions, especially of women: little girls are his passion.'[97] There were marked social contrasts, nevertheless. The working classes seem often to have been more repelled by such behaviour than the wealthy: 'If your daughter is telling the truth', cried a woman, the neighbour of a rag-and-bone man of Saint-Aignan, 'the guillotine would be too good for you!'[98]

Other transgressions were regarded as depravities at the beginning of the Victorian period, then slowly lost their power to shock. The norm of reference was coitus between adults of the opposite sex, without 'immodest acts' or 'unnatural passions'. For the conventional English, sex more than twice a week was a clear sign of animality. The fear of unleashing the beast lying dormant within the human being haunted the moralists. In France, fellatio seems to have been rare and confined to prostitutes in the nineteenth century, but 'oral practices, focused on pleasure rather than reproduction', became common in the twentieth century, spreading from illicit couples to lower-class married couples, then to those awaiting marriage during the inter-war period. Prudish England totally excluded such matters from great literature, confining them to pornography. Described as 'disgusting practices', fellatio and cunnilingus were nevertheless frequently demanded by the clients of brothels and are consequently mentioned in the specialized London guides. On both sides of the Channel, doctors reserved the notion of 'perversities' or 'monstrous things' to onanism and 'sexual inversion', which fascinated them, while ordinary people reserved their strongest condemnation for paedophilia and bestiality but were relatively unperturbed by masturbation.[99]

The use for the first time of the word 'homosexual', in 1869, by the Hungarian physician Benkert, coincided with a surge of scholarly interest in the 'third sex', which had been recognized in a very ambiguous fashion in both London and Paris at the beginning of the eighteenth century.[100] In France, Ambroise Tardieu broke the law of silence in 1857, after which the subject fascinated the medical community from the Second Empire to the First World War.[101] More than a thousand works were devoted to it in Europe between 1898 and 1908.[102] This emergence from limbo coincided with a greater degree of tolerance. In England 'pedication', or anal penetration, was punishable by death until 1828, as long as a witness had actually *seen* the act, unlike mutual masturbation and fellatio, which were more common but considered less serious. Although the courts hesitated to apply the supreme penalty, it was not uncommon for young men to mutilate themselves to avoid such a danger. Havelock Ellis, author with J. Addington Symonds, himself an 'invert', of *Sexual Inversion*, estimated at the end of the nineteenth century that the number of persons concerned was between 2 and 5 per cent of the male population, which is close to the 6 per cent established by the Kinsey Report in 1948.[103] According to Richard von Krafft-Ebing, the prohibitions and the sense of danger induced a nervous irritability in these men, which sometimes drove them to extreme violence. In London they could procure the services of male prostitutes. The latter, often heterosexual, called 'margeries' or 'pooffs' in the early and middle years of the reign of Victoria, operated in Fleet Street, Holburn and the Strand, with recognition signs and specific gestures when they spotted a potential client. In an attempt to combat the general hostility, the outcasts devoted many books to their situation. They tried to acquire greater respectability by using an appropriate vocabulary, speaking, for example, of 'sexual inversion', the 'third sex' or 'uranism'. Coined by Carl Heinrich Ulrich in the 1860s, this last term indicated a female soul in a male body, a topos which became popular in literary fiction.[104] The rare places where homosexuality truly prospered were the English public schools, where certain masters and tutors shared and encouraged it, and also the universities. The students and dons at Oxford and Cambridge, a tiny minority of the population, formed a very juvenile and entirely masculine society. Reading Greek authors, in particular Plato, who extolled the love of one man for another man or for a boy, helped to lift some of the guilt of those involved. Nevertheless, in the second half of the reign of Victoria, three sensational affairs, widely reported in the press, revealed the massive disapproval and bad odour which surrounded the matter: the transvestism of Boulton and Park in 1870, the Cleveland Street scandal of 1889 and, most of all, the three trials of Oscar Wilde, once a student at Oxford, in 1895.[105]

The devotees of sapphism did not encounter such fierce hostility as their male homologues. Nevertheless, at the beginning of the nineteenth century, Parent-Duchâtelet considered 'the lesbians as fallen into the worst degree of vice to which a human being could attain', and the madams of brothels were formally prohibited from allowing women to sleep in the same bed in 1824. But the pressure was subsequently relaxed. The great authors – Balzac, Musset, Baudelaire, Pierre Louÿs, Zola – freely described the phenomenon. The doctors showed little interest in it, except for the monstrous clitorises which had already stimulated the fantasies of their predecessors in the sixteenth and seventeenth centuries. Men wavered between the position of voyeur and that of disappointed chauvinist. The feelings of the former were eroticized by imagining intertwined female bodies; the latter felt challenged in their virility and their capacity to procure pleasure: 'By doing without men, being sufficient in themselves, women will soon do without their love', claimed Dr Chevalier. The model is found in the clandestine literature, incarnated by the eponymous heroine of *Gamiani*. Running to 44 editions between 1833 and 1930, this huge erotic success was falsely attributed by one pamphlet to George Sand, 'the sapphists' colonel'. It was expanded with every new edition, the heroine finally becoming an insatiable rutting beast by the turn of the twentieth century. She acquired her mortal hatred of men, the story goes, after being beaten and raped by some monks. Less colourful, and comparable to the eight examples noted by Krafft-Ebing, 14 cases discovered in the judicial records also reveal the sexual emancipation of the women accused. All but one later than 1910, they involved kept women, women serving in bars and prostitutes, essentially in towns.[106]

Another sign of the way the sexual 'perversions' were becoming more commonplace is provided by the emergence of sadism and masochism, described in 1890 by Richard von Krafft-Ebing, the famous author of *Psychopathia Sexualis* (1886). While expanding the notion of fetishism, Krafft-Ebing suggested that sadism should be considered an exaggeration of normal male behaviour, whereas masochism, which was clinically more common, developed a similar excess peculiar to women. In 1892, he published an essay on sexual dependence in which he distinguished what he called an extreme form of masochistic normality from the earlier pathological type. The problem, he believed, constituted an important cultural fact, very much on the increase, especially in literature. He quoted in this connection the stories of Sacher-Masoch, after whom the phenomenon was named, of his wife, Jean Richepin's *La Glu* and the lyrical works of Johannes Wedde, posthumously published in 1894.[107] He had learned by listening to his patients that the techniques for inflicting pain were well known to prostitutes and that brothels held specific tools, in particular whips.

Flagellation was regarded in Europe as the 'English vice'. It was one of the corporal punishments administered in public schools, especially Eton. The pain it caused also gave rise to a certain sexual pleasure, if we believe the psychologist E. Wulffen. In 1913, he explained that there appeared, after the initial pain, 'a sensation of warmth which envelops the whole of the seat like a soft, warm blanket, producing a pleasurable sensation and this may easily connect up with the sexual area'. Often surprised by what they felt, boys who had been flogged sometimes tried to get the punishment repeated, which risked affecting their libido, he added. No doubt the scholarly interpretation allowed the teachers to explain the obstinacy of certain pupils in choosing not to toe the line. There were many lovers of the whip in London. In 1838, they could select their pleasurable pain in 20 splendid specialized brothels. Mrs Theresa Berkley, who died in 1836, and who ruled hers at 28 Charlotte Street with a rod of iron, as was only proper, was able to amass a small fortune between 1828 and 1836. She had at her disposal a wide range of instruments: flexible switches, whips with a dozen thongs, cat-o'-nine-tails studded with sharp points, straps decorated with tin tacks, stinging plants of every type and, peak of refinement, a flogging machine she had invented herself, 'the Berkley horse'.[108] France was not to be outdone. The great *maisons de tolerance* of the nineteenth century disposed of 'a complete arsenal of sexual tortures': straps with thongs of perfumed leather, silk cords for binding, small bunches of nettles, long needles, thongs studded with pinheads and knotted cords. The women did not only perform fellatio, which the moralists regarded as the most abject of all practices, along with sodomy. They were obliged to pander to every fantasy, including those of homosexuals, and be able to operate all the equipment. In line with scientific progress, they took advantage of modern technology, such as the suction pump of Dr Mondat or machines that administered localized electric shocks, not forgetting dildoes – imported from England, according to Leo Taxil – and the harness that allowed women to be equipped with an artificial penis.[109]

Proletarian pleasures

The sexual pleasures of the mass of the population are less well known. They figure incidentally in the autobiographies, most of which were written by cultivated members of good society. Walter makes many observations on the subject, revealing how deceptive are the conventions, even in the case of his own gilded world. At one point in his life, when he was regularly visiting high-class theatres and restaurants, he attended a masked ball in the Vauxhall Gardens. What gave him most pleasure, he recounts, was 'tipping the watchman to let me hide in the shrubs, and crouching down to hear the women piss. I have heard a couple of hundred do so on one evening, and much of what they said. Such a mixture of dull and crisp baudiness I never heard in short sentences anywhere.'[110] Apart from the information about the lack of lavatories, so that everyone relieved themselves in the bushes, the narrator opens a window onto the most commonplace reality, when the situation did not require that a social role be maintained. Only those offended by the smutty language and games of children when out of their parents' sight will be surprised. A toned-down and very 'soft' version of this scene was regularly included in the famous American TV series, *Sex and the City* (1998–2004), in which four feisty female New Yorkers talked frankly among themselves about their desires.

Several scholars have recently made studies of the sexual lives of the lower classes.[111] The records relating to 1,318 admissions to the London Foundling Hospital between 1850 and 1880 have shed light on the sexual behaviour of the working classes and corrected the accusation of debauchery routinely levelled against them by right-minded people. One observer wrote in 1850: 'There is no form or show of propriety, decency or morality; but, at times, a vitiating and disgusting bestiality unknown to the savages.' Nudity and the exposure of certain types of body hair were especially denounced. The censorious bourgeoisie were shocked to see the tiniest piece of uncovered flesh or the hair on men's chests or in women's armpits.[112] They could not tolerate anything that suggested the animality of the human being and they condemned the poor for ignoring the moral codes of the elites.

The Foundling Hospital received the fruits of sin. The foundlings had all been born out of wedlock. A few were the product of the power relations easily established between a master and a servant girl; many others were the result of perfectly ordinary love affairs between partners of the same social status. Almost all the mothers admitted to having had sex one or more times, confident in the expectation that they would be able to marry their lover, after a courtship often lasting longer than six months, even a year in over half the cases. Their love letters very rarely refer to the act of love or the pleasure it gave.[113] The author concludes rather too hastily that the carnal intemperance for which the 'depraved classes' were habitually criticized did not exist. It is true that tender feelings are frequently expressed and that the surviving letters are influenced – exactly by what process is not clear – by the dominant bourgeois model of romantic love, with its great reticence in the matter of physical effusions. It needs to be remembered, however, that the regulations for admission to the Foundling Hospital required both a personal request by the mother of the child and a written statement attesting to the applicant's 'Virtue, Sobriety and Honesty'.[114] It was essential for the mother to demonstrate her repentance, humility and meekness to prove her good reputation and erase the memory of her sin. The least hint of anything to the contrary in the documents she submitted risked getting her application rejected. The hard fact was that the majority of unmarried mothers did not earn enough to pay for a wet nurse or were unable to go on working with the added burden of a baby. Forced into total destitution, they turned to the only possible means of salvation, adapting their behaviour to the moral requirements this necessitated.

The sources paint a very pessimistic picture of the sexuality of poor young women. If they let themselves believe the words of a lover and eventually consented to sleep with him, in spite of the risks they knew only too well, it was because they were often trapped by cultural contradictions beyond their control. Many women were still influenced by the old rural traditions that allowed a young couple to fondle each other in ways that might go as far as copulation. The

English peasantry of the *ancien régime* practised the ritual of 'bundling', an advanced form of courtship conducted within the family home, with the consent of the parents, in which the young couple often lay undressed on a bed. It was also acceptable for them to mark their special relationship by a public exchange of gifts which was equivalent to a promise of marriage, or even publicly to formalize a prenuptial concubinage by the ceremony of 'pitchering'.[115] This sort of trial marriage was found all over Europe. The law and neighbourhood pressure provided solid guarantees for women by obliging a seducer to marry the mistress he had impregnated or assume financial responsibility for the child if he already had a family.[116] In nineteenth-century London, working-class girls went on believing they could follow their inclinations when they had been given a firm promise of marriage.

They realized too late that, for young men, the rules of the game had changed. The authors of the Poor Law Amendment Act of 1834 were deeply hostile to what they called the popular vices, and the Act included 'bastardy clauses' which withdrew all legal and material assistance from unmarried mothers other than that provided in the workhouses. From then on, paternity suits and breach of promise suits were no longer heard by the courts. This meant that very few seduced girls were able to enforce their rights. Lovers made promises they did not keep, fled when the bans were published or emigrated, for example to America. Some men expressed a deep feeling of guilt at having betrayed their sweetheart due to the sheer impossibility of supporting her and her child. Others, the libertines, 'men who live from day to day', exploited the flaws in the system to seduce their prey and then abandon her without scruple. The Victorian paradox was to have deliberately upset the balance of power in working-class pre-marital relations in the name of morality, and in so doing to have liberated masculine desire at women's expense.[117] The latter were victims both of a new lack of protection if they succumbed to temptation and of the illusions of the romantic model of marriage, which drove them into the arms of womanizers confident they could easily shirk their responsibilities. Nevertheless, a relative degree of equilibrium was restored. The Foundling Hospital offered a way out for a tiny minority who paraded all the signs of repentant virtue. And, though many of their sisters, whose careers were deemed less edifying, swelled the ranks of prostitutes or lived in destitution, family and friends were often sympathetic towards the unfortunate women. They did not condemn as such the loss of virginity, sexual relations outside marriage and concubinage, rural traditions imported into the industrial towns.[118]

It is unfortunate that so little information is forthcoming about the male partners in these tragedies, revealed by a mechanism that was ambiguous, because it was both socially philanthropic and morally punitive. The 1,318 infants rescued from the gutter in 30 years in the huge London metropolis, and their mothers, rescued for the time being from disaster, conceal a host of symbols. The documents reveal a new relationship between the sexes, heavily biased in favour of men. In their case, sexual desire and pleasure were still as acceptable outside marriage as in earlier centuries, according to the customs of their group, and the law no longer compelled them to put right their wrong. Women looked for the pleasures of the flesh and the promise of marriage without being as well protected as in the past if they became pregnant. In essence, the Victorian system that left men the space for sexual freedom by confining women within the cage of matrimony and the moderation of the sexual appetites was strictly adhered to. It can be seen as a clever strategy, complementing the discourse that derided the mass of the people, likely to find favour with men of all social categories, because their virility was clearly privileged in contrast to the obligations weighing on their partners. Women now bore alone all the weight of the transgressions. A few lovers cynically and shamelessly said as much when they learned of the pregnancy: 'I told him and he slighted me and told me to drown myself and that he would help to do so. He did not deny paternity.'[119] Industrialization was no paradise for the working classes, and it had a sexual dimension. The impression of anarchy and lechery given by the denigratory discourse of the upper classes was not entirely false. By destabilizing the relationship between men and women in the name of morality, the censorious helped to intensify the sex war within the working class, giving the former a new feeling of impunity and the latter a feeling of increasing dependence and vulnerability. It served to connect the orgasm and anxiety for women, in the absence of contraception and in spite of the relative compassion of their family and friends and of the severe philanthropists who took in the children of sin.

This study is restricted to one generation, from 1850 to 1880, which was the apogee of Victorian repression in England. Later, the doctors changed their attitude to masturbation and the guardians of the temple found they were unable to prevent the expression of a growing curiosity about the physical pleasures, revealed, among others, by Havelock Ellis. The rigid norms were challenged by a sort of *fin de siècle* 'sexual anarchy', as the homosexuals and the New Women who repudiated marriage asserted their rights.[120] There were similar upheavals at the same time in France. Between 1900 and 1914, doctors showed increasing interest in phenomena that had been ignored or dealt with unobtrusively in the past, such as abortion and mortality among new born babies.[121] Among the working classes, sexual conduct slowly changed in certain ways. New habits mingled with old practices which had been forgotten for a while, or perhaps simply abandoned in order to avoid sanctions and rebukes, and which now re-emerged as cracks appeared in the moral straitjacket.

The most frightening discourses of denigration fail in their purpose if they are too clearly opposed to solidly established habits, especially when these are enjoyable. Workers and peasants paid little attention to the fierce criticism of juvenile masturbation, the loss of virginity by young girls, sex outside marriage, concubinage and adultery. The taboo on nudity, on the other hand, was more easily accepted in the nineteenth century, especially by those wives who were reluctant to undress completely in front of their husband.[122] The greatest successes of the moralists seem to have been in secondary matters. Kissing on the mouth, disapproved of up to the end of the nineteenth century, now emerged from the realm of the forbidden and was added to the armoury of amorous advances, eventually emerging as a sign of their intensity.[123] It seems unlikely that the pleasure of putting one's tongue in a partner's mouth was so slow to be discovered. The phenomenon testifies less to developments in the techniques of lovemaking than to the fluctuation of prohibitions according to period and group. The libertines of the seventeenth century happily engaged in what was called 'Italian kissing' in Paris and 'French kissing' in London. On both sides of the Channel it was practised by the peasantry with equal enthusiasm, for example in Somerset and during bundling in England or *maraîchinage* in the Vendée. The opprobrium later attached to it was probably due to its association with the erotic secrets dispensed by prostitutes during the golden age of the brothel in the great European cities. In the end, it rediscovered some of its innocence and resumed its place among all social classes during the twentieth century.

The first half of the twentieth century was characterized by a growing quest for sensual pleasure. 'The eroticization of the couple can be seen in the triumph of kissing on the mouth, nudity and oral caresses. It is also shown by the spread of sexual relations outside marriage. The growth in pre-marital liaisons is particularly striking, a marginal practice having become a generally accepted ritual.'[124] Women gave the initial impulse by refusing unwanted pregnancies, beginning with the least well-off, working-class women, who were copied one or two generations later by the better-off. Before the contraceptive pill, the 'hedonist wager', practised in France since the Third Republic, was based on a sort of risk-management relying on a combination of masculine caution and feminine prevention, with abortion as a last resort. 'I begged the men to take precautions to avoid becoming pregnant', explained an ironer from Brive in 1900. Coitus interruptus was the chief technique for men. Their partners used tampons and, above all, sponges, only rarely pessaries. If these failed, they 'got rid of' the burden, often before the third month. The number of abortions doubled, rising from 30,000 in 1900 to 60,000 in 1914, after which the increase was even more spectacular. In parallel, the arts of seduction became a more serious business for women. The rise in the use of make-up and hair dyes in the 1920s, and of the cult of the body, youth and a slim figure, are all signs of a desire to love and be loved that has only grown stronger. Pre-marital sex became increasingly common. A quarter of young girls went in for it during the Belle Époque, half around 1950, and 90 per cent by the end of the century.[125]

The collapse of the Victorian system based on the masculine double standard and the subjection of women did not lead to the invention of sexual freedom strictly speaking so much as to the return of what had been suppressed, that is, to more balanced relations between the sexes. The pendulum has swung back in the direction of negotiation between the two parties, as in the peasant societies of the seventeenth century, or in *L'École des filles* of 1655. As the repressive cycle drew to a close, around the middle of the twentieth century, women were still not demanding everything that their heirs would see as natural at the beginning of the twenty-first century. Many taboos persisted, with regard to menstruation, the rejection of sex with the light on, embarrassment at exposing the genital organs in front of the doctor or the gynaecologist and, even more insidiously, the fear of openly expressing one's carnal desires. No woman would have dared to write so smuttily as this young man of Loir-et-Cher in a letter to his sweetheart in 1939: 'I've got a hard-on like a stag. I wish I could fold you in my arms and slip my cock into your pretty little cunt. I reckon that while it was inside I'd give you a good time and we wouldn't half enjoy having it off together . . . you'd feel my fine pair of balls which would be banging you from behind . . . I'm sure you'd go away happy having sucked a fine prick and tickled a pair of balls with some good stuff in them.'[126] The baron de Blot, whose philosophy in 1650 was to eat, drink and fuck, would surely have appreciated, as a connoisseur, this descriptive prose.

The ebbs and flows of desire

The Victorian age is no more than a convenient theoretical notion to describe a long historical period characterized by a dominant medical discourse structured round the necessity of self-control of the sexual desires and needs. The images produced and the stories told spread beyond the circle of experts, gradually convincing many of their contemporaries.[127] The need to avoid 'over-spending', or exhausting oneself, became the central message of the new masters of society and industry. The role model proposed was that of the family where the wife without desires, even frigid, sheltered from a dangerous world, bore and raised the children and watched over the well-being of everyone else. The husband found calm and comfort in her presence, while feeling he had the right to seek erotic pleasure or the illusion of shared love with women of easy virtue. Mother or whore, the Victorian woman was under constant pressure to be far more submissive than her predecessors. Only the whore, however, now bore the burden of original sin, in a modernized form, credited with an insatiable and devouring lust, in contrast to the prudish and chaste wife.

This system was only slowly put in place, reaching its apogee between 1850 and 1880, after which it was increasingly vigorously contested, both by medicine itself, joined by the youthful psychiatry, and by cultural and social realities. The outcasts accused of 'perversion' demanded recognition of their difference. Women began to refuse to be kept in tutelage. They challenged from all directions. The liberated New Woman rejected marriage; working women demanded the right to enjoy themselves without fear of the downfall caused by an unwanted pregnancy and a lover who fled his responsibilities. The first significant cracks appeared between 1880 and 1914. Contradictions and confusions characterized these years of moral turnaround. The censorious raged against pornographic books and the erotic press, but the doctors abandoned the dogma of the morbidity of masturbation and became increasingly interested in normal sexuality as well as the major transgressions, such as sadism and masochism. In France, the 1884 law on divorce opened the way to greater freedom for wives, who made similar demands in England, achieving success in the 1920s. After which, the insidious slide into hedonism only accelerated.

Constraints, prohibitions and taboos are never imposed uniformly or continuously. The first half of the nineteenth century had been much less constrained than the second.[128] Under the impact of the terrible shock of 1914–18 and the need to relieve the accumulated tensions, the inter-war period saw a resurgence of the sexual cultures that had been swept under the carpet, rather than destroyed, by the Victorian offensive. The aristocratic libertines, never vanquished, took advantage of the situation to make refined pleasures, primarily those of sex, central to the Roaring Twenties. Ordinary people, who were now better organized, more demanding and influenced by liberating social ideologies, rediscovered some of the traditions of relative moral freedom they had been urged to abandon. Working women, who had suffered more than their male peers from the burden of the new norms and paid a heavy price in unwanted pregnancies and traumatizing abortions, now gradually restored some balance, to their own advantage, to the business of sharing pleasure. The ground was prepared for a slow liberalization of sexual life up to the sudden accelerations of the 1960s.

Desire and pleasure cannot be regulated. They often frustrate efforts to repress them because they transmit complex existential questions relating to the relationships between the body and the soul. In 1955, King Vidor directed for Universal Studios what is today considered one of the great myths of the Western, *Man Without a Star*.[129] The story is simple: a solitary drifter who obeys only his instincts and his appetites is called on to assist a community of small ranchers threatened by a domineering woman who is seeking to appropriate their land. They try to defend themselves by putting barbed wire round their property. The hero is torn between the primal erotic force by which he is possessed and the demand for justice on the part of the poor, between the search for egotistical pleasure in the arms of an employer determined to instrumentalize him and the sense of collective duty. Amateurs of Freud may see it as an allusion to the power of the unconscious impulses opposed to a sort of cultural superego urging that one transcend narcissism for the general good. In any case, not long before the sexual revolution of the 1960s, the great director King Vidor showed that desire was still a deeply destructive force and in permanent opposition to the objectives of civilization. The hero is doubly crucified, both by revisiting his past and on the metal barbs of the barriers whose existence he denies, carried away by his savage desire for pleasure.

How can we measure the ebbs and flows of desire in our culture? Perhaps revealing an English sense of humour, Desmond Morris suggests that we study the length of women's skirts, as they usually grow shorter during periods of prosperity and longer in times of economic crisis. It is difficult to understand, he gravely remarks, why women want to expose a little more of their legs when the economy is prospering.[130] While waiting for a thesis to be devoted to this tricky problem, we may confine ourselves to the main trends. During the Roaring Twenties, skirts were calf-length; they became significantly longer during the Depression of the 1930s, climbed during the Second World War, descended with the New Look, then grew extremely short during the prosperous sixties, shrinking to a bare minimum that was the delight of male chauvinists in the age of the miniskirt. The petrol crisis and economic collapse of the 1970s spared fashion designers the task of devising a modest embellishment for the crotch, as the tension and skirts fell once again. Since when, dress designers seem to have had great difficulty in predicting the future with their scissors, even when consulting the gurus of Wall Street. What are we to conclude? Are the ups and downs perhaps primarily a sign for interpreting the fluctuations of a moral disapproval that was transformed into a 'magic skin' in the aftermath of the Second World War? Has the miniskirt lifted the last Victorian veil? Have we seen the end of the burning eroticism of women's legs, which the nineteenth-century Briton, prudish to the point of covering up those of pianos, could not even imagine without swooning with delight or choking with rage? Did the sixties initiate a fundamental sexual revolution?

Part IV

REVOLUTIONS? THE HERITAGE OF THE SIXTIES

The notion of pleasure extends beyond the definition of the satisfaction of the needs and the desires to join up with the theme of happiness. Thus, if we are to explore it properly, we need to consider the question of personal and collective morality in the face of life, its joys and its sorrows.[1] Nor can we avoid a close consideration of religion and the way it is experienced by the Subject.

The originality of Europe today, characterized by increasing individualism and intense hedonism, has its roots in the distant past. As the preceding chapters have shown, it all started in the sixteenth century, when a few rare individuals, who stood out from their contemporaries, began to develop a singular image of their Self, in spite of all the pressures of an extremely repressive society, religion and morality. The second major phase led from the libertines of the seventeenth century, who challenged theological dogmas and extolled the joys of physical love, to the *philosophes* of the Enlightenment, who influenced small but dynamic social groups. It included the discovery of sexual pleasure, which brought major transgressions and symbolic fractures to both Paris and London in the last century of the *ancien régime*. Each in his own way, the marquis de Sade and the physician Tissot, campaigner against the dangers of the solitary vice, bear witness to this.[2] At the same time, a part of spiritual transcendence migrated to other spheres, in particular that of politics, with the affirmation of the 'disenchantment of the world'.[3] This was followed by a long period of Victorian sexual glaciation, lasting until the major changes of the 1960s. In our own day, sociologists, psychologists, philosophers and historians describe the dominant cult of the Ego, while constraints fall away and social controls prove much less stifling than in the past.[4] Beauty, health, youth, wealth and eternity are promised to each and every one of us by the consumer society, by advertising and by the media. This produces an ever-increasing thirst to experience a narcissistic epiphany, without which one feels to be failing to achieve total self-fulfilment. Such a world view is based on an implicit belief in a continuous progress of humanity; and that the Self, at the beginning of the twenty-first century, will largely impose its hedonistic desires and its immense appetite for life on political and religious structures increasingly required to adapt to its meteoric rise. Tinged with idealism, this interpretation seriously underestimates the inextinguishable gregarious appetite that characterizes our species. The evident triumph of individualism is in reality a sort of dynamic renegotiation of the social pact and the contract of civilization, an adaptation of Western culture to the challenges of globalization.

Since the early 1990s, many observers have spoken of a new 'Euro-secularity' – that is, an accelerated decline of religious belief in the Old Continent and Canada, in contrast to the United States.[5] According to a survey published in 2000, deep faith in a personal God stands at 36 per cent in Europe (20 per cent in France) as against 69 per cent in the land of Uncle Sam, where simple belief in the existence of a Creator rises to 93 per cent, as against 69 per cent on this side of the Atlantic (57 per cent in France).[6] This spectacular decline seems to derive from a 'spiritual individualism absorbed by the modern culture of self-fulfilment', the principal cause of which is the 'revolution of food satiety'.[7] Having eaten its fill for the first time in history, Western civilization is experiencing a radical transformation of the symbolic relationship – collective or personal – with death and the world. The ideal of achievement is increasingly related to the individual him- or herself. The aspiration to happiness has gone beyond the fear of going hungry, to focus instead on self-fulfilment. The traditional link between hunger, closely associated with the sense of death, and the divine promise to give everyone their 'daily bread' has been broken.[8] Yet the United States does not follow the same pattern of spiritual development, although the majority of its citizens eat as much, if not more, than Europeans. Other variables, essentially cultural and symbolic, need to be considered in order to complete the picture. After the turning-point of the years 1968–70, 'individualism in collective life' became more strongly established in France.[9] Our continent has not experienced the 'culture wars' which have raged in America since the 1990s.[10] With regard to social issues such as abortion, gay marriage and capital punishment, these wars divide the United States into two fiercely opposed camps. The influence of the

South and the Bible belt makes for great intransigence in these matters. A Gallup poll of May 2003 found that 64 per cent of those questioned were in favour of the death penalty (31 per cent opposed it), 93 per cent rejected double adultery and 46 per cent illegitimate births; 44 per cent judged homosexuality acceptable (52 per cent against) and only 37 per cent were in favour of abortion (53 per cent against). There is a widening gulf with neighbouring Canada, which is very close to the European model and equally marked by a strong religious decline, and where many provinces, including Quebec, allow same-sex marriages. The difference is based on something difficult to define: the sense of happiness is not the same on both sides of the frontier. Canada seems socially more relaxed and less dominated by the laws of the market.[11] This is also what most American analysts think about the Old Continent, in particular France. At a French film festival in New York, in March 2004, one critic contrasted the culture of 'imperial chauvinism' conveyed by the cinema of his own country with a rather more feminine epicureanism he claimed to detect in the irreducible land of France.[12] If perhaps a little exaggerated, the distinction at least evokes a current, rather disapproving American view of a search for pleasure which does not conform to the canons of the land of the Star-Spangled Banner. If individualism represents a virtue in both cases, it takes very different forms on either side of the Atlantic.

Some slight shifts are visible, however, at the beginning of the twenty-first century. A timid resurgence of religion seems to be visible in Europe, while there are signs of some wavering in the United States.[13] In this fluid situation, pleasure plays a central but ambiguous role. It is not absolutely certain, half a century later, that the hedonism of the sixties has definitively triumphed in the West. Do the most visible revolutions in the sphere of sexual liberation, in particular a woman's right to orgasm, represent permanent breaks with the past? Are we living through a real revolution in desire and sexual pleasure? Or simply a powerful hedonist surge which might be succeeded by a new repressive offensive, just as the Victorian nineteenth century reversed the triumphant eroticism of the age of Enlightenment?

6

THE ERA OF PLEASURE (FROM 1960 TO OUR OWN DAY)

The sixties were crucial years in both Europe and North America. They saw massive changes, especially in the cultural sphere. At the dawn of the twenty-first century, the founding generation (today's 'oldies', the former baby-boomers) has seen that of its immediate heirs take its place, followed by the offspring of the latter. All three generations have left their own mark on the fabric of our civilization, as the great-grandsons and great-granddaughters of the former baby-boomers are now also beginning to do. These four successive strata should not, therefore, be considered as a single whole. The increasingly rapid changes testify to great diversity, further accentuated by social class, economic capacity and educational and intellectual differences. A whole book would not suffice, however, to explore such nuances. We need to stick to the essentials in an attempt to understand whether the 'revolutions of the sixties' represent the beginning of a radically different Western system or whether they constitute, at most, a permissive phase that might be followed by a period of tightening constraints, on the model of previous cycles.

The story of the break begins in 1948, with the publication in Philadelphia of the first report of Alfred C. Kinsey.[1] Very brave for its time, and fiercely criticized, it opened a window on male sexuality, previously a source of embarrassment and blanketed in silence. Close behind Kinsey came cohorts of researchers who made haste to widen the breach, not without difficulty in the United States, much more easily in Europe. The time was ripe for a scientific analysis of the subject. Later, many investigations highlighted the essential role of female pleasure, liberated from the obligation of motherhood for the first time in human history, depending on the free choice of the woman concerned. This is the true revolution! Though still difficult to evaluate at all precisely, its consequences quickly made themselves felt in every area of human relationships. The shock waves spread to other symbolic spaces. Within 50 years, homosexuality ceased to be regarded as abnormal behaviour, at least in Europe, though it remains a burning issue on the other side of the Atlantic, where gay marriage is the subject of impassioned debate in the first decade of the twenty-first century.

The question of sexuality and pleasure was so crucial in our civilization for centuries that it remained taboo, like the great founding myths. The radical change inaugurated by Kinsey was made possible by a fundamental shift in the perception by the Subject of their relationship to others. This shift became more pronounced as the great ideologies were contested and as the Western-style social contract was forced both to adapt to new challenges on the world stage and to integrate an irresistible aspiration to personal success, a consequence of the spread of a hedonist trend. The body and the soul no longer speak with the same voice at the dawn of the third millennium. Yet the individual-as-king is only a metaphor to explain the transformation of the culture in which that individual exists. Even if it is no longer much influenced by the dilatory responses issuing from the great ideologies or the churches, the quest for instant happiness does not stop people from thinking about transcendence or what happens after death, at the price of contradictions which may prove creative or, on the contrary, painful. Half a century after the discoveries of Kinsey and his team, America, unlike Europe, hesitates on the threshold of defining a new sexual pact, on which every communal tie is based, seeking to preserve the dogma of the heterosexual family and the principle of the strict control of sensual pleasure.

A sexual bombshell: the Kinsey Report

One only need open the first volume of the massive Kinsey Report of 1948 to realize that the United States was then the devoted custodian of the repressive European tradition. In revealing, for the first time, the reality of erotic behaviour in one of the most puritan of universes, the Report opened a veritable Pandora's box. The California of Peace and Love, the movements for sexual liberation, the discovery of female pleasure and the demands for recognition by those who were then labelled as deviants or abnormal – these are only some of the consequences of this veritable seismic shock, particularly violent in a country of marked contrasts.

The origins of the 'culture wars'

Director of the Institute for Sex Research at the University of Indiana, Alfred Charles Kinsey (1894–1956) embarked, in 1938, on a gigantic sociological investigation into human sexual behaviour. The results were published in two volumes, one in 1948 on men, the other in 1953 on women.[2] His method was to present and discuss statistical data observed and compared as a function of every possible parameter – sex, age, geographical origin, educational level, occupation, civil status, etc. The conclusions were recorded in descriptive language devoid of passion. One cannot help but suspect, however, that the readers of the 800 pages devoted to the human male, in 1948, must sometimes have smiled to themselves or, on the contrary, fumed with rage as they worked their way through this simple but precise prose. In the conclusion to the section on sexual contacts with animals, for example, it is noted that their frequency varied tremendously in different parts of the United States and that the figures given applied primarily to the north-eastern quarter of the country. Around 6 per cent of the male population, the Report reveals, engaged in such activities during early adolescence, but the figure dropped to about 1 per cent for single men over the age of 20. In the case of the unmarried male rural population aged between 11 and 15 years, 11 per cent were involved, with a maximum frequency of eight relations a week for the most active individuals – and so on.[3]

The most fascinating aspect of this systematic, scholarly study is the way it defines with exemplary clarity the difference between norms and reality. Kinsey and his team brought out the extremely constrictive repressive dimension of the 'English-American' tradition. Heir to Christian norms, it considered sex solely as a means to procreation and accepted 'no form of socio-sexual activity outside of the marital state'. Even intercourse within marriage was limited to particular times and places and to the techniques most likely to result in conception. As a result, single men, widowers and divorced men had in theory no rights in this sphere, since they could not legally procreate. Homosexuals and masturbators were viewed with disfavour by public opinion for the same reasons, and penalized by the law in case of transgression. The American legislations characterized all pre-marital, extra-marital or post-marital intercourse as abnormal and illicit, calling the acts by such names as rape, fornication, adultery, prostitution, incest, assault and battery or public indecency. Similarly, any homosexual activity or sexual contact with animals was punishable. If brought to the attention of the courts, mouth-genital or anal sex practised by a legally married couple was also penalized. Even if those involved were consenting, heavy petting between adolescents was liable to prosecution as assault and battery or impairment of the morals of minors. The slightest public erotic exhibition, even the viewing of such an activity, could lead to a prosecution for 'delinquency' or public indecency. Masturbation was held in particular abhorrence. In 1905, Indiana decreed that the encouragement of this vice was in itself an offence punishable as sodomy. Some educational institutions imposed physical punishments on those who masturbated; a regulation of June 1940 of the United States Naval Academy at Annapolis considered evidence of it sufficient grounds for refusing admission to a candidate.[4]

The second Kinsey Report emphasized the ambiguity of the prevailing moral and cultural messages regarding sex. Religion, the law, psychologists and psychiatrists, supported by a majority of the public, extolled heterosexual coitus as the most desirable, the most mature and the most socially acceptable form of sexual activity. Yet these same authorities were strongly critical of it if it occurred outside marriage, which confused the issue in the eyes of adolescents. In 1953, most American states still prohibited any copulation between juveniles before the age of majority, which varied from 14 to 21 according to place. The magistrates generally reacted with greater severity if the accused was under the age of 20, belonged to a different social level or was of a different racial group, as they did too if an adult male had sex with a female minor.[5]

The puritanical America of the 1950s emerges as a custodian of the anti-sexual ideology as it had been imposed in Europe in the seventeenth century, in the days of forbidden pleasure.[6] As we have seen, the erotic literature itself had then sanctioned the model of exclusively procreative marriage, so as to ensure that no precious semen was ever lost. The churches and the law labelled all relations outside marriage as impure and criminal, the worst imaginable depravities being homosexuality, bestiality and incest. In the patient expectation of a belated conjugal felicity, young girls were expected to preserve intact the treasure of their virginity, and young boys to shun masturbation. The only major difference compared with the descriptions of Kinsey concerns female sexual pleasure, which had then been considered indispensable to successful conception. The principle was subsequently abandoned when the Victorians proclaimed that the desire for orgasm was found only among prostitutes, never in respectable wives. In the middle of the twentieth century, the United States achieved a normative synthesis of this twofold historical heritage. Not only did religion, prevailing mores and the law impose the exclusive ideal of marriage directed towards reproduction, issuing dire threats against all rebels and deviants, but the Victorian tradition put strict limits on the taste for carnal pleasure, including within marriage, and in particular for women.

However, the Kinsey researchers observed that such restrictive norms and codes were not observed by the majority of their contemporaries. One may suspect that a heavy price was paid in terms of frustration and perhaps the guilt the Subject was made to feel, without being able to take this further, as the investigation stops at this point. Fifty years later, the Puritan legacy still hangs heavy over the land of Uncle Sam. Kinsey was afraid that a literal interpretation of the strict anti-masturbation law of 1905 in Indiana might make it possible to prosecute a scholar for having written that masturbation did no physical harm, on the pretext that such a scientific conclusion might be an encouragement to commit the offence. In December 1994, Joycelyn Elders, United States Surgeon General in the Clinton administration, was fired by the President for having publicly stated, at a United Nations conference on AIDS, that it might be helpful if masturbation were taught in state schools. This, at least, was the reason officially put forward at a press conference in Miami, when the President explained that such an attitude conflicted with the policy of his cabinet and with 'his own convictions'.[7] Dr Elders' remarks shocked both leading Democrats and the most traditionalist of Christians. The taboo remains one of the most powerful and most widespread in the United States.

Other recent cases suggest that 'culture wars' are now being fought between two camps with entrenched opinions – progressives and conservatives – over abortion, the family, gay marriage or simply the sexual rights of the individual. A brilliant athlete selected to enter Vanderbilt University, Marcus Dixon, a young black student from Rome, a largely white community in Georgia, had his life turned upside down in 2004 when he was sentenced to 10 years in prison for having had sexual relations, aged 18, with a white girl at the same school, a minor aged 15 years and 9 months. A jury of nine whites and three blacks acquitted him of the felony charges of rape, but found him guilty of statutory rape and aggravated child molestation. The first charge applied to physical relations with a minor, even if consenting. The maximum sentence was one year's imprisonment, Georgia being one of 35 states which had promulgated 'Romeo and Juliet' statutes decriminalizing or reducing the punishments in the case of adolescent offenders. However, the second charge was extremely serious. Defined in 1995 by the local legislators as one of the 'seven capital sins', it carried a mandatory sentence of 10 years in prison. It had been brought because the victim was a virgin, had bruises in her vagina and cuts to her lips and claimed not to have consented. Few people realized what the consequences would be. The judge explained that he was obliged to apply the law. After the sentence had been announced, five members of the jury declared that they would not have voted as they did if they had realized that Marcus would remain so long behind bars. The punishment was too heavy for a simple act of sex between teenagers, all the more so as there was no recent record of such severity in Georgia's history. The *New York Times* was strongly critical of this example of 'Old South justice'. The district attorney tried to defuse the allegations of racism by claiming that Marcus Dixon was a 'sexual predator', because he had already twice been criticized for 'inappropriate sexual behaviour', once when he had exposed himself in class, the other time when he had put his hands on a female student's bottom.[8]

The old prohibitions surrounding juvenile sex could still be activated in legal form at the beginning of the twenty-first century. Among the criteria defined by Kinsey in 1953, the minority of the 'victim', and the majority and difference in colour of the 'aggressor', continue to weigh heavily. The girl herself had stated that she had not wanted to be seen with Marcus because her father 'was a racist', and she was afraid he would kill them both if he saw her with a Black. But public opinion was not monolithic, as shown by the 'Romeo and Juliet' statutes adopted in the majority of states, the reaction of some members of the jury in Georgia, the shocked article in the *New York Times* and the activities of the Marcus Dixon support committees, which succeeded in obtaining his early release. Though infrequent, even exceptional, such trials are highly symbolic and judged, accordingly, with brutal severity. The reality is that the laws crush a few deviants who are punished as an example, but allow the mass of those who infringe them to go free. Ultimately, permissiveness prevails over the constraining norms and codes, as the Kinsey Reports made plain.

Homosexuality and masturbation

The summary of conclusions to the 1948 study of the American male highlighted the fact that the average widower or divorcee continued to lead an active sex life in spite of the customs, laws and mores prohibiting it. He still conformed to the dominant model for the married man, satisfying his desires 80 per cent of the time with heterosexual sex. For the rest, he masturbated, had wet dreams or, if he was still young, had relations with partners of the same sex, about as often as the single adolescent boy.[9] Kinsey calmly laid out some statistical truths particularly distressing to the moralists by revealing as widespread what some called deviancies, vices or perversions. He refused to divide the male population into heterosexuals and homosexuals, preferring to speak of a continuum and proposing a seven-point scale to describe the possible stages in an individual's sexual orientation during the course of his life. The zero rating was used for men who were exclusively heterosexual, six for those who were exclusively homosexual and three for those who were equally heterosexual and homosexual.[10] Over a third of white males interviewed (37 per cent) had had 'at least some overt homosexual experience to the point of orgasm between adolescence and old age'. This was also the case, on average, for 50 per cent of those who remained single until the age of 35. Educational level was an important factor, as the figure rose to 58 per cent for the better educated. At the other end of the scale, men whose activities were exclusively homosexual from adolescence on amounted to only 4 per cent of the group; Havelock Ellis had estimated the figure at between 2 and 3 per cent at the beginning of the century. However, only 8 per cent were exclusively homosexual for at least three years between the ages of 15 and 55.[11] In other words, in youth, 'nature' or desire was more important than 'culture', that is, the law and the normative codes, after which the matrimonial ideal became increasingly exclusive and constrictive. There are strong echoes here of the European *ancien régime*, when unmarried men, in theory constrained to chastity, enjoyed a tacit tolerance, only to change their habits once they had received the sacrament of marriage. In 1953, Kinsey added some observations on the extreme severity of the law on this subject in most American states. Labelled, as in the seventeenth century, as 'sodomy, buggery, perverse or unnatural acts, crimes against nature', etc., such behaviour was often punished as harshly as violence against persons. One single state, New York, imposed no penalties as long as these acts were confined to adults, in private and with the consent of both parties, as was the case in Scandinavia and other Western countries.[12]

Among the great cultures of the mid-twentieth century, that of North America was considered the most repressive by the Kinsey team. It took a lot of courage to confront, as they did, oppressive prohibitions that had the support of the churches, the courts and public opinion. One of the pebbles calmly thrown into the sea of conformism, regarding masturbation, is still causing ripples today. The 1948 study revealed that nearly 99 per cent of the youngest boys, those aged between 8 and 12, had experimented, and that about 92 per cent of the total male population masturbated to the point of orgasm. The exceptions were predominantly boys from the lower social classes, who had no need to masturbate because they had heterosexual sex at a very early age, and those who were not interested because they got enough sexual pleasure from wet dreams. Globally, the figures accord pretty well with European studies, which put the figure at between 85 and 96 per cent. Masturbation is a formidable taboo in the United States, added Kinsey, which meant that there was deep reluctance to admit to it when questioned, especially among the less well educated.[13]

Such an attitude seems to be directly inherited from the major prohibition proclaimed by Western medicine since Tissot.[14] It combines the notion of sin derived from Christianity with that of a loss of substance damaging both to the individual and to society as a whole. A powerful sense of guilt is felt at the mere mention of the subject, which provokes embarrassment, anxiety or denial in those present. It is by no means certain that this is fully conscious. A sort of automatic reflex has been confusedly perfected in a country that is extremely hostile to any form of sex outside marriage, as Kinsey emphasized. Masturbation is very difficult to detect, obviously, hence to punish and stamp out. An anecdote related in the *New York Review of Books* in 2004 reveals the depth of unease created by any reference to it. The issue of 8 April discussed 'solitary sex' in connection with a book devoted to the subject. The author had been invited to lecture on it at Harvard two years before. This initiative had set off a mini-panic among the instructors who led the seminars and conducted tutorials. A staff meeting to discuss the 'Great Masturbation Crisis' took place in an atmosphere as feverish as it was embarrassed. One instructor declared that it was against his conscience to assign students to read the book or even require them to attend the lecture.[15] Yet the state of Massachusetts is not renowned for the narrowness of its outlook. The local supreme court had even made news, late in 2003, by authorizing gay marriage as from 17 May 2004, the first legal initiative of this type, and fiercely criticized by the neoconservatives. That such deep anxiety should be felt with regard to the solitary vice, in a prestigious university in a supposedly open-minded part of America, makes it possible to appreciate the full extent of the cultural silence on this subject.

The 1953 Kinsey Report on women revealed that about 62 per cent had masturbated at some point in their lives, but only 58 per cent had achieved orgasm. Their number increased with age, probably because they had fewer opportunities for intercourse, but perhaps also, suggested Kinsey, because women acquired greater erotic sensibility as they grew older. One of his most sensational conclusions, quickly seized on by those who demanded the right to sexual enjoyment, concerned the effects of this on the sexual life of a couple. The investigation showed that wives often had more difficulty than husbands in achieving sensual satisfaction. Among the causes suggested was that 36 per cent of them had never experienced any pleasure at all before marriage, whether in a complete relationship, heavy petting, homosexual relations or masturbation. The quality of conjugal relations was closely dependent on some previous experience of orgasm: between 31 and 37 per cent of those who had never masturbated, or never to orgasm, failed to reach orgasm within the first year of marriage, even, in most cases, during the first five years, whereas only 13–16 per cent of those who had masturbated to orgasm fell into this category. Masturbatory techniques among women were also very varied: 84 per cent, compared with 95 per cent of men, had recourse to genital manipulation, 20 per cent to vaginal insertions, 15 per cent to thigh pressures or muscular tensions and 2 per cent to fantasy alone, something extremely rare among men.[16]

A hidden erotic culture

Whereas close to 100 per cent of men achieved orgasm during coitus, the rate was only between 70 and 77 per cent among women. In more than two-thirds of cases, foreplay lasted for between 15 and 20 minutes, in 22 per cent for longer and in only 11 per cent for less than 3 minutes. The most common position was for the man to be on top of his partner, but the interviews of 1953 revealed that women frequently enjoyed two other positions, either being themselves on top of the man (45 per cent) or lying side by side (31 per cent).[17] Other figures revealed a hidden sensual culture, in contradiction with morality and the law. Nudity, for example, was more acceptable among the upper classes than lower down the social scale, where it was even described as obscene by the least well-off and least well educated. Among the former, 90 per cent regularly had sex naked and many of them, especially men, also slept naked.[18] In the case of the lower classes, this should be seen as a belated Victorian heritage, whereas the elites had adopted other habits as a way of distinguishing themselves from ordinary people. Yet, though the taboo on nudity was relaxed within the conjugal intimacy of the upper classes, it remained more important in public than in some European countries, especially Scandinavian. The norms of the Hollywood cinema continue to testify to a puritan prudery which is no longer accepted in the rest of the Western world. Like violence and bloodshed, nakedness, kissing and love scenes are still subject to strict supervision in the United States and rigorously codified in order to warn the public.[19]

The two Kinsey Reports emphasized a social disjunction in the mid-twentieth century. The sexual practices of the affluent were clearly distinguished from those of the mass of the population by a greater freedom and emphasis on the search for erotic pleasure. Deep petting was highly valued by both men and women. The explanation offered is that men are persuaded by talk among friends and by reading marriage manuals that women need intense sensory stimulation if they are to achieve orgasm at the same time as their partner during coitus. As a result, women's breasts and genitalia were almost always manipulated (96 and 90 per cent of cases) at this social level, whereas men from lower down the social scale were less likely to bother with this (79 and 75 per cent). One observation that is of considerable interest, but not discussed, is that the investigation of 1948 indicated that working-class women achieve orgasm more often, yet in the arms of partners who make less effort to encourage them by foreplay. These women were also the most reluctant to manipulate male sexual organs (57 per cent). Among these categories, the author laconically notes, intromission was regarded as the essential activity in 'normal' sexual relations. Ways of kissing also varied with social class. Though common and desirable among the affluent, the practice was much rarer and more superficial among the working class. Whereas the former found deep kissing, with tongue contact and exploration of the interior of the partner's mouth, exciting and exotic (87 per cent), this was seen as dirty and a source of disease by the latter.[20]

There could be no better illustration of the extent to which the whole of human sexuality is always a cultural construct, relating to the values of a given civilization. The deep kiss was part of the ancient art of love. Yet in the nineteenth century it became for the working and middle classes a negative sign of the libidinous sensuality of aristocrats greedy for sex. In the United States around 1950, it was propelled to the top of the social pyramid, where it was seen as proof of an ability to pay attention to the desires of one's loved one. If it was shunned by the working classes, this was probably more to preserve their identity by asserting their attachment to manly values than from a real distaste for intimate contact. Petting had been heavy and varied in the Somerset countryside in the seventeenth century.[21] Only women from the nobility and the prosperous Puritan peasantry had rejected it, to assert both their difference and their disapproval. Such facts should not, therefore, be analysed as absolutes, in the name of a contingent morality. Forms of sexual pleasure constantly adapt to the dominant collective codes, principally as a function of gender, age and social position. What is acceptable or desirable for some becomes unacceptable or reprehensible for others, in a communal process in which sexuality serves both as reference point and proof of normality in the eyes of those one wishes to resemble. When the American elites widely indulged in mild transgressions of the laws and of morality, the ordinary people set themselves up as the latter's defenders, implicitly criticizing the laxity of the elites. The 'culture wars' did not begin in the 1990s. They have their roots in much older antagonisms linked to economic, religious or educational background. The fracture line is even more marked at the beginning of the twenty-first century. If abortion, gay marriage and erotic techniques are its pretexts, they reveal the deep existence of an old hostility between those who want to believe in the prohibitions and norms at all costs and those who disregard them, because they are sufficiently powerful, moneyed and cultured not to be too seriously affected by the legal sanctions or the ostracism promised to deviants. It should be remembered that public, extra-marital petting was defined as indecency in most American states in 1950, even as an offence if it involved intimate touching or mouth-genital contact. Prosecutions might follow cases of denunciation by irate parents or outraged neighbours. In Oregon, all 'perverse' genital contact was a crime against nature. The same was true in Arizona of bodily touching performed in an 'unnatural' manner with a view to arousing sexual desire in a person. In many states, contact between the mouth and the penis or vagina was punished, either as if it was sodomy or because it represented a 'crime against nature'.[22]

Oral experiences within the couple were also proscribed by the laws and statutes of many states. There are cases of married couples being brought before the courts and sentenced because their activities became known to their children and, through them, to the neighbours. The repression in this sphere was so strong in mid-century that it created an extreme reluctance to reply to questions about it, which minimized the extent of the phenomenon.[23] The inhibition has since lost much of its power, as all the surveys of the late 1980s showed that cunnilingus and fellatio were practised by 90 per cent of respondents, married or unmarried. Women even complained about the male obsession with blow jobs.[24]

The remarkable work of the team under Kinsey revealed the basic paradigm of ideal American sexuality around 1950: the heterosexual couple and it alone! The defence of this bastion of the system meant an interdict on pre-marital relations – whereas in Europe, clinicians believed they might have some benefits for the individual and for the community – and also on every type of 'abnormal' pleasure, that is, other than penetration with a view to procreation. The law also penalized adultery, more severely in the north-east of the country than elsewhere.[25] Nevertheless, the reality was very different from the codes, the rules and the social conventions. This second conclusion of the research of Kinsey was also the most detailed, the fullest and the most impressive. It makes it easier to understand the emergence in the 1960s, in California and elsewhere, of a desire for pleasure that was in conflict with the legal and moral imperatives and even more the classic division of the United States into two radically opposed camps. The current 'culture wars' are not purely religious and political. They have many other dimensions, in particular an insurmountable difference with regard to the management of marriage and the carnal freedoms. Those committed to the permanence of the founding heterosexual couple bitterly oppose the 'transgressives' who claim a pre-eminent right to turn into normality what the established legislations and mores still label as sins, attitudes against nature, offences and sometimes even crimes. At the beginning of the third millennium, this is what most distinguishes the United States from Europe, where those opposed to change have already lost the battle, in spite of the rearguard action being fought by traditionalists against contraception and abortion.

The survival of a sexual double standard

When we come to explore the underlying reasons for the institutional, religious and ethical attachment of Americans to the exclusive ideal of the conjugal family, sole permitted site for sensual pleasure, things get more complicated. Kinsey had no difficulty in demonstrating that behaviour conflicted with the repressive theories. This was sometimes on such a massive scale that one wonders why, when everybody, or almost everybody, broke it, the rule continued to exist. This was the case with masturbation and with the systematic prohibitions applying to single, widowed and divorced men, all of whom were in practice almost as sexually active as their married peers. One explanatory hypothesis might be to see the tension between the codes and the realities as a necessary dimension of the American system. Is the constant obligatory confrontation between Good and Evil the principal key to interpreting it? Might permanent trench warfare, without true victors or vanquished, be a necessary prerequisite to achieving a socially effective compromise? For, in the last analysis, while professing to be shocked by them in public, many conformists tolerate concrete modifications to the classic matrimonial system, while the deviants ultimately accept its validity as long as they go largely unpunished for their defiance of the strict laws. It may be that a sort of conflictual consensus is the secret of a country that is both notably puritan in theory and often liberal in practice.

The United States seems to engage en masse in what one might – in homage to the Victorians who invented the notion for the sole benefit of married men – call the sexual 'double standard'. It is only to be expected that in the land of Uncle Sam, home of democracy, this principle should be extended to everyone, not only to women but to 'deviants' and marginals as well. The sole officially accepted norm is that of the heterosexual couple whose main aim is to procreate, not to enjoy sex. But everyone can get as much sex as they need, in the tacit context of an effective tolerance, constantly expanding as a consequence of the battles waged by the relevant pressure groups: racial minorities in the 1960s, then women, more recently homosexuals. Most young people set out to enjoy themselves, Kinsey had observed in 1948. The talk today is not only of the erotic rights of gays and lesbians but also of their social recognition and their access to the sacred institution of marriage, as in Massachusetts since May 2004, while awaiting other advances.

Further, Kinsey tends to underestimate the scale of the resort to women of easy virtue, basis of the Victorian double standard in the nineteenth century. The investigation of 1948 established that about 69 per cent of the white male population had 'some experience with prostitutes', but the discussion is concentrated on the 31 per cent who had never sought contact of this type and the small minority of regular clients of prostitutes, who became increasingly assiduous with age. Previous generations, says the Report, visited specialized houses more frequently, with a variety of aims, not exclusively erotic; they were also seeking relaxation or even simply to form relationships. The conclusion argues that their attraction for men was waning, thanks to an active educational campaign and legal moves. There is also a rather surprising calculation regarding the potential use of the services of these women between adolescence and impotence, which produces the figure of 3,190 visits per week for a town of 100,000 inhabitants. The aim was to demonstrate the impossibility of resolving this problem through police activity.[26] Embarrassed formulations and scarcely resolved contradictions tend to suggest that the male Victorian double standard survived and had even surreptitiously spread to the whole of sexual life. We need to try to imagine the mental and social tension experienced by men when they were required to abandon the status of juvenile transgressor, characterized by masturbation for nearly all boys and homosexual experiences for over two-thirds of them, and don the mantle of custodian of the matrimonial temple. Masturbation and homosexuality then decrease, but other prohibitions are transgressed, especially those on oral sex and on coitus with the woman on top. Successive generations, up to our own day, seem to have accepted a slightly schizophrenic 'double constraint': on the one hand, the dominant message validates the pre-eminent sacredness of marriage and glorifies conjugal sensuality; on the other, it instils guilt in the unmarried, young and old, and officially forbids them any form of carnal pleasure, but this does not prevent them from indulging in it as frequently as married couples. The challenge to this whole system finally came from women, for whom it had not been constructed, when they discovered that their pleasure was very different in nature from that of men.

The discovery of the female orgasm

A huge collective work, the Kinsey Report overturned many received ideas. This cool demystification was rapidly utilized by groups relegated to the margins of society, who drew on the data it assembled to demand their rights. They included the male and female 'third gender', which has since become a major field of study. This has helped date the historical origins of the gay phenomenon in London to around 1700.[27] Others have been grateful to the Kinsey Report for its demonstration that only a minority of the American population was either solely homosexual or solely heterosexual, many people being capable of developing an attraction for someone of the opposite sex at some point in their life. According to the study of 1953, between 3 and 10 per cent of women questioned had some lesbian experience; by the age of 40, 19 per cent had enjoyed at least one deliberate erotic contact with a person of the same sex.[28]

Everything that had been categorized as an unspeakable and reprehensible perversion before Kinsey now occupied a normal, almost banal, place in the great book of sexuality and life. Voices emanating from the margins of society were more clearly heard after this scientific enquiry. The authors openly proclaimed their belief in the notion of sex as a normal biological function, an interpretation popularized by Freud, while admitting that this hardly conformed to the English or American doctrine, which spoke rather of a primitive, materialistic attitude beneath the dignity of a civilized and educated people.[29] This was certainly the reaction of the hostile readers who learned that masturbation was not a vice but a commonplace activity. The ground was now prepared for further studies and open debate, in fact for a quite new view of sexuality, in spite of the scandal Kinsey provoked, or perhaps because of it.

Female pleasure

In 1966, another pebble was thrown into the pond of age-old certainties. William Masters and Virginia Johnson published a biological and psychological investigation, *Human Sexual Response*, which offered the first scientific analysis of female sexual pleasure.[30] The results were based on the reports of 487 women, given in the research laboratory immediately after experiencing orgasm. Three distinct stages were identified. The first began with a sensation of suspension, accompanied or immediately followed by an intense sensual awareness, clitorally oriented, but radiating upwards into the pelvis. Many women reported at this moment a sense of expelling, and a small number believed there had been a real emission of fluid. The authors noted that this might explain the male interpretation, which they believed was erroneous if widespread, that women ejaculated during orgasm. This had been an obsession of Walter, anonymous author of *My Secret Life* at the end of the nineteenth century, who was forever trying to analyse in detail what his many partners had felt – the soul of a sexologist, as it were, in the body of a seducer.[31]

The second stage described by Masters and Johnson consisted of a sort of suffusion of warmth pervading the pelvic area, then progressively spreading throughout the body. The third stage took the form of a feeling of involuntary contraction, particularly marked in the vagina or lower pelvis. Some of the women described two successive moments, a spasm, immediately followed by a 'pelvic throbbing'. Taking their analysis further, the authors came up with what they regarded as a norm, that is, between five and eight vigorous contractions of the orgasmic platform. Between eight and twelve contractions was rated by researchers and subjects as an intense physiological experience, while between three and five was a mild experience, except in the case of post-menopausal women, who rated it more highly. Pregnant women experienced the effects of the orgasm more strongly, especially during the second and third trimesters. Masters and Johnson were still careful to note in conclusion that their clinical description did not allow the degree of subjective pleasure experienced to be adequately measured.[32]

The book had the indirect effect of rehabilitating masturbation, previously, as we have seen, one of the great American taboos. The authors demolished the Freudian thesis that women abandoned this practice as adults, observing that most of them continued to masturbate throughout their sexual life. Further, they were not content with a single orgasm when manipulating the clitoris, but sought orgasms to the point of exhaustion. It was not the aim of the authors to champion the solitary vice, but rather to play down its importance and incorporate it into heterosexual relations. It was to be a long time before this was achieved. Instead, the message was quickly hijacked by the feminist movements and then by gay groups to be used as an argument for erotic freedom and the rejection of the constrictive norms. The next few years saw the publication of numerous radical proclamations it had inspired. In 1970, Anne Koedt published her *Myth of the Vaginal Orgasm*; in 1971, there appeared a veritable bible on the subject, produced by a female collective from Boston, *Our Bodies, Ourselves*, four million copies of which, in 16 languages, were sold within 30 years; in 1974, Betty Dodson produced a bestseller, which had run to six editions by 1996, *Liberating Masturbation: A Meditation on Self-Love*.[33]

The true sexual revolution of the twentieth century primarily concerned women and started in the United States in the 1950s, then accelerating in subsequent decades. Thus it was in a society deeply anxious about the issue that the mechanisms for radical change were established, before being extended to the whole of the Western world. The North American universe is at one and the same time that of the intensely repressive patriarchy described in the Kinsey Reports of 1948 and 1953 and that of the great liberation movement launched in reaction to the oppressive rigidity of the codes and the norms. Looking back on her own youth in an attempt to understand, in 1990, what had happened to the sexual revolution, one expert shrewdly observed that Americans had learned to regard Eros with apprehension, even deep fear, because it was associated with passion, carnal feelings and forces that were dangerous because they seemed so uncontrollable. This is why the notion seems so threatening to family life and why it must be so strictly contained. Our young people, she says, learn at a very early age and in many different ways to limit their desires and to ward off the fear that Eros is a threat to civilization.[34]

In other words, the sexual revolution is today contained in America by traditional forces that remain immensely powerful. The defence of the heterosexual family is one of the priorities of right-minded people and of neo-conservatives. Yet the emphasis on sexuality over the past 50 years has made it the absolute yardstick for the expression of needs and appetites of every kind, well beyond the simple pleasure of the senses. Specialist works are available in their hundreds and some of them are hugely successful. In spite of this, the subject remains shrouded in silence and mystery in private life.[35] The more it is talked about in the public domain, the more enigmatic it becomes at the individual level, proof of a powerful resistance on the part of the old repressive culture, engaged in a long struggle against what challenges it. At the beginning of the twenty-first century, the positions are more entrenched and the camps more hostile than ever, leading to permanent symbolic confrontations.

The contraceptive revolutions

The principal issue is undoubtedly the liberation of women from the tyranny of an obligatorily procreative sexuality. The means had existed since the 1960s. It was still necessary for them to seem acceptable and to be put to use, which is sometimes far from being the case due to the pressure of the dominant familial, social and cultural models.

The first of these processes, the female oral contraceptive, was perfected in the 1950s by an American scientist, Gregory Pincus, and made available to consumers in 1960. The 'pill' is without doubt the most revolutionary product of the twentieth century. For a modest sum, eleven US dollars a month initially, it gave woman the power to control their fertility. Never before in human history had they had this right or this choice.[36] It is not by chance that the work of Pincus was contemporary with that of Kinsey and his team, and only a little earlier than the description of the female orgasm by Masters and Johnson. In the mid-twentieth century, an imperative need came to light in various ways in a North American society that was both very puritanical and deeply uneasy about sex.

Next, in the 1970s, came the psychological means of liberation, not only through that of the body, thanks to the progress of feminist and homosexual claims, but also more institutionally, when the United States Supreme Court legalized abortion in 1973. A bombshell for the American family, the measure continues to make its effects felt to this day, in spite of the fierce resistance of the opposing camp. As well as the right to the pill, the orgasm and solitary practices, women acquired the right not to proceed with a pregnancy that was unwanted or dangerous for their health, though within a strict legal framework. The Catholic Church continues to reject both abortion and contraception. It has long advocated the Ogino (or Rhythm or Calendar) method as the only acceptable way of regulating nature. Women who practise it can now rely on an ingenious modern technique, made available to the public in October 1966: a tiny device with a button that is pressed on day one of the menstrual cycle, and which indicates, when the light changes from green to yellow, that a urine test should be taken; if the light then turns to red, the woman is fertile for the next six to ten days. The advantage is that she can avoid all forms of contraception and the interruption of her ovulatory cycle and decide of her own free will whether or not to have sex when she knows she is fertile. When the morning-after pill is added to the equation, and with other scientific discoveries on the horizon, it becomes clear that the daughters of Eve at last have the means to have sex on equal terms with their male partner, if they choose and if they are psychologically able to do so.[37]

Good vibrations

A new 'technical' frontier in the quest for sexual enjoyment was crossed in the last decades of the twentieth century. America innovated once again, by opening up a lucrative trade previously reserved in the West to the most tolerant countries and to sex-shops: that in objects making it possible to achieve orgasm, alone or not. The first West Coast Good Vibrations, an adult store, opened in California in 1977. Initially modest, around 15,000 dollars a year, its sales reached more than eight million dollars by 2000, at which date the shop sold, among other things, 134,000 vibrators. American customers had by then bought more than a million of them. At the dawn of the third millennium, the country had four large firms manufacturing sex toys, each employing more than 100 people, including the biggest in the world, Doc Johnson. Not to be outdone, Europe had a dozen such firms at the same date. The globalization of pleasure is under way.

One internet site offers on-line silicone dildos modelled on Jesus Christ, the Virgin and Buddha.[38] Masturbation and the erotic delights have not only been normalized by the investigations of sexologists and the plethora of information in the written and visual media and on the internet, but are now the subject of such a flourishing trade that it is doubtful whether its critics can reverse the trend in the name of morality. The laws of the market, it is insufficiently realized, are the principal levers of sexual liberation today − a strange inversion of values, given that masturbation was condemned as wasteful by Tissot and the doctors of the nineteenth century. It has now become a prime principle of capitalist accumulation, which normalizes it very much more than did the reports of Kinsey or Masters and Johnson. In consequence, the taboo is steadily retreating, including in the United States, and in particular among the younger generations. Whereas the Kinsey Report of 1953 indicated that only 40 per cent of women had masturbated before their first carnal experience, more than three-quarters of women and almost all men polled had done so around 1990.[39] Apart from the growth of a practice freed from guilt, the figures also show that it has become easier to talk about it to a pollster, whereas shame and silence had minimized its importance in mid-century.

This is a return of what had been repressed, because dildos and other *bijoux indiscrets*, such as *consolateurs*, then highly prized, were openly sold in the streets of London in the eighteenth century. They were associated with an extreme sensuality, reputedly of French origin, of course. Their recent variants take many forms. Some are American in origin and are actually products of research into human reactions to copulation. These are expensive objects of transparent plastic that make it possible to film inside the vagina; they are electrically powered and equipped with controls to vary the speed and depth of the thrust, in fact machines for never-ending sexual bliss. Others are simple vibrators, but with an apparently anodyne purpose, so they can be bought without embarrassment. Yet others, electrical or not, are artistically carved, in a variety of materials, to present very varied forms. A particularly ingenious type, the *rin-no-tama*, also called *watama* or *ben-wa*, appeared in Japan around 1970. It consists of two hollow balls, roughly the size of pigeon's eggs, one of which contains a small quantity of mercury. The first, empty ball is inserted and pushed well into the vagina, followed by the second, then by a wad of paper or cotton to plug the opening. Thus equipped, a woman can pleasure herself in seeming innocence: all she needs is a swing or a rocking chair to get the balls started on a rhythmic movement that produces a pressure inside her similar to that of a male penis.[40] Lovers of the rope swing had never imagined anything like that! A variant of the 1990s, the Leather Butterfly, is a sort of vibratile electric egg which can be worn invisibly by a woman, for example during a candle-lit dinner.[41] Perhaps the relative lack of success of these techniques, though so discreet, proves right those feminists who prefer the clitoral orgasm and criticize Freud's claims regarding the primacy of vaginal stimulation.

Towards a new sexual contract?

Europe set out on the path towards a generalized sexual freedom earlier than the United States and it has more easily assimilated innovations such as the contraceptive pill, the female orgasm and sex toys. The Protestant countries, in particular Scandinavia and the Netherlands, have for a long time set an example of great tolerance as regards morality, nudity, the open display of pornographic magazines in kiosks and the comprehensive regulation of the world's oldest profession, as shown by the public exposure of prostitutes in the windows of Amsterdam or Hamburg. The Catholic countries have been more reticent, but there has been a sharp falling away of moral rigorism since May 1968. The law has adapted to the changes, in the case of abortion (authorized in France by the Veil Law of 17 January 1975), divorce, the acceptance of homosexuality and forms of legal union allowing two persons of the same sex to live together, for example the PACS (*pacte civil de solidarité*) in the land of Voltaire. The characteristic American tension between strict legislation, retained but rarely enforced, and practices that frequently contravene it, scarcely exists in the Old Continent. Features that are out of line with public opinion rapidly come to be generally tolerated, which leads the legislators to take note of changes having a major impact on the traditional system of the conjugal heterosexual family, age-old foundation of Western civilization.

Changes to the code of love

The sexual contract is being renegotiated on both sides of the Atlantic at the beginning of the third millennium.[42] This contract is a fundamental, though hidden, aspect of the social contract, and, as such, depends less on the wishes of individuals than on the main lines of development chosen by their society. Even the impression of liberty or of liberation, as it has prevailed since 1968 in both Europe and the United States, is in large part a production of the collective world in which the actors move. From this point of view, love is not a uniquely personal feeling, because 'we love and suffer according to cultural imperatives'; it is also a 'code of communication', closely connected to the profound phenomena defining a human community and the ways in which it develops.[43]

In the West, this code confined to the heterosexual couple changed for the first time around the middle of the seventeenth century. From being an elevated ideal, derived from medieval courtly love, it began to incorporate sexuality, now defined as an essential component of the union.[44] In literature, this made it possible to rethink passion and pleasure and, above all, openly assert a difference between them. Another turning point came around 1800, when *amour passion* began to be clearly distinguished from romantic love. Niklas Luhmann sees this as the definitive destruction of a traditional world built on the small family, religion and morality in favour of a modern, functional system in which all the elements – economics, politics, law, art, intimacy, etc. – acquire a high degree of autonomy, while remaining strongly interdependent.[45] His main hypothesis is that such transformations of the semantics of love take place essentially through various methods of symbolic communication. Personal relationships acquire greater intensity as a result of this process. However, what forms persons, their memory and their attitudes can never be wholly accessible to someone else, given that they themselves have only limited access to them. As a result, a large part of communication with others is governed by rules and codes that make it possible to accept or reject the egocentric world view specific to each individual.[46] Walter, narrator of *My Secret Life*, we may remember, often explains his urgent need to write by the fact that he does not know whether his contemporaries experienced the same erotic sensations as him. He frequently notes the difficulty of interpreting what he feels in the absence of a standard of comparison, so powerful were the taboos of English Victorian society.[47]

The code of love continued to evolve in the twentieth century. The growth of individualism would appear to have resulted in greater carnal egoism. Yet nothing is more social than the act of love. Since the liberating sixties, it has become the yardstick by which we measure a person's success. The Western semantics of passion, now globalized,[48] have made sexual pleasure the supreme metaphor for all pleasure, to ensure the epiphany of the Self.[49] The sexual contract assumed quite new forms during the extraordinary upheavals of the late twentieth century. By 1971, it was possible to prophesy the disappearance of the earlier system that was based on an extended prior courtship, no sex between the couple before marriage and the masculine double standard that allowed engaged men, like husbands, to go to prostitutes or sow their wild oats. In the sixties, virginity lost much of its significance for many young girls as a result of advances in contraception, to the point where it might be seen as a sign of sexual inadequacy rather than virtue. In parallel, pre-marital sex came to be accepted among the young, if not always by their parents, who had been brought up in a stricter moral code. The new generations are no longer obliged to confine themselves to heavy petting and they have less reason to resort to masturbation than their predecessors. Some moralists even denounce the 'tyranny of the orgasm'.[50] The requirement to perform is beginning to be an imperative for men as well as for women. Which makes for a laudable equality, as long as the result is not frustration for the producers incapable of fully satisfying the demands of consumers, in a market that has become highly competitive.

The right to sexual pleasure

Thirty years later, at the turn of the twentieth century, the main features of the new sexual and social compromise emerge with much greater clarity. The traditional couple, joined by the sacred tie of marriage, is everywhere in crisis or decline. In an increasing number of cases, official unions end in divorce, both in Europe and in the United States. This has gone so far in America, always motivated by practical considerations and the desire for efficiency, that they have invented a machine, roughly the size and shape of a juke-box, to dispense the necessary legal documents.[51] The rising divorce rate is explained in part by the spectacular increase in life expectancy, which means a long cohabitation much more often than in the past, when, up to the middle of the twentieth century, famine, disease or war brought many marriages to an early and tragic end. Both legal constraints and custom then gave the institution stability, whereas our contemporaries have no hesitation in switching partners so as to conform to the law of pleasure, the consequence of a collective pressure that is as licit as it is constrictive. To enjoy oneself is both a right and a duty. The phenomenon has given rise to a particularly lucrative industry. As well as the market in erotic toys, the land of Uncle Sam has discovered the importance of the market in venal bliss, as in Amsterdam but on a much larger scale. The state of Nevada was first, in 1967, to legalize a brothel. By the end of the century it had no fewer than 36 licensed houses. Discretely situated in isolated locations, they are listed in the *Official Guide to the Best Cathouses in Nevada*. One of them even contains a museum of prostitution. Their success has attracted big investors. In the late 1990s, one financial group was proposing to build a luxury hotel near Las Vegas, complete with golf course, tennis courts and 500 select prostitutes, at a total cost estimated at 130,000,000 dollars. A week's visit, all facilities included, was to cost around 7,000 dollars per head.[52]

All the indications concur in revealing the unprecedented arrival of non-procreative sex. *Homo sapiens* has not, however, become suicidal at the beginning of the third millennium. It is rather that the reproductive function is now clearly differentiated from erotic pleasure. The two spheres are equally important, but they can now be separated without any great difficulty by many people. An abundance of food and the expectation of a long and comfortable life – something unknown to the mass of our ancestors – have made people more demanding in both spheres. The growth of the sensual appetite does not reduce the desire to have a child, rather the contrary. Despite those who preach the apocalypse and denounce the declining birth rate afflicting the white race, children have never been so important in our civilization, or so precious or so generally protected against every threat. The death of a child, though much rarer than in the past, is seen as unacceptable. Paedophilia has become the worst conceivable outrage, a veritable crime against humanity, as revealed by the Dutroux affair in Belgium and by the massive increase in legislation directed against those who commit any form of abuse against minors, especially in the United States. What has changed radically is the fact that it no longer seems necessary to marry in order to have children or to love them. Single parents and same-sex couples step up their demands in this area. Modern techniques for the storage of semen and for impregnation mean that things inconceivable only a few decades ago are now possible. A woman can become pregnant without copulating, and even beyond the age of the menopause. *In vitro* fertilization has become a veritable social phenomenon. In the United States, the number has grown from 64,000 in 1996 to nearly 110,000 in 2001. Specialized clinics proliferate, because it is a highly profitable market: one attempt can cost, in all, as much as 25,000 dollars. But the chances of success decline very rapidly with age, from 35 per cent at the age of 35, to 20 per cent between 38 and 40, and 10 per cent at 41 or 42.[53] Other possibilities are emerging, such as the resort to a surrogate mother,[54] perhaps even, one day, to cloning.

Only ethical and moral rules put down prohibitions, which are themselves likely to change as a function of future renegotiations of the social contract. There are some who dream of seeing the collapse of the final biological barrier which prevents the male from reproducing other than through a female body.

Gay marriage

Yet the couple is not about to disappear. Rather, the reproductive model of our species seems to be monogamous with a degree of flexibility. The exceptions are homosexual couples and also the clergy, who are required to be chaste and of whom, one may well wonder 'how they sublimate their emotions'.[55] The question of the celibacy, paedophilia and homosexuality of priests arises with increasing urgency today. A number of spectacular cases testify to the difficulty – for some the impossibility – of keeping their vows. These are probably signs marking the end of a repressive cycle which began in 1563, at the final sessions of the Council of Trent, when chastity was definitively defined as a touchstone of the Catholic Church and imposed on the secular clergy, not only on monks and nuns, in contrast to the Protestants, whose priests were able to marry. There had often until then been a degree of leniency in practice. The Renaissance popes had fathered illegitimate children. In the first half of the sixteenth century, the pious emperor Charles V legitimized several bastards of bishops and ecclesiastical dignitaries in the Catholic Low Countries. In fact it was several generations before the problem was finally resolved. In Franche-Comté under Spanish tutelage, in the first third of the seventeenth century, many priests separated only with great difficulty and distress from their 'housekeeper', mother of their children, in obedience to instructions that they should turn them out and replace them with morally irreproachable and elderly maidservants.[56] This strong reaffirmation of the principle of the celibacy of the clergy was designed both to counter the virulent Protestant criticism of the debauchery and lechery of the members of the Roman Catholic clergy and to set their chastity up as an ideal for all the faithful. The main aim was to confirm marriage in its status of indissoluble sacrament, which was contested by the reformers. Married couples were more likely to accept a purely reproductive sexuality, under the watchful eye of the confessors, if the pastors of the flock set an example by showing themselves capable of the highest virtue. It is hardly surprising that this system was challenged by the moral liberalization of the sixties. In fact, it was at this very time that the Second Vatican

Council (1962–5) chose significantly less strict moral options than those of the Council of Trent, four centuries before.

Homosexual couples, meanwhile, are increasingly tolerated or accepted in the Western world.[57] In the United States, where resistance is strongest in spite of the long-time existence of large gay communities in San Francisco and New York, it has become a burning issue at the beginning of the twenty-first century.[58] In June 2003, the Supreme Court abolished the laws against sodomy by six votes to three. The Supreme Judicial Court of Massachusetts voted soon after, by four to three, that marriage was possible between persons of the same sex. The decision came into force on 17 May 2004, making this state the pioneer in the field. Since then, virulent opposition has been evident throughout the country. The most radical demand an amendment to the Constitution to prohibit outright any union not between a man and a woman. So far, the battle has been inconclusive. Public opinion remains volatile, as shown by successive *New York Times*/CBS News surveys. That of July 2003 indicated that 54 per cent of those polled believed that homosexual relationships should be legal, as opposed to 41 per cent in the previous survey. This swing, observed for the first time, followed closely on the decision of the Supreme Court mentioned above. At the end of the same year, however, a presidential counter-attack won majority support for the idea of prohibiting such unions by constitutional amendment. The contradiction stems from a fundamental distinction in the minds of the population between the formal notion of liberty, to which many are attached, and the desire of the majority to safeguard the sacred nature of marriage. Those who consider it primarily a religious phenomenon amount to 53 per cent, as against 33 per cent who define it primarily as a legal contract. Among the former, 71 per cent reject outright gay marriage, which is supported by 55 per cent of the latter.[59] In addition to which, there is a geographical frontier separating the generally more liberal north-east from the southern Bible belt.

The debate raged throughout 2004. What was at stake was the 'sanctity of marriage'. Thirty-eight states defined it as purely heterosexual, but five others, including New Jersey on 12 January 2004, and many municipalities, opened a breach in the wall of hostility to homosexual couples by giving legal recognition to their material rights if they cohabited.[60] A law of 1996, however, adopted by Congress in Washington, the Defense of Marriage Act, prohibited federal recognition of gay marriage and relieved every state of the obligation to ratify those legally celebrated outside their jurisdiction. When the jurists rediscovered an obscure statute of Massachusetts, dating from 1913, which annulled any union celebrated in the state if the protagonists did not have the right to marry normally in their own state, a double *cordon sanitaire* was theoretically erected to prevent an extension of the Massachusetts initiative.[61] A pillar of faith, marriage is nevertheless a 'social institution in transition' in the United States. Only 56 per cent of the adult population were in marriages at the beginning of the twenty-first century, as against 75 per cent around 1970, and the proportion of couples with children fell during the same period from 45 to 26 per cent. Added to which, by the early 2000s, one in every two marriages ended in divorce.[62]

The supporters of liberalization attempted to press home their advantage with a flurry of arguments and initiatives. The intellectuals contributed by claiming that homosexuality had a biological basis. Recent research on primates was called on to show that the sexuality of animals was not directed solely towards reproduction. The bonobos, chimpanzees very close to humans, were frequently quoted as an example after the publication of a book which described them as deeply sensual and almost all bisexual.[63] Another scholar claimed that homosexuality had been observed in 450 living species.[64] In 2003, when the Supreme Court heard the case of 'Lawrence *v.* Texas', introduced to contest a law against sodomy in that state, the book was quoted by many groups who supported the initiative and it probably played a role in the decision to annul the incriminating law – proof, if such be needed, of the power of ideas, including in the most unexpected quarters.[65] Other works went further by suggesting that animal homosexuality should be interpreted in the context of the survival of the species. The argument put forward was that the individuals that did not produce their own direct heirs assisted their fellows to feed and raise theirs, thus contributing to the common genetic pool. This is particularly clear in the case of dolphins.[66] Such claims could only horrify the defenders of the sacred nature of heterosexual marriage. A regular contributor to the *New York Times* was assailed by 'a torrent of fire and brimstone' after publishing an article calling for an end to discrimination against gays in which he argued that their behaviour might have a biological basis. He was accused, notably, of blasphemy for having defended vile behaviour denounced by God.[67]

In February 2004, hostilities were exacerbated by a dramatic initiative. Six weeks into his term of office, the young mayor of San Francisco decided to authorize same-sex marriages. Unlike many other governors of big cities, he claimed to have the power to do this because his town was also a county, and because marriage certificates were a county responsibility in the state of California. Although the state laws recognized the validity only of unions 'between a man and a woman', official certificates were issued to homosexual partners from 12 February on. Two lesbians aged 79 and 83 years respectively were the first beneficiaries. Within five days, 2,600 gay marriages had been celebrated in spite of legal attempts to block the action by judges and warnings issued by the Republican Governor, Arnold Schwarzenegger. An opinion poll conducted at this point indicated that an absolute majority of the inhabitants of the San Francisco Bay area approved the initiative, but that the opposite was true of the state as a whole.[68] On 12 August 2004, the California Supreme Court annulled just over 4,000 certificates issued in these circumstances in San Francisco.[69] Nevertheless, a lively national debate on the issue had started all over the United States, and events in Massachusetts and the civil unions found in Vermont and elsewhere were closely followed. The shock waves were felt all over the Western world. 'A first gay couple makes a legal civil marriage', announced the Montreal newspaper, *La Presse*, on 2 April 2004.[70] Many other Canadian provinces followed Quebec in authorizing such marriages. The Netherlands had allowed them since 2001 and Belgium since 2003. In Spain, the new Socialist prime minister obtained the agreement of the lower chamber of Parliament, the Congress of Deputies, on 21 April 2005, for a proposal to promulgate a law to this effect. In France, a debate began about the possibility of amending the Civil Code – now more than 200 years old – to offer the same possibility, as the PACS seemed not to be providing an entirely satisfactory solution. A homosexual wedding officially celebrated in Bègles, near Bordeaux, in June 2004, in the full glare of the media, was promptly declared illegal, and the mayor censured.

The resistance cannot obscure the growing tolerance of homosexuality. It may be that this is connected to the recent huge increase in the human population of our globe, leading our societies unconsciously to relax their hostility towards those who refuse to found a family that has reproduction as its main aim.[71] The growing tolerance of masturbation may have a similar explanation, as current demographics nullify what was once the main objection to it, the squandering of seminal fluid, which had led the doctors of the nineteenth century to fear an exhaustion of the vital forces prejudicial to the common good. This argument is now rarely used except by those alarmed by the declining birth rate in Europe or by minorities who fear the decline of the white race.

Erotic equality and simultaneous orgasm

Meanwhile, the right to pleasure has become an absolute imperative, sometimes resulting in a veritable social tyranny. According to Desmond Morris, we are a species biologically programmed to fall in love and form couples, which are indispensable to raising children. Where does the orgasm fit in? For Morris, it is crucial because it produces a lasting attachment between parents and enables them to raise in optimum conditions offspring who require constant attention for many years before achieving autonomy. As the species has evolved, he maintains, the human couple has developed a deep erotic liaison. Simultaneous orgasm is the principal mechanism by which the family remains united in the long term, assuring the survival of its descendants. It was the chief biological mechanism for loving feelings, and it was based on full sexual equality. However, the changes brought by greater urbanization created a new situation by dividing males into two groups, which Morris calls 'Sexual Givers' and 'Sexual Takers'. The former continue to regard women as their equals in all respects, in private and in public. In late nineteenth-century England, Walter the Victorian – of whose existence Morris was unaware – seems overall to fit this type, although he also possessed some features of the second category. The same would appear to be true of the male authors of the French erotic works of the mid-seventeenth century, such as *L'École des filles*, who are particularly attentive to female pleasure.[72]

The 'Sexual Takers', who are increasingly numerous in the modern urbanized world, seek only their own carnal satisfaction, without considering that of their partners, treating them scarcely better than as aids to masturbation.[73] This was the case with the classic Victorian Englishmen, believers in the sexual double standard, who behaved in this way both towards their wives, described as frigid or scarcely responsive, and towards the prostitutes they exploited without scruple or feelings of guilt. Walter himself partly fits this mould, which might indicate the existence of a third, mixed masculine model, unmentioned by Morris, combining in a conflictual manner the characteristics of both 'Givers' and 'Takers'. In nineteenth-century London, the working-class adolescent boys who seduced girls with promises of marriage, spun out love's young dream for months, even years, then reneged on their responsibilities if the girl told them she was pregnant, were adopting a variety of strategies, sometimes ambiguous. Some were egoistical predators, concealing their evil intentions beneath a smooth tongue, but many were driven by the sheer material impossibility of supporting a wife and child. Their clumsy letters often reveal distress at being forced to behave in this way, even though the law now guaranteed them near-impunity. It was always women from the lower classes who were hardest hit by the Victorian culture of guilt as regards sex outside marriage.[74]

The main recent change, a consequence of the disconnection of reproduction and pleasure, is the return to carnal and cultural equality between the sexes. Even if we distance ourselves from the arguments of Desmond Morris regarding the evolution of the species, the simultaneous orgasm, which he sees as central, now constitutes the fundamental criterion of the relationship between men and women. Admittedly, this is not accepted by everyone or without problems. The old symbolisms and their practical forms are not disappearing in a uniform manner. Age, education, social class and a rural or urban context all have a role in producing an infinitely varied spectrum of sexual attitudes. It is nevertheless the case that the centre of the spectrum is now occupied, especially among the younger generations in the big cities, by an angst-free quest for sexual pleasure on the part of boys and girls alike. It is based on a demanding but flexible affective investment, easily ended if it fails in its purpose. The desire for a child ties in with this configuration, without obligation or exclusivity however, especially since it can be satisfied outside it. At the two extremes are numerically important groups whose sole point in common is that they do not subscribe to all or part of this new sensual and social contract.

On the one hand, the gay and lesbian movements demand their eminent rights, with important differences, in a context which is increasingly favourable to them. As well as those who recognize themselves as such, do they perhaps also attract people made acutely anxious by the demand for orgasmic performance expressed by the other sex, who hope they might discover more tenderness and less competition in relationships with someone of the same sex? Young men in particular sometimes appear disoriented by the uncertainties now surrounding the notion of virility.[75] This helps to explain the growth of chauvinist movements or, in America, male equivalents of the radical feminist groups of the 1960s and 1970s. In France, the poor academic results of boys compared with girls of the same age have been linked to their deeper psychological insecurity in a highly competitive situation.

At the other extreme, among the more conformist, many men and women remain attached to the old archetypes. Predators who care nothing for their partners still prowl the streets. Neither voracious women nor traditional male chauvinists have disappeared as if by magic. Their existence is revealed by occasional dramas, like the John Wayne Bobbit case in the United States in 1993, when, infuriated by his behaviour, his wife Lorena cut off her husband's penis while he was asleep. Bobbit became famous because the penis, which his wife had thrown away, was found and successfully re-attached. Though rare, such cases have nevertheless attracted attention in countries where men still claim to dominate their wives, such as Brazil. In the late 1990s, a young grocer called Mattos suffered the same fate at the hands of his girlfriend, having told her he was leaving her after spending the night with her in a hotel. Mattos, who had the presence of mind to plunge the severed appendage into ice and call the police, recovered his attribute after an operation lasting four hours. He was later awarded the annual prize for the 'greatest male chauvinist in the country' by the Brazilian 'Society of Male Chauvinists'.[76] Nor should we forget 'prudish' or 'frigid' women, those who refuse to accept the importance of the orgasm and interpret the erotic demands of their sisters as signs of decadence, danger or animality. Victorian education in England and Christian morality in France long insisted on the 'natural' absence of sensuality in respectable women and the need to confine sex to procreation. Daughters born in the first half of the twentieth century experienced this type of conditioning to varying degrees, depending on social class, which was intended to prevent them from sinning before marriage. Their own daughters constitute a generation in transition, in a rapidly changing world, because they were also to some extent influenced by the same prohibitions, though more cunningly disguised than in the past, in the form of advice and recommendations: the pill causes cancer; beware of venereal disease; abortion is criminal because it destroys an innocent life, and so on.

The sexual revolution today

There are two possible and opposing ways of viewing the sexual revolution in progress since the sixties, one pessimistic, the other optimistic. As always in the history of the West, some are tempted to take a gloomy Hobbesian view, others prefer a Rousseauist idealism. America inclines rather to the former. The sex wars and the culture wars will happen. In fact, they have already begun. This is the gloomy conclusion emerging from the impassioned and highly controversial feminist works of Shere Hite.[77] After *The Hite Report on Female Sexuality*, in 1976, *The New Hite Report*, published in

2000, claimed that sexual behaviour is determined not by biology but by culture, and emphasized the importance of external or clitoral stimulation to enable a woman to achieve orgasm.

The Hite Report on the Family, published in 1994, explained that the institution is not in the process of collapsing, simply of changing by generating different types of couple. Yet the overall tone of the book suggests a certain despondency.[78] The research was based on 3,000 responses to questionnaires, 50 per cent from the United States, 35 per cent from Europe (including 14 per cent from England, 10 per cent from Germany, 6 per cent from the Netherlands and 2 per cent from France), the rest from eight other countries. The Protestant world massively outnumbered the Catholic world, which accounted for less than 10 per cent of the total, and the North-American mass skews the results.

Girls and boys learn at a very early age, and for life, not to touch their parents, especially if they are naked and in particular in the genital area, or to rub up against them. It is this, says Hite, that later produces an unremitting need for intimate loving contact, body to body. Similarly, she links sadomasochistic tendencies to the frequency and intensity of physical punishments, common from an early age in the United States and England, whereas in Scandinavia, for example, parents who dare to resort to them can be prosecuted at law. Returning to an old Victorian idea, she claims that the flow of blood to the buttocks in such circumstances causes genital sensations, especially in girls. The experience is all the more likely to be eroticized because it is the only way of obtaining an intense degree of intimacy with the father or the mother.[79] If these observations are accurate, they highlight a difference in kind between the Anglo-Saxon countries and the hedonist Europe that protects, touches, caresses and cajoles its children. If, instead, it is an American fantasy reported by the subjects of the study, it speaks volumes as to the permanence of a fear of bodily contact and of sexuality in general. In either case, an old conflictual erotic system, dominated by the male, is evoked. Further, some specialists believe that domestic and conjugal violence, common in the land of Uncle Sam, results from the punitive practices employed against young children and adolescents.[80]

A second deeply pessimistic aspect of the report concerns the definition of a male fear of love linked to a traumatic puberty. The little boy masturbates regularly between the ages of 10 and 12, as the Kinsey Report had already shown, but in secret, and experiencing shame, at the very age when he is being told that he must 'leave' his mother, behave in a manly fashion and not be a sissy. These related phenomena induce a confused type of sexuality, mingling attachment and hatred, guilt feelings and anger. Many adult men are consequently afraid of falling deeply in love with a woman, a prospect they find more frightening than attractive. Many do not marry the woman they love and brag about it publicly in order to demonstrate their attachment to masculine group values.[81]

The explanations are gloomier still with regard to the formation of the female libido. It all begins well. Lots of little girls enjoy a marvellous period of independence and freedom up to adolescence, because they have the right to behave like tomboys. Things go wrong when the family suddenly urges them to become 'good girls', around the time of their first menstruation. Yet this last remains completely taboo, passed over in total silence, at the very moment when these girls are secretly indulging in masturbation, equally unmentionable, and when they suffer physical punishments which have a powerful sensual effect. Every power over their own body is denied them. The sole example held up to them is that of the mother, defined in a totally asexual manner within the household. Every conjugal unit thus reproduces the masculine double standard so dear to the Victorian bourgeoisie. Still in force in the United States, it divides women into two radically opposed groups, the 'good', in the image of the Virgin Mary, the pure mother or the obedient daughter, and the 'bad', dangerous because they do not control their carnal impulses. Young girls develop a double identity, for fear of revealing things that are strictly forbidden, that they have repressed under constant pressure from an unceasing sensual and gestural education. 'Keep your legs together', is the constant injunction between the ages of 3 and 13. The well-brought up adolescent girl who behaves as such in public can only express her true desires and sensuality in private.[82] Once again, if Shere Hite is evoking a myth more than a reality, it is one that is sufficiently powerful to haunt American society. In 2004, a film of Gary Winick, starring Jennifer Garner, *13 Going on 30,* told how a little girl of 13, who made a wish when she was shut up in the toilets by naughty boys, turns into a vamp of 29, while preserving the mind and gaucherie of her 13 years. Classified PG-13 for 'slight sexual content and references to drugs', the film is a sentimental piece which seeks to touch a sensitive chord by playing on the two successive and fundamentally different personalities American girls are expected to adopt.

Although elsewhere she signals her desire to break with such 'patriarchal' pressures,[83] linked, she believes, to the old domestic icons organized round the image of an asexual mother, Shere Hite here offers a very gloomy conclusion. The sex wars and the culture wars are surely inevitable in the United States if the two genders are really and massively 'programmed' in this way, within the institution of marriage, at the end of the twentieth century.

Other researchers offer a more optimistic vision of things. While accepting the idea that the American education associates love and the flesh with the fear of a threat to the family and civilization, one specialist calls for an end to the confrontations and the creation of a new social consensus, recalling that the sexuality of each individual is intimately bound up with the role – masculine or feminine – defined by society. We are finally learning, she says, that to eat alone will not assuage our hunger.[84] In 1971, Desmond Morris described love as a complex two-way process, which cannot be satisfied with substitutes, and claimed that human beings always have need of true intimacy, even if only with one single person, or else they will suffer.[85] A quarter of a century later, he emphasized the recent return to sensual equality, after the interlude of the great urbanization which had relegated women to a secondary position. But it is, he believes, a new type of equality. In the past, women had been at the centre of traditional society, while men had hunted or practised agriculture around the village. Now, women leave the house and join men in the new work places and compete with them by demanding equality, except when motherhood returns them to the home.[86]

The truth perhaps lies on the side of neither Hobbes nor Rousseau. Far from the moral judgements that may be implied by the pessimistic or optimistic visions, the historian first observes the scale of the changes, then notes the fluidity of the situation at the beginning of the twenty-first century. Torn between its pre-eminent traditions, which accord a sacred value to marriage, and the challenges of the world today, Western civilization may simply be in the process of producing new syntheses, concealed by superficial conflicts. More slowly in the United States than in Europe, younger generations are renegotiating the social contract through the redefinition of the sexual contract. Women's liberation, not only in the sphere of eroticism but in access to employment, is vigorously rattling the cage of the matrimonial traditions. The separation of the procreative principle and the pleasure principle opens up a quite new space. The whole of society is gradually feeling the effects, because the competition for jobs presupposes readjustments to the domestic unit, as women will no longer either sacrifice their maternal instincts or return alone to the home to look after the children. The Victorian masculine double standard is not dead, especially in America, but it is holed below the water line, and sometimes even turned to their own advantage by girls and women. The tyranny of pleasure and the almost mystical quest for the simultaneous orgasm further contribute to the destabilization of the institution of marriage, now no longer accepted as the sole effective system for bringing up children. Confrontations intensify between the two 'genders', each increasingly demanding of the other. The insecurity is especially unsettling for young men, who are living through a difficult period of transition because they are called on to adapt waning chauvinist certainties to the egalitarian claims of women of their own age. The groups previously rejected or marginalized for an eroticism diverted from reproductive ends are becoming increasingly established, amid the ruins of the patriarchal family so sombrely described by Shere Hite.

The future is not written in books. At the very most, one can appreciate the formidable scale of the changes taking place before our eyes. The god of pleasure may now be worshipped free from anxiety by women, which they have never been able to do before, since the beginnings of humanity. It is still necessary for them to want this. Cultures are made up of heavy strata piled one on top of the other. A new layer of civilizing soil does not destroy the germinative power of its predecessors, nor do innovations cause age-old traditions suddenly to disappear. The beginning of the third millennium certainly appears an extraordinary period of change, but observers rooted in their own epoch can perceive it only imperfectly, for the most part through the most spectacular ruptures or the conflictual dialogue taking place between the many different forces. They do not know in what direction or how far the change will go. The future remains open and impossible to predict.

CONCLUSION: THE NARCISSISTIC SOCIETY

An exhibition at the New York Metropolitan Museum of Art, in 2004, *Dangerous Liaisons. Fashion and Furniture in the 18th Century*, emphasized the sensuality that dominated clothing and the decorative arts in France under Louis XV and Louis XVI. The title chosen, and some rather acid comments appearing in the *New York Times* to coincide with the opening, reveal the gulf existing between the current American conception of pleasure, still marked by Puritanism, and the epicurean hedonism that is supposed to prevail in the land of the Declaration of the Rights of Man. In the United States – 'a nation with the soul of a church', in the famous phrase of G. K. Chesterton[1] – the neoconservatives and the Christian fundamentalists condemn decadent 'old Europe' more generally, by contrast with the moral and religious virtues they defend. In reality, their fellow-Americans are divided into two very distinct camps, separated by a grey area: the traditionalists based on the Bible belt of the Deep South, and the supporters of greater freedom, well represented in New York and in the north-east. It might be said that the intellectuals and the champions of the two groups are engaged in an eternal 'remake' of the great spiritual confrontation between the tolerant ethos of the eighteenth-century *philosophes* and the guilt-inducing interdictions imposed by the Protestant and Catholic Churches in the sixteenth and seventeenth centuries. There is a whiff of Counter-Reformation[2] in the American air at a time when the minorities are trying to shake off the lead weight of conformism bearing down on them. In contrast, the cause is won in our peaceable continent, heading towards unification at the beginning of the third millennium. In spite of the major differences that persist between North and South and between East and West, Europe has collectively opted for the optimistic and hedonistic legacy of the Enlightenment. The project for a European constitution put forward in 2004 spoke of 'cultural, religious and humanist heritages', without explicit reference to Christianity. The desire for peace, entente and the enjoyment of the things of this world has made rapid progress in an area ravaged by incessant wars for centuries, up until 1945. This is also one of the great dissimilarities with the United States, which had not experienced such traumas on its own soil between the end of the War of Secession in 1865 and 11 September 2001.

The two parts of the West do not share the same view of life, happiness and pleasure. To try to understand the reasons for the differences, it is necessary to plunge deep into the symbolic and social depths of each. Individualism prevails in both, but it does not mean the same thing, because it is not rooted in the same constructions of the communal tie and because it conveys values that are often very different. In Northern Europe, it is perfectly compatible with a strong civic sense, a powerful feeling of belonging to the community and great sexual permissiveness. In France, it displays greater egoism and is more inclined to reject the rules, while largely opening up to freedom of morals. In the United States, it is accompanied by a strong group-awareness, as in Scandinavia, but it does not result in sexual liberation, in spite of the minorities who are actively demanding it.

Narcissism, however, is everywhere the rule. Yet the convergence is in large part illusory, because on this side of the Atlantic the notion expresses a desire to live happily here and now, while on the other it expresses a fragility of the Self encoded in a 'culture of survival', sometimes leading to veritable pathologies.

The values of the hedonists

For the historian or the sociologist, individuals do not exist alone, because they are always 'constructs'. Their freedom, however, is to be constantly in the process of fulfilling themselves and of being able to choose from among the various pressures bearing down on them.[3] If the individual occupied centre stage in the 1970s, it is because the individual had been promoted as such by a euphoric society, driven onwards by the motor of consumption and by technical, scientific and medical discoveries. Well-being, self-fulfilment and the quest for pleasure have become cult values.[4] Constraints began to reappear in the mid-1980s, in the wake of the excesses of globalization, global warming and rising unemployment.[5] A generational effect has probably been added to the new sufferings for the heirs of permissive and individualistic parents when they are suddenly confronted by an intensely competitive world of work, with exacting rules. Psychologists tell us that the recent adolescent fashion for tattooing and piercing reveals both the awareness of being part of an age group and the desire to differentiate themselves from certain parents afflicted by 'youthism' and reluctant to grow up.[6] Passing the baton is not easy for two groups separated by different perceptions of life. The hedonism of today is more feverish than that of the sixties. In addition to which, success is harder for children of parents who are often still very present, due to increased life expectancy, and who have often refused the authoritarian role of father or mother in rejecting the model of the patriarchal family.

It is hardly surprising, in these circumstances, that the Europe of the first decade of the third millennium is changing while at the same time hesitating on a number of points. The most recent European Values Survey, carried out in 1999, reveals rather tentative changes.[7] The only clear and indisputable conclusion is that individualism is advancing everywhere on the continent. Some commentators draw a rather pessimistic conclusion from this, speaking of a 'culture of retreat' and a fear of the outsider leading to a 'fragilization of democracy'.[8] Nevertheless, what people value most highly is the family, by 86 per cent of those polled, followed by work (54 per cent) and then by friends and relations (47 per cent), with religion (17 per cent) and, even more, politics (8 per cent) lagging well behind. For France on its own, the figures are not systematically different from the general average, but regard for family, work and friends has increased since the previous survey of 1990, unlike faith, which is rated less highly (down from 14 per cent to 11 per cent).[9] Reading these figures, one notes an attachment to social values that is still dominant but has assumed a different form, now focused on the units of local life – home, close family, friends and work groups – while trust in the large structures constituted by the churches or political parties has collapsed. Described as 'individualization', this shift is in no way a retreat to a desert island. Rather it suggests the desire to take refuge in protective cocoons, on a human scale and concretely perceptible. The shrinking of the ideal social network is not evidence of a desire to be rid of communal pressures. These last are, on the contrary, strengthened by the effect of proximity, although theoretical and remote citizenship and the attachment to global ideological systems have declined in importance.

CONCLUSION

It is in the light of this basic trend that we should consider the information in the same survey relating to the continued retreat from religion, a phenomenon already visible in similar surveys of 1981. It affects all countries, but is most marked in France, Belgium, the Netherlands and Sweden and generally more widespread among Protestants than among Catholics. The situation is similar in Eastern Europe. On the other hand, 'believing without belonging', to use a phrase coined in relation to Great Britain,[10] has continued to grow since its appearance in the figures for 1990. Where the decline of observance has been most marked, this 'spiritual autonomy' is primarily characteristic of the young, between 18 and 29 years of age. In this group, more of those who claim they belong to no denomination said in 1999 that they believed in God, a life after death, reincarnation and the existence of Hell and Paradise. Arguing also from the partial return to devotion of the generation of baby-boomers, one commentator has detected the beginnings of a halt to 'European exceptionalism', especially as surveys conducted between 1991 and 1998 suggest that the United States may be experiencing a 'slight religious retreat'.[11] It seems more likely that significant generational differences are emerging, between the baby-boomers, founders of individualism, who have in part returned to faith, their immediate heirs, aged between 35 and 49, who have the lowest levels of belief, and the grandchildren of the baby-boomers, who feel the need for a sort of 'off-piste' sacred. It has to be said that the content of this spirituality remains distinctly vague. The needs of this one or that one hardly match up to the great Christian verities. A CSA poll for *Le Monde* and the daily paper *La Vie* in 2003 showed that the latter have systematically lost ground since an identical survey conducted in 1994. This applies in the case of the divinity of Christ, his Resurrection (47 per cent believe in it, compared with 51 per cent in 1994), Hell (25 per cent as opposed to 33 per cent) and the Devil (27 per cent and 34 per cent). These changes have not been to the benefit of parallel beliefs, which have sharply declined over the same period. Astrology attracts no more than 37 per cent of those polled (60 per cent in 1994) and witchcraft has declined from 41 per cent to 21 per cent.[12]

Yet many observers still speak of a 'return to religion' and morality, sometimes even interpreted as a halt to the fall from grace of the Christian heritage.[13] I see it rather as the expression of a growing unease among the young, signalled by the increase in hopes of survival after death among this age group; and also as a sign of a search for values of proximity, because the trend helps to produce social ties in a threatening and disenchanted world. The failure of the great collective ideologies, the dread of unemployment and the fears associated with the growing risks of the pollution of the planet and global terrorism combine to make people feel much greater anxiety than during the 'Thirty Glorious Years', the age of economic progress after the Second World War. The individualism practised by those of our contemporaries who came of age in 2000 is fundamentally different, more sombrely experienced than that of the two previous generations.

The 1999 survey also analysed levels of trust between people, in other words, the types of relationships that individuals establish with their society.[14] The author of the synthesis used six criteria for this: spontaneous trust, trust in institutions, altruism, civic-mindedness, liberalism of morals and selectivity in social relations (accepting or rejecting proximity with deviant or different people). He suggests a typology of Europeans into five main groups, sometimes more strongly represented in one country than another: the 'integrated moderns', such as the Protestants with a strong civic culture in the upper ranks of the Nordic states; the 'hyper-permissives', mostly aged between 30 and 49, politically to the left, without religion, numerous in Scandinavia, Spain and Austria; the 'permissive individualists', characterized by values inherited from the past, well represented in the Mediterranean regions; the 'integrated traditionalists' of Central and Southern Europe, elderly, of rural origins, believers and on the right; and the 'scarcely integrated traditionalists', without strong ideological or political commitment, for example Italian small businessmen.

The profiles of the 'modern integrated' and the 'hyper-permissives' are fairly similar. Together they represent more than two-thirds of the inhabitants of Scandinavia and the Netherlands, whose populations are also distinguished by greater tolerance in matters of morality, in particular with regard to homosexuality, divorce, abortion, suicide and euthanasia. Germany and Great Britain have a structural resemblance, the two categories in question accounting for a little over a third of the total, while the traditionalists, integrated or not, account for slightly more than half, and individualists for 11 per cent. The other states remain deeply impregnated by the old values, in particular the Mediterranean countries and the two Irelands. France is an exception, with 48 per cent 'integrated moderns' and 'hyper-permissives', 32 per cent 'traditionalists' of both types and 19 per cent 'individualists'. This last figure is almost twice the general average. Further, the French are the least civic-minded of all Europeans and the most mistrustful of others. Unlike the Nordic countries, the very pronounced retreat of established values is not largely compensated for in France by the appearance of new and altruistic commitments. The rapid collapse of the Catholic moral framework, especially since 1990, has been accompanied by an unstoppable growth of permissiveness in the sphere of morality, but the trend is accompanied by a weakening of the feeling of social integration.

In whatever form, civic-minded or egoist, the advance of individualism paves the way for sexual freedom. The most spectacular example is homosexuality, totally condemned by 44 per cent of those questioned in 1981, but only by 24 per cent in 1999.[15] It should be remembered that 52 per cent still regarded it as unacceptable in the United States in 2003. In these circumstances, pleasure has been promoted to the rank of new god in the Old Continent. Many people worry about this or denounce its 'tyranny';[16] others simply pretend to be offended, as they know that the exacting quest for sexual enjoyment opens up a huge consumer market. Sexologists, psychologists, laboratories manufacturing Viagra, firms specializing in making aging penises perform and a host of others rush to solve the problems of couples, at a high price. Happiness may be accessible to all, but only if you are able to keep at it without flagging until orgasm, simultaneous of course.

I myself have the feeling that individualism and permissiveness are stratagems of our culture to orient bodies and hearts, some would say souls, towards new, more direct and stronger forms of social tie, primarily through the phenomenon of the family, which is changing dramatically before our eyes. Far from revealing a decadence of our civilization, as grumpy moralists complain, these innovations prove rather its dynamism and its capacity to adapt. To live better, longer and more intensely, with deeper and more refined satisfactions: hedonism skims lightly over a continent sated with suffering for centuries. It is taking hold, clearly, in the wake of the global market. It was the heavyweight Japanese economic journal *Ekonomisuto* that published an article entitled 'Love between men and women, key to the revival of demand' in which its author called on his compatriots to rediscover 'the spirit of pleasure' which had been one of the great features of Japanese society until the middle of the nineteenth century.[17] To sustain the luxury industry, still buoyant in spite of the crisis, he proposed restoring to the elderly, who hold 60 per cent of the nation's savings, the taste for life, for desire and for love; and he recalled the essential symbolic role of these forces when the eighteenth-century Western aristocracy spent fortunes on curios, lace, silks and other superfluous objects that were indispensable to the art of love.

Can pleasure be absorbed into hedonism? Not entirely, we may be sure, because it is also a unique personal experience, partly incommunicable, as emphasized by Masters and Johnson at the end of their study of the female orgasm. But the collective dimension of the recent European experience, based on the search for happiness and sensory delight, is sweeping throughout Western civilization and suggests to the Subject, who has free access to them, that he or she achieve a bliss unknown to their ancestors before the second half of the twentieth century. Do the animals not set us an example? The discovery of the sensuality and bisexuality of the bonobos has cast doubt on the moralizing conception of a life ruled strictly by the reproductive principle. Among the new forms of permissiveness, the most important is undeniably that which liberates women from the curse they have borne since Eve. Not only do they no longer need to believe they give birth in sin, but it is now possible for them to de-couple the procreative function from the orgasm and to achieve fulfilment in both. This unprecedented revolution has transformed the relationships between the two biological genders, challenged the traditional structures of marriage and reintegrated the 'sexual deviants', once stigmatized under such labels, into the heart of a society that is increasingly conciliatory in such matters. It is true that the younger generations suffer from a loss of reference points at a time of massive upheavals and a rise in anxieties. They sometimes display a tendency to retreat or to flee towards an egoistic individualism.

Narcissism and culture

Before it came, in the eyes of various analysts, to characterize the American universe in the last decades of the twentieth century, narcissism appeared primarily as a mental illness, defined by Freud, his colleagues and his successors. Clinical cases became more numerous at the end of the Second World War. Although they were then often described by British and American specialists, they did not seem to result from a specific national context. Things changed in the early 1970s with the publication in the United States of works by practitioners in the field. Among the most important were those of Heinz Kohut.[18] He described the narcissistic pathology of his patients as presenting four features: perverse fantasies, together with a lack of interest in sex; an inability to form and maintain significant social relationships, even delinquent activities; lack of humour, of a sense of proportion, of empathy for other people's needs and feelings, a tendency towards attacks of uncontrolled rage, pathological lying; and hypochondriacal preoccupations with one's physical and mental health.[19] He maintained that the origin of this behaviour lay in severe traumas in childhood. So as not to suffer further, the patient established a mental structure based on one idea, 'I am perfect', which counterbalanced the idealized parent imago, 'You are perfect, but I am part of you.' Kohut named this the 'grandiose self'. His aim was to heal this illness by psychoanalytical cures, transferences, which he presented and discussed in his works.[20]

The appearance of such clinical observations coincided in the United States with the upheavals of the sixties and the traumas associated with the Vietnam War. They were seized on by writers seeking to explain the evolution of their civilization. In 1978, Christopher Lasch characterized America as 'the culture of narcissism'.[21] Criticizing the emptiness of the modern Subject in his country, he attributed it to post-war abundance, the retreat of the Victorian patriarchal ethos which had produced autonomous souls and a modernity that promised to abolish all constraints and satisfy every desire. His argument was based on the grandiose conception of the Self in the child, which produced the desire for wealth, beauty and omnipotence. Such images, buried in the unconscious mind at an early age, are foundations of the personality for the whole of life, especially its second part.[22] More fearful of dependence than others, and needing the sort of constant admiration usually reserved for youth, these people find it very hard to confront the ravages of age and death.[23] Lasch also denounced the introduction of the spirit of economic competitiveness into the very heart of relations of proximity. Sociability is turned into social combat. The demand for sexual performance and for satisfaction is installed within the family. In moralizing mode, he even speaks of 'emotional manipulations' of others to seek a specific advantage. Ultimately, he describes the extension to the whole of private life of the laws of competition and consumption which govern the market. The pursuit of self-interest is no longer limited to the accumulation of wealth. It has also become 'a search for pleasure and psychic survival'.[24]

Against a backdrop of the extension to the masses of the luxurious habits reserved, a century earlier, to the elites, a culture develops that is centred on individuals and their dissatisfactions, concrete and psychic. Lasch puts the blame for this on the absence of the father from the American family, which has the effect of distorting the relationships of the children with a mother who assumes the masculine role, leading to 'Momism'. However, this custodian of the family is too often narcissistic, from having tried to please her own mother by replacing the absent father. Thus, with little involvement in practical functions, she is also very remote from her offspring in affective terms.[25] The pessimism that permeates such conceptions is also found in the writings of Shere Hite on the patriarchal family in the United States and on the role of the mother in the traumas suffered by sons and even more by daughters, torn between the 'good' model she offers and the sensual desires that must never be mentioned.[26] On the other hand, the hedonism of the 1960s and 1970s liberated the female libido. Lasch sees this as a new cause for anxiety among men, especially since the Masters and Johnson Report, which 'depicts women as sexually insatiable' by showing their capacity to experience repeated orgasm.[27] The fear expressed here is characteristic of an old masculine dread. The medicine of the Victorian period had soothed it by assuring husbands that 'normal' wives were frigid or had little inclination for sex. This had not been the general view between the sixteenth and the eighteenth centuries, when doctors had emphasized the necessity of female pleasure for successful conception. It is true that contraception and, most of all, the pill had radically changed things by 1978, just when Lasch was writing. This made the return to female pleasure, without the risks of the past, doubly alarming for men, because it really did foreshadow the end of erotic inequality. The sex wars can only be exacerbated in these circumstances. Added to which, in the United States, men's fears are aggravated by the demands of the radical feminists and continue to be rooted in a maternal image that is itself disquieting. For Lasch, the narcissistic personality constitutes a collective pathological form, characteristic of a society that has lost its interest in the future. It seems to him to explain the intensity of the mid-life crisis: 'Americans experience the fortieth birthday as the beginning of the end.' Incapable, he goes on, of taking an interest in what will happen after their death, they seek eternal youth and 'no longer care to reproduce themselves'.[28]

In both the United States and Europe there is a growing and sustained interest in understanding the Self; it has become a veritable social phenomenon.[29] After two millennia, the discourse that valorized the eternal soul and distrusted the mortal flesh has lost its monopoly, allowing a more positive conception of the latter to emerge. In a postmodern society from which risks and fears have not disappeared, what seems at first sight to be a narcissistic vision of the body reveals, at a deeper level, a need to understand it, construct it and control it.[30] The analyses of this reality are contradictory, so rapidly does the situation change. In 1991, the sociologist Anthony

CONCLUSION

Giddens linked the growing need for security to the breaking down of the protective framework of the small community and tradition, and their replacement by much larger, impersonal organizations.[31] The survey of the values of Europeans of 1999, however, saw them as, on the contrary, valorizing the cocoons on a human scale, family and friends, to the detriment of politics and the sacred. The indications also point to a greater attachment among the young to the notions of order, and civic values tend in the same direction: the Subject invests at the local level as a way of controlling his or her anxieties. Other scholars, especially in America, cultivate an alarmist view of the Self as fragile and fragmented.[32] For them, narcissism reveals a hatred of oneself rather than admiration, even if the individual is constantly seeking proofs of the latter from others. There is a need for permanent reassurance to compensate for the feeling of emptiness which coexists with the feeling of being grandiose. In subsequent works, Lasch has further developed the pessimistic aspects of his interpretation, no longer speaking of narcissism but of a culture of survivalism. In the face of the increasing risks run by humanity, he detects the development of a siege mentality, apocalyptic and paralyzing. Some observers emphasize the role of shame to explain the narcissistic mentality. This quality is only 'the other side' of pride and, like it, is founded in the social bond. Linked to the ideal Self, that is, to the 'Self as I want to be', in the words of Kohut, it produces insecurity and existential anxiety when a goal is not achieved. The grandiose personality then feels seriously threatened when its possessor thinks he has lost value in the eyes of others.[33]

The overall conclusion is probably valid for the United States at the beginning of the twenty-first century, where self-esteem and national pride merge. It is hardly applicable in Europe. Narcissism exists here, but it does not greatly impact on human relations. On the contrary, the northern countries pull the continent in the direction of a greater moral freedom that does not preclude a high level of civic-mindedness, whereas the countries more strongly marked by traditionalism, including Germany and England, retain, by that fact, solid safeguards against the disruptive phenomena described by Lasch. Only France might perhaps partly fit such an analysis, because of its high percentage of individualists, which does not prevent religion from collapsing and the flesh from exulting.

Is sexuality 'the key to modern civilization'?[34] I believe the answer to be yes, and that it was the same, in very different cultural forms, in the past. It has been one of the best-kept secrets since the appearance of Christianity. It was also one of the most closely guarded, because its liberating emergence would have challenged the fundamental dogma of the superiority of mind over body. The libertines of the seventeenth century perfectly understood this, like all those who were – and still are – accused of endangering divine morality by seeking pleasure instead of preparing for their eternal salvation. The repression of the lascivious appetites was a constant in the West until very recently. The Mental Deficiency Act passed in Great Britain in 1913 was responsible for the despatch of thousands of unmarried women – poor, homeless or simply 'immoral' – to institutions or asylums, because they had become pregnant. It was widely believed that illegitimate pregnancy was in itself a sign of mental subnormality.[35] Things have changed radically in Europe since the last decades of the twentieth century. Sexuality is no longer seen as 'a great continent of normality surrounded by small islands of disorder', but rather as an archipelago composed of islands of different sizes.[36] In the first decade of the third millennium, the notion of perversion is in rapid retreat, unlike in the United States, where the powerful resistance to gay marriage shows that the minorities have a fierce struggle on their hands if they are to gain recognition of their right to the public expression of their desires.

Love and sensuality are essential facts in human societies. Not only do they permit their reproduction, but they also constitute an indispensable cultural 'communication code'.[37] The latter assures the progress in the West of a 'plastic sexuality'. Liberated from reproductive obligations, women are its principal beneficiaries, because for them pleasure has been freed from all the fears that surrounded it. Their affective and erotic behaviour has changed much more radically than that of men of a similar age, in particular in the United States, where the contrast between the successive female generations is striking.[38]

No one yet knows in which direction the situation will evolve. One may equally well worry or rejoice at seeing sexuality disconnected from the 'cosmic processes of life and death'.[39] In either case, it is sure to retain its primordial role in our civilization. After all, the biological discourses themselves find a place for a sort of transcendence, under cover of the perpetuation of the species. Desmond Morris's hypothesis regarding the essential role of the orgasm in the durability of the human couple, so as to provide the best chances of growth to the children, fits such a perspective. His conclusions regarding the 'natural' equality of desire, damaged during the recent phase of urbanization, then rehabilitated since the sixties, are accompanied

CONCLUSION

by an explicit condemnation of carnal egoism, which he sees as devoid of significance.[40] But has this not always been the case in our societies? The recent collapse of religious prohibitions is not that of all morality. New systems of meaning are put in place to teach us the infinite social value that should be accorded to bodily intimacy. Some simply offer a means of survival to individuals entangled in the contradictions of their world of reference. Thus American narcissism provides a global response to the intolerable tension existing between the puritanical norms deemed inviolable and their permanent transgression, cause of an existential anxiety through strong feelings of guilt. Others emphasize the necessity of managing physical love in a way that makes it a factor promoting self-esteem and enriching relationships with one's fellows. The European Values Survey of 1999 suggests (or allows one to hope) that the continent is in the process of choosing this type of solution, far from the schizophrenic pressures of the American system. The retreat to the revamped family would then not be a sign of fragility. Rather it would be the mark of an investment by the Subject in a complex of emotions and relations of proximity destined to compensate for the coldness and hardness of modernity; a way of dealing with the contradiction that results from plastic sexuality by offering as a desirable ideal a cocoon centred on a physical and affective partnership, wrapped in the relational 'onion skins' formed by friends, neighbours, parents, even ex-partners with whom one has had children, and so on.

The present exit from religion gives men and women the choice to use their bodies as they wish. Things are not quite so simple, however, because their free will is limited by social and cultural pressures. Radically different from in the past, permissive and no longer repressive, these still determine the future of every citizen. The laws of the economic market drive them into fiercer competition so as to assert their identity and get as much pleasure as possible whatever their age. The codes of romantic and erotic equality demand that they give as much as they receive, so as to culminate once again and always in orgasm. They must continue to perform by remaining eternally youthful and desirable in order to hold onto the other half of a couple that remains fundamental, if potentially weakened by the fact that it is no longer obligatorily linked to procreation or the raising of children. Everyone is now much more demanding in the spheres of sensuality, the emotions and the passions. The age of love à la carte seems to have arrived, of a contract constantly under threat from the requirement for perfection and completeness so insistently formulated by our whole civilization. It could certainly be argued that sexuality today retains a weak echo of the transcendence that shrouded it when it assured the survival of the species, consequently surrounding the search for physical pleasure with an aura of nostalgia and disillusion. But that would be to admit that its profound transformation symbolizes the failure of a civilization dedicated to economic growth and technical control.[41] The observation is valid only for the United States. On this side of the Atlantic, although we, too, see a fragilization of the personality among young men who have lost the chauvinist reference points of their elders, and who are confronted with the need to perform on all fronts by the young women of their generation, it does not result in a clear growth of pathological narcissism. On the contrary, we see a revival of the values of proximity and the definition of a code of love based on fulfilling oneself through the Other.

Attitudes towards carnal enjoyment are highly informative with regard to social choices. The heirs of the New World remain viscerally attached to a Western repressive system in which religion and the family born of the sacrament of marriage are the twin pillars of tradition. Yet the escalation of demands is badly shaking a fractured world. The culture of narcissism seems to reflect the transcription at the personal level of this great collective weakness. The Kinsey Reports of 1948 and 1953 had already shown that the laws and rules, particularly harsh in matters of morality, were constantly transgressed. Fifty years later, the same 'double constraint' continues to have negative consequences, even though there have been some liberal openings, especially in the case of female sexuality.

Hedonist Europe, meanwhile, has deliberately chosen the permissive path. The visible excesses do not prevent the new values from being integrated into the social fabric and from producing additional social cement. The growth of the taste for pleasure goes hand in hand with the mending of the relational web damaged by modernity. The recent valorization of close and warm structures reveals the existence of new negotiations between the individual who yearns for security and the entities which are best able to provide it, beginning with the couple, whose survival seems assured, on condition it adapts to great changes.

Never have the people of the West been so powerfully oriented and determined by their group as at the beginning of the twenty-first century. Individualism appears to triumph, but individuals are doomed by the laws of the economic market and the tyranny of the orgasm to become athletes in personal success, constantly required to demonstrate to others that they can do even better. Yet never have

CONCLUSION

they had so much freedom of choice, at least in Europe, to expand, to make the most of their bodies and live out their desires in a newly possible erotic equality between men and women or between partners of the same sex. The perpetual renegotiation of the communal bond, stratagem of a dynamic and inventive culture, now means that we all have to take account of the best-kept secret since the origins of Christian civilization: the pleasure we call carnal.

NOTES

INTRODUCTION

1 Nylan, 'On the politics of pleasure', pp. 73–5. I would like to thank the author for drawing my attention to this article and for kindly giving me the benefit of his knowledge.
2 In Europe, the concept only became important with the Enlightenment; it was combined with the theme of progress in the run-up to the French Revolution: Mauzi, *L'Idée de bonheur*.
3 Foucault, *History of Sexuality*, vol. I: *The Will to Knowledge*.
4 Weber, *The Protestant Ethic and the Spirit of Capitalism*.
5 Elias, *The Civilizing Process*.
6 Foucault, *Madness and Civilization*; *Discipline and Punish*.

PART I THE ORGASM AND THE WEST

1 Lionel Tiger recalls the formula of Edmund Burke, repeated in *The Oxford English Dictionary*, 'Pain and pleasure are simple ideas, incapable of definition': Tiger, *The Pursuit of Pleasure*, p. 17.
2 Tiger and Fox, *The Imperial Animal*.

CHAPTER 1 CARNAL KNOWLEDGE

1 Morris, *The Discovery of the Individual*, pp. 158–9.
2 Kramer and Bynum, 'Revisiting the twelfth-century individual', pp. 84–5. See also Bynum, *Jesus as Mother*, ch. 3: 'Did the

twelfth century discover the individual?' I am grateful to Caroline Bynum for these references.
3 Burckhardt, *The Civilization of the Renaissance in Italy*.
4 Weber, *The Protestant Ethic and the Spirit of Capitalism*.
5 Ibid., p. 73.
6 Muchembled, *Passions de femmes*.
7 Greenblatt, 'Fiction and friction'; *Renaissance Self-Fashioning*, pp. 1, 256.
8 Davis, 'Boundaries and the sense of self in sixteenth-century France'.
9 Oscar Bloch and Walther von Wartburg, *Dictionnaire Etymologique de la Langue Française* (Paris: PUF, 1968), p. 337: 'individual' is dated to 1242, 'individuality' to 1760 and 'individualist' to 1836.
10 Hume, *A Treatise of Human Nature*, quoted by Lyons, *The Invention of the Self*, p. 21.
11 See esp. Freud, 'Beyond the pleasure principle'; Rose, 'Assembling the modern self'; Meyer, 'Myths of socialization and of personality', p. 209; Dumont, *Essais sur l'individualisme*.
12 Elias, *The Civilizing Process*; *The Court Society*; *La Dynamique de l'Occident*; *The Society of Individuals*. See also Muchembled, *La Société policée*. For the past 10 years Elias's disciples have published a journal in Amsterdam with the title *Figurations. Newsletter of the Norbert Elias Foundation*. The most forceful critique of his theories is that of Hans-Peter Duerr, *Nackheit und Scham* (*Nudité et Pudeur*).
13 Elias, *The Civilizing Process*: 'Changes in attitude toward relations between the sexes', pp. 169–91 (quotation p. 180).
14 Zohar, *The Quantum Self*, p. 154.
15 Freud, 'The ego and the id', *Complete Psychological Works*, vol. 19, p. 24.
16 Freud, 'Beyond the pleasure principle', *Complete Psychological Works*, vol. 18 (quotation pp. 51–2).
17 Rose, 'Assembling the modern self', pp. 225, 254–7, 268.
18 These ideas of Freud are analysed and discussed in Zohar, *The Quantum Self*, pp. 160–1.
19 Lasch, *Culture of Narcissism*. This work was inspired by psychoanalytic practices of the 1960s, as described esp. by Heinz Kohut (see his *The Analysis of the Self*; *The Restoration of the Self*). These themes are developed in Layton and Schapiro (eds), *Narcissism and the Text*, esp. pp. 1–32. On the connections

between this pathology and artistic creativity, see Kris, *Psychoanalytic Explorations in Art*.
20 For a powerful critique of Lasch's argument, see Holland, 'On Narcissism from Baudelaire to Sartre', p. 165.
21 Foucault, *History of Sexuality*, vol. I: *The Will to Knowledge*.
22 Ibid., p. 35.
23 Ibid., passim.
24 Ibid., pp. 37, 140–1.
25 Foucault, *History of Sexuality*, vol. II: *The Uses of Pleasure*; vol. III: *The Care of the Self*. The back cover of the first volume, in 1976, announced five further volumes to complete the project. The second and third were to be called *The Flesh and the Body* and *The Children's Crusade*; in the end, however, Foucault chose to devote them to Classical Greek thinking and to the Greek and Latin authors of the first two centuries AD.
26 Foucault, *History of Sexuality*, vol. I: *The Will to Knowledge*.
27 Ibid., pp. 104–5.
28 Freud, 'Three essays on the theory of sexuality', *Complete Psychological Works*, vol. VII, p. 238.
29 Pitt-Rivers, *The Fate of Shechem*, for an anthropological approach to the subject of the law of shame and the gaze of the others.
30 Bakhtin, *Rabelais and His World*; Muchembled, *L'Invention de l'homme moderne*, pp. 61–76; Flandrin (ed.), *Les Amours Paysannes*.
31 Ariès, *Centuries of Childhood*; Daumas, *Le Mariage amoureux*; Ariès and Duby (eds), *A History of Private Life*, vols III–V; Pollock, 'Living on the stage of the world', pp. 79, 81.
32 Tiger, *The Pursuit of Pleasure*, p. 75.
33 For a summary of the main debates on this subject, see Dupâquier (ed.), *Histoire de la population française*, vol. II: *De la Renaissance à 1789*. For England, from an impressive body of work, see esp. three books of Peter Laslett, *The World We Have Lost*; *Family Life and Illicit Love in Earlier Generations*; and *The World We Have Lost: Further Explored*. See also Wrigley, *English Population History from Family Reconstitution*. Sexuality is also discussed in three books by Flandrin, *L'Église et la Contrôle des Naissances*; *Les Amours Paysannes*; and *Le Sexe et l'Occident*.
34 Daumas, *Le Mariage amoureux*, pp. 138–46.
35 The formulation is that of Philippe Ariès at a conference in 1976: see Sullerot (ed.), *Le Fait féminin*, pp. 382–3; Fox, *The*

Red Lamp of Incest, pp. 198–203 of 1983 edn. I have found the same pattern in the villages of Artois: Muchembled, *La Violence au village*. See also Muchembled, *L'Invention de l'homme moderne*, ch. 5: 'De père en fils'.
36 Rossiaud, *Prostitution médiévale*, pp. 26–40.
37 Stone, *The Family, Sex and Marriage in England*; Shorter, *The Making of the Modern Family*.
38 Quaife, *Wanton Wenches and Wayward Wives*, p. 246.
39 Muchembled, *Passions de femmes*, pp. 213–15.
40 Bercé, *Fête et révolte*.
41 Flandrin (ed.), *Les Amours paysannes*.
42 Trumbach, *Sex and the Gender Revolution*, vol. I, p. 22.
43 Ibid., pp. 409. See the virulent review of this book by Thomas Laqueur in the *American Historical Review*.
44 Trumbach, *Sex and the Gender Revolution*, vol. I, pp. 14–17, 19, 22–3, 430.
45 Claverie and Lamaison, *L'Impossible Mariage*; Ploux, *Guerres paysannes en Quercy*.
46 Lionel Tiger shows that the phenomenon also existed in other cultures, with particular reference to the case of the Japanese geishas: *Pursuit of Pleasure*, p. 143.
47 Claus, *The Sorrow of Belgium*.
48 Belluck, 'Massachusetts gives new push to gay marriage'.
49 *Something's Gotta Give* (dir. Nancy Meyers).
50 Trumbach, *Sex and the Gender Revolution*, vol. I, p. 13.
51 Héritier, *Masculin-féminin*. For the golden age of marriage, see Daumas, *Le Mariage amoureux*.
52 See her Preface to the volume of conference proceedings: Sullerot (ed.), *Le Fait féminin*, p. 21. The conference was held at the Centre Royaumont pour une science de l'homme.
53 Sullerot (ed.), *Le Fait féminin*, p. 383. This observation by Massimo Livi-Bacci was made in discussion. See also his contribution: 'Le changement démographique et le cycle de vie des femmes': ibid., pp. 467–8.
54 Sullerot, 'En guise de conclusion': in ibid., p. 515. One notes her unhappiness at having had to avoid such questions, because she calls for there to be, one day, a quite different work, devoted to the 'female subject'.
55 Tiger, *Pursuit of Pleasure*, p. 74.
56 A commercial on American TV in Autumn 2000 urged people to watch the programme 'Guilty Pleasures' by repeating the slogan: 'Imagine, for the moment, that you have everything –

NOTES TO PP. 45–53

but will need more!' Cited by Nylan, 'On the politics of pleasure', pp. 79–80 and n. 15.

CHAPTER 2   MASCULINE, FEMININE: INDIVIDUALS AND THEIR BODIES

1   Burckhardt, *The Civilization of the Renaissance in Italy*.
2   Some historians are fighting a rearguard action against the idea of an emergence of the individual in the Renaissance, for example the medievalist David Aers, whose arguments are a little vague: Aers (ed.), *Culture and History*, esp. his own article, 'A whisper in the ear of early modernists'.
3   Greenblatt, *Renaissance Self-Fashioning*, pp. 2–3.
4   Castiglione, *Book of the Courtier*.
5   Burke, 'Viewpoint. The invention of leisure in early modern Europe', esp. p. 149. See also Nardo, *The Ludic Self in Seventeenth-Century English Literature*.
6   Greenblatt, *Renaissance Self-Fashioning*, pp. 8–9, 202–3, 256.
7   Burke, 'Representations of the self'.
8   Fogel, *Marie de Gournay*.
9   Muchembled, *Passions de femmes*, pp. 42–3.
10 Burke, 'Representations of the self', pp. 24–6.
11 Muchembled, *Passions de femmes*, pp. 126–8; Muchembled, *Le Temps des supplices*.
12 Silverman, *Tortured Subjects*.
13 Hanson, *Discovering the Subject in Renaissance England*, esp. pp. 13, 19, 40, 55, 60, 74, 88, 91.
14 Heale, *Autobiography and Authorship in Renaissance Verse*, pp. 8, 11, 40, 155, 171.
15 Webber, *The Eloquent 'I'*, pp. 4–9. English Baptism resembled Anabaptism; the Levellers came from the austere Protestant sect of independents, who rejected all hierarchy and were among the most radical partisans of absolute equality at the time of the Revolution.
16 Monluc, *Commentaires*: see esp. Preface, pp. ix–xxi.
17 Dragstra, Ottway and Wilcox (eds), *Betraying Ourselves*, esp. Introduction, pp. 8–9 and Epilogue, pp. 198–9, 210–11. See also Bourcier, *Les Journaux privés en Angleterre*; Yates, *The Art of Memory*; Kuperty-Tsur, *Se dire à la Renaissance*; Briot, *Usage du monde, usage de soi*.
18 Fraser, *The Weaker Vessel*, p. 1. This book paints an extremely evocative picture of women in England from 1603 to 1702.

19 My definition is close to that of Anthony Fletcher in his excellent book, *Gender, Sex and Subordination in England*, pp. xv–xvi. See also on this subject, Wiesner, *Women and Gender in Early Modern Europe*; Shoemaker and Vincent (eds), *Gender and History in Western Europe*.
20 Fletcher, *Gender, Sex and Subordination*, p. 27.
21 Muchembled, *Passions de femmes*, p. 59.
22 Ibid., pp. 137–66. For London and masculine anxiety, see Fletcher, *Gender, Sex and Subordination*, pp. 27, 110, 339.
23 Matthews-Grieco, *Ange ou diablesse?*
24 Fletcher, *Gender, Sex and Subordination*, p. 29; Febvre, *Amour sacré, amour profane*, esp. pp. 310–11.
25 Muchembled, *La Sorcière au village*, esp. p. 120, for the stereotype defined in 1595 in a mandate of Philip II for the Low Countries.
26 Muchembled, *Passions de femmes*, pp. 62–3; Hanley, 'Engendering the state'.
27 Belsey, *The Subject of Tragedy*, p. 147.
28 Rossiaud, *La Prostitution Médiévale*.
29 Fletcher, *Gender, Sex and Subordination*, p. 93.
30 Gowing, *Domestic Dangers*, esp. p. 40. See also Crawford and Gowing (eds), *Women's World in Seventeenth-Century England*; Gowing, *Common Bodies*.
31 Muchembled, 'Au malheur des dame' ['The unhappiness of women'], in *Passions de femmes*, pp. 51–82; see also pp. 117–22 for a well-documented case of conjugal violence.
32 Muchembled, *Les Derniers Bûchers*, pp. 187–216.
33 Farge, *Vivre dans la rue à Paris au XVIIIe siècle*.
34 Gowing, *Domestic Dangers*.
35 Fletcher, *Gender, Sex and Subordination*, p. 362.
36 Belsey, *The Subject of Tragedy*, pp. 135, 140–1, 185.
37 Fraser, *The Weaker Vessel*, p. 419.
38 Jardine, *Still Harping on Daughters*.
39 Steinberg, *La Confusion des sexes*.
40 Jardine, *Still Harping on Daughters*, p. 9 (for Rainoldes), 20–1, 24.
41 Trumbach, *Sex and the Gender Revolution*, vol. I; see also ch. 1 above.
42 See ch. 1 above: 'Frustrated young men'.
43 Muchembled, 'Nerf de boeuf et chandelier: Renée?' ['Cosh and candlestick: Renée?'], in *Passions de femmes*, pp. 117–22.

44 Helen Wilcox in Dragstra, Ottway and Wilcox (eds), *Betraying Ourselves*, p. 116.
45 Muchembled, *Passions de femmes*, p. 39.
46 Ibid., 'The unhappiness of women', pp. 51–82.
47 Belsey, *The Subject of Tragedy*, p. 223.
48 Fletcher, *Gender, Sex and Subordination*, pp. 347, 354.
49 Helen Wilcox in Dragstra, Ottway and Wilcox (eds), *Betraying Ourselves*, pp. 117, 4.
50 Graham, *Her Own Life*, pp. 87–99, for a discussion and extracts from the memoirs of Margaret Cavendish.
51 Ibid., pp. 35–53, for Anne Clifford. The extracts are from the years 1616–17 and the portrait of herself she commissioned is on p. 36. See also the comments of Helen Wilcox, 'Her own life, her own living? Text and materiality in Englishwomen's writings', in Dragstra, Ottway and Wilcox (eds), *Betraying Ourselves*, pp. 105–19, esp. pp. 110–11; Spence, *Lady Anne Clifford*.
52 She had wanted the inheritance to go to her grandsons. Her memory remains strong to this day: tourists can walk in her footsteps from Skipton to Brougham on 'The Lady Anne Clifford Walk', between the Yorkshire Dales and the Eden Valley.
53 The painting, probably by Jan van Belcamp, is now in Appleby Castle.
54 Wray, '[Re]constructing the past', in Dragstra, Ottway and Wilcox (eds), *Betraying Ourselves*, pp. 148–9.
55 Quoted in the excellent Paster, *The Body Embarrassed*, p. 8.
56 Ibid., pp. 8–9; Laqueur, *Making Sex*, pp. 19–20; Fletcher, *Gender, Sex and Subordination*, chapter entitled 'Fungible fluids, heat and concoction'.
57 Laqueur, *Making Sex*, pp. 25, 171–4.
58 Steinberg, *La Confusion des sexes*.
59 Sawday, *The Body Emblazoned*, plate 29, p. 97.
60 Paster, *The Body Embarrassed*, p. 10.
61 Roper, *Oedipus and the Devil*, p. 107.
62 Sawday, *The Body Emblazoned*, p. 20.
63 Ibid., pp. 23, 28–9; Sawday, 'Self and selfhood in the seventeenth century', pp. 34–6 (for Caravaggio), 46–8 (for the consequences of the ideas of Harvey and Descartes).
64 Belsey, *The Subject of Tragedy*, pp. 18, 20, 23, 33–4, 42–3.

65 Sawday, *The Body Emblazoned*, illustration no. 5 (see also no. 6, 'The Anatomy Theatre of Leiden, 1609').
66 Ibid., p. 107.
67 Ibid., pp. 9, 11.
68 *The Secret Miracles of Nature* (first Latin edn 1559, first Italian edn 1560, first French edn 1556, first German edn 1569, a further Latin edn 1605–51, and first English trans. 1658). There were frequent reprints soon after publication. References here are to the French edition of 1574: *Les Occultes Merveilles et Secretz de nature* (Paris: Galot du Pré, 1574), with detailed pictures.
69 Lemnius, *Les Occultes Merveilles*, fols 155, 166v.
70 Sawday, *The Body Emblazoned*, pp. 10, 222, 224.
71 Paster, *The Body Embarrassed*, pp. 19, 21, 23–7, 40–1, 95.
72 Ibid., pp. 14–16 (for Elias and Bakhtin); Elias, *The Civilizing Process*; Bakhtin, *Rabelais and His World*.
73 Greenblatt, *Shakespearean Negotiations*, pp. 78–93.
74 Fletcher, *Gender, Sex and Subordination*, pp. 32, 54–7, for an excellent summary of the subject. See also Berriot-Salvadore, *Un Corps, un destin*; Gent and Llewellyn (eds), *Renaissance Bodies*.
75 Paster, *The Body Embarrassed*, pp. 134–5, 161.

CHAPTER 3 CARNAL PLEASURES, MORTAL SINS

1 *L'École des filles*, in Prévot (ed.), *Libertins du XVIIe siècle*, vol. I, pp. 1179–80.
2 Muchembled, *La Société policée*.
3 Molière, *L'École des femmes* (1662), V, iv, 1516–19.
4 Ibid., II, v, 600.
5 For an excellent synthesis, see Prévot (ed,), *Libertins du XVIIe siècle*, vol. I, pp. 1672–80.
6 Shorter, *The Making of the Modern Family*; Stone, *The Family, Sex and Marriage in England*. For a critique of both books, see Quaife, *Wanton Wenches and Wayward Wives*, pp. 243–8.
7 Reprinted in 1959 with the title *Les Secrets de l'amour et de Vénus*.
8 Flandrin, *Un Temps pour embrasser*, pp. 124–7.
9 Boaistuau, *Le Théâtre du monde*, pp. 59ff, 100–5.
10 Muchembled, *Passions de femmes*, ch. 2; Hanley, 'Engendering the state'.

11 Muchembled, *A History of the Devil*, esp. ch. 1.
12 Matthews-Grieco, *Ange ou diablesse?*
13 This is the title and theme of a film of Jean Eustache, *La Maman et la Putain* (1973), in which the hero hesitates between two loves, two types of woman, one maternal, the other given to hedonistic pleasure and drink. It cleverly evokes the break with the old model of the masculine double standard following the changes of the 1960s (see ch. 6 below).
14 Flandrin, *L'Église et la contrôle des naissances*; Noonan, *Contraception*.
15 I have discussed this at length in Muchembled, *Le Temps des supplices*, pp. 135, 139–45.
16 For these female crimes, in particular concealment of pregnancy and witchcraft cases, see Muchembled, *Passions de femmes*, chs 2 and 7.
17 For a more detailed analysis of rape and adultery cases, see ibid., pp. 76–81.
18 Deregnaucourt and Poton, *La Vie religieuse en France* (for the consistories, see pp. 263–73).
19 Quaife, *Wanton Wenches and Wayward Wives*, pp. 38–43.
20 Elias, *The Civilizing Process*; Bakhtin, *Rabelais and His World*.
21 Stone, *The Family, Sex and Marriage in England*.
22 Quaife, *Wanton Wenches and Wayward Wives*, pp. 193, 248.
23 Ibid., pp. 25, 29.
24 Muchembled, *La Violence au village*, pp. 31–2, 398–9.
25 John Addy modestly presents similar results for the bishopric of Chester, on the basis of the same types of document: *Sin and Society*, esp. pp. 112–58. For Wiltshire, Martin Ingram demonstrates the importance of the documentation while criticizing Quaife's overall view with arguments closer to morality than history: see *Church Courts, Sex and Marriage in England*, esp. pp. 159–61. The opinion of demographers like Peter Laslett (*Family Life and Illicit Love in Earlier Generations*) regarding a strict 'personal discipline' are apparently dogma for many scholars, in spite of the discovery of new sources and new and less puritanical approaches to sexuality. The archives of the London ecclesiastical courts have been used in an original manner by Laura Gowing for adultery, seen from the woman's side: see *Domestic Dangers*, esp. pp. 180–231. For francophone regions, there is some evidence of a sexual life as 'amoral'

as in Somerset in judicial records from the upper valley of the Meurthe and the region round Saint-Dié: see Diedler, *Démons et sorcières en Lorraine*, pp. 28–32 (for the many adulteries and boasts of Gérard Grivel, who claimed that 'if all the women and girls he had slept with held hands, they would stretch as far as the faubourg of the Vieux Marché', 15 kms away), pp. 36–7 (for frequent female infidelities), etc.

26 Quaife, *Wanton Wenches and Wayward Wives*, pp. 56–8. See also Laslett, *The World We Have Lost: Further Explored*, for a classic view of sexuality in the village (though amended and corrected in this revised edition).
27 Goubert, *La Vie quotidienne des paysans au XVIIe siècle*, p. 93. See also Dupâquier (ed.), *Histoire de la population française*.
28 Quaife, *Wanton Wenches and Wayward Wives*, pp. 181–3, 186, 249.
29 Ibid., pp. 175–7.
30 For homosexuality and masturbation among young unmarried men, see the works of Jean-Louis Flandrin.
31 Quaife, *Wanton Wenches and Wayward Wives*, pp. 165–9.
32 Ibid., pp. 124–42, 171, 246.
33 Ibid., pp. 146–58 (this female subculture also appears in the diocese of Chester: see Addy, *Sin and Society*, p. 138, for the case of Ann Savage, a servant at Northenden).
34 Quaife, *Wanton Wenches and Wayward Wives*, pp. 119–21, 171–2.
35 There is a long list in Bougard, *Érotisme et amour physique*, pp. 193–8.
36 Viala, *Naissance de l'écrivain*; Jouanna, *Le Devoir de révolte*.
37 Prévot (ed.), *Libertins du XVIIe siècle*, vol. I, pp. 1672–80; and the works of Lachévre, *Le Libertinage au XVIIe Siècle*, vol. VII: *Mélanges*, pp. 90–1, 116–21.
38 Dubost, *L'Académie des dames*.
39 Bougard, *Érotisme et amour physique*, pp. 12–13, 78–9.
40 'Il nous faut gagner Paradis. / Nous y foutrons chacun un Ange, / Dont le c . . . sent la fleur d'orange.' Lachévre, *Le Libertinage au XVIIe siècle*, vol. VI: *Disciples et successeurs de Théophile de Viau*, III, *Les Chansons Libertines de Claude de Chouvigny*, pp. xxvi–xxix, 12, 16, 20.
41 'De rencontrer ce vit rouge comme un rubis! / Mais l'ayant éprouvé: "Bran de ce vit! dit-elle, / Il n'est pas assez gros; j'aime mieux la chandelle, / Ou l'engin de velours de quoi je me

fourbis".' Bougard, *Érotisme et amour physique*, pp. 13, 182.
42 Ibid., p. 142.
43 'Ce fut alors qu'ils se pâmèrent / De l'excès des contentements; / Que cinq à six fois ces amants / Moururent ou ressuscitèrent; / Que bouche à bouche et corps à corps, / Tantôt vivants et tantôt morts / Leurs belles âmes de baisèrent, / Et que par d'agréables coups / Entre eux ils se communiquèrent / Tout ce que l'amour a de doux.' Ibid., pp. 181–4.
44 Prévot (ed.), *Libertins du XVIIe siècle*, vol. I, pp. 1124–6, 1128.
45 Ibid., pp. 1129, 1136.
46 Ibid., pp. 1147–1202 (p. 1186 for the soul dragged downwards).
47 As argued by Laqueur, *Making Sex*.
48 Shoemaker, *Gender in English Society*, p. 9. See also Laqueur, 'Orgasm, generation, and the politics of reproductive biology', p. 112; Turner, *Fashioning Adultery*.
49 Roecke, *Forbidden Friendships*, pp. 234–5.
50 Ibid., p. 235.
51 See ch. 4 below for London and Paris.
52 Pintard, *Le Libertinage érudit* (revised edn), pp. 22–5.
53 Ibid., pp. 440, 576.
54 Prévot (ed.), *Libertins du XVIIe siècle*, vol. I, pp. 1221–46 (for Théophile and the records of his trial); Lachévre, *Le Libertinage devant le Parlement de Paris. Le Procès du poète Théophile de Viau*; Lachévre, *Le Libertinage au XVIIe siècle. Une seconde révision des oeuvres du poète Théophile de Viau*.
55 Lachévre, *Le Libertinage au XVIIe siècle*, vol. VI: *Les Chansons libertines de Claude de Chouvigny*, pp. xxvii, 19, 22.
56 Ibid., p. xxvii.
57 Lachévre, *Le Libertinage au XVIIe siècle*, vol. II: *La Vie et les Poésies libertines inédites de Des Barreaux*.
58 Lachévre, *Le Libertinage au XVIIe siècle*, vol. VII: *Mélanges*, pp. 90–121; Prévot (ed.), *Libertins du XVIIe Siècle*, vol. 1, p. 1672; Bougard, *Érotisme et amour physique*, pp. 162, 173.
59 Sauvy, *Livres saisis à Paris*, p. 33.
60 Prévot (ed.), *Libertins du XVIIe Siècle*, vol. I, p. 1673.
61 Lachévre, *Le Libertinage au XVIIe siècle*, vol. V: *Les Oeuvres libertines de Claude Le Petit*.
62 Foxon, *Libertine Literature in England*, p. 48.

63 See the fine book by Michel Jeanneret: *Éros Rebelle*.
64 For this subject, see Muchembled, *La Société policée*, ch. 4, pp. 123–80.
65 Hunt (ed.), *The Invention of Pornography*, pp. 30, 40.
66 Foxon, *Libertine Literature in England*, pp. 5–6.
67 Hunt (ed.), *The Invention of Pornography*, p. 21.
68 Foxon, *Libertine Literature in England*, pp. 52–63.

CHAPTER 4 THE EROTICISM OF THE ENLIGHTENMENT

1 Elias, *The Civilizing Process*.
2 Jeanneret, *Éros Rebelle*.
3 Foxon, *Libertine Literature in England*, pp. 43–4.
4 Hunt (ed.), *The Invention of Pornography*, Introduction, pp. 10–11; Jacob, 'The materialist world of pornography', pp. 158–9, 182.
5 Foxon, *Libertine Literature in England*, pp. 44, 49; Underwood, *Etherege and the Seventeenth-Century Comedy of Manners*.
6 Flandrin, *Le Sexe et l'Occident*, p. 298.
7 Jacob, 'The materialist world of pornography', p. 183; Norberg, 'The libertine whore', pp. 229, 243.
8 Wagner, *Eros Revived*, p. 7.
9 Muchembled, *La Société policée*.
10 Goulemot, *Forbidden Texts*, pp. 36–8.
11 Trumbach, 'Erotic fantasy and male libertinism', p. 266.
12 Wagner, *Eros Revived*, p. 175; *Forbidden Texts*, pp. 142–4.
13 Hunt, 'Pornography and the French Revolution', in Hunt (ed.), *The Invention of Pornography*, pp. 302–4, 339. See also Wagner, *Eros Revived*, pp. 246–7 (quoting the work of Ronald Paulson, who establishes a connection between the political violence of the age and the moral revolt of pornography: see his *Representations of Revolution*).
14 *Justine ou les Malheurs de la vertu* (1791) and *La Philosophie dans le boudoir* (1795).
15 Goulemot, *Forbidden Texts*, pp. 30–5 and figure 2.1.
16 Wagner, *Eros Revived*.
17 Cressy, 'Literacy in context', pp. 313–14.
18 Wagner, *Eros Revived*, pp. 22–3.
19 Ibid., pp. 26–7.
20 Ibid., pp. 48–9, 58–9.
21 Ibid., p. 80.

22 Ibid., pp. 92–3.
23 Ibid., pp. 114–15.
24 See below, 'Demonized biographies'.
25 Wagner, *Eros Revived*, pp. 160–1.
26 Ibid., p. 220.
27 Cameron, *London's Pleasures*, esp. pp. 17, 82, 141; Porter and Hall, *Facts of Life*, pp. 22, 25, 31.
28 Ibid., p. 16. For the separate spheres, see Davidoff and Hall, *Family Fortunes*.
29 Porter, 'Material pleasures in the consumer society', pp. 34–5.
30 With the title *La Fable des abeilles, ou les Fripons devenus honnêtes gens, avec le commentaire où l'on trouve que les vices des particuliers tendent à l'avantage du public, traduit de l'anglais sur la sixième édition*, and published in London by J. Nourse.
31 Porter, 'Enlightenment and Pleasure', pp. 5, 8–13, 18.
32 Mauzi, *L'Idée de bonheur*, pp. 16, 21, 179.
33 Ibid., pp. 386–7.
34 Ibid., pp. 393–9, 413–17.
35 Flynn, *The Body in Swift and Defoe*, p. 49.
36 Mauzi, *L'Idée de bonheur*, pp. 417, 422, 430–1, 646.
37 Fillon, *Les Trois Bagues au doigt*.
38 Flandrin, *Le Sexe et l'Occident*, pp. 84–5, 94–5.
39 Ibid., p. 130.
40 Porter and Hall, *Facts of Life*, pp. 65–90, esp. pp. 36, 66, 69, 76.
41 Tarczylo, *Sexe et liberté*, pp. 82–5.
42 Ibid., pp. 71–3.
43 Fletcher, *Gender, Sex and Subordination*, p. 407.
44 Ibid., pp. 29, 340. The double standard is described in many works in English, esp. those by Randolph Trumbach and Robert Shoemaker, but has signally failed to attract the interest of French historians.
45 Trumbach, *Sex and the Gender Revolution*, vol. 1, pp. 384–5.
46 Ariès, *Centuries of Childhood*.
47 Shoemaker, *Gender in English Society*, pp. 66–7.
48 Trumbach, *Sex and the Gender Revolution*, vol. I, pp. 111, 196, 275, 392, 422, 430 for the three London generations.
49 Fletcher, *Gender, Sex and Subordination*, p. 339; Norton, *Mother Clap's Molly House*.
50 Turner, *Fashioning Adultery*, pp. 5, 15, 96, 115, 127, 197, 202–3.

51 Fletcher, *Gender, Sex and Subordination*, pp. 400, 407.
52 Elias, *The Civilizing Process*.
53 Jordanova, *Sexual Visions*.
54 Fletcher, *Gender, Sex and Subordination*, p. 383 (for details and an additional bibliography in English).
55 This is the opinion of Randolph Trumbach: *Sex and the Gender Revolution*, vol. I. See ch. 1 above.
56 Ibid., p. 394.
57 In spite of the excellent work of Michel Rey, 'Police et sodomie à Paris au XVIIIe siècle'.
58 See ch. 3 above.
59 Muchembled, *Le Temps des supplices*, p. 140.
60 Porter and Hall, *Facts of Life*, pp. 7, 42.
61 Mainil, *Dans les règles du plaisir*, p. 176.
62 Not 80, as claimed by Van Ussel: *Histoire de la répression sexuelle*, p. 199.
63 Trumbach, *Sex and the Gender Revolution*, vol. I, pp. 63–5; Tarczylo, *Sexe et liberté*, pp. 108–9. See also Van Ussel, *Histoire de la répression sexuelle*.
64 Shoemaker, *Gender in English Society*, p. 67; Trumbach, 'Erotic fantasy and male libertinism', p. 266.
65 Tarczylo, *Sexe et liberté*, pp. 112–13, 228–9. Tarczylo says that Tissot's treatise appeared in France only in 1792, but the third edition, of 1764, allegedly published in Lausanne, was actually published clandestinely in Paris: Stengers and Van Neck, *Masturbation*.
66 Ibid.
67 Samuel-Auguste Tissot, *Onanism, or a Treatise upon the Disorders Produced by Masturbation: or, the Dangerous Effects of Secret and Excessive Venery* (London: Varenne, 1761); for the French edition of 1764, see n. 65 above.
68 Mainil, *Dans les règles du plaisir*, pp. 184–91.
69 Ibid., pp. 194–7.
70 Ibid., pp. 198–9.
71 Porter and Hall, *Facts of Life*, pp. 92–3.
72 Staël, Anne-Louise-Germaine de, *De l'Influence des passions sur le bonheur des individus et des nations*. I would like to thank Veit Elm for drawing my attention to this text.
73 Lejeune, *L'Autobiographie en France*; Lejeune, *Le Pacte autobiographique*; Mathieu-Castellani, *La Scène judiciare de l'autobiographie*.

NOTES TO PP. 146–159

74 Muchembled, *La Société policée*. For all these themes, see chs 2 and 3 above.
75 Rawlings, *Drunks, Whores and Idle Apprentices*, pp. 18–19, 22, 40–1.
76 Ibid., p. 23.
77 Flynn, *The Body in Swift and Defoe*, pp. 5–6, 25. For France, see Etlin, *The Architecture of Death*.
78 Flynn, *The Body in Swift and Defoe*, pp. 26–7.
79 Preston, *The Created Self*, pp. 7, 13.
80 Bastien, 'Le Spectacle pénal à Paris au XVIIIe siècle'.
81 Sorbier, 'De la potence à la biographie'.
82 Ibid., pp. 266–71.
83 Mascuch, *Origins of the Individualist Self*, pp. 180–1.
84 Faller, *Turned to Account*, pp. x–xi.
85 Faller, *Crime and Defoe*, pp. 70–3.
86 Ibid., pp. 211–15.
87 Ibid., p. 225.
88 Elias, *The Civilizing Process*. Michel Foucault, in many works, and at his most pessimistic, discusses this same phenomenon by linking it to the advance of the power to 'discipline and punish'.
89 Faller, *Turned to Account*, pp. 191–3.
90 Faller, *Crime and Defoe*, pp. 6–8, 10.
91 Brewer, *The Pleasures of the Imagination*, pp. xxii–xxiii, 82–5, 111, 180–1, 194.
92 Ibid., pp. 262–3, 270–3.

CHAPTER 5 BENEATH THE VICTORIAN VEIL (1800–1960)

1 Gay, *The Bourgeois Experience*. The definition appears in the Introduction to vol. V, intended to synthesize the whole work. For 'Gustavus Flaubertus, Bourgeoisophobus', see p. 25.
2 Gay, *The Bourgeois Experience*, vol. V: *Pleasure Wars*, pp. 138, 238–41.
3 Elias, *The Civilizing Process*.
4 Sennett, *Fall of Public Man*; idem, *Authority*.
5 Sennett, *Fall of Public Man*.
6 Staffe, *Usages du Monde*. The use of a titled female name gave extra credibility to such manuals (as it still does today); see Muchembled, *La Société policée*. ch. 6.

7 Sennett, *Fall of Public Man.*
8 The view that medicine was a new religion of the nineteenth century appears in Putnam, *Reason, Truth and History*, p. 185. Sander L. Gilman qualifies this argument, while accepting the author's view that medicine is modelled by the culture from which it springs: *Sexuality: An Illustrated History*, p. 9. Ronald Pearsall also emphasizes the power of the doctors, whom he calls arrogant, over a credulous middle class: *The Worm in the Bud*, p. XII.
9 Porter and Hall, *Facts of Life*, pp. 202–3.
10 Gilman, *Sexuality: An Illustrated History*, p. 3.
11 Laqueur, *Making Sex*, pp. 149–50, 191–2.
12 Marcus, *The Other Victorians*, pp. 2–3, 29–31.
13 Porter and Hall, *Facts of Life*, pp. 202–3, 212–13.
14 Sohn, *Du premier baiser à l'alcove*, pp. 84–5 (various examples); Pearsall, *The Worm in the Bud*, p. 345.
15 Stora-Lamarre, *L'Enfer de la IIIe République*, p. 183.
16 Pearsall, *The Worm in the Bud*, pp. 104–6, 350–1.
17 *My Secret Life*, Part 1, p. 293 of 1998 Grove edn.
18 Pearsall, *The Worm in the Bud*, pp. 412–13, 423.
19 Sohn, *Du premier baiser à l'alcove*, pp. 89, 94.
20 Pearsall, *The Worm in the Bud*, p. 422.
21 Although Sohn devotes a chapter to the various fears, especially of venereal disease: *Du premier baiser à l'alcove*, pp. 109ff.; Alain Corbin also refers to this anxiety in his *Women for Hire*, pp. 28–9, 250–2.
22 Pearsall, *The Worm in the Bud*, pp. XII, 416 (where ch. 9, entitled 'The Psychology of Victorian Sex', has as its first subheading 'Anxiety'); Marcus, *The Other Victorians*, pp. 17, 272.
23 Rosenman, *Unauthorized Pleasures*, p. 13.
24 Marcus, *The Other Victorians*, pp. 22, 273.
25 Pearsall, *The Worm in the Bud*, pp. xiv.
26 Ibid., pp. xv, 186.
27 Corbin, *Women for Hire*, p. 193 (author's underlining).
28 Marcus, *The Other Victorians*, pp. 3, 9; Porter and Hall, *Facts of Life*, p. 132.
29 The notion of 'civilized morality' is applied to the United States of the beginning of the twentieth century by Bullough, 'The development of sexology in the USA', pp. 303–4.
30 Corbin, *Women for Hire*, p. 212.
31 Hauser, 'Krafft-Ebing's psychological understanding of sexual behaviour', pp. 210, 217. The first English edition of

Krafft-Ebing's *Psychopathia Sexualis*, unexpurgated, says the editor, translated from Latin, dates from 1965.
32 As argued by Porter and Hall, *Facts of Life*, p. 275.
33 Gallagher and Laqueur (eds), *The Making of the Modern Body*, p. viii. See also Laqueur, 'Orgasm, generation, and the politics of reproductive biology', pp. 1–41, where he summarizes the argument put forward in 1990 in his *Making Sex*, pp. 149–243.
34 Corbin, 'Commercial sexuality in nineteenth-century France', pp. 210–11.
35 Muchembled, *A History of the Devil*, p. 146.
36 Quoted in Aron and Kempf, *La Bourgeoisie*, p. 170.
37 Agnolo Bronzino, *Venus, Cupid, Folly, and Time*, c.1545, National Gallery, London.
38 Gilman, *Sexuality: An Illustrated History*, pp. 48 London, 9.
39 See ch. 4 above; Laqueur, *Solitary Sex*, pp. 25, 32, 84, 179.
40 Ibid., p. 39, where Laqueur notes 61 editions in various languages, including 35 in French, without counting various abbreviated Latin editions or adaptations.
41 Ibid., quoting Tissot, *L'Onanism*.
42 Stengers and Van Neck, *Masturbation* (the quotations are in the addenda, p. 196).
43 Gilman, *Sexuality: An Illustrated History*, p. 270 and illustration no. 286; the article in question was by T. D. Savill, 'Hysterical skin symptoms and eruptions', *The Lancet*, 20 January 1904.
44 Sohn, *Du premier baiser à l'alcove*, pp. 39–41.
45 Ibid., p. 159; Roy Porter, 'The literature of sexual advice before 1800', in Porter and Teich (eds), *Sexual Knowledge, Sexual Science*, p. 150; Wagner, *Eros Revived*.
46 See ch. 4 above, n. 60.
47 Gilman, *Sexuality: An Illustrated History*, illustrations nos. 260, 27–82 for Jack the Ripper.
48 Stora-Lamarre, *L'Enfer de la IIIe République*, pp. 39, 69.
49 The best book on the subject is that of Thomas Laqueur (*Solitary Sex*). That of Stengers and Van Neck (*Masturbation*) is often confined to description and does not explore the relationship with the anti-sexual 'bourgeois' dread. See also the older work of Jos Van Ussel, *Histoire de la répression sexuelle*.
50 Stengers and Van Neck, *Masturbation*, p. 17 and plates from *Le Livre sans titre*, after the edition of 1844.
51 Ibid., pp. 16–17.
52 Ibid., pp. 118–18.

53 Ibid., pp. 22–3; Porter and Hall, *Facts of Life*, illustrations 12, 13, pp. 146–7 (of Milton); Gay, *The Bourgeois Experience*, vol. I: *Education of the Senses*, illustrations, p. 182 (from Milton and the house of Mathieu catalogue of 1904).
54 Stengers and Van Neck, *Masturbation*, pp. 122–5.
55 Ibid., p. 127; Porter and Hall, *Facts of Life*, p. 147, on the subject of clitoridectomy in Great Britain.
56 Ibid., pp. 149, 160, 282–3.
57 Ibid., pp. 134–5, 142–3, 160–3, 177. See also ch. 6 below.
58 Stengers and Van Neck, *Masturbation*, addenda, pp. 198–9.
59 Sullerot (ed.), *Le Fait féminin*, pp. 443–4 (discussion between Évelyne Sullerot, Jean-Paul Aron and Michelle Perrot). For England, see Pearsall, *The Worm in the Bud*, p. 425.
60 Ibid., pp. 250–1, 258–9, 264–5.
61 Ibid., pp. 258–9. Prostitution has been much studied in England: Walkowitz, *Prostitution and Victorian Society*; *City of Dreadful Delight*; Weeks, *Sexuality and its Discontents*; Mason, *The Making of Victorian Sexuality*.
62 Corbin, *Women for Hire*, p. 6. The situation in Paris at an earlier period is unusually well known thanks to the work of Erica-Marie Benabou, *La Prostitution et la Police des moeurs*.
63 Corbin, *Women for Hire*, p. 10.
64 Foucault, *Discipline and Punish*.
65 Corbin, *Women for Hire*, pp. 10–11, 21–3, 27–8, 130–1. In London, in the mid-nineteenth century, police statistics also divided prostitutes into 'regulars' and 'irregulars': Pearsall, *The Worm in the Bud*, p. 276.
66 Corbin, *Women for Hire*, pp. 135–8.
67 *My Secret Life*, pp. 318–19 of 1998 Grove edn.
68 Corbin, *Women for Hire*, pp. 168, 188, 192–3, 200–1.
69 Pearsall, *The Worm in the Bud*, p. 277. See also Porter and Hall, *Facts of Life*, pp. 224–5, for the failure of the Contagious Diseases Acts, and p. 231 for the treatment of syphilis in the period 1905–9.
70 Huysmans, *En Ménage*.
71 Corbin, *Women for Hire*, pp. 250–2, 261–3, 267–8, 275. See also Sohn, *Du premier baiser à l'alcove*, p. 109.
72 Corbin, *Women for Hire*, graph on p. 116, pp. 348–9.
73 The 1966 Grove edition has lxiii–2,359 pages. *My Secret Life* has been discussed in detail by Steven Marcus (*The Other Victorians*), who sees it as a true confession, like most later commentators, with the exception of Peter Gay, who speaks of

the erotic imagination of a Victorian, without producing any real arguments in support of this view: *The Bourgeois Experience*, vol. I: *Education of the Senses*, p. 468.
74 *My Secret Life*, Preface, p. 7 of 1998 Grove edn.
75 Ibid., vol. I, Preface; Marcus, *The Other Victorians*, pp. 82–3, 111–14.
76 Ibid., p. 115; Rosenman, *Unauthorized Pleasures*, pp. 168–9.
77 See n. 67 above.
78 Marcus, *The Other Victorians*, p. 120; Rosenman, *Unauthorized Pleasures*, p. 171.
79 There is a long scene of this type in *My Secret Life*, pp. 686–92 of Arrow edn, part II, vols V–VIII.
80 Marcus, *The Other Victorians*, pp. 150, 155, 158–9, 164, 172, 176; Rosenman, *Unauthorized Pleasures*, pp. 175, 183, 186–8. The full account of the homosexual experience is pp. 588–601 of Arrow edn, part II, vols V–VIII, of *My Secret Life*.
81 *My Secret Life*.
82 Ibid., p. 598 of Arrow edn, part II, vols V–VIII.
83 Ibid., p. 564; Rosenman, *Unauthorized Pleasures*, pp. 194–6.
84 *My Secret Life*, Introduction to part II of Arrow edn.
85 Marcus, *The Other Victorians*, pp. 182–5.
86 Sigel, *Governing Pleasures*.
87 Porter and Hall, *Facts of Life*, pp. 152–3.
88 Pearsall, *The Worm in the Bud*, pp. 364–5, 415; Marcus, *The Other Victorians*, pp. 34–5, 163. See also Gay, *The Bourgeois Experience*, vol. I: *Education of the Senses*, pp. 358–9.
89 Marcus, *The Other Victorians*, pp. 272–3, 283–4.
90 Ibid., pp. 34, 38; Stora-Lamarre, *L'Enfer de la IIIe République*, pp. 14–15.
91 See ch. 3 above.
92 Stora-Lamarre, *L'Enfer de la IIIe République*, pp. 24–5.
93 Ibid., pp. 36–7.
94 Ibid., pp. 24, 39.
95 Ibid., pp. 70–1, 132–3, 158–9.
96 Ibid., pp. 192–3, 204–5, 211.
97 Pearsall, *The Worm in the Bud*, p. 289.
98 Sohn, *Du premier baiser à l'alcove*, p. 78.
99 Ibid., pp. 30, 38, 40–1, 102–3; Pearsall, *The Worm in the Bud*, pp. 238, 520; Aron and Kempf, *La Bourgeoisie*, pp. 62–3.
100 See chs 1 and 4 above.
101 Sohn, *Du premier baiser à l'alcove*, pp. 41–7; Aron and Kempf, *La Bourgeoisie*, pp. 84–5.

102 Pearsall, *The Worm in the Bud*, p. 448.
103 See ch. 6 below.
104 Pearsall, *The Worm in the Bud*, pp. 448–51. For Havelock Ellis, see Porter and Hall, *Facts of Life*, pp. 160–1.
105 Pearsall, *The Worm in the Bud*, p. 458–9.
106 Aron and Kempf, *La Bourgeoisie*, p. 90; Stora-Lamarre, *L'Enfer de la IIIe République*, pp. 35–6; Sohn, *Du premier baiser à l'alcove*, pp. 54–5.
107 Hauser, 'Krafft-Ebing's psychological understanding of sexual behaviour', pp. 210–11, 216–19.
108 Pearsall, *The Worm in the Bud*, pp. 328–35. For the pornographic literature devoted to this subject, see Marcus, *The Other Victorians*, ch. 6: 'A child is being beaten'.
109 Corbin, *Women for Hire*, pp. 124–5.
110 *My Secret Life*, p. 290 of 1998 Grove edn.
111 Sohn, *Du premier baiser à l'alcove*, for France between 1850 and 1950; Barret-Ducrocq, *Love in the Time of Victoria*.
112 Ibid., ch. 1: 'Labouring classes, depraved classes' (quotation is p. 21) (pp. 36, 240 of French edn). See also below 'Nudity and body hair'.
113 Barret-Ducrocq, *Love in the Time of Victoria*, ch. 2: 'The foundling hospital', ch. 3: 'Love and marriage' (pp. 86, 108, 117, 130, 159 of French edn).
114 Ibid. (pp. 242, 244 of French edn).
115 Ibid., p. 86. (p. 117 of French edn).
116 See ch. 3 above, with regard to Somerset.
117 Barret-Ducrocq, *Love in the Time of Victoria*, pp. 138, 156 (pp. 181, 202 of French edn).
118 Ibid., 'Family and friends', pp. 165ff. (pp. 231–2 of French edn).
119 Ibid., p. 132 (p. 174 of French edn).
120 Rosenman, *Unauthorized Pleasures*, p. 2.
121 Sullerot (ed.), *Le Fait féminin*, pp. 440–1 (discussion between Évelyne Sullerot and Michelle Perrot).
122 Sohn, *Du premier baiser à l'alcove*, p. 84–5.
123 Ibid., p. 108.
124 Ibid., p. 308.
125 Ibid., pp. 129, 131–4, 186–7, 224.
126 Ibid., pp. 308–9.
127 Jordanova, *Sexual Visions*, p. 158.
128 Rosenman, *Unauthorized Pleasures*, p. 2.
129 *Man Without a Star* (1955), directed by King Vidor, with Kirk Douglas, Jeanne Crain and Claire Trevor.

130 Morris, *The Meaning of Human Gestures*, p. 221, with a graph depicting skirt lengths in the twentieth century.

PART IV REVOLUTIONS? THE HERITAGE OF THE SIXTIES

1 Rey, *Histoire de la douleur*.
2 Mainil, *Dans les règles du plaisir*.
3 Gauchet, *The Disenchantment of the World*.
4 Kaufmann, *Ego. Pour une sociologie de l'individu*.
5 Berger (ed.), *The Desecularization of the World*; Davie, *Religion in Britain Since 1945*; Davie (ed.), *Predicting Religion*; Davie and Hervieu-Léger, *Identités Religieuses en Europe*.
6 Figures quoted by Hervieu-Léger in *Croyances religieuses, morales et éthiques*, p. 11.
7 Hervieu-Léger, *Le Pèlerin et le Converti*.
8 Hervieu-Léger develops these arguments in *Croyances religieuses, morales et éthiques*, p. 17.
9 Singly, *Libres ensemble*.
10 Hunter, *Culture Wars*.
11 Krauss, 'Canada's view on social issues is opening rifts with the US'.
12 Holden, 'An Epicure's 15-course French feast'.
13 See the Conclusion below.

CHAPTER 6 THE ERA OF PLEASURE (FROM 1960 TO OUR OWN DAY)

1 That is, in Pennsylvania, whose official motto is, with good reason, 'Virtue, Liberty, Independence', as is proclaimed on the reverse of the new quarter (or 25 cent piece), each new issue of which now bears the symbol of the state of the union in which it is struck.
2 Kinsey et al., *Sexual Behaviour in the Human Male*; *Sexual Behaviour in the Human Female*. The data was later carefully verified, sometimes corrected, and then published: Gebhard and Johnson, *The Kinsey Data*. The Institute for Sex Research of the University of Indiana has 18,000 individual cards on which these studies are based; Kinsey dreamed of collecting 100,000. For Kinsey himself, initially a specialist in a type of wasp (the *cynipidae*), see the huge, at once admiring and highly critical, biography by James Jones, *Alfred Kinsey*; also the film, *Kinsey*.

3   Kinsey et al., *Sexual Behaviour in the Human Male*, p. 262.
4   Ibid., pp. 263–4.
5   Kinsey et al., *Sexual Behaviour in the Human Female*, pp. 285, 324–5.
6   See ch. 3 above.
7   Kinsey et al., *Sexual Behaviour in the Human Male*, p. 264. For the Elders case, see Greenblatt, 'Me, myself and I'.
8   Jacobs, 'Student sex case in Georgia stirs claims of Old South justice'. Thanks to the activities of defence committees, Marcus Dixon was freed after 18 months in detention.
9   Kinsey et al., *Sexual Behaviour in the Human Male*, p. 296.
10 Ibid., pp. 639, 656. The Kinsey scale has provoked an abundant literature. Other rating scales have been proposed, esp. by Coleman et al. Many internet sites are devoted to discussion of these questions, including The Kinsey Institute for Research in Sex, Gender, and Reproduction (University of Indiana), where the Kinsey scale is presented, with a large critical bibliography: http://www.kinseyinstitute.org/resources/akhhscale.html.
11 Kinsey et al., *Sexual Behaviour in the Human Male*, pp. 650–1.
12 Kinsey et al., *Sexual Behaviour in the Human Female*, p. 483.
13 Kinsey et al., *Sexual Behaviour in the Human Male*, pp. 313, 499.
14 See ch. 5 above.
15 Greenblatt, 'Me, myself and I'.
16 Kinsey et al., *Sexual Behaviour in the Human Female*, pp. 142, 174, 371.
17 Ibid., pp. 392–3.
18 Kinsey et al., *Sexual Behaviour in the Human Male*, p. 366.
19 R (Restricted) for violence, sexual content, impiety, use of drugs or alcohol (the details are specified: *Dogville*, directed by Lars von Trier, was classified as R for violence and sexual content in 2004, as was Quentin Tarantino's *Kill Bill, Volume 2*, in this case for impiety, violence and drug use); PG (Parental Guidance) for slight sexual content, ribald language or crude humour (in 2004, *Ella Enchanted*, based on the book by Gail Carson Levine, a variation on the Cinderella story, was awarded this rating for coarse humour and ribald language); PG-13 (Parents Strongly Cautioned) for adult themes, crude and sexual humour, impiety, nudity, explicit sex, use of drugs or alcohol

(applied, for example, to *The Girl Next Door*, with Emile Hirsch, or even *Bon Voyage*, with Gérard Depardieu, for violence).
20 Kinsey et al., *Sexual Behaviour in the Human Male*, pp. 367–9.
21 See ch. 3 above.
22 Kinsey et al., *Sexual Behaviour in the Human Female*, pp. 262–3, esp. nn. 32–4.
23 Kinsey et al., *Sexual Behaviour in the Human Male*, p. 577.
24 Rubin, *Erotic Wars*, pp. 120–1.
25 Kinsey et al., *Sexual Behaviour in the Human Male*, pp. 559, 599.
26 Ibid., pp. 598–9, 602–3.
27 Trumbach, *Sex and the Gender Revolution*, vol. I; see also ch. 1 above.
28 Kasl, *Women, Sex and Addiction*, p. 208.
29 Kinsey et al., *Sexual Behaviour in the Human Male*, p. 263.
30 Masters and Johnson, *Human Sexual Response*.
31 For Walter and *My Secret Life*, see also ch. 5 above. Specialists are today agreed that during a particularly powerful orgasm, some women may expel a liquid which is not urine, but produced by the Skene's glands: Morris, *The Naked Woman*.
32 Masters and Johnson, *Human Sexual Response*, pp. 136–7.
33 Laqueur, *Solitary Sex*, pp. 74–7.
34 Rubin, *Erotic Wars*, pp. 120–1.
35 Ibid., pp. 187–9.
36 Morris, *The Human Sexes*, pp. 226–7.
37 Ibid., p. 227.
38 Laqueur, *Solitary Sex*, pp. 78.
39 Rubin, *Erotic Wars*, pp. 20–1.
40 Morris, *Intimate Behaviour*, pp. 208–9.
41 Morris, *The Human Sexes*, pp. 122–3.
42 Pateman, *The Sexual Contract*.
43 Luhmann, *Love as Passion*, pp. 4, 20.
44 Ibid., pp. 43, 45.
45 Ibid., pp. 5, 43, 45.
46 Ibid., pp. 13, 21.
47 For Walter, see ch. 5 above.
48 The whole planet has followed the adventures of the six main characters of the cult American TV soap, *Friends*, since 1994 (NBC definitively ended it on the evening of 6 May 2004, during a skilfully presented programme watched by more than 50 million viewers in the United States).

49 Rubin, *Erotic Wars*, pp. 187, 199. See also Weeks, *Sexuality and its Discontents*.
50 Morris, *Intimate Behaviour*, pp. 84–7.
51 Morris, *The Human Sexes*, pp. 90–1 (with a photo of the Quick-court divorce-dispensing machine).
52 Ibid., pp. 100–1.
53 Kolata, 'The heart's desire'.
54 As in the last episode of *Friends*, on 6 May 2004, when Chandler and Monica were presented with a boy and a girl carried by another woman. As American TV has very strict audience requirements and must therefore be closely in tune with the public mood, this is evidence that the issue raised in this extremely popular series constitutes a social phenomenon. And morality is safe, as Chandler and Monica are married.
55 Morris, *The Human Sexes*, pp. 116–17.
56 The legitimations of Charles V and the cases of the female servants of priests in Franche-Comté are found in Series B of the Archives du Nord in Lille (see the impressive printed summary).
57 Morris, *The Human Sexes*, pp. 120–1.
58 The literature on the subject is huge. For a résumé of the situation soon after the sexual revolution of the sixties, see White, *States of Desire*.
59 Selye and Elder, 'Strong support is found for ban on gay marriage'.
60 'Partnership rights for gays'.
61 Belluck, 'Massachusetts gives new push to gay marriage'; Liptak, 'Bans on interracial unions offer perspectives on gay ones'.
62 Kipnis, 'Should this marriage be saved?'
63 Waal, *Bonobo: the Forgotten Ape*.
64 Bagemihl, *Biological Exuberance*.
65 Smith, 'Love that dare not squeak its name'.
66 Ibid. See also Zuk, *Sexual Selections*.
67 Kristof, 'Lovers under the skin'.
68 Marshall, 'More than 50 gay couples are married in San Francisco'; Murphy and Marshall, 'Gay weddings continue in San Francisco'; Murphy, 'San Francisco mayor exults in move on gay marriages'; 'San Francisco judge rules gay marriages can continue'.
69 Murphy, 'California Supreme Court rules gay unions have no standing', *New York Times*, 13 August 2004.

70 Leduc, 'Un premier couple gai se marie civilement au palais de justice'.
71 As argued by Desmond Morris: *The Human Sexes*, p. 121.
72 See chs 3 and 5 above.
73 Morris, *The Human Sexes*, pp. 124–5, 220–1, 224. See also, for the body in general, Morris, *Bodywatching*.
74 Barret-Ducrocq, *Love in the Time of Victoria*.
75 Mosse, *The Image of Man*.
76 Morris, *The Human Sexes*, pp. 224–6.
77 Shere Hite recently took German nationality.
78 Hite, *The Hite Report on the Family*.
79 Ibid., pp. 14–15, 42.
80 Straus, Gelles and Steinmetz, *Behind Closed Doors*.
81 Hite, *The Hite Report on the Family*, pp. 231–2.
82 Ibid., pp. 59, 97, 274, 351.
83 Hite, *Women as Revolutionary Agents of Change*. See also Hite, *Women and Love*.
84 Rubin, *Erotic Wars*, pp. 195, 198.
85 Morris, *Intimate Behaviour*, p. 243.
86 Morris, *The Human Sexes*, p. 241.

CONCLUSION: THE NARCISSISTIC SOCIETY

1 Huntington, *Who Are We?* (discussion of the Anglo-Protestant heritage in American history up to the present).
2 The reference is to the Council of Trent (1545–63), whose systematic policy of Catholic reconquest of territory lost to Protestantism led to a century of inexpiable wars of religion in France, the Low Countries, Germany, etc.
3 Lahire et al., *Portraits sociologiques*.
4 Lipovetski, *L'Ère du vide*.
5 Lipovetski, *Les Temps hypermodernes*.
6 Vincent, 'Ados à fleur de peau'. See also Anzieu, *Le Moi-peau*.
7 The results are analysed in a special issue of the journal *Futuribles*, 'Les valeurs des Européens'. For France, see also Bréchon (ed.), *Les Valeurs des Français*; Galland and Roudet (eds), *Les Valeurs des jeunes*.
8 Bréchon, 'Les inégalités dans les sociétés européennes fragilisent la démocratie'.
9 *Futuribles*, 'Les valeurs des Européens'.
10 Davie, *Religion in Britain Since 1945*.

11 Lambert, 'Religion: l'Europe à un tournant'.
12 Ternisian, 'En une décennie, les croyances ont reculé en France'.
13 Lambert, 'Un certain retour de la morale'.
14 Galland, 'Les dimensions de la confiance'.
15 Galland, 'L'individualisation progresse partout'; the author distinguishes between the individualization of morals and individualism, in the sense of egoism.
16 Vincent, 'La tyrannie du plaisir'.
17 Discussed in Pons, 'Cupidon, moteur de la relance économique', *Le Monde*.
18 Kohut, *The Analysis of the Self*; *The Search for the Self*; *Self Psychology and the Humanities*.
19 Kohut, *The Analysis of the Self*, p. 23.
20 Ibid., pp. 26–9.
21 Lasch, *Culture of Narcissism*. See also the older work of David Riesman, *Individualism Reconsidered*.
22 The description of the damaging effects of narcissism in the second part of life is inspired by Kernberg, *Borderline Conditions and Pathological Narcissism*.
23 Lasch, *Culture of Narcissism*, pp. 38–41.
24 Ibid., pp. 65, 69.
25 Ibid., pp. 73, 174–5.
26 See ch. 6 above.
27 Lasch, *Culture of Narcissism*, p. 193.
28 Ibid., pp. 204–5, 210–11.
29 Among a very abundant literature, see Sanford, *Self and Society*; Popper and Eccles, *The Self and its Brain*; Taylor, *Sources of the Self*; Sulloway, *Jane Austen and the Province of Womanhood*; Fireman, McVay and Flanagan (eds), *Narrative and Consciousness*.
30 Giddens, *Modernity and Self-Identity*, pp. 3, 7.
31 Ibid., p. 33.
32 This is the opinion of Christopher Lasch (*Culture of Narcissism*) and Richard Sennett (*Fall of Public Man*).
33 Giddens, *Modernity and Self-Identity*, pp. 65–7, 169, 172–3.
34 Giddens, *Transformation of Intimacy*, p. 158.
35 Ibid., p. 77.
36 Ibid., p. 33, quoting Weeks, *Sexuality and its Discontents*.
37 Luhmann, *Love as Passion*.
38 Giddens, *Transformation of Intimacy*, pp. 2, 9–10, 27. The themes were already outlined in his earlier book, *Modernity*

and Self-Identity (pp. 162, 164, 206, 219). For generations of women in the United States, see Rubin, *Erotic Wars*.
39 Giddens, *Modernity and Self-Identity*, p. 206.
40 See ch. 6 above and Morris, *The Human Sexes*.
41 This is argued by Anthony Giddens: *Transformation of Intimacy*, p. 203.

BIBLIOGRAPHY

Addy, John, *Sin and Society in the Seventeenth Century* (London: Routledge, 1989).
Aers, David (ed.), *Culture and History, 1350–1600: Essays on English Communities, Identities and Writing* (New York: Harvester Wheatsheaf, 1992).
Aers, David, 'A whisper in the ear of early modernists; or reflections on literary critics writing the "history of the subject"', in Aers, *Culture and History*, pp. 177–201.
Anzieu, Didier, *Le Moi-peau* (Paris: Dunod, 1985).
Ariès, Philippe, *Centuries of Childhood* (London: Jonathan Cape, 1962).
Ariès, Philippe, and George Duby (eds), *A History of Private Life*, 5 vols (Cambridge, MA: Belknap, 1987–94), vol. III: *Passions of the Renaissance*, vol. IV: *From the Fires of Revolution to the Great War*, vol. V: *Riddles of Identity in Modern Times*.
Aron, Jean-Paul, and Roger Kempf, *Le Pénis et la Démoralisation de l'Occident* (Paris: Grasset, 1978), reprinted with the more academic and less provocative title *La Bourgeosie, le Sexe et l'Honneur* (Brussels: Complexe, 1984).
Bagemihl, Bruce, *Biological Exuberance: Animal Homosexuality and Natural Diversity* (New York: Saint Martin's Press, 1999).
Bakhtin, Mikhail, *Rabelais and His World*, trans. H. Iswolsky (Bloomington: Indiana University Press, 1984).
Barret-Ducrocq, Françoise, *L'Amour sous Victoria. Sexualité et classes populaires à Londres au XIXe siècle* (Paris: Plon, 1989), trans. John Howe as *Love in the Time of Victoria. Sexuality and Desire Among Working-Class Men and Women in Nineteenth-century London* (London: Verso, 1991; Harmondsworth: Penguin, 1992).
Bastien, Pascal, 'Le spectacle pénal à Paris au XVIIIe siècle' (unpublished thesis, supervised by Robert Muchembled and Claire Dolan, Université de Paris-Nord and Laval University, Quebec, 2002). The author is preparing a book on the death penalty for the Éditions du Seuil.

Belluck, Pam, 'Massachusetts gives new push to gay marriage in strong ruling', *New York Times*, 5 Feb. 2004.
Belsey, Catherine, *The Subject of Tragedy* (London and New York: Methuen, 1985).
Benabou, Erica-Marie, *La Prostitution et la Police des moeurs au XVIIIe siècle*, with a preface by Pierre Goubert (Paris: Perrin, 1987).
Bercé, Yves-Marie, *Fête et révolte. Des mentalités populaires du XVIe au XVIIIe siècle* (Paris: Hachette, 1976).
Berger, Peter L. (ed.), *The Desecularization of the World: Resurgent Religion and World Politics* (Grand Rapids: W. B. Eerdmans Pub. Co., 1999).
Berriot-Salvadore, Evelyne, *Un Corps, un destin: la femme dans la médecine de la Renaissance* (Paris: Champion, 1993).
Boaistuau, Pierre, *Le Théâtre du monde* [1558], ed. Michel Simonin (Geneva: Droz, 1981).
Bougard, Roger R., *Érotisme et amour physique dans la littérature française du XVIIe siècle* (Paris: Gaston Lachurié, 1986).
Bourcier, Élizabeth, *Les Journaux privés en Angleterre (1600–1660)* (Paris: Publications de la Sorbonne, 1976).
Brantôme [Pierre de Bourdeille, seigneur de], *Vie des dames galantes*, text established on the basis of the original edition by Jacques Haumont (Paris: J. de Bonnet, 1972).
Bréchon, Pierre (ed.), *Les Valeurs des Français. Évolutions de 1980 à 2000* (Paris: A. Colin, 2000).
Bréchon, Pierre, 'Les inégalités dans les sociétés européennes fragilisent la démocratie', *Le Monde*, 14 Oct. 2002.
Brewer, John, *The Pleasures of the Imagination: English Culture in the Eighteenth Century* (London: Harper Collins, 1997).
Briot, Frédéric, *Usage du monde, usage de soi. Enquête sur les mémorialistes d'Ancien Régime* (Paris: Éditions du Seuil, 1994).
Bullough, Vern L., 'The development of sexology in the USA in the early twentieth century', in Porter and Teich (eds), *Sexual Knowledge, Sexual Science*, pp. 303–22.
Burckhardt, Jacob, *The Civilization of the Renaissance in Italy* (first German edn 1860), trans. S. G. C. Middlemore (Penguin Classics, 1990); Modern Library Classics (New York: Random House, 1982; new edn 2002 with Introduction by Peter Gay).
Burke, Peter, 'Viewpoint. The invention of leisure in early modern Europe', *Past and Present*, 146 (Feb. 1995), pp. 136–50.
Burke, Peter, 'Representations of the self from Petrarch to Descartes', in Porter (ed.), *Rewriting the Self*, pp. 17–28.
Bynum, Caroline W., *Jesus as Mother. Studies in the Spirituality of the High Middle Ages* (Berkeley: University of California Press, 1982).
Cameron, David Kerr, *London's Pleasures: from Restoration to Regency* (Stroud: Sutton, 2001).

BIBLIOGRAPHY

Carnal Knowledge, film, directed by Mike Nichols, with Jack Nicholson, Arthur Garfunkel, Ann Margret, Candice Bergen (1971).

Castiglione, Baldassare, *Book of the Courtier* [1528] (Harmondsworth: Penguin, 1967).

Claus, Hugo, *The Sorrow of Belgium* (London: Viking, 1990; New York: Pantheon Books, 1990) (first pub. 1983 as *Het Verdriet van België*).

Claverie, Élisabeth, and Pierre Lamaison, *L'Impossible Mariage. Violence et parenté en Gévaudan, XVIIe, XVIIIe et XIXe siècles* (Paris: Hachette, 1982).

Corbin, Alain, *Les Filles de noce: misère sexuelle et prostitution, XIXe et XXe siècles* (Paris: Aubier, 1978), trans. Alan Sheridan as *Women for Hire: Prostitution and Sexuality in France after 1850* (Cambridge, MA, and London: Harvard University Press, 1990).

Corbin, Alain, 'Commercial sexuality in nineteenth-century France: a system of images and regulations', in Gallagher and Laqueur (eds), *The Making of the Modern Body*, pp. 209–19.

Crawford, Patricia, and Laura Gowing (eds), *Women's World in Seventeenth-Century England* (London: Routledge, 2000).

Cressy, David, 'Literacy in context: meaning and measurement in early modern England', in John Brewer and Roy Porter (eds), *Consumption and the World of Goods* (London and New York: Routledge, 1993).

Croyances religieuses, morales et éthiques dans le processus de construction européenne (Paris: La Documentation Française, 2002).

Daumas, Maurice, *Le Mariage amoureux. Histoire du lien conjugal sous l'Ancien Régime* (Paris: Colin, 2004).

Davidoff, Leonore, and Catherine Hall, *Family Fortunes: Men and Women of the English Middle Class, 1780–1850* (London: Hutchinson, 1987).

Davie, Grace, *Religion in Britain Since 1945: Believing Without Belonging* (Oxford: Blackwell, 1994).

Davie, Grace (ed.), *Predicting Religion: Christian, Secular and Alternative Futures* (Oxford: Blackwell, 1994).

Davie, Grace, and Danièle Hervieu-Léger, *Identités religieuses en Europe* (Paris: La Découverte, 1996).

Davis, Natalie Zemon, 'Boundaries and the sense of self in sixteenth-century France', in Heller, Sosna and Wellbery (eds), *Reconstructing Individualism*, pp. 53–63.

Deregnaucourt, Gilles, and Didier Poton, *La Vie religieuse en France aux XVIe–XVIIIe siècles* (Paris: Ophrys, 1994).

Diedler, Jean-Claude, *Démons et sorcières en Lorraine. Le bien et le mal dans les communautés rurales de 1550 à 1660* (Paris: Éditions Messene, 1996).

Dragstra, Henk, Sheila Ottway and Helen Wilcox (eds), *Betraying Ourselves: Forms of Self-Representation in Early Modern English Texts* (New York: St Martin's Press, 2000).

Dubost, Jean-Pierre, *L'Académie des dames ou la Philosophie dans le boudoir du Grand Siècle* (Arles: Éditions Philippe Picquier, 1999).
Duerr, Hans-Peter, *Nackheit und Scham: der Mythos vom Zivilisationsproze* (Frankfurt am Main: Suhrkamp Taschenbuch Verlag, 1988); trans. as *Nudité et pudeur. Le mythe du processus de civilisation* (Paris: Maison des Sciences de l'Homme, 1998).
Dumont, Louis, *Essais sur l'individualisme: une perspective anthropologique sur l'idéologie moderne* (Paris: Éditions du Seuil, 1983).
Dupâquier, Jacques (ed.), with Jean-Pierre Bardet and others, *Histoire de la population française* (Paris: PUF, 1988).
École des Filles, L', published anonymously in 1655, printed in full in Prévot, *Libertins du XVIIe siècle*, pp. 1099–1202.
Elias, Norbert, *The Civilizing Process* [1939], trans. E. Jephcott (Oxford: Blackwell, 1978).
Elias, Norbert, *The Court Society* [1969], trans. E. Jephcott (Oxford: Blackwell, 1983).
Elias, Norbert, *La Dynamique de l'Occident* (Paris: Calmann-Lévy, 1975).
Elias, Norbert, *The Society of Individuals* (Oxford: Blackwell, 1991).
Etlin, Richard, *The Architecture of Death: the Transformation of the Cemetery in Eighteenth-Century Paris* (Cambridge, MA: Harvard University Press, 1984).
Faller, Lincoln B., *Turned to Account. The Forms and Functions of Criminal Biography in Late Seventeenth- and Early Eighteenth-Century England* (Cambridge: Cambridge University Press, 1987).
Faller, Lincoln B., *Crime and Defoe. A New Kind of Writing* (Cambridge: Cambridge University Press, 1993).
Farge, Arlette, *Vivre dans la rue à Paris au XVIIIe siècle* (Paris: Gallimard-Julliard, 1979).
Febvre, Lucien, *Amour sacré, amour profane. Autour de l'Heptaméron* [1944] (Paris: Gallimard, 1971).
Fillon, Anne, *Les Trois Bagues au doigt: amours villageoises au XVIII siècle* (Paris: R. Lafont, 1989).
Fireman, Gary D., Ted E. McVay and Owen J. Flanagan (eds), *Narrative and Consciousness: Literature, Psychology, and the Brain* (Oxford: Oxford University Press, 2003).
Flandrin, Jean-Louis, *L'Église et la contrôle des naissances* (Paris: Flammarion, 1970).
Flandrin, Jean-Louis (ed.), *Les Amours paysannes: amour et sexualité dans les campagnes de l'ancienne France (XVIe–XIXe siècles)* (Paris: Gallimard-Julliard, 1975).
Flandrin, Jean-Louis, *Le Sexe et l'Occident: évolution des attitudes et des comportements* (Paris: Éditions du Seuil, 1981), trans. Sue Collins as *Sex in the Western World: the Development of Attitudes and Behaviour* (Philadelphia: Harwood Academic Publishers, 1991; Reading, 1991).

Flandrin, Jean-Louis, *Un Temps pour embrasser: aux origines de la morale sexuelle occidentale (VIe–XIe siècle)* (Paris: Éditions du Seuil, 1983).

Fletcher, Anthony, *Gender, Sex and Subordination in England, 1500–1800* (New Haven: Yale University Press, 1995).

Flynn, Carol Houlihan, *The Body in Swift and Defoe* (Cambridge: Cambridge University Press, 1990).

Fogel, Michèle, *Marie de Gournay* (Paris: Fayard, 2004).

Foucault, Michel, *Madness and Civilization: A History of Insanity in the Age of Reason*, shortened version, trans. Richard Howard (Random House: New York, 1965), and, more recently, complete trans. Jonathan Murphy and Jean Khalfa as *History of Madness* (London: Routledge, 2007).

Foucault, Michel, *History of Sexuality*, vol. I: *The Will to Knowledge* (Harmondsworth: Penguin, 1998; page citations in the text are from the 1990 Penguin edition) (first published as *An Introduction* (New York: Random House, 1982)); vol. II: *The Use of Pleasure* (Harmondsworth: Viking, 1986); vol. III: *The Care of the Self* (New York: Pantheon, 1986).

Foucault, Michel, *Discipline and Punish. The Birth of the Prison*, trans. Alan Sheridan (Vintage: New York, 1977).

Fox, Robin, *The Red Lamp of Incest: An Enquiry into the Origins of Mind and Society* (Notre Dame: University of Notre Dame Press, 1980; new edn 1983).

Foxon, David, *Libertine Literature in England* (New Hyde Park, New York: University Books, 1965).

Fraser, Antonia, *The Weaker Vessel* (New York: Alfred Knopf, 1984).

Freud, Sigmund, 'Three Essays on the Theory of Sexuality' [1905], *The Standard Edition of the Complete Psychological Works of Sigmund Freud*, vol. VII (London: The Hogarth Press, 1955).

Freud, Sigmund, 'Beyond the Pleasure Principle' [1920], *The Standard Edition of the Complete Psychological Works of Sigmund Freud*, vol. XVIII (London: The Hogarth Press, 1955), pp. 7–64.

Freud, Sigmund, 'The Ego and the Id' [1923], *The Standard Edition of the Complete Psychological Works of Sigmund Freud*, vol. XIX (London: The Hogarth Press, 1955).

Futuribles, 'Les valeurs des Européens. Les tendances de long terme', special edn, directed by Pierre Bréchon and Jean-François Tchernia, 277 (July–Aug. 2002).

Gallagher, Catherine and Thomas Laqueur (eds), *The Making of the Modern Body: Sexuality and Society in the Nineteenth Century* (Berkeley: University of California Press, 1987).

Galland, Olivier, 'Les dimensions de la confiance', *Futuribles*, 277 (July–Aug. 2002), pp. 15–40.

Galland, Olivier, 'L'individualisation progresse partout, les différences culturelles restent fortes', *Le Monde*, 14 Oct. 2002.

BIBLIOGRAPHY

Galland, Olivier, and Bernard Roudet (eds), *Les Valeurs des Jeunes. Tendances en France depuis Vingt Ans* (Paris: L'Harmattan, 2001).
Gauchet, Marcel, *Le Désenchantement du monde. Une histoire de la religion politique* (Paris: Gallimard, 1985), trans. Oscar Burge as *The Disenchantment of the World: A Political History of Religion* (Princeton: Princeton University Press, 1999).
Gay, Peter, *The Bourgeois Experience: Victoria to Freud*, 5 vols; vol. I: *Education of the Senses*; vol. II: *The Tender Passion*; vol. II: *The Cultivation of Hatred*; vol. IV: *The Naked Heart*; vol. V: *Pleasure Wars* (New York and Oxford: Oxford University Press, 1984–98).
Gebhard, Paul H., and Alan B. Johnson, *The Kinsey Data: Marginal Tabulations of the 1938–1963 Interviews Conducted by the Institute for Sex Research* (Philadelphia: W. B. Saunders Co, 1979).
Gent, Lucy, and Nigel Llewellyn (eds) *Renaissance Bodies: The Human Figure in English Culture c.1540–1660* (London: Reaktion, 1990).
Giddens, Anthony, *Modernity and Self-Identity: Self and Society in the Late Modern Age* (Cambridge: Polity, 1991).
Giddens, Anthony, *The Transformation of Intimacy. Sexuality, Love and Eroticism in Modern Societies* (Cambridge: Polity, 1992).
Gilman, Sander L., *Sexuality: An Illustrated History. Representing the Sexual in Medicine and Culture from the Middle Ages to the Age of AIDS* (New York: Wiley, 1989).
Goubert, Pierre, *La Vie quotidienne des paysans au XVIIe siècle* (Paris: Hachette, 1982).
Goulemot, Jean-Marie, *Ces livres qu'on ne lit que d'une main. Lecture et lecteurs de livres pornographiques au XVIIIe siècle* (Aix-en-Provence: Alinea, 1991); trans. James Simpson as *Forbidden Texts: Erotic Literature and its Readers in 18th-Century France* (Cambridge: Polity, 1994).
Gowing, Laura, *Domestic Dangers: Women, Words and Sex in Early Modern London* (Oxford: Clarendon Press, 1996).
Gowing, Laura, *Common Bodies. Women, Touch and Power in Seventeenth-Century England* (New Haven: Yale University Press, 2003).
Graham, Elspeth (ed.), *Her Own Life: Autobiographical Writings by Seventeenth-Century Englishwomen* (London: Routledge, 1989).
Greenblatt, Stephen, *Renaissance Self-Fashioning: From More to Shakespeare* (Chicago: University of Chicago Press, 1980).
Greenblatt, Stephen, *Shakespearean Negotiations: The Circulation of Social Energy in Renaissance England* (Berkeley: California University Press, 1988).
Greenblatt, Stephen, 'Fiction and friction', in Heller, Sosna and Wellbery (eds), *Reconstructing Individualism*, pp. 30–52.
Greenblatt, Stephen, 'Me, myself and I', *New York Review of Books*, 56: 6 (8 Apr. 2004): a review of Thomas Laqueur's *Solitary Sex: a Cultural History of Masturbation*.

Hanley, Sarah, 'Engendering the state: family formation and state building in early modern France', *French Historical Studies*, 16 (1989), pp. 4–27.

Hanson, Sarah, *Discovering the Subject in Renaissance England* (Cambridge: Cambridge University Press, 1998).

Hauser, Renate, 'Krafft-Ebing's psychological understanding of sexual behaviour', in Porter and Teich (eds), *Sexual Knowledge, Sexual Science*, pp. 210–29.

Heale, Elizabeth, *Autobiography and Authorship in Renaissance Verse. Chronicles of the Self* (New York: Palgrave Macmillan, 2003).

Heller, Thomas C., Morton Sosna and David E. Wellbery, *Reconstructing Individualism: Autonomy, Individualism, and the Self in Western Thought* (Stanford: Stanford University Press, 1986).

Héritier, Françoise, *Masculin-Féminin*, vol. I: *La Pensée de la Différence*; vol. II: *Dissoudre la Hiérarchie* (Paris: O. Jacob, 1966 and 2002).

Hervieu-Léger, Danièle, *Le Pèlerin et le Converti. La Religion en Mouvement* (Paris: Flammarion, 1999).

Hite, Shere, *Women and Love: A Cultural Revolution in Progress* (New York: Knopf, 1987).

Hite, Shere, *Women as Revolutionary Agents of Change: The Hite Report and Beyond* (Madison: University of Wisconsin Press, 1994).

Hite, Shere, *The Hite Report on the Family: Growing Up Under Patriarchy* (London: Bloomsbury, 1994).

Holden, Stephen, 'An Epicure's 15-course French feast', *New York Times*, 12 Mar. 2004.

Holland, Eugene, 'On narcissism from Baudelaire to Sartre: ego-psychology and literary history', in Layton and Schapiro (eds), *Narcissism and the Text*.

Hume, David, *A Treatise of Human Nature, Reprinted from the Original Edition in Three Volumes and Edited, with an Analytical Index, by L. A. Selby-Bigge* (Oxford: Clarendon Press, 1896 [1729]).

Hunt, Lynn, 'Pornography and the French Revolution', in Hunt *The Invention of Pornography*.

Hunt, Lynn (ed.), *The Invention of Pornography: Obscenity and the Origins of Modernity, 1500–1800* (New York: Zone Books, 1993).

Hunter, James Davison, *Culture Wars: the Struggle to Define America* (New York: Basic Books, 1991).

Huntington, Samuel P., *Who Are We? The Challenges to America's National Identity* (New York: Simon and Schuster, 2004).

Huysmans, Joris-Karl, *En Ménage* (Paris: G. Charpentier, 1880).

Ingram, Martin, *Church Courts, Sex and Marriage in England, 1570–1640* (Cambridge: Cambridge University Press, 1987).

Jacob, Margaret C., 'The materialist world of pornography', in Hunt (ed.), *The Invention of Pornography*.

Jacobs, Andrew, 'Student sex case in Georgia stirs claims of Old South justice', *New York Times*, 22 Jan. 2004.

BIBLIOGRAPHY

Jardine, Lisa, *Still Harping on Daughters: Women and Drama in the Age of Shakespeare* (Sussex: Harvester Press, 1983).
Jeanneret, Michel, *Éros rebelle. Littérature et dissidence à l'ère clasique* (Paris: Éditions du Seuil, 2003).
Jones, James H., *Alfred Kinsey. A Public/Private Life* (New York: W. W. Norton and Company, 1997).
Jordanova, Ludmilla J., *Sexual Visions: Images of Gender in Science and Medicine Between the Eighteenth and Twentieth Centuries* (Madison: University of Wisconsin Press, 1993).
Jouanna, Arlette, *Le Devoir de révolte. La noblesse française et la gestation de l'état moderne, 1559–1661* (Paris: Fayard, 2001).
Kasl, Charlotte Davis, *Women, Sex and Addiction: A Search for Love and Power* (New York: Ticknor and Fields, 1989).
Kaufmann, Jean-Claude, *Ego. Pour une sociologie de l'individu. Une autre vision de l'homme et de la construction du sujet* (Paris: Nathan, 2001).
Kernberg, Otto F., *Borderline Conditions and Pathological Narcissism* (New York: J. Aronson, 1975).
Kinsey, Alfred C., Wardell B. Pomeroy and Clyde E. Martin, *Sexual Behaviour in the Human Male* (Philadelphia: W. B. Saunders Co, 1948).
Kinsey, Alfred C., Wardell B. Pomeroy, Clyde E. Martin and Paul H. Gebhard, *Sexual Behaviour in the Human Female* (Philadelphia: W. B. Saunders Co, 1953).
Kinsey, film, directed by Bill Condon, with Liam Neeson and Laura Linney, 2004.
Kipnis, Laura, 'Should this marriage be saved?', *New York Times*, 25 Jan. 2004.
Kohut, Heinz, *The Analysis of the Self. A Systematic Approach to the Psychoanalytic Treatment of Narcissic Personality Disorders* (New York: International Universities Press, 1971).
Kohut, Heinz, *The Restoration of the Self* (New York: International Universities Press, 1977).
Kohut, Heinz, *The Search for the Self: Selected Writings of Heinz Kohut, 1950–1978*, ed. with an Introduction by Paul H. Ornstein (New York: International Universities Press, 1978).
Kohut, Heinz, *Self Psychology and the Humanities: Reflections on a New Psychoanalytic Approach*, ed. with an Introduction by Charles B. Strozier (New York: W. W. Norton, 1985).
Kolata, Gina, 'The heart's desire', *New York Times*, 11 May 2004.
Krafft-Ebing, Richard von, *Psychopathia Sexualis: A Medico-Forensic Study* (New York: Putnam, 1965; 1st German edn, 1886).
Kramer, Susan R. and Caroline W. Bynum, 'Revisiting the twelfth-century Individual. The inner self and the Christian community', in Gert Melville and Markus Schürer (eds), *Das Eigene und das Ganze. Zum Indviduellen im mittelalterlichen Religiosentum* (Dresden: Lit, 2002), pp. 57–85.

Krauss, Clifford, 'Canada's view on social issues is opening rifts with the US', *New York* Times, 2 Dec. 2003.
Kris, Ernst, *Psychoanalytic Explorations in Art* (New York: Schocken, 1952).
Kristof, Nicholas D., 'Lovers under the skin', *New York Times*, 3 Dec. 2003.
Kuperty-Tsur, Nadine, *Se dire à la Renaissance. Les mémoires du XVIe siècle* (Paris: Vrin, 1997).
Lachèvre, Frédéric, *Le Libertinage devant le Parlement de Paris. Le procès du poète Théophile de Viau (11 juillet 1623 au 1 septembre 1625)*, 2 vols (Paris: H. Champion, 1909; repr. Geneva: Slatkine, 1968).
Lachèvre, Frédéric, *Le Libertinage au XVIIe siècle. Une seconde révision des oeuvres du Poète Théophile de Viau* (Paris: H. Champion, 1911; repr. Geneva: Slatkine, 1968).
Lachèvre, Frédéric, *Le Libertinage au XVIIe siècle*, vol. II: *Disciples et successeurs de Théophile de Viau*, I, *La Vie et les poésies libertines inédites de Des Barreaux (1599–1673), Saint-Pavin (1595–1670)* (Paris: H. Champion, 1911).
Lachèvre, Frédéric, *Le Libertinage au XVIIe siècle*, vol. V: *Disciples et successeurs de Théophile de Viau, Les Oeuvres libertines de Claude Le Petit, Parisien brûlé le 1er Septembre 1662, précédées d'une notice biographique* (Paris: E. Capiomont et Cie, 1918).
Lachèvre, Frédéric, *Le Libertinage au XVIIe siècle*, vol. VI: *Disciples et successeurs de Théophile de Viau*, III, *Les Chansons libertines de Claude de Chouvigny, baron de Blot-l'Église (1605–1655)* (1919).
Lachèvre, Frédéric, *Le Libertinage au XVIIe siècle*, vol. VII: *Mélanges* (Paris: H. Champion, 1920; repr. Geneva: Slatkine, 1968).
Lahire, Bernard, et al., *Portraits sociologiques. Dispositions et variations individuelles* (Paris: Nathan, 2002).
Lambert, Yves, 'Religion: l'Europe à un tournant', *Futuribles*, 277 (July–Aug. 2002), pp. 129–60.
Lambert, Yves, 'Un certain retour de la morale, en particulier chez les jeunes', *Le Monde*, 17 Apr. 2003.
Laqueur, Thomas W., *Making Sex: Body and Gender from the Greeks to Freud* (Cambridge, MA: Harvard University Press, 1990).
Laqueur, Thomas W., 'Orgasm, generation, and the politics of reproductive biology', in Shoemaker and Vincent (eds), *Gender and History in Western Europe*.
Laqueur, Thomas, review of Trumbach, *Sex and the Gender Revolution*, in *American Historical Review*, 106: 4 (Oct. 2001), pp. 1456–7.
Laqueur, Thomas, *Solitary Sex: A Cultural History of Masturbation* (New York: Zone Books, 2003).
Lasch, Christopher, *The Culture of Narcissism: American Life in an Age of Diminishing Expectations* (New York: Norton, 1978).
Laslett, Peter, *The World We Have Lost* (London: Methuen, 1965).

Laslett, Peter, *Family Life and Illicit Love in Earlier Generations* (Cambridge: Cambridge University Press, 1977).
Laslett, Peter, *The World We Have Lost: Further Explored*, 3rd edn (London: Methuen, 1983).
Layton, Lynne, and Barbara Ann Schapiro (eds), *Narcissism and the Text: Studies in Literature and the Psychology of the Self* (New York: New York University Press, 1986).
Leduc, Louise, 'Un premier couple gai se marie civilement au palais de justice', *La Presse* (Montréal), 2 Apr. 2004.
Lejeune, Philippe, *L'Autobiographie en France* (Paris: A. Colin, 1971).
Lejeune, Philippe, *Le Pacte Autobiographique* (Paris: Éditions du Seuil, 1975).
Lemnius, Levinus, *The Secret Miracles of Nature*. First Latin edn 1559; first French trans. Lyon: Jean d'Ogerolles, 1566, then Paris, 1567 (three repr. before 1575); first Italian trans. 1560 (four others before 1570); first German trans. Leipzig, 1569 (three others before 1580, five more between then and 1605); a further Latin edition Amsterdam, 1605–51; English trans. London, 1658.
Lipovetski, Gilles, *L'Ère du vide. Essais sur l'individualisme contemporain* (Paris: Gallimard, 1983).
Lipovetski, Gilles (with Sébastien Charles), *Les Temps hypermodernes* (Paris: Grasset, 2004).
Liptak, Adam, 'Bans on interracial unions offer perspectives on gay ones', *New York Times*, 17 Mar. 2004.
Locke, John, *Essay Concerning Human Understanding* [1690], ed. Roger Woolhouse (Harmondsworth: Penguin, 1997).
Luhmann, Niklas, *Love as Passion: The Codification of Intimacy*, trans. from German by Jeremy Gaines and Doris L. Jones (Cambridge: Polity, 1986).
Lyons, John O., *The Invention of the Self: The Hinge of Consciousness in the Eighteenth Century* (Carbondale: Southern Illinois University Press, 1978).
Mainil, Jean, *Dans les Règles du plaisir . . . Théorie de la différence dans le discours obscène romanesque et médical de l'ancien régime* (Paris: Éditions Kimé, 1996).
Maman et la Putain, La, film, directed by Jean Eustache, with Bernadette Lafont, Jean-Pierre Léaud and Françoise Lebrun (1973).
Man Without a Star, film, directed by King Vidor. With Kirk Douglas, Jeanne Crain, and Claire Trevor. USA: Universal Studios (1955).
Mandeville, Bernard de, *The Fable of the Bees: or Private Vices, Publick Benefits* (London: Hundert, 1714).
Marcus, Steven, *The Other Victorians: A Study of Sexuality and Pornography in Mid-Nineteenth Century England* (New York: Basic Books, 1966).

Marshall, Carolyn, 'More than 50 gay couples are married in San Francisco', *New York Times*, 13 Feb. 2004.
Mascuch, Michael, *Origins of the Individualist Self: Autobiography and Self-Identity in England, 1591–1791* (Cambridge: Polity, 1997).
Mason, Michael, *The Making of Victorian Sexuality* (Oxford: Oxford University Press, 1994).
Masters, William, H., and Virginia E. Johnson, *Human Sexual Response* (Boston: Little, Brown, 1966).
Mathieu-Castellani, Gisèle, *La Scène judiciare de l'autobiographie* (Paris: Presses Universitaires Françaises, 1996).
Matthews-Grieco, Sarah F., *Ange ou diablesse? La représentation de la femme au XVIe siècle* (Paris: Flammarion, 1991).
Mauzi, Robert, *L'Idée de bonheur dans la littérature et la pensée française du XVIIIe siècle* (Paris: A. Colin, 1960; 2nd edn 1965).
Meyer, John W., 'Myths of socialization and of personality', in Heller, Sosna and Wellbery (eds), *Reconstructing Individualism*, pp. 208–21.
Molière, *L'École des femmes*, in *Théâtre complet*, notes of Maurice Rat (Paris: Le Livre de Poche, 1963), vol. II, pp. 5–82.
Monluc, Blaise de, *Commentaires, 1521–1576*, with a preface by Jean Giono (Paris: Gallimard, 1964).
Morris, Colin, *The Discovery of the Individual, 1050–1200* (New York: Harper & Row, 1979).
Morris, Desmond, *Intimate Behaviour* (New York: Random House, 1971).
Morris, Desmond, *The Meaning of Human Gestures* (New York: Harper & Row, 1979).
Morris, Desmond, *Bodywatching: A Field Guide to the Human Species* (New York: Crown, 1985).
Morris, Desmond, *The Human Sexes: A Natural History of Man and Woman* (London: Network Books, 1997).
Morris, Desmond, *The Naked Woman: A Study of the Female Body* (London: Jonathan Cape, 2004).
Mosse, George L., *The Image of Man: The Creation of Modern Masculinity* (Oxford: Oxford University Press, 1996).
Muchembled, Robert, *La Sorcière au village (XVe–XVIIIe siècle)* (Paris: Gallimard-Julliard, 1975; new edn Gallimard, 1991).
Muchembled, Robert, *Les Derniers Bûchers. Un village de Flandre et ses sorcières sous Louis XIV* (Paris: Ramsay, 1981).
Muchembled, Robert, *L'Invention de l'homme moderne. Culture et sensibilités en France du XVe au XVIIIe siècle* (Paris: Fayard, 1988; repr. Hachette, 1994).
Muchembled, Robert. *La Violence au village (XVe–XVIIe siècle). Comportements populaires et mentalités en Artois* (Turnhout: Brepols, 1989).
Muchembled, Robert, *Le Temps des supplices. De l'obéissance sous les rois absolus, XVe–XVIIIe siècle* (Paris: A. Colin, 1992).

Muchembled, Robert, *La Société policée. Politique et politesse en France du XVIe au XXe siècle* (Paris: Éditions du Seuil, 1998).
Muchembled, Robert, *A History of the Devil from the Middle Ages to the Present*, trans. Jean Birrell (Cambridge: Polity, 2003).
Muchembled, Robert, *Passions de femmes au temps de la Reine Margot, 1553–1615* (Paris: Éditions du Seuil, 2003).
Murphy, Dean E., 'San Francisco mayor exults in move on gay marriages', *New York Times*, 19 Feb. 2004.
Murphy, Dean E., 'San Francisco judge rules gay marriages can continue', *New York Times*, 21 Feb. 2004.
Murphy, Dean E., 'California Supreme Court rules gay unions have no standing', *New York Times*, 13 Aug. 2004.
Murphy, Dean E., and Carolyn Marshall, 'Gay weddings continue in San Francisco as lawyers argue', *New York Times*, 18 Feb. 2004.
My Secret Life: see 'Walter'.
Nardo, Anna K., *The Ludic Self in Seventeenth-Century English Literature* (New York: State University of New York Press, 1991).
Noonan, John T., *Contraception. A History of Its Treatment by the Catholic Theologians and Canonists* (Cambridge, MA: Harvard University Press, 1965).
Norberg, Kathryn, 'The libertine whore: prostitution in French pornography from Margot to Juliette', in Hunt (ed.), *The Invention of Pornography*.
Norton, Rictor, *Mother Clap's Molly House: the Gay Subculture in England, 1700–1830* (London: GMP, 1992).
Nylan, Michael, 'On the politics of pleasure', *Asia Major* (Academia Sinica, Taiwan), 3rd series, vol. 14, part 1 (2001), pp. 73–124.
Oeuvres anonymes du XVIIIe siècle, vol. I: *Histoire de Dom Bougre, portier des chartreux*; *Mémoires de Suzon, soeur de Dom Bougre, portier des chartreux*; *Histoire de Marguerite, fille de Suzon, nièce de Dom Bougre*; *La Cauchoise*, preface by Hubert Juin, Michel Camus and Jean-Pierre Dubost (Paris: Fayard, 1985).
'Partnership rights for gays', *New York Times*, 13 Jan. 2004.
Paster, Gail Kern, *The Body Embarrassed: Drama and the Discipline of Shame in Early Modern France* (Ithaca: Cornell University Press, 1993).
Pateman, Carole, *The Sexual Contract* (Cambridge: Polity, 1997).
Pearsall, Ronald, *The Worm in the Bud: The World of Victorian Sexuality* (London: Weidenfeld and Nicolson, 1969).
Pintard, René, *Le Libertinage érudit dans la première moitié du XVIIe siècle* (Paris: Boivin, 1943; new revised edn Geneva: Slatkine, 1983).
Pitt-Rivers, Julian, *The Fate of Shechem, or, The Politics of Sex* (Cambridge: Cambridge University Press, 1977).
Ploux, François, *Guerres paysannes en Quercy. Violences, conciliations et répression pénale dans les campagnes du Lot (1810–1860)* (Paris: Bibliothèque de l'Histoire, 2002).

Pollock, Linda A., 'Living on the stage of the world: the concept of privacy among the elite of Early Modern England', in Adrian Wilson (ed.), *Rethinking Social History: English Society, 1570–1920* (Manchester: Manchester University Press, 1993).

Pons, Philippe, 'Cupidon, moteur de la relance économique', *Le Monde*, 30 Jan. 2002.

Popper, Karl R., and John C. Eccles, *The Self and its Brain* (London: Routledge and Kegan Paul, 1977).

Porter, Roy, 'Enlightenment and Pleasure', in Porter and Roberts (eds), *Pleasure in the Eighteenth Century*, pp. 1–18.

Porter, Roy, 'Material pleasures in the consumer society', in Porter and Roberts (eds), *Pleasure in the Eighteenth Century*, pp. 19–35.

Porter, Roy (ed.), *Rewriting the Self: Histories from the Renaissance to the Present* (London: Routledge, 1997).

Porter, Roy, and Lesley Hall, *The Facts of Life: the Creation of Sexual Knowledge in Britain, 1650–1950* (New Haven: Yale University Press, 1995).

Porter, Roy, and Marie Mulvey Roberts (eds), *Pleasure in the Eighteenth Century* (Basingstoke: Macmillan, 1996).

Porter, Roy, and Mikulas Teich (eds), *Sexual Knowledge, Sexual Science: The History of Attitudes to Sexuality* (Cambridge: Cambridge University Press, 1994).

Preston, John M. A., *The Created Self: The Reader's Role in Eighteenth-Century Fiction* (London: Heinemann, 1970).

Prévot, Jacques (ed.), *Libertins du XVIIe siècle*, vol. I (Paris: Gallimard, 1998).

Putnam, Hilary, *Reason, Truth and History* (Cambridge: Cambridge University Press, 1981).

Quaife, Geoffrey Robert, *Wanton Wenches and Wayward Wives. Peasants and Illicit Sex in Early Seventeenth-Century England* (London: Croom Helm, 1979).

Rawlings, Philip, *Drunks, Whores and Idle Apprentices. Criminal Biographies of the Eighteenth Century* (London: Routledge, 1992).

Rey, Michel, 'Police et sodomie à Paris au XVIIIe siècle: du péché au désordre', *Revue d'Histoire Moderne et Contemporaine*, 29 (1982), pp. 113–24.

Rey, Roselyne, *Histoire de la Douleur* (Paris: La Découverte, 1993).

Riesman, David, *Individualism Reconsidered, and Other Essays* (Glencoe: Free Press, 1954).

Roecke, Michael, *Forbidden Friendships: Homosexuality and Male Culture in Renaissance Florence* (Oxford: Oxford University Press, 1996).

Roper, Lyndal, *Oedipus and the Devil. Witchcraft, Sexuality and Religion in Early Modern Europe* (London: Routledge, 1994).

Rose, Nikolas, 'Assembling the modern self', in Porter (ed.), *Rewriting the Self*, pp. 224–48.

Rosenman, Ellen Bayuk, *Unauthorized Pleasures: Accounts of Victorian Erotic Experience* (Ithaca: Cornell University Press, 2003).
Rossiaud, Jacques, *La Prostitution médiévale* (Paris: Flammarion, 1988).
Rubin, Lillian B., *Erotic Wars: What Happened to the Sexual Revolution?* (New York: Farrar, Straus, and Giroux, 1990).
Sanford, Nevitt, *Self and Society; Social Change and Individual Development* (New York: Atherton Press, 1966).
Sauvy, Anne, *Livres saisis à Paris entre 1678 and 1701* (The Hague: Martinus Nijhoff, 1972).
Sawday, Jonathan, *The Body Emblazoned: Dissection and the Human Body in Renaissance Culture* (London: Routledge, 1995).
Sawday, Jonathan, 'Self and selfhood in the seventeenth century', in Porter (ed.), *Rewriting the Self*, pp. 29–48.
Secrets de l'Amour et de Vénus, Les (Paris: Cercle du Livre Précieux, 1959).
Selye, Katherine Q., and Janet Elder, 'Strong support is found for ban on gay marriage', *New York Times*, 21 Dec. 2003.
Sennet, Richard, *The Fall of Public Man* (New York: Knopf, 1977; London: Faber and Faber, 1986).
Sennet, Richard, *Authority* (London: Faber and Faber, 1993).
Shoemaker, Robert, *Gender in English Society, 1650–1850: The Emergence of Separate Spheres* (London and New York: Longman, 1998).
Shoemaker, Robert, and Mary Vincent (eds), *Gender and History in Western Europe* (New York: Arnold, 1998).
Shorter, Edward, *The Making of the Modern Family* (New York: Basic, 1975).
Sigel, Lisa Z., *Governing Pleasures. Pornography and Social Change in England, 1815–1914* (New Brunswick, NJ: Rutgers University Press, 2002).
Silverman, Lisa, *Tortured Subjects. Pain, Truth, and the Body in Early Modern France* (Chicago: University of Chicago Press, 2001).
Singly, François de, et al., *Libres ensemble: l'individualisme dans la vie commune* (Paris: Nathan, 2000).
Smith, Dinitia, 'Love that dare not squeak its name', *New York Times*, 7 Feb. 2004.
Sohn, Anne-Marie, *Du premier baiser à l'alcove: la sexualité des français au quotidien, 1850–1950* (Paris: Aubier, 1996).
Something's Gotta Give, film, directed by Nancy Meyers, with Jack Nicholson and Diane Keaton (2003).
Sorbier, Françoise du, 'Récits de gueuserie et biographies criminelles de Head à Defoe' (doctoral thesis, University of Paris VII, 1977: Lille, Atelier national de reproduction de thèses, University of Lille III; Paris: Didier Èrudition, 1984).
Sorbier, Françoise du, 'De la potence à la biographie, ou les avatars du criminel et de son image en Angleterre (1680–1740), *Études Anglaises*, 32

(1979), pp. 252–71 (based on the author's thesis, 'Récits de gueuserie et biographies criminelles de Head à Defoe').
Spence, Richard T., *Lady Anne Clifford, Countess of Pembroke, Dorset and Montgomery, 1590–1676* (Woodbridge: Sutton Publishing, 1997).
Staël, Anne-Louise-Germaine de, *De l'influence des passions sur le bonheur des individus et des nations* (Lausanne: J. Mourer, 1796).
Staffe (baronne), *Usages du monde. Règles du savoir-vivre dans la société moderne*, revised, corrected and augmented edn (Paris: Flammarion, 1899).
Steinberg, Sylvie, *La Confusion des sexes. Le travestissement de la Renaissance à la Révolution* (Paris: Fayard, 2001).
Stengers, Jean, and Anne Van Neck, *Masturbation: The History of a Great Terror*, trans. Kathryn Hoffmann (New York: Palgrave, 2001).
Stevenson, Robert Louis, *Strange case of Dr Jekyll and Mr Hyde* (London: Longmans, Greene, & Co., 1886).
Stone, Lawrence, *The Family, Sex and Marriage in England 1500–1800* (New York: Harper & Row, 1977).
Stora-Lamarre, Annie, *L'Enfer de la IIIe République: censeurs et pornographes (1881–1914)* (Paris: Imago, 1989).
Straus, Murray, Richard Gelles and Susanne Steinmetz, *Behind Closed Doors: Violence in the American Family* (New York: Simon and Schuster, 1980).
Sullerot, Évelyne (ed.), with Odette Thibault, *Le Fait féminin. Qu'est-ce qu'une femme?*, preface by André Lwoff (Paris: Fayard, 1978).
Sulloway, Alison G., *Jane Austen and the Province of Womanhood* (Philadelphia: University of Pennsylvania Press, 1989).
Tarczylo, Théodore, *Sexe et liberté au siècle des lumières* (Paris: Presses de la Renaissance, 1983).
Taylor, Charles, *Sources of the Self: The Making of Modern Identity* (Cambridge, MA: Harvard University Press, 1989).
Ternisian, Xavier, 'En une décennie, les croyances ont reculé en France', *Le Monde*, 17 Apr. 2003.
13 Going on 30, film, directed by Gary Winick, with Jennifer Garner (2004).
Tiger, Lionel, *The Pursuit of Pleasure* (Boston: Little, Brown, 1992).
Tiger, Lionel, and Robin Fox, *The Imperial Animal*, with a New Introduction by the authors (Transaction Publishers: New Brunswick-London, 1998; 1st edn 1971).
Tissot, Samuel-Auguste-David, *L'Onanisme; ou dissertation physique sur les maladies produites par la masturbation. Nouvelle édition annotée d'après les nouvelles observations par les docteurs Gottlier, Vogler, etc.* (Paris: Chez les Marchands de Nouveautés, 1836).
Trumbach, Randolph, *Sex and the Gender Revolution*, vol. I: *Heterosexuality and the Third Gender in Enlightenment London* (Chicago: University of Chicago Press, 1998).

BIBLIOGRAPHY

Trumbach, Randolph, 'Erotic fantasy and male libertinism in Enlightenment England', in Hunt (ed.), *The Invention of Pornography*.

Turner, David M., *Fashioning Adultery: Gender, Sex, and Civility in England, 1660–1740* (Cambridge: Cambridge University Press, 2002).

Underwood, Dale, *Etherege and the Seventeenth-Century Comedy of Manners* (New Haven: Yale University Press, 1957).

Van Ussel, Josef, *Histoire de la Répression Sexuelle* (French trans.) (Paris: R. Laffont, 1972).

Viala, Alain, *Naissance de l'Écrivain. Sociologie de la littérature à l'âge classique* (Paris: Éditions de Minuit, 1985).

Vincent, Catherine, 'La tyrannie du plaisir', *Le Monde*, 21 May 2003.

Vincent, Catherine, 'Ados à fleur de peau', *Le Monde*, 9 July 2003.

Waal, Frans de, *Bonobo: The Forgotten Ape* (Berkeley: University of California Press, 1997).

Wagner, Peter, *Eros Revived: Erotica of the Enlightenment in England and America* (London: Secker and Warburg, 1988).

Walkowitz, Judith, *Prostitution and Victorian Society: Women, Class, and the State* (Cambridge: Cambridge University Press, 1980).

Walkowitz, Judith, *City of Dreadful Delight: Narratives of Sexual Danger in Late Victorian London* (Chicago: University of Chicago University Press, 1992).

'Walter', *My Secret Life*, 2 vols (New York: Grove Press, 1966; repr. 1998); also 3 parts (London: Arrow, 1994–5).

Webber, Joan, *The Eloquent 'I'; Style and the Self in Seventeenth-Century Prose* (Madison: University of Wisconsin Press, 1968).

Weber, Max, *The Protestant Ethic and the Spirit of Capitalism*, trans. Talcott Parsons (1st German edn 1904–5) (Oxford: Blackwell, 2002).

Weeks, Jeffrey, *Sexuality and its Discontents* (London: Routledge and Kegan Paul, 1985).

White, Edmund, *States of Desire: Travels in Gay America* (New York: Dutton, 1980).

Wiesner, Merry E., *Women and Gender in Early Modern Europe* (Cambridge: Cambridge University Press, 2nd edn 2000).

Wray, Ramona, '[Re]constructing the past: the diametric lives of Mary Rich', in Dragstra, Ottway and Wilcox (eds), *Betraying Ourselves*, pp. 148–65.

Wrigley, E. A. et al., *English Population History from Family Reconstitution, 1580–1837* (Cambridge: Cambridge University Press, 1997).

Yates, Frances A., *The Art of Memory* (Chicago: University of Chicago Press, 1966).

Zohar, Dana (with I. N. Marshall), *The Quantum Self: Human Nature and Consciousness Defined by the New Physics* (New York: Morrow, 1990).

Zuk, Marlene, *Sexual Selections: What We Can and Can't Learn about Sex from Animals* (Berkeley: University of California Press, 2002).

INDEX

'abbeys of misrule' 25, 59
abortion 201
   16th and 17th centuries 89
   1800–1960 200, 203
   1960s to present day 230
   right to 35
   United States 34, 208–9, 228
abstinence
   as remedy for syphilis 183
Académie des dames, L' 91
Acton, William 161, 166, 174
actors, boy 58–9
Addison, Joseph 130
adolescents *see* young men; young people
adultery 81
   16th and 17th centuries 54, 82–3, 84, 95
     punishment for 85
   18th century 139
   United States 209, 222
   see also extra-marital sex
age differences
   in love 35
   see also elderly; young men; young people
AIDS 32, 183
alcohol abuse
   16th and 17th centuries 85
Alembert, Jean d' 153

Amiel, Henri-Frédéric 171
Amsterdam 117
   homosexuality in 27
anal penetration 193
anal sex
   16th and 17th centuries 74
     rejection of 91–2, 95
   United States 213–14
   see also sodomy
anarchy, sexual
   1800–1960 200
anatomy
   16th and 17th centuries 69–74
Anatomy Theatre of Leiden, The 71–2
Anglican church
   marriage 57–8
   surveillance 85
animals
   homosexuality 236
   in Kinsey Report 213
   sexuality 251
Anne of Austria 92–3, 102
anxiety 33–4
   16th and 17th centuries 58
   18th century 137, 145
   1800–1960 161, 165–9, 188
   1960s to present day 249, 253
   young people 239, 244, 251, 257

INDEX

Apollinaire, Guillaume 190
apprentices
  18th-century biographies 146–8
Arditi, Sebastiano 48
Aretino, Pietro 122
Aristotle's Masterpiece 141–2, 172
art
  Renaissance 46
  18th century 154–5
    pornographic 127
  1800–1960
    collecting 158
    pleasure and death in 173
    venereal diseases in 182
  definitions of femininity in 80–1
  sense of touch in 169–70
  sensuality in French 244
  as sublimation 21–2
  see also paintings; portraits
asceticism *see* celibacy
Ashbee, Henry Spencer *see* Pisanus Fraxi
astrology 248
Augustine, St 46
autobiographical writings
  16th and 17th centuries 46, 47, 48–9, 51–2
    women 61
  18th century 146
  1800–1960
    lower classes 196
    My Secret Life 157, 183, 184–9, 196, 225, 231
  religious 47
  spiritual 15
autonomy 19
  16th century 15–16
  spiritual 248

Bakhtin, Mikhail 73, 85
Balzac, Honoré de 169, 178, 194
Barrin, Jean 116
Barthélemy, Auguste 173
bastards *see* illegitimacy
Bayle, Pierre 131

Beaumarchais, Pierre 125
Belgium
  retreat from religion 248
  same-sex marriage 237
Benedicti, Jean 133
Berkley, Theresa 195
Bernard, Claude 174
bestiality 81, 82
  16th and 17th centuries 99
  in 18th-century pornography 121
  1800–1960 193
  in rural areas 26
Bienville, M. D. T.
  Nymphomania 142
bigamy 81
biographies, criminal
  18th century 146–53
birth control *see* contraception
blasphemy 101–2
Bloch, Marc 45
blood
  in 18th-century pornography 125–6
  menstrual 72, 78, 81
Blot-l'Église, Claude de Chouvigny, baron de 76, 90, 102–3, 107, 113
  sexual morality of 92–4
Boaistuau, Pierre 78
boarding schools 29–30, 173
Bobbit case 240
Boccaccio, Giovanni 54
body
  in 18th-century literature 148
  1800–1960 157, 169, 185
    control of 162–4
    fear of 172–3
    as machine 165
  Christianity's distrust of 43
  as cultural entity 9
  duality with soul 10, 13, 16, 18–19, 70, 71
  fluids 69–74, 81, 144
  humoral perception of 45
  narcissistic view of 253

body (*Cont'd*)
  tattooing and piercing 247
  torture 50
  women 35
    16th and 17th centuries 72
    in erotic literature 75–6
Boswell, James 129
Botticelli 80
bourgeoisie *see* middle classes
boy actors 58–9
boys
  flagellation 195
  masturbation 5, 142
    1800–1960 164, 171, 172
    United States 218
Brantôme, Pierre de 15
  Dames galantes, Les 49, 52
breach of promise suits 198
Brieux, Eugène
  Avariés, Les 182
Bronzino, Agnolo
  Venus, Cupid, Folly and Time 169–70
brothels 84
  18th century 118, 123, 129, 137, 141
  1800–1960 178, 180
    closure of 183
  in French literature 166
  sadism and masochism in 195–6
  United States 232–3
Browne, Thomas 70
bundling 197–8
  see also petting
Burckhardt, Jacob 14
Burnett, Frances Hodgson
  Little Lord Fauntleroy 171
Bury, Elizabeth
  journals 61

Calvinism 2, 14
  body and soul in 70
Canada
  same-sex marriage 209, 237

capitalism 38
  and individualism 14–15
  pairing with Christianity 2–3
  see also consumer culture
Caravaggio, Michelangelo
  culture of dissection 70–1
Carroll, Lewis 163
Cartouche 152
Casale, Giambattista 48
Castiglione, Baldassare, Count
  Book of the Courtier 17, 47
Castle of Perseverance, The 71
castration complex 177
Catholic Church
  abortion and contraception 228
  celibacy 234
  decline in influence 37
  marriage 22, 78
Catholic countries
  sexual tolerance 230
cauterization
  for masturbation 175
Cavendish, Margaret
  autobiography 62
celibacy
  17th century 24–5
  clergy 22, 234–5
  monks 22, 77
Cellini, Benvenuto
  autobiography 46, 48
cemeteries 148
censorship
  France 191–2
extra-marital sex
  18th century 126–7
  United States 214
  see also adultery
Chausson, Jacques 104–5
chauvinist movements 239
children and childhood 21
  1960s to present day 233
  prostitution 192
  purity and corruption in 1800–1960 171
  syphilis 183

304

see also infant mortality; infanticide
China, ancient
  pleasure 1
Chorier, Nicolas 107
  Satyra Sotadica 77, 106, 116, 117
Christian, Jules 176
Christianity
  body and soul duality 13
  confession 83
  control of carnal pleasure 3–4
  distrust of body 43
  individual self-control 22
  pairing with capitalism 2–3
  procreative sex 24
  prohibitions 77–9
  retreat from 248
  sin 76–7
  see also specific forms e.g. Catholic Church
chroniques scandaleuses 125
civilizing process 3, 16–17, 73, 84–5
  18th century 116, 140
  1800–1960 158
class, social
  and prostitution 180–1
  18th century 115
  United States 219–21
  see also lower classes; middle classes; upper classes
Claus, Hugo 30
Cleland, John
  Fanny Hill 108, 118–19, 126, 128, 132
clergy
  celibacy 22, 234–5
Clifford, Anne 69
  autobiographies 62–7
Clifford, Francis 65, 66
cloning 233
clothing
  sensuality in 244
colleges 29–30, 173

colonialism 9–10, 31
Combe, Mary 88–9
communication code 255
Compleat Collection of Remarkable Tryals, A 150
Compleat Collection of State Tryals, A 150
concubinage 81
conduct manuals see courtesy manuals
confession 83
confession manuals 50, 83
  denunciation of masturbation 26
confinement, women
  16th and 17th centuries 56–7
consent, parental
  to marriage 79
constraints see repression
consumer culture 207–8
  emergence of 112
  Europe 38–9
  and private life 252
  rejection of moderation 38
  and sexual enjoyment 250
  United States 34
Contagious Diseases Acts (1864, 1866, 1869) 166
continence
  periods of obligatory 77, 79
contraception 34, 35
  16th and 17th centuries 89, 98
  1800–1960 172, 201
  revolutions 227–8
contract, sexual
  1960 to present day 230–44
  see also sexual system
Copie d'un bail et ferme 89–90, 94–5
Corbin, Alain 179
Corneille, Pierre 95, 98, 153–4
corruption and pleasure
  1800–1960 172–3
couples
  1960s to present day 6
  in biological programme 238

couples (*Cont'd*)
  heterosexual
    decline of 232
    eroticization of 200–1
    sexuality 231
    United States 222
  role of orgasm in 255–6
  same-sex
    children 233
  see also marriage
courtesy manuals 17, 47, 107
  18th century 140, 146
Cranach, Lucas, the Elder 80–1
Cranach, Lucas, the Younger 49
criminal justice 76
  16th and 17th centuries 50
    France 81–3, 101–8
    homosexuality 100–1
    women in 57, 67
  see also records, judicial
criminals
  18th-century biographies 146–53
  in 18th-century pornography 125–6
Cromwell, Oliver 66, 67
cuisine, French 113
culture
  16th and 17th centuries
    erotic 91, 108
    and individual 46–9
    women 99–100
  18th-century upper classes 153–4
  and narcissism 251–8
  United States
    hidden erotic 219–22
culture wars
  United States 208–9, 215–16, 221, 222, 240–3, 244
Cumberland, Earl of 62, 67
cunnilingus 193, 221–2
Curll, Edmund 120, 123

da Vinci, Leonardo 46
Daily Telegraph 163
Darwin, Erasmus 129–30

Dashwood, Francis 154
d'Aubigné, Françoise 90–1
d'Aubigné, Théodore Agrippa 15
  autobiography 49, 51
death
  in 18th-century pornography 125–6
  carnal pleasure linked with 18–19, 43, 168, 169, 172–3
  of children 233
  fear of 161
  and hunger 208
death instinct 10, 13, 18–19, 43
death penalty
  16th and 17th centuries 81, 82, 84, 102
  18th century 149–50
  homosexuality 100
  Le Petit 104–5
  United States 208–9
debauchery 81
Debay, Auguste 174
Defoe, Daniel 126, 131, 147, 148
  Colonel Jack 152
  criminal biographies 151–2
  Moll Flanders 149, 151–2
  Roxana 152
demimondaines 180
depression, women
  1800–1960 159
Descartes, René 71
de-sexualization
  in 17th century 24
dildos 75, 98, 123–4, 196, 229
Dilettanti, Society of 28, 154–5
discourses
  Foucault 20
disease
  1960s to present day 32
  carnal pleasure linked with 18–19
  fear of 161
  see also sickness; venereal diseases
disorders, sexual 167

dissection 70–1
  women's bodies 72
divorce
  18th century 136, 139
  1800–1960 166, 202–3
  1960s to present day 230, 232
  United States 166, 236
divorcees
  United States 216–17
  see also widowers
Dixon, Marcus 215–16
Dodson, Betty 226
domestic sphere *see* spheres
domination, male
  16th and 17th centuries 55–6, 57, 82–3
  18th century 134–5
  1800–1960 161, 162, 168, 187
Donne, John 69
Dorset, Richard Sackville, Earl of 62–3, 65, 67
double standard
  16th and 17th centuries 55, 68, 80, 94
  18th century 112–13, 115, 134–8
  1800–1960 5, 157, 162, 166–7, 185, 238
  present day 243–4
  United States 222–4, 242, 257
Drysdale, George 176
du Barry, Madame 125
Du Camp, Maxime 180
Dunton, Elizabeth
  journals 61
Dürer, Albert 46, 49

École des filles, L' 75–6, 77, 88, 90, 91, 108
  authorship 103–4
  sexual education in 96–9
economics
  and individualism 14–15
  pairing with spirituality 2–3
  and private life 252, 256
  see also consumer culture

economy, sexual
  18th century 111, 130
  1800–1960 156–7, 165, 169
effeminate men ('mollies') 27, 142
effigies, funerary 49
ego and egoism 19, 36, 38
  appearance of 17
  cult of 207
  since 1960s 5
ejaculation
  by women 99, 185, 225
elderly 250
Elders, Joycelyn 215
Elias, Norbert 3, 16–17, 73, 84–5, 140
Elizabeth I
  and Anne Clifford 62, 63–4, 67
  social role 60
Ellis, Henry Havelock 174, 177, 193, 199–200, 217
  Sexual Inversion 176
embarrassment
  in Elizabethan theatre 73
England
  carnal pleasure in 3
  colonialism 31
  divorce 166
  family 55
  masturbation 142–3
  middle classes 156, 158
  narcissism 254
  nudity 162–3
  oral sex 193
  patriarchy 53
  pornography 118, 189
  sexual repression 83–4
  Somerset peasants 84, 85–9, 221
  venereal diseases 182
  see also London
engravings
  definitions of femininity in 80
  pornographic 122
enjeu
  Foucault 20
epicureanism 38, 130–1

INDEX

equality
  erotic 238–40
  gender 243
equilibrium
  1960s 32
Erasmus, Desiderius 46, 48, 78
  On Good Manners for Boys 17, 73
Eros 10, 43, 177, 226–7
euphemisms
  1800–1960 163–4
Euro-secularity 208
Europe
  carnal pleasure in 5–6, 37–9
  hedonism 244–5
  individualism 257–8
  narcissism 254
  pairing of economics with spirituality 2–3
  social values 254
  see also specific countries
European Values Survey 247, 256
Europeans
  typology of 249–50
evacuation, medicine of
  16th and 17th centuries 74
excess, sexual
  1800–1960 169, 170
executions 112, 149–50
exhibitionists, Victorian 172
extra-marital sex 28
  Renaissance 22
  16th and 17th centuries 55
  18th century 126–7
  1800–1960 238–9
  United States 214
  see also adultery

'Fait féminin, Le' 36
family
  16th and 17th centuries 55, 56–7
  1960s to present day 241, 250, 256
  defence of 36
  Europe 247
  management of sexuality 23–5
  United States 227
famine, end of 32
Farrar, Frederic William
  Eric, or Little by Little 174
father, absence of 252–3
Father Paul and the Blue-Eyed Nun of Saint Catherine 125
fellatio 192–3, 196, 221–2
femininity
  16th and 17th centuries 56–7, 71, 79–81
fetishism, Victorian 163, 195
Feuillade, Louis 173
Fielding, Henry
  Jonathan Wild 151
flagellation
  18th century 123, 127, 138
  1800–1960 164, 195–6
Flandrin, Jean-Louis 77
Flaubert, Gustave 158, 172
Florence
  homosexuality in 100, 101
fluids, body 69–74, 81
  and masturbation 144
fondling *see* petting
food abundance 32, 208
foreplay
  United States 220
forgers 152–3
Foucault, Michel 1, 4
  paradigms 20–1, 23
foundlings 196–7
  see also illegitimacy
Fouquet, Nicolas 90, 104
Fournier, Edmond 183
Fowler, O. Q. S. 160
Fracastoro, Girolamo
  Syphilis 173
France 209
  art and clothing 244
  arts 154
  carnal pleasure 3
  colonialism 31
  contraception 89

308

divorce 166
erotic literature 89–95
illegitimate births 24
individualism 15, 245
male insecurity 239
marriage 55, 79
  same-sex 237
masturbation 143–5
middle classes 156, 158
moderation 130–1
narcissism 254
nudity 162
oral sex 192–3
patriarchy 53
pre-nuptial pregnancies 86
prostitution 166–7, 182, 183
repression 101–8
retreat from religion 248
sexual repression 81–3
sexual violence 56
social values 247, 249–50
sodomy and bestiality 26
venereal diseases 182–3
see also Paris
freedom
  of individuals 39
  sexual
    1960s to present 250
    male 86
  women
    16th and 17th centuries 88–9
French Revolution
  and pornography 120
Freud, Sigmund 138, 157, 164, 169
  life instinct and death instinct 10, 13
  masturbation 142
  narcissism 251
  sublimation 17
friendship, masculine 140–1
frigidity, female
  1800–1960 5, 178, 185–6, 202, 207
  1960s to present day 240

frustrations
  1800–1960 166, 168–9
  young unmarried men 25–7
fusion, theme of 98

Gamiani 194
Gautier, Théophile
  Roman de Violette, Le 190–1
Gay, John
  Beggar's Opera, The 151
Gay, Peter 158
gay *see* homosexual desire and homosexuality
gay and lesbian movements 239
gay marriage *see* marriage, same-sex
gender revolution
  London 138
generations
  relations between 35
  religion 248
Genuine Memoirs of the Celebrated Miss Maria Brown 126
geography
  16th and 17th centuries 71
Germany
  middle classes 158
  narcissism 254
  social values 249
Giddens, Anthony 253–4
Giovio, Paolo 49
girls
  masturbation 142, 171, 172
  sexual exploitation of 163
Gladstone, W. E. 170–1, 179
Goncourt, Edmond de 166
Gougon, Jean 80–1
grand tours 154
grandiose self 252
grandparents 35
Great Britain
  social values 249
  see also England
Green, Julien 177
green sickness 159

Greenblatt, Stephen 46, 47, 73
Gregory the Great 77
groups
   relationship with individual 9
guilt
   16th and 17th centuries 83
   18th century 111
   homosexuality 101
   and masturbation 26, 218
   rejection of 38, 39
   role of religion 4
   United States 224

hair, body
   lack of pubic 163, 171
   Victorian lower classes 197
happiness
   18th century 129–30, 131
   aspiration to 4
   Canada 209
Hart, James 73
Harvard 218
Harvey, William 71
Haussonville, comte d' 166–7
hedonism 33, 207, 208, 209
   18th century 128, 129, 154–5
   1960 to present day 212
   advance of 158
   emergence of 23
   European 5, 244–5
   values of 246–51
hell, literary 190
Herbert, Philip, Earl of Pembroke
   and Montgomery 65–6, 67
Hickey, William 128
highwaymen tales 152
Histoire de Dom B., L' 119, 124,
   127, 132
Hite, Shere 242–3, 253
   reports 240–1
Hoby, Lady Margaret
   journals 61
Hogarth, William 128, 129, 148,
   154, 170
   Idleness and Industry 146–7

Rake's Progress, A 124
Holbein, Hans, the Elder 49
home *see* spheres
homosexual desire and
   homosexuality 23, 27–8, 36
   16th and 17th centuries 24, 59,
      81, 87, 100–1
   18th century 115, 138, 141
   1800–1960 173, 186, 191, 193–
      4, 200
   1960s to present day 5, 33, 212,
      230, 250
   animals 236
   biological basis 236
   continuum of 217
   United States 33, 209, 223, 224,
      250
   see also sodomy
human race
   survival of 36–7
humanism
   end of 50–1
   Renaissance 46
humours 45, 69–70
hunger
   and death 208
husbands
   16th and 17th centuries
      adultery 82–3
      murder of 58
   1800–1960
      control of sexual power 5
      benefits of sexual system 20, 31
Huysmans, Joris-Karl 166, 182
hygiene, manuals of
   1800–1960 174
hypocrisy, middle class
   1800–1960 165–6
hysteria 21, 159, 178

identities
   Anne Clifford 63
   women
      16th and 17th centuries 59–60,
         68

INDEX

double 242
illegitimacy 28
  Renaissance 22
  16th and 17th centuries 24, 84, 85
  18th century 132, 139
  1800–1960 198
  United States 209
  see also foundlings
imagination, pleasures of
  18th century 153–5
impotence
  18th century 145
in vitro fertilization 233
incest 81, 82
  16th and 17th centuries 83, 84, 87
  punishment for 85
  1800–1960 192
individual and individualism 207, 208, 209
  16th and 17th centuries 45–52
    women 45, 53–68
  1960 to present day 212, 231, 246–51
  duality of 19
  emergence of 4, 10–11, 13–19
  Europe 245, 257–8
  freedom of 39
  links with states 20–1
  relationship with group 9
  United States 245
individuality
  1800–1960 158–9
individualization 247
industrial revolution 28
infant mortality
  1800–1960 200
infanticide 81–2
  Victorian prostitutes 178
infertility
  18th century 145
  1960s to present day 233
infibulation
  for masturbation 175–6
insanity, masturbatory 174

insecurity *see* anxiety
intellectuals
  16th and 17th centuries 50–1
  middle-class criticisms of 158
introspection
  16th and 17th centuries 48–9
  18th century 153
irenicism 78
Italy
  autobiographies 48

Jack the Ripper 173, 189
James I
  and Anne Clifford 65, 67
Japan 250
Johnson, Charles 150
Johnson, Virginia *see* Masters, William
Jones, Inigo 71
Joubert, Laurent 54
journals
  women
    16th and 17th centuries 61–8
  see also autobiographical writings
justice *see* criminal justice; records
juveniles *see* young men; young people

kingdoms of misrule 25, 59
Kinsey Report (1948) 193, 211, 212–14, 216–18, 220, 256
Kinsey Report (1953) 214–16, 219, 220, 256
kissing on the mouth
  1800–1960 164, 200
  United States 220–1
Knight, Richard Payne 28
  Account of the Worship of Priapus, An 154–5
knowledge, masculine
  of feminine pleasure 96–9
Koedt, Anne 226
Kohut, Heinz
  narcissism 251–2

Krafft-Ebing, Richard von 169, 176, 193, 195
  Psychopathia Sexualis 167

La Bretonnière, François Chavigny de 116
Lachèvre, Frédéric 75–6
lactation 144, 164
La'mert, Samuel 174, 176
Lancet, The 171, 176
Landucci, Luca 48
L'Ange, Jean 90, 103–4
language
  of homosexuality 193–4
  Victorian euphemisms 163–4
Larpent, Anna 153–4
Lasch, Christopher 252, 254
Laslett, Peter 86
Le Nismois
  Association de demivierges 191
Le Petit, Claude 103, 106
  Bordel des Muses, Le 105
  execution of 104–5
legislation
  1960s to present day 230
  against abuse of children 233
  United States 213–14, 221–2
  homosexuality 217
legs 163
Leighton, Frederic 162–3
leisure, invention of 47
Lemnius, Levinus 72, 73–4
lesbianism
  18th century 139, 144
  1800–1960 194
  United States 224
  see also homosexual desire and homosexuality
Lesbos, Georges 173
letters
  16th and 17th centuries 48–9
Lewis, Thomas 148
liberation, sexual 209, 226–7
  and repression, cycles of 2, 4, 5, 21, 31–2, 112, 157–8
  of women 4, 37, 251
liberation, women's 34, 243
libertines 28
  16th and 17th centuries 76, 101–2, 106, 107, 207
  1800–1960 198, 200, 203
libido, female
  1960s to present day 253
  formation of 242
life expectancy
  1960s 32
  and divorce 232
life instinct 10, 13, 18–19, 43
Lillo, George
  London Merchant, The 151
literacy
  18th century 123
literature
  16th and 17th centuries
    and individuality 47–8
    use of first person singular 51
  18th century
    influence of France 153–4
  erotic 10, 89–95
  lesbians in 194
  on prostitution 166–7
  venereal diseases in 182
  see also medical texts; pornography; *specific authors*
Livre sans titre, Le 173–4
Locke, John 131
London 3
  18th century 112, 113, 128
  1800–1960 157, 238–9
  arts 154
  colonialism 31
  criminal justice 57
  homosexuality in 27–8, 30, 59
  pornography 117
  prostitutes 178–80
  sex toys 229
  sexual system 20

sexual violence 56
young people in 147–8
London Foundling Hospital 196–7, 198
loss, fantasy of
  Victorian 169, 172–3
love, romantic 167, 243
  18th century 132–4, 138–41
  1800–1960 197
  1960s to present day 231
  fear of 241–2
lower classes
  1800–1960 157
    masturbation 171–2
    sexual pleasures 196–202
  individuality 60
  United States 219–21
  see also peasants
Ludwig, Carl 159
Luhmann, Niklas 231
Luther, Martin 46
Lyly, John
  Gallathea 58

machine, body as 165
magazines, pornographic 189, 192, 230
Maintenon, Madame de 90–1
maisons de rendez-vous 182
maisons de tolérance 195–6
Malthus, Thomas Robert 28
Man Without a Star 203–4
Mandeville, Bernard de 131
  Fable of the Bees 115, 130
Mandrin 152
manners, good
  Victorian 156, 159
  see also courtesy manuals
Marguerite de Navarre 124
Marguerite de Valois 15
  autobiography 48–9, 51–2
  social role 60–1
market see economics
Marlowe, Christopher 47
  Doctor Faustus 59, 71

marriage 29
  16th and 17th centuries 50, 55, 56–7, 57–8, 81, 83
    controls on 77–9
  18th century 121, 132–4, 136, 138–9
    in 18th-century pornography 126
  1960s to present day 5
  Catholic Church 22
  clandestine 79
  destabilization of 244
  emphasis on 20
  management of sexuality 23–5
  moderation in 4, 24
  same-sex
    1960s to present day 234–7
    Canada 209, 237
    United States 33, 208–9, 212, 218, 223, 235–7, 255
  trial 79, 198
  United States 236
  see also husbands; wives
Mary, Virgin
  devotion to 54
masculinity
  16th and 17th centuries 55–6, 56–7, 71
masochism
  Victorian 164, 169, 195, 202
Masters, William and Virginia Johnson
  Human Sexual Response 225, 253
masturbation 21, 38
  16th and 17th centuries 24, 81, 87–8, 94
  18th century 112–13, 115, 138, 141–6
  1800–1960 157, 164, 165, 169–77, 184–5, 193
  1960s to present day 177, 229, 237, 241–2
  boys 5, 142, 164, 171, 172, 218
  United States 214, 215, 218–19, 224, 226

313

masturbation (*Cont'd*)
  unmarried young men 26
  women 142, 219, 226
Matrimonial Causes Act (1857) 166
Maudsley, Henry 177
Maupassant, Guy de 166
Mauriac, Charles 176
medical texts
  18th century 140
    masturbation 143
  as manuals of instruction 172
  as pornography 123
medicine and medical profession
  16th and 17th centuries 45, 74
  1800–1960 5, 157–8, 160–2, 164, 169, 202
  abortion and infant mortality 200
  body fluids 69–71, 81
  masturbation 173–6
  power of 167
  procreative sex 24
men
  16th and 17th centuries
    sexual freedom of 86, 87
  1800–1960 199
  anxiety 33–4, 58, 137, 253
  as authors of pornography 190
  benefits of sexual system 20, 31
  effeminate ('mollies') 27, 142
  masculine friendship 140–1
  today 33–4
  see also domination; father; husbands; masculinity; young men
menstrual blood 72, 78, 81
menstruation 242
mental subnormality
  of unmarried pregnant women 255
micturition *see* urination
mid-life crises 253
middle classes
  18th century 135

  double standard 136–8
    1800–1960 156, 158
    hypocrisy of 165–6
    masturbation 171, 177
    prostitution 180–1, 182
    social roles 158–60
  migration
    young unmarried men 31
  Millot, Michel 90, 91, 103, 113
  Milton, J. Laws
    On Spermatorrhoea 175
  Mirabeau, Honoré 120
  mistresses, kept
    Victorian 178–9, 180, 182
  model man
    Renaissance 46–7
  moderation
    18th century 111, 112, 124, 127, 128–31, 135, 145
    1800–1960 5, 156–7, 158, 160–1
    ideal of 2
    in marriage 4, 24
  modernity
    challenges of 6
    repression as element of 2
  modesty, Victorian 162
  Molière 76
  'mollies' 27, 142
  monks
    celibacy 22, 77
    in pornography 124
  Monluc, Blaise de
    autobiography 51–2
  Montaigne, Michel de 15, 69
  Montluc, Blaise de 15
  morality 207
    Victorian 164, 167
    for young men 173–4
  Morande, Charles 125
  More, Thomas 78
  Morlière, chevalier de la 131
  Morris, Desmond 204, 238, 243, 255–6
  mothers
    narcissism 252–3

nurturing role of 144
unmarried
    execution of 81–2
    in institutions 255
    Victorian 197, 198
'motts' 178, 179
murders
    of husbands 58
    see also infanticide
My Secret Life 157, 183, 184–9, 196, 225, 231
mystery, sexual 21
mythology
    in Victorian paintings 162–3

names, women
    16th and 17th centuries 60
narcissism 18, 19, 208, 245
    and culture 251–8
    Europe 254
    features of 251–2
Nerciat, Andrea de 120, 121
Netherlands, the
    retreat from religion 248
    same-sex marriage 237
    sexual tolerance 230
    social values 249
neuroses, Victorian 157, 164, 169, 188, 189
    of medical profession 176
    of women 178
New Women 200, 202
Newgate Calendar, The 126, 150
Newton, Richard
    Wearing the Breeches 126
Nichols, T. L. 160–1
Nietzsche, Friedrich 158
norms
    in pornography 191
    and reality 213
nudity
    United States 219–20
    Victorian 162–4
        lower classes 197, 200
nuns 190

Onania 142, 170
onanism *see* masturbation
Onanisme, L' 170
oral sex
    16th and 17th centuries 99
    1800–1960 192–3, 196
    United States 213–14, 221–2
orgasm
    16th and 17th centuries 99–100
    18th century 132–4
    female 35
        discovery of 224–30
        since 1960s 5
        United States 214–15
        pregnant women 226
    simultaneous 95, 97
        1960s to present day 238–40
    and reproduction 74
    tyranny of 232

paedophilia 193
    1800–1960 192
    1960s to present day 233
Paget, James 176
pain 77
    and pleasure 4, 43–4, 123
    see also suffering
paintings
    Anne Clifford 66–7
    bodily functions in 73
    culture of dissection in 70–1
    nudity in 78, 162–3
    see also portraits
Parent-Duchâtelet, Alexandre 168, 179, 194
Paris 3
    18th century 113, 128, 129
    1800–1960 157
    colonialism 31
    executions 112
    homosexuality in 27, 28
    pornography 117–18, 190
    prostitutes 178–80
    sexual system 20
    women's identities 60

Parnasse des poëtes satyriques, Le 102
Paster, Gail Kern 73
paternity suits 198
patriarchy
   16th and 17th centuries 53, 56–7, 59–60
   1800–1960 167
   United States 226
Pearl, The 163, 189
peasants
   16th and 17th centuries 78, 82
   celibacy 24–5
   sexual system 25–7, 28
   Somerset 84, 85–9, 221
   women 57, 60
penetration
   anal 193
   16th and 17th centuries 91, 97, 98
penis
   cutting off 240
Pepys, Samuel 108, 128
permissiveness
   1960s to present day 250, 251
personality, culture of 158–9
perversions
   1800–1960 169, 191, 195–6
   retreat of notion of 255
   see also masochism; sadism
petting
   1800–1960 191, 197–8
   Somerset 221
   United States 220
philosophy of life
   libertines 107
piercing, body 247
pill, contraception 35, 227
Pincus, Gregory 227
Piot, Louis, the Younger 103, 104
Pisanus Fraxi
   Index librorum prohibitorum 189, 190

pleasure, carnal 5
   16th and 17th centuries 4–5, 10, 22–3, 75–108
   definition of 73–4
   18th century 10, 23, 115–55
   women 133
   1800–1960 5, 10, 156–204
   1960s to present day 5–6, 10, 23, 32–4, 211–44
   women 32–9
   in ancient China 1
   characteristics of 3–4, 13–39
   right to 232–4
   United States 3, 5–6, 34–5, 38, 244–58
pleasure principle 18
Poor Law Amendment Act (1834) 198
popes 234
population growth 28
pornographic turn 106–8
pornography 5
   18th century 117–27, 137–8, 192
   1800–1960 157, 162, 164, 165, 186, 187–8, 189–92
   pleasure and death in 173
   anti-aristocratic 124, 125
   anti-religious 124–5
portraits
   16th and 17th centuries 49
pre-marital sex
   18th century 147–8
   1800–1960 200–1, 238–9
   1960 to present day 232
   United States 214, 215–16, 222
   young men 25–7, 29–30, 55–6
predestination, doctrine of 14
pregnancy
   1800–1960
      lower classes 199, 203
      prostitutes 178
   concealment of 81–2
   outside marriage
      16th and 17th centuries 85–6

18th century 132
  as mental subnormality 255
pregnant women
  orgasm 226
Priapus, cult of 28, 154–5
priests
  celibacy 234–5
private sphere *see* spheres
Proceedings 149, 150
Proclamation Society 120–1
procreative sex 21
  16th and 17th centuries 24, 74, 92, 99
  1960s to present day 213
  role of religion 4
  separation from pleasure principle 6, 233–4, 243, 251
  United States 214–15
prohibition 3–4
  16th and 17th centuries 76–7, 77–84, 97, 108
  1800–1960 165, 203
prostitutes and prostitution 29
  16th and 17th centuries 54–5, 57, 83
    names of 60
    types of 88
  18th century 113, 118, 129, 137, 141
  18th century biographies 147
  in 18th-century pornography 126
  1800–1960 5, 162, 163–4, 166–7, 168, 178–83, 184
    male 193
  1960s to present day 230
  child 192
  in French literature 166–7
  guides 179
  United States 223–4
  in urban areas 30–1
Protestant Church
  celibacy 234
  decline in influence 37
  and individuality 47
  marriage 78
  repression 2–3
Protestant countries
  sexual tolerance 230
Protestant United Provinces
  colonialism 31
prudery, Victorian 163
psychoanalysis 169
  castration complex 177
pubic hair
  lack of 163, 171
public schools
  flagellation in 195
  homosexuality in 194
public sphere *see* spheres
Puisieux, Madam de 131
punishment
  16th and 17th centuries 79, 84, 85
  and female libido 242
  homosexuality 100–1
  linked to sadomasochism 241
  see also flagellation
purging
  16th and 17th centuries 74
Puritanism 5, 14, 85
  marriage 57–8
  United States 244

Quaife, Geoffrey 84, 85, 87
Quakers
  autobiographies 52
Queyrat, Dr 183

Rabelais, François 46, 54, 78, 80, 85, 124
race
  differences of, in love 35
  United States 215–16
rakes 113, 124
Rann, Sixteen-String Jack 152
rapes
  16th and 17th centuries 55, 79, 81, 82, 84
  by unmarried young men 25–6

rebellion and pleasure
  16th and 17th centuries 4
rebels, women
  16th and 17th centuries 59–68
Rebuffé, Eustache and Pierre 105
records, judicial 77
  lesbianism 194
  sexual repression 81–3
Régnier, Mathurin 89
regulatory system
  prostitution 180, 183
religion 207
  and anatomy 72
  and individualism 46–9
  retreat from 208, 248, 256
  return to 209, 248–9
  and self-control 3–4
  see also specific forms, e.g. Christianity
religions
  sociology of 14–15
religious colleges
  sodomitic practices in 30
Religious Wars 51
Rembrandt
  culture of dissection 70
Rémond le Grec 131
Renaissance 22, 43
  and individuality 14–15, 46–7
  and self-control 16–17
  sense of touch in art 169–70
  women in 54
repression 13, 21–3, 30, 255
  16th and 17th centuries 101–8
  1800–1960 157, 162–4
    women 159
  cause of 20
  in criminal records 81–3
  disappearance of 39
  European 2–3
  Freud 19
  and liberation, cycles of 2, 4, 5, 21, 31–2, 112, 157–8
  period of 1–2

United States 257
urban areas 22–3
reproduction
  1960s to present day 233–4
  see also procreative sex
revolutions
  1960s 32–4, 211
  contraceptive 227–8
  sexual 226–7, 240–4
Rich, Charles 68
Rich, Mary, Countess of Warwick 62
  diary and autobiography 67–8
Richardson, Samuel 147, 148
  Pamela 139
Richepin, Jean 195
rin-no-tama 229–30
roles, social
  Victorian 158–60
  see also wives, role of good
Rops, Félicien 182
Rousseau, Jean-Jacques 131, 144
  Confessions 146, 153
Rubens, Peter Paul 81
rural areas
  Victorian 184
  see also peasants
Ruskin, John 163
Russell, Margaret 63, 64, 65, 66

Sacher-Masoch, Leopold von 195
Sade, Donatien, comte de (marquis de) 28, 121, 131, 207
sadism, Victorian 164, 169, 186, 195–6, 202
sadomasochism
  linked to physical punishment 241
Sanchez, Alonso 133
sapphism see lesbianism
Scandinavia
  physical punishments 241
  sexual tolerance 230
  social values 249
  see also Sweden

INDEX

Scarron, Paul 90, 104
schools 173
  see also boarding schools; public schools
science
  human body 70
  sexuality 36
sciences, human
  individualism 10–11
  research into carnal pleasure 5
Secretaires 48
security
  growing need for 253–4
seduction, arts of 201
self-consciousness
  development of 159
self-control 22, 28–9
  18th century 111, 116, 124, 137, 151
  1800–1960 156–7, 159–60, 202
  increasing acceptance of 16–17
  role of religion 3, 4
  in towns 4
self-portraits
  16th and 17th centuries 49
sex and sexuality 20–32
  fear of 30
  stages of 21–3
  Victorian
    as sickness 164–204
  see also adultery; extra-marital sex; procreative sex
Sex and the City (television) 196
sex-shops 228
sex wars 240–3, 253
sexes
  difference of genders 1800–1960 167
  relations between 35, 38
    16th and 17th centuries 45
    18th century 115, 132, 145–6
    in 18th-century pornography 126
    1800–1960 199
    1960s to present day 251

'Sexual Givers' 238
sexual system
  1700–1960s 20, 28–32
  peasant 25–7, 84, 85–9, 221
  see also contract, sexual
'Sexual Takers' 238–9
Shakespeare, William 53, 73
  male anxieties in 47
  sonnets 51
  transvestism in 59
  treason in 50
shame, role of 254
she-devils 54, 80
Short, Thomas 147
sickness, sexuality as
  Victorian 164–204
silence, conspiracy of
  Victorian 166, 185, 188, 190
Simon, Dr 174
sin and sins 16, 76–7
  16th and 17th centuries 4, 99–108
  18th century
    weakening of 117
  1800–1960
    secularization of 160–1
  linked to pleasure 4
  and marriage 77
  punishment of 79
  seven capital 80
single parents 233
skirts, length of
  and desire 204
smell
  Victorian prostitutes 168
  women 72
Smith, Adam 130
Smith, Alexander
  Lives and Histories of the Most Noted Highwaymen, The 150
social control
  16th and 17th centuries 106–8
  18th century 127, 128, 145
  and individuality 47–8

social order
  and pornography 120
Society for the Suppression of Vice 121
sodomy 82
  16th and 17th centuries 59, 74, 81, 87, 99, 101
  18th century 115
  in colleges 30
  in rural areas 26
  see also homosexual desire and homosexuality
soliloquies 71
Somerset 84, 221
  peasant eroticism in 85–9
soul *see* body
Spain
  same-sex marriage 237
spheres, public and private 23–4
  18th century 135, 137
  1800–1960 156–7, 159
Staël, Anne-Louise-Germaine de 145–6
states
  links with individual 20–1
  obedience to 4
  use of torture 50
  see also specific countries
stepfamilies 35
Sterne, Laurence 148
  Tristram Shandy 128
Stevenson, R. L.
  Doctor Jekyll and Mister Hyde 177, 189
stigmata diaboli 171
sublimation 28
  17th century 24
  1800–1960 5
  in Christianity 4
  as driving force 13, 21–2, 23, 31
  Elias 17
  European 2–3
  Freud 19
  United States 34

suffering
  and identity 68
  and pleasure 4
  see also pain
suffocation
  as aid to orgasm 123
Sullerot, Évelyne 36
super-male
  democratization of 33
surgery
  as remedy for masturbation 175–6
surrogacy 233
surveillance, systems of
  16th and 17th centuries 83–4, 85
survivalism, culture of 254
Sweden
  retreat from religion 248
Symonds, J. Addington 193
syphilis 170, 178, 182–3

Tardieu, Ambroise 193
tattooing, body 246
Thanatos 10, 43, 177
theatre
  16th and 17th centuries 71
  boy actors in female roles 58–9
  representation of women 72–3
13 Going on 30 (film) 242
Tissot, Samuel-Auguste 207
  Onanisme, L' 143–5, 170
Todd, Mabel Loomis 158
torture 50
touch, sense of
  1800–1960 169–70
  today 241
Towneley, Charles 155
towns *see* urban areas
toys, sex 228–30
trade system
  introduction of 14
tragic man, figure of 19
transgression
  16th and 17th centuries 5, 77, 81–3, 97

INDEX

and 18th-century pornography
  117–18
and individualism 15–16
taste for 4
transsexualism
  in 18th century pornography 121
transvestism
  16th and 17th centuries 58–9
  in 18th-century pornography 121
treason
  16th and 17th centuries 50
Trent, Council of (1563) 22, 50–1,
  78–9, 234
trust 249
truth
  16th and 17th centuries 50
Tyburn Chronicle, The 126, 150

Ulrich, Carl Heinrich 193
unconscious, the 177
  power of 203
United States
  abortion 34, 208–9, 228
  brothels 232–3
  carnal pleasure in 3, 5–6, 34–5,
    38, 244–58
  culture wars 208–9, 215–16,
    221, 222, 240–3, 244
  divorce 166, 236
  homosexuality 33, 209, 223,
    224, 250
  masturbation 214, 215, 218–19,
    224, 226
  narcissism 19, 252
  religion 208, 248
  same-sex marriage 33, 208–9,
    212, 218, 223, 235–7, 255
universities 173
  homosexuality in 194
  sodomitic practices in 30
upper classes
  16th and 17th centuries
    social control of young men 47
  18th century 116, 128, 129, 136
    culture of 153–4

1800–1960 157
erotic literature 90
phases of repression and
  libertarianism 31–2
United States 219–21
see also rakes
uranism 193–4
urban areas 28
  16th and 17th centuries 4
    adultery 82
    women in 54–5, 57
  18th century 115–16, 128–9,
    148
    expansion of 112
    pornography 117
  1800–1960 184
    prostitutes 30–1`
    repression in 22–3
urination
  women 73
Usages du Monde 159

values, social
  Europe 247, 249–50, 254, 256
vampires 173
vamps, cinema 173
veil, image of
  Victorian 157
venereal diseases 28
  18th century 139, 145, 147, 148
  1800–1960 164, 166, 170,
    182–3
Venette, Nicolas 135
  Tableaux de l'amour conjugal
    133–4
Vénus dans le cloître 90, 106, 116
Verville, François Béroalde de 89
Vesalius, Andreas 69–70
Viau, Théophile de 90, 91, 102
vibrators 228, 229–30
Vidor, King 203
violence
  16th and 17th centuries 55–6,
    68, 85
  cause of 241

321

violence (Cont'd)
  and self-control 16–17
  by young unmarried men 26
virginity
  1960 to present day 232
virtue
  18th century 131
Voltaire 131, 149, 153

Walker, Elizabeth
  journals 61
Walpole, Horace 154
'Walter' see My Secret Life
war 32
wars of religion 78
Weber, Max
  on capitalism 2
  sociology of religions 14–15
Wedde, Johannes 195
Weemes (Wemyss), John 72
white sickness 159
Whitney, Isabella 51
Whythorne, Thomas 48, 51
widowers
  16th and 17th centuries 60
  United States 216–17
widows
  16th and 17th centuries 54, 55, 60
wife sales
  18th century 136
Wilde, Oscar 192, 194
witch-hunts 29, 54
witches and witchcraft 80, 82, 248
  16th and 17th centuries 55, 58, 70, 170
  stigmata diaboli 171
wives
  16th and 17th centuries 88
  18th century 113
  1800–1960
    frigidity of 5, 178, 185–6, 202, 207
    role of good 29, 80, 87

  16th and 17th centuries 54, 57, 61
  18th century 139, 141
  1800–1960 166, 168, 178
women 29
  16th and 17th centuries 86–7
  autonomy of 16
  roles of 45, 53–68
  sexuality 79–81
  18th century 115, 133, 134–6, 144, 145, 151
  inferiority of 113
  1800–1960 159, 161–2, 165, 185–6, 199, 202
  lower classes 184, 197–8
  two opposed types of 167–8
  1960s to present day 32–9, 211–12, 240, 255
  autobiographies 48
  bodies 35, 72, 75–6
  formation of libido 242
  hysteria 21, 159, 178
  masturbation 142, 219, 226
  menstrual blood 72, 78, 81
  orgasm
    discovery of 224–30
    in rural areas 27
  sex toys 229–30
  sexual liberation of 4, 34, 37
  sexuality of 75–6
  United States 219, 226
  see also femininity; mothers; prostitutes; wives
women's liberation 34, 243
Woodward, George 131
  Padlock, The 126
workers' movements 177
working classes see lower classes
world, conception of
  16th and 17th centuries 71

Yellowlees, Dr 175–6
Young, Edward 131
young men 29–30
  16th and 17th centuries

aggression 55–6
social control 47
18th century 145
1800–1960 238–9
  lower classes 198
  medical morality for 173–4
1960s to present 32–3
  anxiety 257
  insecurity 239, 244
as actors in female roles 58–9
migration 31

rural pre-industrial 25–7
see also apprentices
young people
  in 18th-century London 147–8
  anxiety 251, 257
  religion 248–9
  social values 254
  United States 214, 215–16
youthism 247

Zola, Émile 166, 194